Edited by

Sarah Whatley, Natalie Garrett Brown and Kirsty Alexander

Published in this first edition in 2015 by:
Triarchy Press
Axminster, EX13 5PF
England

+44 (0)1297 631456
info@triarchypress.net
www.triarchypress.net

A catalogue record for this book is available from the British Library.

Paperback ISBN: 978-1-909470-63-7
ePub ISBN: 978-1-909470-64-4
pdf ISBN: 978-1-909470-65-1

Cover image: Christian Kipp (see p.188 for details).

CONTENTS

www.triarchypress.net/attending-to-movement

CONTRIBUTORS

Kirsty Alexander studied law and then trained in contemporary dance. She performed with a diverse range of artists including Gill Clarke, Rosemary Butcher, Gaby Agis, Michael Clarke, Station House Opera and Michel Laub. Her own choreographic work is generally site specific and in collaboration with artists from other disciplines. She has been involved in educating dancers within the higher education sector for over 15 years, including as Head of Undergraduate Studies at Laban from 2000-2004, and as Assistant Director of London Contemporary Dance School from 2005-2010. As a certified teacher of Skinner Releasing Technique, Kirsty's approach to the philosophy of education has been significantly influenced by somatic practice and she is Associate Editor of the *Journal of Dance and Somatic Practices*. She undertook the MA Values in Education at the Institute of Education, London. In October 2010 she was awarded a University of Stirling PhD studentship, and is currently drawing on kinaesthetic experience to reconsider the dynamics of pedagogical experience.

Nadra Assaf received her MFA in Dance from Sarah Lawrence College, and a Doctorate of Education from Leicester University. She has been teaching at the Lebanese American University since 1991. Her recent dance productions include: *STS: Space-Time-Shape* (2012), *I Matter: An Audience Interactive Performance* (2010), *The Faces of EVE* (2008-2009), and *Majnoun Leila* (2007). She is the Artistic Director and founder of Al-Sarab Alternative Dance School (1991 to date). In April 2011 she organised and implemented the first annual International Dance Day Festival in Lebanon. Among her publications are: 'The Meanings of a Modern Dance: An Investigation into the Communicative Properties of a Non-Verbal Medium' (2009) and '"I Matter": An Interactive Exploration of Audience-Performer Connections' (2012).

Fiona Bannon PhD trained as a community dance practitioner and later transferred these skills to lecturing in Dance. She is Senior Fellow of the Higher Education Academy and Senior Lecturer in Dance at the University of Leeds, where she teaches undergraduate and postgraduate courses in research methods, collaboration, choreography. As Chair of DanceHE she represents and advocates for dance in higher education in various forums. She is a member of the editorial board of *Research in Dance Education* and regularly reviews articles for several publications. She writes and presents work on a range of topics; recent projects have included reflections on choreographic practice, collaboration, aesthetics and relational ethics.

Adam Benjamin is a choreographer and improviser. Adam is a founder member of 'Five Men Dancing' and he has performed and taught with Kirstie Simson, Rick Nodine, Kim Itoh, Jordi Cortés and Russell Maliphant. He was joint founder/artistic director of CandoCo Dance Company (with Celeste Dandeker) and has made work for community groups and professional companies around the world including Vertigo Dance Company and Scottish Dance Theatre. In South Africa, shortly after the dismantling of apartheid, he founded Tshwaragano Dance Company and also choreographed for Remix Dance Project in Cape Town. In Ethiopia he developed the integrated strand for the Adugna Dance Theatre Company. Adam has been a Wingate Scholar, an Associate Artist at The Place and a Rayne Fellow (2006-8). In 2013 he was awarded a National Teaching Fellowship. He lectures at Plymouth University (UK).

Carol Brown is a choreographer, a performer, an Associate Professor at the University of Auckland, New Zealand and a visiting Reader at Roehampton University, UK. Her work evolves through dialogue, experimentation and creative research in response to contemporary issues of space and becoming. After completing a practice-led PhD at the University of Surrey, Carol was invited to be Choreographer in Residence at the Place Theatre, London. While there, she developed Carol Brown Dances. Carol's dance theatre and performance installation works have toured internationally, and she has been commissioned to create large-scale works for urban contexts in Barcelona, Athens, Perth, Prague and Auckland. Her writings on dance, space, technology and sexuality are published widely.

Penny Collinson MA is a Senior Lecturer and Course Leader of MA Dance & Somatic Wellbeing: Connections to the Living Body, an ISMETA Approved Training Programme at the University of Central Lancashire, UK. Penny has worked as a contemporary dance performer and lecturer since 1992. She trains with Linda Hartley, holding a Diploma from the Institute for Integrative Bodywork and Movement Therapy (IBMT) and is now an external assessor for the programme. She practices Authentic Movement, and was fortunate to receive the Lisa Ullmann Travelling Scholarship Fund (2002) to study at the Authentic Movement Institute in Berkeley, whilst completing her MA by Research. Penny is a registered Somatic Movement Educator with ISMETA, and runs a private practice in Lancashire offering supervision and client work.

Bernadette Cronin is a theatre practitioner-researcher. Her interdisciplinary performance work is carried out in the main with Gaitkrash performance group, of which she is a founder member. She holds a PhD in Drama from the University of Exeter, an acting diploma from LAMDA, and publishes in the areas of Performance Studies and Adaptation Studies. Bernadette's most recent collaboration, *Playing the Maids,* (with the Llanarth Group and Theatre P'Yut) will tour in Wales during 2015 funded by Arts Council Wales. She teaches in the department of Drama & Theatre Studies at University College Cork, where she is currently head of department.

Cath Cullinane is originally from Liverpool. She has worked as a Performance Technician for over 20 years in theatres, colleges and festivals in the UK and Europe. She has worked as Senior Theatre Technician / Skills Instructor at Coventry University and has recently moved to Armagh.

Sally E. Dean has been a performer, performance maker and teacher for over fourteen years – in university, professional and community settings. Informed by somatic-based practices, Sally's work interlinks the fields of health, movement, expression, culture and performance. She is a certified teacher of Skinner Releasing Technique, an Amerta Movement practitioner (trained with Suprapto Suryodarmo from Java), and is a British Wheel of Yoga certified Scaravelli teacher. She also has a background in butoh, physical theatre, improvisation and playwriting. Sally's ethos is interdisciplinary and transcultural collaboration. Her teaching and performance work integrate site, object, nature and costume. She also is the director of the 'Kolaborasi Project', which facilitates performance and teaching collaborations among American, European and Asian artists (www.kolaborasi.org), with recent projects in Sri Lanka and Indonesia. She has been supported by the Arts Council England and the British Council.

Martha Eddy CMA, RSMT helped to register the field of Somatic Movement Education & Therapy with the United States Department of Labor in 1992 as a board trustee of ISMETA. She maintains a somatic movement practice with neo-nates to the hospice. She taught with Irmgard Bartenieff and Bonnie Bainbridge Cohen before founding and directing the Dynamic Embodiment Somatic Movement Therapy Training which she created in 1990 blending LMA and BMC. DE-SMTT is now in Cologne, Germany. Eddy writes about dance and somatic education, perceptual-motor development, kinaesthetic intelligence, vision enhancement, peace studies and conflict resolution (doctoral research – The Role of Physical Activity in Educational Violence Prevention for Youth.) Her dance methods Body-Mind Dancing and Moving For Life are featured on national radio and television in the USA and in journals internationally.

Natalie Garrett Brown is Principal Lecturer in Dance at Coventry University, where she contributes to the dance provision and co-ordinates postgraduate study for the Performing Arts Department. She holds a BA and MA from the Laban Centre of Movement and Dance, London alongside a doctorate from Roehampton University. Natalie is Associate Editor for the *Journal of Dance and Somatic Practices* and sits on the board for the Dancelines section in *Research in Dance Education*. Natalie has completed her Somatic Movement Educators Training in Body-Mind Centering with Embody Move Association, UK and is co-convener for the International Conference for Dance and Somatic Practices, held biannually at Coventry University. Alongside this she is a founding member of 'enter and inhabit', a collaborative site responsive project with dance artist Amy Voris and photographer Christian Kipp and the Corporeal Knowing Network; an international exchange between theatre and dance artists and scholars interested in embodied writing practices.

Jools Gilson is an Interdisciplinary Artist Scholar. Her writing, performance and visual art work has been produced, performed and exhibited internationally, supported by multiple awards from the Arts Council of Ireland/England and others. She is also an award-winning radio broadcaster and has made successful documentaries for RTÉ Radio One and BBC Radio 4. She holds a PhD in Theatre and Performance Studies, and publishes in the fields of Performance Studies, Creative Writing and Visual Culture. She teaches in the School of English at University College Cork, where she is the Associate Director of the MA in Creative Writing.

Nicole Harbonnier-Topin has been, since 2004, Professor in Movement Studies and, between 2009 and 2014, Director of the Graduates' Programs in Dance and in Somatic Education in the Dance Department of the University of Quebec in Montreal (UQAM). She has a doctoral degree in Science Education (2009, Conservatoire National des Arts et Métiers, Paris). She is certified in Functional Analysis of the Dancing Body (Analyse fonctionnelle du corps dans le mouvement dansé AFCMD - Paris, 1997). She was a dance performer (1982-2004), a contemporary dance teacher (1985-2004) and a dance teacher's instructor in the field of AFCMD at several institutions in France (1997-2004), mainly in the Centre National de la Danse in Lyon.

Duncan Holt MA (Laban), Doctor of Chiropractic (McTimoney) is a Fellow of the McTimoney Chiropractic Association and a Senior Fellow of the Higher Education Academy. He lectures in Dance at the University of Hull. He has worked as a professional dancer in the UK, Canada and Australia, and as Dance Artist in residence in North Wales. His research interests include choreographic practice in relation to aspects of modernism with references to Duchamp. His work shows his interest in technology in live performance. He has written considerations of the manner in which dance and chiropractic relate in the context of wellbeing and artistic practices.

Thomas Kampe PhD has worked internationally as performer, performance-maker and educator for more than 30 years. He currently works as Senior Lecturer at Bath Spa University. Thomas trained as a visual artist in Germany and studied dance at the Laban Centre in London, and worked for 13 years with Austrian Ausdruckstanz pioneer and Holocaust survivor Hilde Holger (1905-2011). He was awarded Associate Professorship (2011) at London Metropolitan University for developing a somatic-informed dance/movement curriculum. He is a qualified practitioner of the Feldenkrais Method, which forms a foundation for his teaching, research and artistic practice.

Christian Kipp is a photographer based in Essex. He splits his time between working on his own in the natural landscape and collaborating with a variety of dance artists. He is interested in the ways that these two areas feed and reflect each other. He has exhibited his work at Laban, Clarence Mews, Oxford House, Moving Arts Base and at the London Independent Photography Exhibition.

Hilary Kneale is an independent artist who draws on a background in fine art, movement and shamanism as resources to support her work. She has collaborated with artists of varied backgrounds and disciplines for over twenty years and is interested in and inspired by the creative tension and resulting dialogue that can emerge through collaboration as the meeting place to call the 'muse'. For the last fifteen years she has included herself within her work as she creates and inhabits installations or works in the natural environment through movement, performance and ritual. The written word is also a strong part of her ongoing practice and is combined into her work in multiple ways. Hilary Kneale is an accredited teacher of the 5 Rhythms, has practised Walk of Life non-stylised movement in the landscape for ten years and is a shamanic practitioner and healer. She is a Decoda associate artist.

Lalitaraja (Joachim Chandler MA) lectures in dance at Roehampton University where he teaches choreography, contact improvisation and improvisation. Performance credits include Scottish Ballet, Michael Clark, Adventures in Motion Pictures, Laurie Booth, Yolande Snaith and Charles Linehan, among others. He has presented more than 25 choreographic works and continues to choreograph and perform. The name Lalitaraja was given on ordination into the Triratna Buddhist Order. He has been meditating for nearly thirty years and he teaches meditation and Buddhism in London.

Lizzy Le Quesne's work is an examination of embodied inter-subjectivity—in movement, text and photography. Her work has been presented internationally including at What Now, the National Gallery of Modern Art Prague, Kyoto Arts Centre, and the Preview Berlin Art Fair. Her writing on dance and contemporary art has been published in *Afterall, Contemporary, Dance Magazine, Intelligent Life, State of Art, Dance Theatre Journal, Journal of Dance and Somatic Practices, Prague Post, Tanz, Tanecni Zona* (of which she was also Editor-in-Chief 2003-5) and *Umulec International*. Lizzy was British Council Artist in Residence at the Prague Academy of Performing Arts, guest teacher at the Conservatory of Modern Dance Prague and lecturer at Brighton University and London Metropolitan University in movement and critical theory. She is a core associate of social choreography project RICE on Hydra (Greece). She has danced for Ricochet Dance Productions, Susanna Szperling, Wally Cardona, Rosemary Lee, Tino Sehgal, Michael Kliën and Florence Peake. She is a certified teacher of Skinner Releasing Technique and teaches internationally.

Jennifer Mackerras teaches Alexander Technique in the pre-College and undergraduate programmes at Royal Welsh College of Music and Drama, Cardiff. Jennifer studied Theatre at the University of New England (Australia), and gained a PhD in Drama from Bristol University. She worked in Theatre-in-Education and Disability Arts before focusing on teaching Alexander Technique. She teaches privately as 'Activate You' and has worked for Bristol City Council, Southampton NHS Trust, University of the West of England and Bristol Old Vic Theatre School. She is author of the ebook *Four Words to Conquer Stage Fright*.

Juan M. Aldape Muñoz is a PhD student of Performance Studies at the University of California, Berkeley. His current work focuses on movement, migration and mapping discourses as they relate to undocumented bodies. Most recently, he co-founded 'A PerFarmance Project', site-specific collaborations between farmers and performers researching the concept of food security from rural and urban perspectives. He is an active member of both the International Federation for Theatre Research's Performance as Research working group, and the Latino Advisory Council for Minneapolis-based Mixed Blood Theatre. He holds an MA in International Performance Research from the University of Warwick (UK).

Róisín O'Gorman is a theatre artist and lecturer at University College Cork, Ireland. She studied theatre in the USA and returned to Ireland in 2007. Róisín's current research lives between embodied practices and theoretical understandings of performance. She explores this interdisciplinary terrain through the somatic practice of Body-Mind Centering (BMC) which offers an embodied ground to her theoretical and media-based work. Róisín completed her Somatic Movement Educator certification in BMC with Embody-Move Association in the UK with support from UCC and The Arts Council of Ireland.

Sara Reed is Head of the Department for Performing Arts, Coventry University (UK). Her career has spanned a wide range of contexts including freelance dance artist, performer, choreographer, teacher, college principal and consultant and she has been a participant in the Clore Leadership Programme. Originally trained at Laban she has an MA in Performing Arts (Middlesex University) and PhD (University of Surrey). Sara's research interests include, though not exclusively, education and pedagogy, somatic practices, the training of performers, dancers' health and fitness and the development of creative practice. Sara practices Scaravelli yoga and is a Feldenkrais Awareness Through Movement teacher.

Jennifer Roche is a Lecturer in Dance at Queensland University of Technology, Brisbane. Her research focus is the creative practice of contemporary dancers, exploring the specific nuances of this career from multiple perspectives including philosophical approaches, somatics and narrative inquiry. She has worked extensively as a contemporary dancer since the 1990s and was artistic director of Rex Levitates Dance Company, Ireland, (now Liz Roche Company) which she co-founded with her sister Liz Roche in 1999. She completed her PhD at Roehampton University, London in 2010. From 2007 to 2011 she was dance adviser to the Arts Council of Ireland.

Carolyn Roy is a London-based, independent dancer and landscape designer with over twenty years' experience of making and performing, teaching, writing and designing. Ongoing practice research is rooted in dance improvisation and the body's encounter with the environment. In addition to her own projects she has performed with Gaby Agis and Co, the Pacitti company, Graeme Miller, Tino Sehgal and Joe Moran and is at present working with Florence Peake and Botanic Dances. She is a regular teacher and researcher for Independent Dance and currently running courses in live art and somatic practice developed specifically for the adult education context of Morley College.

Helen Simard is a Montreal-based performer, choreographer and dance researcher. Since 2000, her choreographic work has been presented across Canada, as well as in England, France and Switzerland. Helen has over fifteen years teaching experience as a street dance, contemporary dance and Pilates instructor. She has a BFA in contemporary dance from Concordia University (2000), an MA in dance studies from University of Quebec in Montreal (2014), and is currently doing a PhD in Étude et pratique des arts (Study and practice of arts) at University of Quebec in Montreal.

Jane Toms is an Alexander Technique teacher and a Chartered Physiotherapist. Her Alexander Technique practice includes private pupils, working in occupational settings and university teaching. As a physiotherapist she worked in clinical practice for 20 years, completed a Masters and moved into academia in 2001. Her passion for working with dancers began when she collaborated with Natalie Garrett Brown in 2007. Their joint delivery of a Master's module 'Embodying Dance and Performance Practice' led to a presentation at a performing arts conference in Melbourne 2012 on group learning in the Alexander Technique as a means of facilitating self-agency and reflexivity.

Amy Voris is a dance-artist based in Manchester. Her practice is process-oriented and collaborative. She works with photographer Christian Kipp, composer James Buchanan, lighting designer Cath Cullinane and is a co-founder of the 'enter inhabit', 'L219' and 'aMiGaEnterPrises' projects. She has worked in higher education for over a decade and recently completed training in Integrative Bodywork and Movement Therapy with Linda Hartley. She is currently pursuing a practice as research PhD at the University of Chichester.

Sarah Whatley is Professor of Dance and Director of the Centre for Dance Research (C-DaRE) at Coventry University. Her research interests include dance and new technologies, dance analysis, somatic dance practice and pedagogy, and inclusive dance practices. Her current AHRC-funded project is 'InVisible Difference; Dance, Disability and Law'. She is also leading a major EU-funded project (EuropeanaSpace), exploring the creative reuse of digital cultural content She led the AHRC-funded Siobhan Davies digital archive project, RePlay, She is also Editor of the *Journal of Dance and Somatic Practices* and sits on the editorial boards of several other Journals.

Contact details for the authors can be found via this book's web page:

www.triarchypress.net/attending-to-movement

EDITORS' INTRODUCTION

This edited collection draws together contributions from the second Dance and Somatic Practices International Conference[1], held at the Centre for Dance Research[2], Coventry University, UK, July 2013, in association with Independent Dance[3]. The title of the edited collection is taken from the conference theme and includes writings by somatic practitioners, dance artists and scholars from a range of subject domains interested to consider what embodied thinking and action can afford to philosophical and socio-cultural inquiry.

As with the conference, the book aims to investigate the potentials of embodied thinking and action, to provoke new questions and to develop new ways of engaging with wide ranging trans-disciplinary concerns. In taking this approach the book celebrates and builds upon the work of visionary UK dance artist, teacher and scholar Gill Clarke (1954 –2011)[4], who championed the value of somatic approaches within and beyond dance education and creative practice. Several of the authors directly discuss the influence of Clarke's work upon their own and others' practice while other contributors engage with her provocation that 'attending to movement' holds the potential to illuminate understandings of relationship, ethics and knowledge -generation more broadly.

The book is arranged in five parts, each including a variety of solo and collaboratively authored chapters speaking from a range of perspectives and disciplines. The five sub-themes of the book, which comprise its five parts, are: ***Intercultural Dialogues***, ***Somatic Practices in the Wider Social Context***, ***The Interplays of Practice and Writing***, ***Pedagogy Perspectives*** and ***Lived Lineages***. They are indicative not only of Clarke's work but also speak to current research interests within the field of dance and somatic practices. In publishing this collection and continuing the series of Biennial Dance and Somatic Practices Conferences our interest is to further the development of this burgeoning field of scholarly and artistic inquiry, which extends increasingly across geographical and disciplinary borders.

Part One – Intercultural Dialogues

Opening with a chapter by Carol Brown, one of the conference keynote presenters, **Intercultural Dialogues** offers four accounts of attending to the cultural context of movement. In Brown's writing 'So, Remember the Liquid Ground' this is explored through a consideration of her own choreographic work in Auckland, New Zealand, while the second chapter by Lalitaraja, 'Thinking, Reflecting and Contemplating With the Body', considers how Buddhist teachings inform his practice as a UK-based dance artist engaged in performance, improvisation, choreography and contact improvisation.

---

1 *The Journal of Dance and Somatic Practices* is published by Intellect – http://bit.ly/tpMove95. The conferences are hosted at Coventry University, UK – http://bit.ly/tpMove94.

2 The Centre for Dance Research (C-DaRE) – http://bit.ly/tpMove93.

3 Independent Dance, London, UK – http://bit.ly/tpMove92.

4 Further publications featuring Clarke's work include: *Journal of Dance & Somatic Practices*, Vol 3.1 & 3.2, 2012 (Barnard, Clarke & deLahunta, 'A conversation about choreographic thinking tools') and Diehl, I. & Lampert, F. (ed) (2011) *Dance Techniques 2010*, Tanzplan.

Nadra Assaf's contribution for Chapter 3 'Not Without my Body' brings into view socio-political positioning of the dancing body and reflects upon contemporary dance performance in the Middle East. The fourth and closing chapter of this part by Juan Aldape, 'Embodied Migratory Acts Across the USA-Mexico Border', further extends the engagement with choreographic practice present in Brown and Lalitaraja's writing while extending the focus to include interrelated ethnographic field work.

Part Two – Somatic Practices in the Wider Social Context

Part Two draws together three authors interested in the potential of somatic practices to enact or invite change in society. Thomas Kampe begins with a discussion of the Feldenkrais Method as a critical practice arguing in his chapter, 'The Art of Making Choices' that it has the potential to 'provide the conditions for inquiry, un-knowing and embodied self examination'. Chapter 6, 'An Intricate Field', by Lizzy Le Quesne continues the discussion with her reflection on a choreographic project informed by Skinner Releasing Technique, positioning this as a political act. The closing Chapter, 'Embodied Adventures in and out of the Irish Countryside', is a multi-authored account of an ongoing project by the Somaticats. Through image, reflective accounts and poetry, they invite the reader to consider their own relationship to the body, place and story within the everyday.

Part Three – The Interplay of Practice and Writing

This part contains seven perspectives on somatically-informed dance makers and performers interested in the relationship between movement and language, dancing and modes of inscription. Chapter 8 by Adam Benjamin, 'The Fool's Journey and Poisonous Mushrooms', begins by exploring metaphor as a way to talk about the 'getting lost' of improvisation. The next Chapter, 'At Dusk, the Collaborative Spills and Cycles of L219', by Amy Voris, Natalie Garrett Brown and collaborators considers writing and photography as an integral part of the ongoing creative practice. Carolyn Roy weaves scholarly references and reflective writing to explore the significances of embodied walking practices in her Chapter, 'As My Attention is Wandering'. Like Roy, Sally E. Dean brings scholarly writing in conversation with her own practice to chart her collaboration with costume and visual artists in Chapter 11 'Amerta Movement and Somatic Costume; Gateways into Environment'. Hilary Kneale's contribution, Chapter 12, 'The Daily Round, the Common Task', investigates the interrelationship between writing and making within her own creative practice, situating this work within the context of the visual arts. Sarah Whatley's Chapter 'Motion Capture and The Dancer; Visuality, Temporality and the Dancing Image' closes this part of the book with a discussion of how Motion Capture technology can "unearth something of the poetics in the SRT [Skinner Releasing Technique] pedagogy and the dancers' own philosophies of movement" in the work of Gibson and Martelli.

Part Four – Pedagogy Perspectives

Part Four offers a collection of four writings considering the influence of somatic practices within a range of educative contexts. Chapter 14 'Attending to Movement; The need to make dance that was different from that which went before' by Sara Reed charts the interrelationship between somatic practices and the development of

British New Dance while exploring the legacy of this within the UK higher education system. Fiona Bannon and Duncan Holt's contribution, 'Attending to Ethics and Aesthetics in Dance' frames dance education as "relational practice" or "thinking through motion" and thus able to "facilitate affective and significant personal and cultural growth", while Penny Collinson's Chapter, 'Re-sourcing the Body; Embodied Presence and Self-care in Working with Others', resonates with Bannon and Holt's interest in ethics and explores the role of creative and improvisational practices within a one-to-one / client and therapist context. Chapter 17, 'Towards a Constructive Interaction between Somatic Education and Introspective Verbalisation', by Nicole Harbonnier-Topin and Helen Simard completes this part and brings into view the importance of language use within somatically-informed dance education.

Part Five – Lived Lineages

The final part of the book, ***Lived Lineages***, includes four chapters interested in embodied histories and legacies. It begins with 'Disorganising Principles; Corporeal Fragmentation and the Possibilities for Repair' by Jenny Roche, who considers how somatic practices might support the dancer to "recalibrate and rebalance" when required to embody multiple choreographic movement vocabularies as a free-lance dance artist. Chapter 19, 'Myth-Busting; Using the Alexander Technique to Free Yourself from Detrimental misconceptions in the Performing Arts' by Jennifer Mackerras and Jane Toms holds a similar concern for embodied histories to Roche and proposes The Alexander Technique as a 'paradigm for honouring and using what is useful from our heritage, while acknowledging the 'myths' we acquire in our day to day living. Duncan Holt's writing in Chapter 20 'A Moving and Touching Career in Dance and Chiropratic' brings into conversation his own lived lineages as a dancer and chiropractor to explore the overlap within and between these two forms. The book and this part concludes with a contribution by Martha Eddy, an invited speaker at the conference. In this chapter 'Early Trends; Where Soma and Dance Began to Meet – Keeping the Meeting Alive', Eddy begins by tracing the varied lineages of the somatic and dance community that exist in the USA and Europe today. Eddy's chapter ends with a return to the opening theme of the book 'Intercultural Dialogues' as she reminds us of the varied cultural roots of the different somatic practices often drawn upon by dance artists. In doing so she echoes the conference theme in her assertion "...that the somatic process is not only a journey of awareness and self-acceptance, but also that the somatic process can lead to cultural empathy and societal balance".

Our aim in bringing together this collection is twofold. We hope the variety of perspectives and experiences encapsulated in the writing extends and deepens knowledge about the place of somatic philosophy within dance studies. We also hope that it generates further debate and curiosity about this fertile field of thought and practice, stimulating more moving and writing, to enliven our living in this world.

Kirsty Alexander
Natalie Garrett Brown
Sarah Whatley

April 2015

PART ONE

Intercultural Dialogues

CAROL BROWN

So, Remember the Liquid Ground

> We are grounded in a relationship with the environment which is changing constantly, what is coming into the present is us and the environment ... in conversation.
> (Gill Clarke in Lee & Davies [2011])

Standing on a beach, at the gifting line,
the receding tide leaves its debris of shells, seaweeds, fish bone, and jellyfish
and the discarded waste of human lives
plastic bottles and wrappings, fragments of ceramics and shards of sea smoothed glass

Feet sink into coarse-grained sand
Like sponges
Incoming water pools around toes
a wintery wind blows the foam caps off incoming waves

Face to sea and horizon line extending
Roaring, scudding saltwater
The same as the tears in our eyes
Before me, the shimmer of an obsidian sea
And behind me, the reflective glint of a grid of honeycombed windows
Polaroids at the ready, the glare-stare of the city meets the sea

Fig. 1: Becca Wood, *1000 Lovers*, Auckland, 2013. Photo: Cathy Carter

Knowledge of a sea like knowledge of a city, its patterns and pulses, its rhythms and riptides comes from embodied experience – I can study oceanography but I need the choreography of encounter to make sense of it – it is through practices like sea swimming and urban navigation that my knowledge of the unpredictability, changeability and readability of the environments we inhabit becomes incorporated.

In living in a city surrounded by sea – Auckland, Aotearoa New Zealand – it is impossible to ignore the circadian rhythms of our cosmos as the time of the sea, its incoming and outgoing rhythms expressed as a twelve-hour tidal flow, forms a counterpoint to the quotidian patterns of urban life. As a choreographer, I have had a long-standing preoccupation with working with the kinaesthetic sense of a liminal threshold between water and land. From early attempts at choreographing the shifting push/pull of tidal rhythms as a metaphor for love in the duet *O Seaswell of Love* (University of Otago, 1984); to *Manuhiri* with Bronwyn Judge inspired in part by the long breaking surf swells at Kaitiaki Beach in North Otago (Dunedin, 1990); to

Ocean Skin (The Place Theatre, London, 1997), a solo with video monitor and film of myself submerged in a bottomless pool; to the development of a constantly evolving virtual sea in *SeaUnSea* (Dance Umbrella, 2006), a real-time interactive performance and installation premiered at Siobhan Davies Studios; and that same year *Deep and Beneath* (2006) at the Roundhouse with an inter-disciplinary team of artists and young people in response to Cunningham Dance Company's presentations of *Ocean,* dances in dialogue with a sense of the sea have been a longstanding preoccupation. The sea has made a good dance partner. Most recently, this preoccupation has emerged in a series of urban performances that navigate the fluid borders of the edge of the land in Auckland, a city built on a narrow isthmus between two harbours. The works, *Blood of Trees* (World Water Day, 2012); *1000 Lovers* (Auckland Arts Festival, 2013); and *Tuna Mau* (Oceanic Performance Biennale, 2013) are variations of a performance cycle initiated in Perth in Western Australia through *Tongues of Stone* (Perth Dancing City, 2011). As an extended performance research event in collaboration with designer Dorita Hannah, sound artist Russell Scoones and local dancers in Perth and Auckland, these choreographies have been developed through a sustained attention to patterns of movement between bodies, cities, histories and nature.

As choreographer, water has not just formed a conceptual trigger and thematic content for these works but also provided me with rich kinaesthetic material through strong corporeal memories of a childhood spent sea swimming, lifesaving, surfing and diving. At a somatic level thoughts of the sea bring to mind the primacy of our own corporeal history in the internal sea of the amniotic fluids and in the inter-cellular processes of breathing. But the shifting edge of where the sea meets the land is also an inestimable, indefinable contour that constantly changes and shifts, like the outline of a body.

Politically, in the 21st century, water as an elemental force of nature has become mired in issues of scarcity and management. When the Conservative government came to power in the UK in 1979, water changed from being understood as a common good to becoming a commodity. Ten years later water was offered for sale to a public that already owned it collectively (Ward in Strang 2004: 10). Historical analyses of water resource management in the UK and elsewhere reveal a consistent pattern of lost agency and ownership. In Aotearoa New Zealand issues of water ownership and management are characterised by multiple languages, two distinct ones are those of indigenous and European cultures. For the former, *wai* or water is co-extensive with human life, is life giving and healing, a carrier of meanings, of stories and of *mauri* (spirit). For the European settlers who colonised New Zealand, water was understood as a resource to be drained, managed, channelled and systematically controlled or ,alternatively, as a source of leisure for bathing, surfing, boating and swimming.

What if paying attention to the fluid membranes of our bodies, to the liquid ground of our beginnings, to the connection between the salt of our tears and the salt of the sea, to the pathways to and from as well as along the shifting edge of the sea formed the basis for a choreography that navigates between the diverse histories and meanings of water and convenes a relationship between that which is considered fluid and that which is considered grounded?

This writing refracts recent work in the field of urban performance in Aotearoa New Zealand at the quick edge where the sea and land meet, with notions of repair and concepts of space and materiality emerging in recent critical thought.

Fig. 2: Sophie Williams, *1000 Lovers*, Auckland, 2013. Photo: Carol Brown

what can urban performance do?

> For innovation in creative work, we need inhabitation – of our bodies, of the places we live and love, and of the ideas we want to bring responsibly back to community.
> (Andrea Olsen 2014: 3)

The way I move is an ongoing response to what is around me. I feel, we feel, the force of movement take form in the thresholds of choreographic thinking. Knowing the world means paying attention to it, its reverberations, its textures, its colours and its patterns. *Worlding* this knowing through the choreography of encounter means inviting others to pay attention too.

Dancing in dialogue with the forces of the world in sensuous landscapes, urban terrains and civic sites holds the potential for transforming the sensory impulses of the body into performative moments that allow the forces and textures of the world to be re-embodied and invested with meaning and significance whilst at the same time drawing attention to the material dimensions of non-organic life, including water.

Performing ***Mnemosyne*** *in Prague (Prague Quadrenniale 2011), I carry a bucket of water. Holding it aloft between me and visitors to the gallery I take the hands of strangers and carefully rinse them in the water before touching my head with their hands. Hand, head and heart form a nexus of contact in this moment, momentarily a language of touch creates a constellation of meaning within the quotidian environment.*

Fig. 3: Carol Brown, *Mnemosyne*, Prague Quadrenniale, 2011. Photo: Russell Scoones

In Perth, Catherine Piue performing as 'sloshy' manages two buckets of water and a harness of water-filled balloons. The task of carrying water in multiple containers is heavy, cumbersome and makes her stagger as she moves down the lane. An impossible task, balloon sacs drop and break on the paving stones, their split membranes releasing a small flood of water that the audience navigate around as they journey behind her. The sacs become grotesque bladders, organs of release that leak and spill.

Fig. 4: Catherine Piue, *Tongues of Stone*, Perth, 2011. Photo: Christophe Canato

new forms of agency

As a choreographer I see performance as holding the potential to intensify the experience of sensation, both *subtly* and *spectacularly*. In the context of site-responsive performance this occurs by drawing attention to the co-presence of the human and the non-human across a relational field of joint agency. Reflecting on each of the choreographed situations above, I note that their 'taking place' is predicated upon a watery threshold that forms a liminal space of encounter with bystanders.

As these instances of performances indicate, I am interested in choreographic practices that return us to our animal lineage and to the sensuality of the environments we inhabit: practices that are not purely bound up with concepts but reside in our capacities to be attuned to material life. In passing from nature to culture, from the satisfaction of instinctual needs to the sharing of desires, these dances in public spaces are in part formed by a desire to bring *beings and non-beings into relation*. In other words they are concerned with moving beyond the anthropocentric.

This concern follows the work of French feminist philosopher Luce Irigaray (2012) who, like Elizabeth Grosz, calls for a *new epoch* in our human evolution, an era in which art, philosophy and spirituality are endowed with meaning and put into a practice in ways different from those that we have known in the past (2012: 22).

A chorus of 'river-runners' holding stainless steel buckets filled with water run through busy urban streets. The water sloshes and spills over the side of the buckets splashing onto the pavement and disrupting passers-by.

Fig. 5: River Runners, STRUT Dance, *Tongues of Stone*, 2011. Photo: Christophe Canato

If dance is a place I go to, to know myself, my surroundings and environment, what is it to form a sense of place through liquid ground? For Luce Irigaray, a forgetting of air and of fluids is part of our inheritance of Western philosophical thought. In her recent writing she describes a loss of sensory intelligence in our relations with nature and the other; and that we are trying to find it again:

> I think that we are trying to find *the crossroads* at which we have taken the wrong path. (Irigaray 2012: 145)

If Western philosophy has historically denied the sensory intelligence of the body, so too has the so-called 'civilising' influence of industrial economies in their relationship to resources. Paul Carter describes this legacy as 'dry thinking' that held an aversion to the damp, humid, sodden and swampy.

> The history of Western civilisation is a history of desiccation. All civilisations require water, and many are literally built upon it. But modern Western cultures have defined themselves increasingly by setting water apart, as a necessary, but foreign object or resource, rather than as a constituent and accomplice of human life. European culture has grown ever more suspicious of the moist and damp. (Carter 2005: 107)

And yet, our bodies are composed primarily of fluid. The cells of our tissues live within the interstitial fluid, our internal sea. As Emilie Conrad described it, 'we are basically fluid beings that have arrived on land' (cited in Olsen 2014: 13). A denial of the damp, the leaky and the fluid is part of a long legacy of somatophobia in the West. Overcoming this denial, paying attention to the wetness of our eyes, the moisture in our mouths and lips, forms part of a movement towards a more visceral and corporeal state of awareness and way of knowing.

Is the source of your movement arising from the effortless internal flow of fluid through your tissues or is it restricted due to hardness, dryness, stagnation, collapse or stress and effort? Body-Mind Centering is a practice that focuses on the movement of the body's fluids acknowledging and opening the potential for blood, lymph, cellular, interstitial and cerebral-spinal fluids. Each fluid has a specific rhythm and tonal range. According to Body-Mind Centering techniques the mind of the fluids is flow, rhythm and ease in the ever-changing conditions of our lives including in relation to environment.

On Munster Lane a chorus of river-runners pour water onto the laneway paving stones and crouch down; unfastening their headscarves they wash these in the water, allowing the red inky marks of their messages to bleed onto the ground below.

Fig. 6 *Tongues of Stone* Perth 2011. Photo: Christophe Canato

Each of these recent works – *Tongues of Stone* (Perth Dancing City 2011), *Mnemosyne* (Prague Quadrennial 2011), *Blood of Trees* (Fluid City, Auckland 2012), *1000 Lovers* (White Night Auckland Arts Festival 2013) and *Tuna Mau* (Oceanic Performance Biennale, Auckland 2013) – involved water as a performative agent, both physically and conceptually. In reflecting on these collaborative performances collectively, I see that the movement of water, its hidden and visible presence within the choreography, formed a liminal threshold through which meanings and significance was developed. I would like to propose that this emphasis on the material presence of water and its agency within these works invites consideration of a fluid subjectivity, uncontained from the privileged ground of an 'earthed' terrestrially centred dancing. As a critical spatial poetics this choreographic approach might be considered to move towards a partial and provisional response to the challenge of working in post-colonial and decolonising cities where indigenous thinking exists alongside and in tension with settler, new immigrant and global cultures.

corporeal history

> Landscape can be the basis of our identity; it can also be a mythology. (Park 2006: 76).

As a Pākehā (European New Zealand) choreographer and performer living in Aotearoa New Zealand, a country undergoing a process of decolonisation from a colonial past rooted in the values of Victorian England, I am in dialogue with the question of 'how not to be imperial?'. This task solicits from me the requirement to research and gather the coordinates of movement within the cosmology of the southern hemisphere despite being educated, trained and incorporated into the cultural forms of a largely Western European history.

> *Choreography class begins with the invitation for students to name the mountain and river that they identify with or were born in proximity to and then to orientate themselves in the studio in relation to these places. One student of Pacific island descent responds, 'my river is inside me'.*

Where does the sun rise? The imposition of a colonial geography is everywhere evident in the so-called New World. 19th- and early 20th-century urban planners designed cities from London and exported the blueprints for houses orientated towards a northern hemisphere sun to the colonies. The house I grew up in was, consequently, facing the wrong way. Though these were historical practices, many in the Southern Hemisphere cities of Australia and New Zealand continue to live with this altered sense of place in cities which recall other cities and that carry the nomenclature of Edinburgh, London and the colonial fathers who settled here. As a dance-artist, this history invites the question, 'how does the dis-placement of one place with another affect our corporeal identity and orientation within space?'.

Part of *tikanga Māori* or Māori philosophy involves locating who one is in relation to genealogy (*whakapapa*) and land (*whenua*). In asking students to name geographical touchstones – mountains (*maunga*) and river (*awa*) rather than the built environment (cities or towns) – as their places of origin, I am encouraging a sense of location that connects to a geophysical and spiritual sense of place and to remember the natural origins of life. Such an orientation to the world initiates a return to nature and, arguably, recognises a maternal genealogy that is concealed by a Western preoccupation with mastery over environment. In exploring becomings not based on forgetting, Irigaray proposes we are returned to the beginning: the mother (2012: 112).

A maternal genealogy favours the values of life, of generation, of growth. Irigaray describes our estrangement from home as being in part to do with our projections of a world that is constructed and that little by little substitutes itself for us. The denial of a maternal identity is also a denial of the liquid ground of our primordial belongings. This is not a call for a return to an essentialist understanding of the feminine; what Irigaray sees as important is a return to our own bodies, our own breath, our own sexuate identities. Such a return calls for a reciprocity between the sexes, between desire and love and more generally in humanity in relation to nature.

If indigenous cultures consciously articulate the natural environment through their creativity and perceive a continuity between humans and the natural environment including seas, land, rivers, mountains, flora and fauna, then their relationship to environment is founded on a belief in reciprocity. Pre-European Māori 'ate from the forest and fished from the sea: forest and sea flowed through them' (Park 2006: 89). Yet the Europeanisation of New Zealand through the colonial project enshrined the imperialist principle that 'people and nature are irreconcilably opposed, and that the victory of one necessarily entailed the vanishing of the other' (Park 2006: 86).

The colonial city, Dunedin, where I was born, was originally modelled on Edinburgh in Scotland. The shadow of this history is everywhere from the statue of Robbie Burns in the centre of the city to the street names and kilt wearing of schoolgirls. My mountain, which I was born under, like my father was, is Mount Cargill. It was named after Captain Cargill, an early colonist and leader of the province of Otago. Built from layers of fluid lava flows accumulated from an extinct volcano more than 10 million years old, its distinctive form was named Kapukataumahaka by local Māori (*Ngai Tahu*). The name refers to the snaring of kereru or pigeons by Māori as the birds ate the berries of the native kapuka tree.

At the level of a body politic, corseted Victorian women arrived from the 1840s in New Zealand. Their experience was extreme. Sarah Mathew, wife of the chief surveyor of Auckland Felton Mathew, on seeing the land around Auckland described it as, 'the most dreary and desolate looking country eye ever beheld' (Mathew in Rutherford 1940: 150).

Though many indigenous names were written over by early colonial settlement, their recovery and reiteration, as New Zealanders come to terms with the different dimensions of landscape, conceptual as well as physical in a bi-cultural country, has led to an effective re-imagining of a cultural coexistence of indigenous and settler ways of belonging. Far from the imperial city of London, there has evolved since the early colonial period a desire to re-imagine the landscape: 'Pākehā New Zealanders peering into the 21st century have, like white Australians, a history that now requires them to re-imagine their community, to rethink their nation's responsibility to its indigenous peoples – as Māori are indeed fast rethinking their responsibility to Pākehā' (Park 2006: 91).

Ideas about landscape, about place, align with our beliefs, values and intuitions for survival. At a physical level we hold embodied memories of place through the kinaesthetic imagination. For Māori, a sense of who you are in the world starts with a relation to Papatuanuku, an oceanic-island earth mother, and the word for land, *whenua*, is also the word for placenta. The/her body *is* home and land. As a descendent of colonial immigrants from England and Ireland I might look to Ninhursaga, the

Sumerian mountain goddess, or Arianrhod, the Celtic goddess of fertility, to a much older inheritance through a mobile culture that was nomadic, uprooted and more placeless than the ties to place and boundaried land that colonial settlement enforced.

Paul Carter asks how our once nomadic and migratory species should have founded its "polity, its psychology, its ethics and even its poetics on the antithesis of movement; on the rhetoric of foundations, continuity, genealogy, stasis?" (Carter in Park 2006: 92). He draws attention to the paradox that a culture intent on global colonisation should, at the same time, associate movement with the 'unstable, the unreliable, the wanton and the primitive' and seek to fix boundaries with the precision of a theodolite. Like the foundations of anatomy for medical science being the cadaver on the slab, so the land as a body was historically surveyed through quantification as a fixed entity (*ibid*: 92). This inheritance is something I know intimately well as my father was a quantity land surveyor, responsible for drawing up maps of previously 'unmapped' (according to European values) terrain. And yet the quick edge of the sea defies our attempts to fix a limit and draw a line that cannot be breached and broken. How do you create an accurate measurement of a constantly changing limit?

> Breathing out the poet puts into words what the swimmer already knows. (Nepia 2012: 1:24)

Given a history of contested rights to land and occupation, my right to perform, in dialogue with place, must be negotiated through an acknowledgement of the pre-European and contemporary spiritual values attached to *moana* (sea) and *whenua* (land).

How, I ask, might we develop practices of dance that are truly de-centred, that move away from a 20th-century inheritance that emphasises weight, gravity and ground as core to our moving and that exclude our liquid corporeal history?

unearthed

> The body's texture is spatial; and reciprocally the texture of space is corporeal. (Gil 2006)

Choreographer Sue Healey's feature length film *Virtuosi,* about New Zealand dancers and their nomadic lives, portrays eight artists who purportedly display a strong sense of 'groundedness' and 'weightedness' in their movement and their attitude to dance. This sense, the film proposes, was acquired through a history of growing up in bare feet and small country towns far from the metropolises of elsewhere. The relation to place expressed as a style of 'earthy', grounded dancing is however counterpointed by images of dancers moving in water as if the unconscious flipside of their grounded movement qualities was a more liquid sense of a moving identity that holds strong affinities with water. New Zealand, like England and Ireland, is an island nation. And yet, much of our cultural identity is founded upon territorial conquest, rights of occupation, property ownership and surveyors' peg marks.

If dancing is a state of unstable flux, it is also something that cannot be given in advance, that cannot be contained. To dance is to systematically take and take-away ground. Whilst we can know in an embodied way that dancers' movements evolve in spaces other than in objective space, how much do we acknowledge the 'liquid ground' of their formation:

> In me everything is already flowing and you flow along too if you only stop minding such unaccustomed motion, and its song … So remember the liquid ground. (Irigaray 1991: 37)

In making work I make leaps between things, edges bump up against and dissolve into each other, movements come and go, are washed away and return. I attempt to create zones of heightened possibility. My interdisciplinary dance practice is concerned with a spatial poetics that *tracks* corporeal knowing through choreography that returns again and again to a watery source, a liquid ground. As interdisciplinary performances that attend to the sensate city this work is a form of creative re-membering, a putting back together of other places, lineages and bodies with the multiple layers and specificities of each site (Carter 2004). It is choreography written from the perspective of corporeal longings that fold historical, ancestral and embodied memories through interaction in the local specific context. In these contexts, I constantly slip up on the debris of history at the broken edge of the land. Thoughts of repair haunt me. Not so much repair as restoration, but repair which leaves an awareness and sensitivity of the original fault; repair in this way might be as simple as a performance journey that evokes past, present and future.

unless

> "But *now*", says the Once-ler,
> "Now that *you're* here,
> the word of the Lorax seems perfectly clear.
> UNLESS someone like you
> Cares a whole awful lot,
> Nothing is going to get better.
> It's not.
> (Dr Seuss 2009, n.p.)

In *Small Acts of Repair* (2007) the former Chicago-based company Goat Island describes the development of performative thought experiments to engage systematically with the conundrum of the possibility of the impossibility of repair. In the process of making *When will the September roses bloom? Last night was only a comedy*' (2004) they asked: How do you make a repair? Their approach, given the scale of the problems confronting the world, was to start small at the level of micropolitics. This was not an indication of an absence of ambition or will to tackle the question of repair, but rather of an interest in bearing witness to the problems themselves. Repair was not about recovery, wherein an original state is restored and the fault or loss forgotten, but a reparative act that leaves an awareness and sensitivity of the fault in place (Bottoms & Goulish 2003: 95).

Like many other artists working in the terrain of a performance ethics, there is a strong desire to incorporate and address what has been excluded, denied or repressed by the forces of a neo-colonial globalisation and consumer capitalism. The ethical turn of performance in the West has involved a complex set of relays between the aesthetic-affective, the micropolitics of perception, and the intersections between performers, the public and the social.[1] In returning to live in New Zealand with my children after an absence of more than 22 years, I find myself also in this conundrum of how to reconfigure relationships between corporeal identity and land.

According to cultural theorist Richard Sennett, there is a close connection between making and repairing. In his recent book, *Together: The Rituals, Pleasures and Politics of Cooperation* he describes the three ways to perform a repair: first by making a damaged thing seem just like new; second by improving the operation of that which is damaged; and third by altering it altogether. These three strategies consist

1 See for example Cull (2013).

of *restoration, remediation* or *reconfiguration*. The first is governed by the thing's original state; the second substitutes better parts or materials while preserving an old form; the third re-imagines the form and function of the thing whilst fixing it (Sennett 2012: 212).

Reconfiguration is the most radical kind of repair. It is a term commonly found in computer applications to describe for instance the wiring in of a switchboard or the peripherals attached to a computer. In a digital age the term also recalls the capacity of dreams to reconfigure waking consciousness by 'filing' and assembling memories in such a way that we can make sense of experience. I like to use this term in thinking about how our performances on the waterfront might reconfigure urban dwellers' relationships with the edge of the land and its meanings. In these contexts the waterfront becomes a liminal threshold for performative acts of repair.

A liminal space is a viscous zone of encounter with the other. It is a truly productive space from which to work. Performing liminality thus evokes a material transformation of space and energy marking a passage in time and within and between spaces. In this context, that which is broken becomes an occasion for remaking differently.

> Radical repairs of this sort … occur through small, surprising changes which turn out to have larger implications. (Sennett 2012: 214)

However these kinds of repairs do not offer the consolations of redemption.

somatic stutter beyond redemption

So how might an engagement with somatic dance open a space for the reconfiguring of relations between nature and culture and the possibility of repair?

If somatics reconfigures understandings of the body-as-organism and in flux, somatic-informed dance can be said to frame this subject in dialogue with culture and nature. Somatic-aware dance can be generative of compositional strategies, ways of thinking about movement, time, gesture, space, rhythm, patterns and space as well as expanding the potential of the body to produce meaning. However I believe that such an approach, if it is to catalyse and effect change, needs to move beyond self-discovery and the confines of the studio and towards a material engagement with the forces of the world and its socio-political, spiritual and non-Western horizons.

> Destruction is more exciting than repair.
> (Bottoms & Goulish 2007: 23)

A young choreographer tells me she is making a solo about shame, another wears her too tight mother's wedding dress as a metaphor for all the bodies she has had to fit into (Irigaray's words, 'with your milk mother I drink ice' echo in my mind).

But as philosopher and psychoanalyst Luce Irigaray explains, persistent representations of pain and anger, though necessary, even cathartic, leave us bare, denuded and without adequate resources for renewal and repair.

What if our question of how to repair the world starts small, as Lin Hixson suggests, at a cellular level, with how to repair the relationship between soma and psyche and from this threshold improvises its way to consider wider issues of the relations between soma and city, the local and the global, the world and its cosmology, even the indigenous and the non-indigenous?

What if, through spatio-corporeal thresholds of performing the city in dialogue with its subterranean fluids, we renew our resourcefulness for repair?

critical homes

In rethinking performative agency distributed across multiple dimensions, spaces and materials within a dispersed and de-centred locale, I turn to materialist theory to find a critical home.

A radical reappraisal of the stuff of life or what matters to us, materialist theory has emerged in the wake of recognition that dominant constructivist theories of postmodernism and postmodern feminism are inadequate for thinking about matter, materiality and political change. A materialist theory of agency calls for a sensory attentiveness to nonhuman forces operating outside and inside the human body (Bennett 2009: xiv) and would seem an appropriate critical partner to somatic approaches to dance and, in particular, site-responsive dance.

A reconfigured relation between theory and materiality expressed by this new materialism aligns with many of the drivers of somatic-aware dance as well as offering critical ballast for a non-essentialist understanding of embodiment within place-responsive work. But what is particularly challenging in the offer emerging from new materialism, perhaps specifically for a somatic-informed practice that has been historically located in embodiment, is the call for a shift away from anthropocentrism and a subject-centred identity politics.

Elizabeth Grosz is one of a number of theorists calling for a moratorium on the subject, the self and talk of identity as a tactic for moving beyond identity politics, the epistemological and the perceived limits of deconstruction and 'postmodern feminism'. Her position is clear:

> To focus on the subject at the cost of focusing on the forces that make up the world is to lose the capacity to see beyond the subject, to engage with the world, to make the real … I am *not* what others see in me, but what I do, what I make. (Grosz 2011: 84–85)

But what does new materialism do to us in terms of practice? Irigaray, one of the key thinkers aligned with the new materialism through Grosz's writing, describes yoga practice and a culture of breath as a way to facilitate this shift through listening to the other(s). If we do not listen to the other we deprive them of breathing, even of living. Through her psychoanalytic practice and theorisation of sexuate difference, Irigaray discusses how yoga helped her create a 'living third' space between her and her patient, in the air. She describes how yoga brings understanding of the relation between two bodies that is reduced neither to a fusional maternal empathy nor to animal attraction, but that is two autonomous worlds that enter into relation whilst remaining two, which she describes as creating something *other than children*.

What Irigaray elaborates is a new understanding of the movement from nature to culture, one that is not tied to violent forces of mastery, containment and control. In this context, culture is understood, not as the domination of nature but as its cultivation, its enhancement and its expansion. As Grosz sees it, culture must be more than the reduction of nature to a dead commodity (2012). Material thinking can be seen to align with an indigenous view of the world through which people are an integral part of nature and there are intricate linkages between customary resources and biodiversity. However, coming to grips with nature as a source of spiritual kinship and identity holds complex challenges for descendants of a European romantic view of landscape as a background to action.

What somatic knowledge can contribute to this discourse is a thickened understanding of the visceral affects and sensations of working with the material and immaterial forces of life. The relationship between the external movement of the body through space, the internal movement of the tissues, organs and fluids, and the movement of mind as we attend to performing outside, tracks a choreographic re-patterning of our relationships to/with the natural and built environment – just as a 'somatic materialism' unfolding in thought and practice, choreographing encounters where land meets sea, re-patterns relationships that are historically fraught and contested.

Hine carries a long rope. She unwinds it, creating a long line on the ridge of landscaped ground above the reedbeds. She lies beside this line, her body forming a horizon, at the edge. The widow picks up the other end of the rope and tugs at it pulling her. Hine leans back resisting the force of this staged 'tug of war' until she is standing opposite. Eyes meet and the rope is loosened, only to be gathered up in Hine's arms and carried towards the sea. Later she will throw the rope to a swimmer (eel-man) and pull him into shore.

swampy thinking

How can we connect the somatic with social-political-historical forces? In returning to live in Aotearoa, I have been compelled to reconsider my own research practice through an urgent need to build relationships across different practices, materialities, knowledges and spaces; to acknowledge and incorporate Pacific thinking and practice without appropriating it. This has been part of an ongoing creative project to unsettle the flattened ground of colonialism.

The grand-daughter of Irish farmers who settled on the East Cape near where Captain James Cook first sighted New Zealand, Tolaga Bay, and the daughter of a land surveyor, who drew some of the first maps of south Otago, this is a personal as well as a political quest.

> It does not matter how maps are redrawn unless they are drawn differently. Unless they incorporate the movement of forms that characterize the primary experiences of meeting and parting. (Carter 2009: 7)

In March 2013, with performance designer Dorita Hannah and composer Russell Scoones, we premiered *1000 Lovers*, a site-responsive performance that journeyed from the sea to the city for a mobile public listening to a soundscape played on headphonics.

1000 Lovers draws its title from Auckland's Māori name *Tāmaki Makaurau,* which means 'Isthmus of one thousand lovers' but may also be understood as the place of many lovers. It followed a walkable route over 50 minutes, starting at Silo Park and ending with audience and bystanders on the steps of Karanga Plaza as the performers crossed the bridge into the central business district. In crossing this strip of reclaimed harbour we imagined a movement from a primordial past through the encounters of colonialism towards an unknown future.

The life cycle and movement patterns of the tuna or eel formed a central motif for the choreography alongside the pan-Pacific story of inter-species love between Hine and Tuna (the eel-man). New Zealand's freshwater eels breed in deep water near Tonga. Their larvae float on tides back towards New Zealand where they mature into glass eels to enter estuaries. As they head upstream to the lakes they turn a darker colour metamorphosing into elvers. Elvers are small enough to climb waterfalls up to 50m and continue their journeys until they reach the inland lakes where they grow into mature eels. After many years in fresh water they migrate back towards the sea, often crossing land masses with the suction pads on their bellies pulling them along to reach the ocean and swim to their breeding place in the sea, between Tonga and Fiji.

Fig. 7 Sophie Williams (Hine), *1000 Lovers*. Photo: Dean Carruthers

Swaying
A tangle of spines, overlapping, intersecting
Swishing
A chorus of elvers moving, around, between, through
Sinews
Remember the route from stream to sea
Slicing
Air like water
Sequential
Unfurling across liquid ground

'Hine and the Eel-man' is a story of Hine's love for a mythical part-man part-eel, Tuna. Her husband Maui, on discovering this forbidden love, mutilates the eel-man. His body forms different fish and flora in the New Zealand environment, his head becoming the conger eel, his whiskers the long grasses and his blood the red stain in the rimu tree.

> *In the most recent iteration of this work a chorus of performers stand on the steps of the harbour and watch red stains bleed into the seawater.*

For the audience, inhabiting the soundworld and following the performers on this journey invited co-presence, being with rather than looking at. In making dynamic exchanges between bodies and places the emphasis was on an encounter between the material reality of the lived world and 'other' worlds, which were invoked to destabilise the familiar. Listening to eels move in the waterways that surround us and kinaesthetically empathising with their movement patterns, our bodies become host to their affective trace, their otherness. Through waterfront movement research becoming eel is evoked in ancestral stories of place through the 'eel-man' and is a method for inter-species exchange at the level of inter-corporeal identity.

Fig. 8: *Tuna Mau,* Auckland, 2013. Photo: Cathy Carter

> *It makes you fall in love with your city again.*
> (Audience member)

If theatrical space is a concentration of space, focusing inwards from an outside, site-responsive dance is concerned with a more open relational space that takes us literally outside. In her countering of Heidegger's metaphysical privileging of the ground of a dwelling as a dense solid plane, Irigaray proposes the spreading, nourishing and infinite substance of air as that which is neglected:

> Is there a dwelling more vast, more spacious, or even more generally peaceful than that of air? (Irigaray 1999: 40)

What happens when we shift our attention from the plane of the horizontal ground to particles of air in dialogue with the movement of breath? Moving with a sense of viscous, thick air in dialogue with breath changes my movement, just as moving outside with the unpredictability of the weather, with wind, rain, clouds and sunshine, alters my sensory experience. Breathing connects to the inter-cellular fluids of our bodies and is the basis of a liquid ground for corporeal identity. Moving in this way holds potential for going beyond the legacies of anthropocentric thought and understandings that hold their foundations in a solid plane.

Beneath our urban infrastructures course natural subterranean fluids, moving through layers of geological strata. With rapid urbanisation, however, falling rainwater is channelled through concrete stormwater drains where it collects concentrations of lead, zinc and copper. Metal and organic contaminants in stormwater run-off to accumulate in the tissues of shellfish, eels, birds and other invertebrates and contribute to the build up of toxins in the sediment and silt of our harbours (Kelley 2010).

> You're glumping the pond where the Humming fish
> hummed!
> No more can they hum, for their gills are all gummed.
> So I'm sending them off. Oh, their future is dreary.
> They'll walk on their fins and get woefully weary
> In search of some water that isn't so smeary.
> I hear things are just as bad up in Lake Erie.
> (Dr Seuss, *The Lorax* 2009)

*During the making of **1000 Lovers** the dredging of the harbour stirred up silt and contaminated the water with heavy-metal sediments. Where once the dancers could swim it was no longer safe to do so.*

Everyday life is saturated with water and we engage in intimate interactions with it through ingestion and expulsion, contact and immersion. In a recursive relationship nature and culture literally flow into each other.

This is not new to contemporary dance or somatic practice. Water and air, those most incorporeal of substances, are intrinsic to the lexicon of dance and somatics practices. But what happens when we take this knowledge outside, *into the open air?*

As I write, we find ourselves in an era of erosion of our natural and spiritual dwellings. We urgently need to learn how to respond to the call of the other person, of the nonhuman, the animal and the natural world in an ethical way. Grosz, Irigaray, Braidotti and other contemporary writers in the 'turn to matter' recognise that we need to return to a different concept of nature through an interdisciplinary, posthumanist approach. Irigaray furthers this potential by proposing an intercultural philosophy of breath as a kind of ground through which we meet (Skof and Holmes 2013: 11). This sustained critique of a history of Western dominance over nature can be proactive in listening to indigenous voices that have been largely ignored by a history of colonialism. Māori values of *kaitiakitanga*, or guardianship over the land as *tangata whenua* (people of the land), propel me to tread carefully when working in the physical, including the urban, landscape. Here, ancestral stories and ways of telling and naming the land and seascape hold vital knowledge about its material and spiritual values; they can also provide routes for moving beyond the unsustainability of the colonial project. At the quick edge of the land we also encounter a complex history of migration, negotiation and contested rights that are played out through our bodies.

Returning to Goat Island's thought experiments, though performance as an act of repair or reconciliation may prove impossible, how might choreography at the quick edge of the land catalyse a *reconfigured relationship between soma and city, nature and culture*, opening spaces for altered senses of place and a state of attention to the continuous process of change?

The choreography we create in these times of change is filled with intersecting messages of our commitments, corporeal habitations and positions on the future. Each becomes a figure of possibility.Attending to the liquid ground of corporeality brings us into dialogue with what history has forgotten, opening a potential space for siting difference at a threshold between outside and inside and catalysing reparative acts of becoming.

References

'1000 Lovers': http://bit.ly/tpMove25

'Tongues of Stone': http://bit.ly/tpMove24

Bennett, J. (2009) *Vibrant Matter:A Political Ecology ofThings*, Duke University Press

Bottoms, S.J. & Goulish, M. (eds.) (2007) *Small Acts of Repair: Performance, Ecology, and Goat Island*, Routledge

Brannigan, E. (2010) *Moving Across Disciplines: Dance in the Twenty-first Century*, Currency House

Carter, P. (1994) 'From Collage to Fold:A Poetics of Place', *Periphery*, no. 20, pp. 3-7

_______ (2004) *Material Thinking*, Melbourne University Press

_______ (2009) *Dark Writing : Geography, Performance, Design*, University of Hawaii Press

Coole, D. & Frost, S. (eds) (2010) *New Materialisms: Ontology,Agency and Politics*, Duke University Press

Cull, L.(2013) *Theatres of Immanence: Deleuze and the Ethics of Performance*, Palgrave Macmillan

Daly,A. (2000) 'Feminist Theory across the Millennial Divide' *Dance Research Journal* Vol.32,1, pp.39-42

Garrett, N. (2007):'Somatic Informed Choreographic Practice', Unpublished PhD thesis Roehampton University, UK

Gil, J. (2006) 'Paradoxical Body', *TDR:The Drama Review*,Vol. 50, No. 4 (T 192),Winter2006, pp. 21-35

Grosz, E. (2011) *Becoming Undone: Darwinian Reflections on Life*, Barnes and Noble

Irigaray, L. (1999) *Why Different?*, Semiotexte

_______ (2012) *In the Beginning She Was*, Bloomsbury

Kelly, S. (2010) *Ecological Impacts from Stormwater in the Auckland Region*, Auckland Regional Council

Lee, R and Davies, S. (2011) 'Gill Clarke', Obituary http://bit.ly/tpMove26

Nepia, P.M. (2012) 'Te Kore – Exploring the Māori concept of void' Unpublished PhD thesis, AUT University, Aotearoa/New Zealand

Olsen, A. (2014) *The Place of Dance*, Wesleyan University Press

Park, G. (2006) *Theatre Country: Essays on Landscape and Whenua*, Victoria University Press

Phillips, M. (2011) dancing city—traceries in stone, *RealTime* #103 June, http://bit.ly/tpMove28

Rutherford, J. (ed.) (1940) *The founding of New Zealand: The journals of Felton Mathew, First Surveyor-General of New Zealand, and his wife, 1840-1847*, A.H. & A.W. Reed

Sennett, R. (2012) *Together: The Rituals, Pleasures and Politics of Cooperation*, Yale University Press

Seuss, Dr. (2009) *The Lorax*, Harper Collins

Skof, L. & Holmes, E.A. (2013) *Breathing with Irigaray*, Bloomsbury

Strang, V. (2004) *The Meanings of Water*, Berg

Wilderness Magazine http://bit.ly/tpMove27

LALITARAJA

Thinking, Reflecting and Contemplating With the Body

Introduction

This chapter sketches out reflections on cultivating wisdom through listening, thinking/ reflecting and contemplating – a teaching drawn from the Buddhist tradition – and explores them in relation to dance practice. These reflections exist within an ongoing attempt to integrate a lived practice of Buddhism with being a dance artist/educator. My lived experience is that they are not separate. To articulate what arises out of that is the challenge this chapter seeks to meet. These articulations are intended to speak both to Buddhists about the synergies between dance practice and spiritual practice and to those engaged in dance practice to show how much of Buddhism might be implicitly known to them already.

As well as laying down some basic ideas about reflection and wisdom in Buddhism this chapter will put things into context in relation to the work of Gill Clarke and through the range of core dance practices that I engage with: performance improvisation, choreography, and contact improvisation, including the structure of Nancy Stark Smith's underscore.

Clarke was a constant presence in my career from the early 1980s onwards. As advocate, performer, maker and as a researcher she embodied and modelled what an intelligent, articulate, concerned and wise dancer could be like – she is sorely missed. Clarke was the bearer not just of a physical intelligence but the holder of bodily wisdom. Over many years of *dharma* practice I have been humbled on many occasions by the presence and compassion of dancers who were not directly engaged in formal spiritual practice; Clarke was the strongest example of this. She committed to her practice wholeheartedly, was pragmatic in her method and it was important for her to share the work. There was a period (early 1990s) when the extent of the breadth and depth of Clarke's investigations into somatic practices such as Feldenkrais, Alexander and Klein (amongst others) became very apparent. Watching her move at that time was a weighty and convincing argument in favour of these practices and many of us soon found ourselves squeezing into her classes and following a similar trajectory. Her wholehearted investment in establishing practice as the primary means to understanding and to wisdom is an example that I still follow today.

What is wisdom in Buddhism and how does one get it?

Known as the three kinds of wisdom, listening, reflecting and meditating comprise one of Buddhism's many lists. This list presents a model for developing wisdom by attending through listening, reflecting and then meditating with regard to the matter in hand, be it conceptual formulations of the teaching or investigating lived experience as it happens. The process starts with *sutamayā paññā* (Wisdom-by-means-of-hearing) – wisdom acquired through listening, reading, studying and thinking about what has been heard. Next, *cintāmayā paññā* (Wisdom-by-means-of-reflecting) includes thinking deeply, dialogue, slow reading and deep listening. Finally there is *bhāvanāmayā paññā* (Wisdom-by-means-of-contemplation or meditation), where distilled reflections are subjected to an absorbed and deeply refined consciousness and knowledge is turned into insight. Versions of this teaching go right back to the time of the Buddha (*Sangiti sutta*).

What is being indicated here is something that, while quite natural in itself, is yet more than the conventional wisdom acquired through experience, good judgement and knowledge – not that this is unworthy of our seeking. Pierre Hadot, in surveying ancient philosophy, says:

> the normal natural state of men should be wisdom, for wisdom is nothing more than the vision of things as they are, the vision of the cosmos as it is in the light of reason, and wisdom is also nothing more than the mode of being and living that should correspond to this vision. (Hadot 1995: 58)

Compare this with Sangharakshita outlining the Buddhist path as beginning with "a vision of the nature of existence, the Truth or the reality of things" which leads one to follow the path of transformation: "the transformation of one's whole being in all its heights and depths, all its aspects, from top to bottom, in accordance with this insight and this experience" (Sangharakshita 1968). What this 'reality' consists in is the subject of a huge corpus of literature and teaching in Buddhism. For example one could start with the teachings on impermanence, which are simple and observable. It is not hard to extrapolate from these that having a fixed sense of self is problematic (*anatman*) and that relying on a false sense of permanence is going to cause anguish (*dukkha*) of one kind or another. The overcoming of anguish/suffering by seeing through impermanence is one way that the Buddhist path is characterised.

Listening

> He that hath ears to hear, let him hear.
> (Gospel of Matthew 11.15)

Listening can extend to hearing, reading and even waiting... One must first be prepared to listen; to be listening is to be receptive – open and ready – ready then for thinking. When Martin Heidegger asks "what calls us to thinking?" it counts for nothing if we are not ready/not intending/desiring to hear the call (Heidegger 1950: 126).

Listening requires attending, giving our attention fully in order to hear. Hadot points out "the theme of the value of the present instant plays a fundamental role in all the philosophical schools. In short it is a consciousness of inner freedom" (Hadot 1995: 69). Whether it is in meditation, in dialogue, giving or receiving bodywork, dancing alone or dancing with others, attentional stability is required to be able to stay present and alert to what is happening and to listen to the body. But this attention to the present moment requires diligence, clear knowing and a putting aside of distractions – to paraphrase the Buddha on mindfulness (Analyo 2003).

In dancing, whether it's in performance, improvisation or choreographic practices, all require this attending, this wakefulness, as a prerequisite: being ready to hear the call to think through the body into space/time/form. What calls us to moving? What calls us to think through the body? It is the practice of being ready to see what comes. In improvisation and contact improvisation this is immediately apparent because decisions are being made in real time in every passing moment, because the processing of impulse into movement is faster than thinking and because our safety is dependent upon being alive to what is happening.

The Underscore, too, begins with arriving into presence and sensation not just as a physical task but an arriving into the present state of the body as it is in itself. In the Minding Motion project Clarke reveals, "even if I am not dealing with improvisation, I am concerned with an improvisational mind" (Clarke 2011: 202). An improvisational mind attends fully and is ready to think through the body in real time.

In listening, information becomes available, information of all kinds: sensations, thoughts, ideas, concepts, feelings. But more than this, hearing encompasses listening to and coming into direct relationship with the basic experience of being alive. There is a coming to know the ground on which one stands physically and ontologically. One cannot come to know oneself, or indeed the world, unless one is prepared to listen as well as look. Whether it is dance practice, Buddhism, philosophy or the many somatic practices, this listening – this mindful attention – is a prerequisite for acquiring knowledge.

Thinking/Reflecting

> What is most thought-provoking in these thought-provoking times is that we are still not thinking.
> (Heidegger 1950: 4)

According to Buddhism, reflection is ideally done from a state of attending fully with a quiet and concentrated mind. In order to reflect effectively one needs a mind that is already present, relaxed and pliable.

Thinking can form a bridge between the activities of listening and reflecting; when processing what has been heard, sensed and/or learned before it is possible to reflect effectively. Clarifying what one thinks and what one is experiencing is an essential prelude to being able to reflect deeply. Making the distinction between different modes of thinking and feeling raises the question as to whether thinking is always a high level cognitive activity. Somatic work such as a dance class involves listening to instructions and seeking guidance through words or directly through hands, followed by processing what has been heard or felt in the body. In the processing, any idea of the mind and body being separate falls away. Sometimes the processing happens directly in the body and yet it feels as if the mind is still active in the processing. It is here that the work of embodiment begins and the development of body-wisdom becomes possible. Clarke's teaching was exemplary in this processing: the detailed instructions, the invitation to investigate in and through movement, then to think through the body to the point where thinking becomes a wordless reflection on the principles in motion.

> The information accumulates within the body. And it needs time for new information to first arrive in the body as sensation or awareness, and then to be applied and tested in practice and then to allow another layer of information to come in, in relationship to this ... if it is only ever met superficially, then it is only going to be an idea in the head, not experiential knowledge thought through the body. (Clarke 2011: 202)

Buddhist teacher Reginald Ray insists on the necessity of working with the body in meditation. In his view the body is the only vehicle through which we can come into relationship with our most authentic inner being and, through that, find a connection to reality itself. Ray's thesis is that the Buddhist tradition has always had a somatic education embedded within it but that this got lost along the way especially as it came to the West (Ray 2007). Jeffrey Maitland echoes Ray's view of the body: "My experience is that transformation, at whatever level it occurs, from psychological transformation to experiences of creativity to spiritual illumination is always a bodily event." (Maitland 1995: xv). Clarke, Ray and Maitland share a view of the importance of being able to think through the body, processing sophisticated ideas and concepts into a knowledge that is deeply embedded in the physical to allow insights to arise.

A lot of thinking is simply rehearsing a sense of identity. Our sense of self is created and recreated from moment to moment based on a view constructed from a lifetime of experiences, including thinking. These views are often quite resistant to change; the cosmetics industry for example seems to rely on this resistance. The litany 'I'm that sort of person', 'I'm not that kind of dancer' seems characteristic of an engrained self-view. But it's just a view; we are not our thoughts, thoughts are constantly changing. Feeling is constantly changing. All of the sensory data is constantly changing. If one can attend fully to the changing nature of experience it is possible to loosen the grip of unhelpful and unrealistic views on life that are based on fixed, unchanging ideas about who we are. Buddhism holds the view that what is experienced as 'I' is the nexus of complex networks of conditioning factors. A single thought is conditioned by every thought that has previously arisen in the mind or been heard, read or seen to have been had by another. Education, upbringing, friends, enemies and much else besides condition it.

To give a personal example: once while I was sitting in the midst of an intensive silent meditation retreat a stray thought arose that brought a smile. This in turn set off a reflection 'Whose thought is this?', 'Where does this sense of humour come from?'. Then a memory arose that was a perfect fit. I remembered watching 'The Two Ronnies' with my grandmother; it was her favourite programme. In remembering us laughing together when I was 8 years old, I knew that the stray thought and the smile it gave rise to were deeply influenced by this experience. There was no 'me' as such that this sense of humour belonged to, it was conditioned by experience. In daily life, it's convenient, even important, to operate with a conventional sense of 'me', 'mine' and 'I' but to investigate further and to develop wisdom it is necessary to come closer to the truth of the way things really are. Here is a short exercise to illustrate this (it is worth taking a good ten minutes over it).

> *Sit quietly ... observe ... take a moment...settle your attention in a relaxed way on your experience of the body and the breath ... Note feelings and the general tone of mind ... let them be as they are whilst encouraging the intention to stay with experience for a few moments more ... Here are some questions – take time between each, leaving space to explore ... Next time a thought passes into awareness ask: 'Whose thought is this? ... Where did it come from? ... Where is the thinker of this thought?' ... If the mind gets busy then come back to the breath and settle ... Next time the mind wanders, repeat the questions ...*

Exploring questions in movement practice can also provide rich material to reflect on. From where did this impulse arise? Who is moving me? Who is observing these sensations? To try to contemplate without having a clear view or without having processed one's thinking can be like trying to listen to a radio broadcast when there is a lot of interference. It becomes difficult to understand what is going on and easy to misunderstand. Thinking can help gather the thoughts and sort them for investigation and reflection. Reflecting can help sift through the thoughts and test them for relevance and importance; it can help to 'clear' the ground – a kind of purification or refining process.

> If one wants to know the nature of a thing, one must examine it in its pure state, since every addition to a thing is an obstacle to the knowledge of that thing. When you examine it, then, remove from it everything that is not itself; better still remove all your stains from yourself and examine yourself ... The seer no longer sees his object, for in that instant he no longer distinguishes himself from it; he no longer has the impression of two separate things, but he has, in a sense, become another. (Plotinus in Hadot 1995: 100-101)

When dancing the Underscore, the mapping out of the changing states of each phase is an ongoing reflection on change. In the final Reflection/Harvest one gathers the experiences through writing, moving, drawing and thinking before coming together in the circle once more to share the fruits of the 'harvest'. This gathering of thoughts and feelings can lead directly into a more contemplative state in itself.

Reflection in this sense is not quite the same thing as reflective practice as found in the academy although there is plenty of overlap. Reflection becomes clearer, starts to slow down and become quieter, less insistent and more spacious. This happens quite naturally. In moving further into the region of reflection there is the sense that, "Reflection is always personal" (Ratnaguna 2010: 44). In attending to thinking and to experience more deeply one relies more and more on first person engagement with the materials, one becomes more subjective in that engagement and the lines between thinking and feeling become less distinct. "One cannot speak of wisdom either in terms of 'knowing' or of 'feeling'. It is both an intuitive understanding and also an intuitive feeling." (Sangharakshita 2013: 11). The process of reflection refines understanding and feeling so that both can be held ever more lightly, making them ready for contemplation.

For reflection to transform understanding into wisdom, one must be ready to be called to it and be open to being transformed by it. The Pāli Canon has many records of discussions and dialogues with the Buddha. It becomes clear that the questioner needs to be receptive: do they really want an answer or do they just want to test this teacher? The Buddha would also enter into dialogue by asking questions; the questions clear the ground for discussion and the teaching that follows. For example in the *Samaññaphala Sutta* we find King Ajatasattu visiting the Buddha in the dead of night. When he arrives he asks the Buddha about the fruits of the spiritual life that can be seen here and now. The Buddha answers by asking a series of counter-questions, which lead the king to find answers for himself (Samaññaphala Sutta 1997).

Dialogue is a key skill in reflection whether with oneself or with others. The kind of dialogue that can take us into reflection is not simply a conversation but that which requires "man in his wholeness wholly attending" (D H Lawrence in Ratnaguna 2010: 19). It requires speaking from the depths of experience, which in turn relies on a profound attending to that experience. Dialogue here is a thinking/reflecting through relational engagement and can include bodywork and somatic practice as well as contact improvisation and group improvisation. Insight meditation teacher Gregory Kramer has developed a whole approach of meditative dialogue and suggests that, "... because interpersonal meditation works with the moment-to-moment experience of interacting with another, it brings the liberating dynamic of meditation into our interpersonal lives" (Kramer 2007: 4).

Themes of liberation and freedom are common to Buddhism, early philosophy and somatic practices. Buddhism talks in terms of freedom, release and liberation (mokṣa) from all that holds us back and causes anguish. Somatic practices aim to produce freedom of movement and release the poor functioning that leads to pain and dis-ease. And early philosophy, as Hadot remarks, "presented itself as a method for achieving independence and inner freedom (*autarkeia*)" (Hadot 1995: 266).

Contemplation

> To arrive at the simplest truth ... requires years of contemplation. Not activity. Not reasoning. Not calculating. Not busy behaviour of any kind. Not reading. Not talking. Not making an effort. Not thinking. Simply bearing in mind what it is that one needs to know.
> (Brown in Claxton 1977)

The roots of the word contemplation go back to the space cleared for divination. One needs to clear-a-space for what takes place in reflection, the sense that the ground needs to be prepared in order to go deeper. As Plotinus points out, "If one wants to know the nature of a thing, one must examine it in its pure state" (Hadot 1995: 100). Characteristically, contemplation is minimally discursive. Settling the mind and clearing a space through reflection, allowing it to rest there, enables the contemplated object to percolate through deeper layers of our being. Classically Buddhist meditation works through *samatha* (calming, stilling, integrating) and *vippassana* (seeing through, insight). In practice this means first getting calm and concentrated so that one can then enter into contemplation (*vippassana*). Although couched in Buddhist language the early Buddhists were here articulating phenomena that are observable and verifiable by anyone. And one finds these principles articulated in other places and at other times. Hadot, in recovering the contemplative possibilities that come from the ancients, reflects on the discipline of the Stoics:

> Attention to the present moment is, in a sense, the key to spiritual exercises. It frees us from the passions ... attention to the present moment allows us to accede to cosmic consciousness, by making us attentive to the infinite value of each instant, and *causing us to accept each moment of existence from the viewpoint of the universal law of the cosmos.* (1995: 84-85; emphasis added)

In Heidegger there is also a good deal of resonance and apparent sympathy with contemplative practice. For example the distinctions between calculative and meditative thinking and work with *gelassenheit* (openness or release) and *aletheia* (truth, revealing: arises with *gelassenheit* as prerequisite) are striking in their apparent fit with *samattha/vippassana* (Heidegger 1927). His later work, *What is Called Thinking?*, presents an approach to thinking that has informed this chapter, especially when he asks, "What is it that calls us to think?" (Heidegger 1950: 126). It seems that Heidegger is directing thinking back towards our actual experience, towards presence, and he sets out receptivity as a prerequisite for thinking.

Studio practice

In the studio I am continually engaging with the ongoing process of making decisions, asking questions and interrogating what presents itself for thinking through the body. In sifting through what is present, one clears a space where it's possible to focus on distilled thoughts, images and concepts. Discursive modes of investigation die away as we move into contemplation.

Knowing and developing wisdom through the body starts with attending to the ever-changing landscape of sensation and feeling tone, and in itself can be *vipassana* practice. So it is no surprise to meet so many people overlapping between contemplative disciplines, improvisation and somatic practice. Therapeutically and for spiritual exercise the overlaps are plain but also in performance practice, clarity of intention and presence are vital. Ellen Langer in *A Call for Mindful Leadership* says, "In more than 30 years of research, we've found that increasing mindfulness increases charisma and productivity" (Langer 2010). To make explicit the link between presence and 'stage presence' confirms something that performers know intuitively.

In 2002, after having experienced several bereavements within the space of a few years, *After the Dogs the Dead* was created. In the studio I practised contemplating death meditatively and from there went seamlessly into moving and finished with journal recording. Several key images emerged from this that described my experience in the practice of moving/contemplating death. List poems arose and memories were awakened from various funerals such as dogs barking and the sound of feet treading pebble paths. I also incorporated as much as I could into a score. The score is set through images that are particular to each section but leave a lot of space for interpretation in performance.

Exploring contemplative modes of studio practice is ongoing. The first of two collaborations with Annie Lok – *Turf* (2006) – began with travel correspondence that set up themes of territory, home, place and displacement. In the studio we used Barbara Dilley's contemplative dance score as a base line for working and developing a score. Work on *Notebook notes for two solos* (2008) began with different meditation instructions to see how different states might be set up.

Writing from the practice

More recently I've been exploring moving and thinking and writing, moving and reflecting and writing and moving from contemplation and writing. Documentation and writing has long been a part of my practice and I enjoy the differences between writing in the studio and writing at a desk. Improvisation has become practice where I can reflect and think effectively, so if I'm in front of a computer and getting stuck, taking the problem/question into the studio and moving can shift things. Improvisation has become a way for me to clear a ground for thinking. Working on this chapter there were a few such sessions and I want to include a sample to illustrate what happens. In what follows I was speaking out loud as I moved. When I sat down with my notebook afterwards, I (surprisingly) could recall most of what I had said.

> What do I think? ... Concerns about government and corporate greed as the dominant power base in the world. But I'm not an activist (at least not in a direct way).
>
> So what kind of work do I make that honours these responses?
>
> Do I fall in behind Rainer's No manifesto? Or Guy Debord?
>
> How should I move? I want to move with less density, less insistent on my past, this leads me to reflect on how I got here, slowing down ... Accessing my bio-mythologies, the traces left by all the dances I've danced and all the choreographers I've worked with.
>
> Can I honour my journey and still take a stand?
>
> What should I present? I don't want pointy feet or 5th position except ironically. I don't want to do style or dance the 'cool' body.
>
> Is it enough to demonstrate a way of moving? No!
>
> Is it enough to be an expert practitioner doing their thing? No!
>
> Do I have anything to say?
>
> If not, great, I can go home now!
>
> *Dance, when you're broken open.*
>
> *Dance, if you've torn apart.*
>
> *Dance in the middle of the fighting.*
>
> *Dance in your blood.*
>
> *Dance, when you're perfectly free.*
>
> What is the relationship between thinking and moving?
>
> How can I use moving to think and thinking to move?
>
> When does thinking become reflection? How does that change moving? When does contemplation come in?
>
> In richness ... the shift from reflection into contemplation feels similar in tone to the shift into moving.
>
> Changes of state?

Thinking/reflecting on bio-mythologies, contemplating embodiment of states of being, on moments of remembered fragments of dancing, devising, making.

Thinking/reflecting on aesthetics, values, meaning and having something to say …

Thinking/reflecting on composition, composing and … thinking.

What is thinking?

I've been thinking.

I've been thinking about dancing.

I've been thinking about dancing for a long time actually. I didn't realise that was what I had been doing until more recently.

I've got all these thoughts stored in my body as bio-mythologies of a sort, my history, all the choreographers, all the dances … it's all in there somewhere being processed whenever I move.

That is what I seek to process, I want to understand it, perhaps that is a prerequisite; I want to know. I am available to thinking.

When I know what I think can I reflect more deeply? Or is it that I reflect in order to know what I think?

I've done it both ways; perhaps what calls me to thinking is wanting to know what I think.

I think therefore … nothing.

I think therefore I … make assumptions?

I think therefore I … am … making assumptions again …

Who is the I that thinks that it is? Can it be found? All I can find is assumptions and habits.

I am a habit or the sum total of my habits. I am a bad habit?

… I want to see deeply into the matter … This is slower and takes more time...

Conclusion

To understand something takes time and effort, to develop wisdom takes longer … The three ways of developing wisdom overlap a great deal and in experience they are available just as much outside formal practice as in it. I was discussing this with a Buddhist friend and we both spoke about reflecting on one or two topics for many years. We both had our own favourite themes that contribute a lot to the distinctiveness of our respective practice. I think that is very much what Clarke was about, working on a few key themes over many years and going deeper and deeper into her understanding of them and becoming more and more distinctive and insightful in revealing her understandings. In *What is Called Thinking?* Heidegger quotes Hoelderlin "who the deepest has thought, loves what is most alive" (Hoelderlin in Heidegger 1950: 20). Although Clarke is no longer with us, her love of *what is most alive* continues to inform and inspire.

References

Analyo, (2003) *Sathipatthana: The Direct Path to Realization,* Windhorse Publications

Clarke, G., Cramer, F.A. & Müller, G. (2011) 'Gill Clarke – Minding Motion' in: *Tanztechniken 2010 – Tanzplan Deutschland* (2011)

Claxton, G. (1998) *Hare Brain, Tortoise Mind,* Fourth Estate

Gospel of Matthew: King James Bible (1611) http://bit.ly/tpMove34

Hadot, P. (1995) *Philosophy as a Way of Life* (trans. M. Chase), Blackwell Publishing

Hartley, L. (1995) *Wisdom of the Body Moving: An Introduction to Body-Mind Centering,* North Atlantic Books

Heidegger, M. (1950/1968) *What is Called Thinking* (trans. F. D. Wieck & J. G. Gray) Harper & Row

_______ (1927/1967) *Being and Time* (trans. J. Macquarrie & E. Robinson) Blackwell

Kramer, G. (2007) *Insight Dialogue: The Interpersonal Path to Freedom,* Shambala Publications

Langer, E. (2010) *A call for mindful leadership* http://bit.ly/tpMove33

Lawrence, D.H. (1972) *D. H. Lawrence: Selected Poems* (ed. K. Sagar) Penguin Books

Maitland, J. (1995) *Spacious Body: Explorations in Somatic Ontology,* North Atlantic Books

Ratnaguna (2010) *The Art of Reflection,* Windhorse Publications

Ray, R. (2007) *Touching Enlightenment: Finding Realization in the Body,* Sounds True

Rumi (1995) *The Essential Rumi* (trans. C. Barks *et al.*) HarperCollins

Samaññaphala Sutta: The Fruits of the Contemplative Life (trans. Thanissaro Bhikkhu) (1997) http://bit.ly/tpMove29

Sangharakshita (2013) *Living Wisely,* Windhorse Publications

Sangharakshita (1968) 'Right Understanding' on Free Buddhist Audio http://bit.ly/tpMove30

Sangiti Sutta: The Recital (trans. T. W. & C. A. F. Rhys Davids) (1921) http://bit.ly/tpMove31

Stark, H. E. 'A Thematic Unity for Heidegger's Was Heisst Denken?' *PAIDEIA: Contemporary Philosophy* http://bit.ly/tpMove32

Stark Smith, N. & Koteen, D. (2008) *Caught Falling: the confluence of Contact Improvisation, Nancy Stark Smith and other moving ideas,* Contact Editions

Performances

Lalitaraja (2002) *After the dogs, the dead*

Lalitaraja & Annie Lok (2006) *Turf*

Lalitaraja (2008) *Notebook notes for two solos*

NADRA ASSAF

Not Without My Body

The Struggle of Dancers and Choreographers in the Middle East

Fig. 1:A scene from the 2 March 2007 performance of Majnoun LaylaAssaf

> *No culture can exist until there is freedom. For culture, freedom is tantamount to an existential imperative. Not to be free is to be separated from cultural creativity by a boundless chasm. Where there is no freedom, culture could become anything but culture. It could become an ideology of deception and polemics; a stammering discourse, mumbling esoteric, apologetic locutions; a decorative folklore; or something – anything – that falls short of what makes culture culture: the urge to express and disclose, to reveal what is hidden, to unveil what is veiled, and to perform a human act and an esthetic, social function.*
>
> (Marcel Khalife 2007)

In the above quotation Khalife mentions the urge to express and reveal what is hidden and this has never been easier than it is today where interaction across cultures and languages spreads quickly via the internet. As a result, cultural exchange has moved far beyond the limitations of space, body and mind. Thus prior dedication to enhancing the placement of the body across disciplines has become even more prominent.[1] Thomas Hanna and Brenda Farnell's variations on Descartes' famous 17th-century aphorism elevate the status of the human body in the 21st century: "I think, therefore I move" (Hanna 1970) and "I move, therefore I am" (Farnell 2012).

What began in the late 20th century as a movement to enhance the importance of body-mind connection resulted in a new realm for the body, for which Hanna coined the term 'somatics'. Somatics firmly placed the body (previously only prominent in anthropology and dance) in the fields of sociology, psychology, education and communication. Recent research, (particularly in the West) has taken the body to relative extremes of articulation[2], whereas in the past researchers placed linguistic, visual and aural learning in that position (Sellers-Young 1998). Previously, physicality was viewed as something that needed to be suppressed to allow intellectual performance to excel (Stinson 1995). This is no longer the case, as we can see from more recent work in areas such as kinaesthetic empathy, embodied knowledge, and mirror neurons. However, the work being done in these fields is located mainly in the Western hemisphere.

As a dancer and choreographer who has spent the majority of her career in the Middle East, the debates surrounding the body-mind connection are pivotal to me. I began my dance-movement journey through a long and intense education in the United States and moved to Lebanon in 1991 with the hope of augmenting the dance community in the region. I am of mixed ethnicity (Native American-Indian and Lebanese) and this cultural mixture is dichotomous: the West gives prominence to the body where the Middle East tries to hide it. Yet even with the prominence afforded it, the body is still struggling in the West. For example, Bryan S. Turner has written extensively on the body within social processes and cultural theories (2008, 1991) and in particular argues that dance is "quintessentially a performance involving all the senses" (2008); Helen Thomas says that most of academia ignores the body except for anthropology which considers the body a crucial element in cultural development (2003); Merleau-Ponty says that the body "is and is not ourselves"(1973) and highlights the fact that body and body image are valued in proportion to the project at hand (1962). Generally, the dance projects I work on are presented in the Middle East, where most countries are strongly influenced by Islam which considers the human body as something of a taboo or haram (legally forbidden by Islamic Law). Despite the struggles the body faces in the West, it is considered an ever growing, always engaged factor in the world (Weiss 1999). The

1 Blakeslee and Blakeslee 2008; Clarke 1997; Foucault 1980; Gallagher 2003; Gardner 1993; Halprin 2003; Hanna 1970, 1979; Hartley 2004; Johnson 1987, 2007; Johnson, D.H. 1993; 1995; Knaster 1996; Mangione 1993; McHose & Frank 2006; Merleau-Ponty 1962; Schusterman 2008; Turner 2008; Varela, Thompson & Rosch 1992; Weiss 1999.

2 Brodie & Lobel 2012; Eddy 2002; 2009; Farnell 2003; 2011; 2012; Foster 2005; 2010; Hanna 2000; 2001; 2003; 2005; 2007; 2008; 2012; Kress 2003; 2006; Olsen 2014; Parviainen 2007; 2009; 2010; 2011; Johnson 2007; Press 2002; Hahn 2007; Halprin 2003; Ross 2007.

somatic view of the body is that it can help us better understand life, as clearly stated by Thomas Hanna: "Far from demeaning the phenomenon of life and robbing it of its significance, such a viewpoint leads to the discovery that life, in its manifestations as the soma, takes advantage of these universal laws and then uses them for its advancement" (Hanna 1993). However, Hanna's soma is not Middle Eastern and, while these ideas about the body and its functions are valid and progressive, this is not the case in the Middle East.

So how does a choreographer, whose canvas is the human body, communicate across this gulf of contention where the body is censored? In the 21st century when visions and images of moving bodies are readily available on YouTube and other internet sources, what can be expected from the Middle East where the body is predominately taboo? How should viewers/audiences react to body predominant performances? Can the socio-political religions of the region continue to keep the body under wraps? I believe the answers to all these questions are important. Consequently, given that in the West dance is a valid form of art and communication and the Middle East has a corpus of dancers and choreographers struggling to communicate, this chapter is an attempt to look more deeply at the social and communicative dilemma of the dance artist's use of the body in countries where exhibiting the body is *haram*. What follows is an attempt to clarify the struggle a dancer faces in the Middle East by examining the reactions to a contemporary dance show entitled *Majnoun Layla* performed in Bahrain in 2007.

The Body and Communication

The starting point for this examination is the growing bond between anthropology and linguistics. As far back as 1960, Dell Hymes was already pointing to the tension between the advocates and opponents of the idea that there are connections between linguistics and other areas like cognitive science and the study of expressive behaviour, in particular of the sort one sees in dance. The mid-1980s saw the beginning of a movement that emphasised different 'intelligences' of which kinaesthetic intelligence was the only one involving the body (Gardner 1983). Around that time, dance researchers such as Susan Leigh Foster and Judith Lynne Hanna began to point to correlations between linguistic functions and dance functions. Since then, the movement has continued, and is currently gaining more prominence and support from many different areas of research. Brenda Farnell, for example, is an anthropologist who researches the body and issues pertaining to dance and physical communication and emphasises the body within cultural and phenomenological realms.

From the communication perspective Hymes explains that an outsider to any group must learn how the group functions in order to be able to communicate effectively (1968). Thus, when adding movement to a mix that includes verbal ideas or musical melodies, both the dancer and the choreographer must understand the context in which the movement will be perceived by the audience. Figure 2 (below) is a representation of Berlo's communication model. This model applies to dance as much as to any other mode of communication; both dancer and choreographer have an understanding of the message they want to convey to the audience, but if the audience does not share the code (Jakobson 1981) they will be unable to decipher and comprehend the message. Thus in cultures where Islam prevails, it can be difficult to acquire the code needed to decipher the message or interpret the creative intent as it is used in other cultures. This lack of knowledge of the code renders dance incomprehensible to audience members.

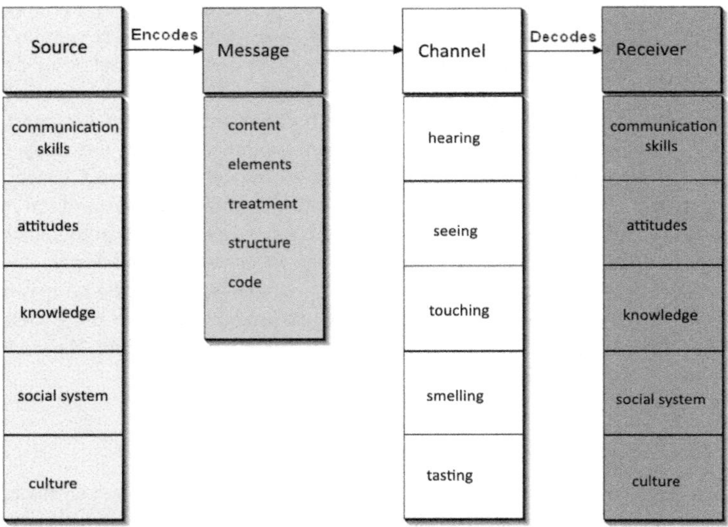

Fig. 2: Simplified from David K. Berlo, *The Process of Communication*. 1960

Cultural connections allow for differences that exist based on personal experiences and different ways of knowing.[3] Examples of such things are: corporeal expression, technology and vocabulary. Audience reactions are directly linked to embodied knowledge. Where the code is not known, however, the information (no matter how elaborate) is simply noise. The feelings an audience member develops while watching movement are referred to as kinaesthetic empathy. Kinaesthetic empathy is actually the knowledge we have of the movement we see and what that makes us feel. Michael Polanyi's assertion: "we know more than we can tell", puts this in the context of "tacit knowledge" (2009). This knowledge amasses in our bodies over time, and is often referred to as body or muscle memory and is a motivating principle in somatics. Thus through reference to our past embodied experiences, we infer what others mean verbally as well as physically. According to Foster, "these patterns represent a way of knowing in a given cultural context, a form of embodied knowledge" (2011). This also depicts dance as a different mode of communication (Gardner 1988). Mangione considers the historical connection between the birth of modern

3 Phenomenological understanding: Edmund Husserl, Martin Heidegger, Maurice Merleau-Ponty, Jean-Paul Sartre, *et al.*

dance and the development of somatic theories and practices and explains the similarities between the two with their "body-based forms that value the whole human being" (Mangione 1993). Thus modern dance, just like modern art, is open to interpretation.

Social context is important in all modes of communication but especially in artistic modes such as dance. Psycho-social linguist James Paul Gee posits that languages differ as to the context of delivery. Theoretically, one adopts different versions of who one is according to the social context. This highlights the crucial importance of understanding the cultural context in which the utterance or communicative form is being delivered. Similarly, the anthropologist Mary Douglas writes: "We allow social institutions (including language) to do much of our thinking for us. We could not live if we consciously made every decision involved in communication and other social behaviour, any more than we could dance if we thought out each step as we did it" (1986). When a dancer performs, s/he is no longer thinking of the 'steps' involved in the execution, but rather of the emotion involved in the theme or idea. Thus, the dancer is not involved in the social conflicts of the audience.

The sociology theorist Arthur Frank considers the body to be the most modern concern in fields of education and human understanding. In his discussion of body types he proposes dance as an example of what he calls the communicative body (1991). He exemplifies the communicative aspect by stressing the production of dance and its association with the individual's body, which is then transferred to the bodies of those watching (1991) through kinaesthetic empathy. This is discussed in detail by Tomie Hahn (2007) who advocates it as the main idea behind dancer/teacher closeness. Unlike in other forms of communication, a dancer needs to experience – and be physically close to – the movements the teacher or leader is creating: in this way, dancers sympathetically align their muscles to resemble those of the teacher. This can be difficult when social norms do not allow the body to be observed.

In the same vein, Gee (1996) points out that who we are and how we communicate is directly related to three important factors: 1. the social or cultural group to which we belong; 2. the social language(s) we use; 3. the context in which we are communicating. This delineation applies to dance as well, for, clearly, one must have a common understanding with the choreographer and/or dancer in order to be able to understand the dance. This could be the cultural or social unit, the spoken language or the body language (here being a particular type of dance), or the actual context in which the performance is being given. Anthropology observes socio-cultural norms and understandings while sociology studies norms, acceptance and retribution. It would be difficult to deny the importance of these categories to comprehension and communication amongst cultures. The point here is the dilemma caused by the separation of mind and body in Islam.

The Body, Dance and the Islamic Perspective

The importance Western culture has placed on the body in the realm of artistic communication is not replicated globally. In the Middle East, Saudi Arabia is the country that adheres most strictly to a literal interpretation of Islam. According to Richard Schifter, the restrictive regime began around 1902 with Abdul Aziz Ibn Saud's alliance with the followers of Muhammad Ibn Abdul Wahhab who prohibited all dance, music and children's games (2004). Other Middle Eastern countries enforce these laws less strictly. However from a global perspective, artists should understand the difference between the *intent* and the *interpretation* of a message. Some social and cultural contexts may widen the gulf of understanding when specific forms of art, like dance, are entirely unaccepted. However, this is not limited to Islamic countries; even liberal countries have restrictions on what is accepted: for example, the UK's ban of an advertisement for Beyoncé's latest perfume in 2010 on the grounds that it was too sexually explicit. Sociologist Bryan Turner states, "The uniqueness and authenticity of a work of art is a function of its embeddedness in the social context of a stable traditional culture" (2008). Turner argues that society's understanding of the body is a product of what is deemed acceptable and acceptance varies not only between regions of the world but within them as well.

Liberal countries may have rules shielding people from extreme sexual explicitness but in Islam dancing is *haram* and has been given no value historically, whereas modern Western dance is perceived to have developed since 1926 in "a lineal way which brought it from rite to entertainment, from the village main square to the palaces of the powerful" (Dox 2006). In the West, dance has long been a part of social rituals, social bonding and cultural ceremonies and historically has been held to have educational as well as physiological value. By contrast, the Middle East, due mainly to social and religious restrictions, has no such clear agreement on the role of dance in cultural ritual and social custom.

According to the *Encyclopaedia of Islam*, dance is 'frowned upon' due to the historical connection of dance and the ecstatic religious experience of the sort one sees in traditional dervish dancing. There are variations on this point of view between specialists in Islamic studies. Su'ad Salih (2009), Professor of Islamic Jurisprudence at Al-Azhar University, writes: "Islam is a religion of moderation; it does not prevent singing and dancing, but it forbids anything that stimulates people's desires, whether it be among men or women". Similarly, Salim Ahmad Salamah adds:

> It is permissible for women to dance and sing as long as there are no males around ... Men and women dancing together is absolutely *haram* in all cases, except when a wife dances in front of her husband. The reason behind this prohibition is that with mixed dancing bodily contact is close and improper sexual desires are aroused. This has been strictly forbidden by Islam in an attempt to block the way against evil. (Salamah 2009)

How does creative and artistic dance fit into this description? Take for example the choreography of Wayne McGregor who has been described as using dance "as a primary motivation to communicate" (May 2010). His piece, *Entity,* stems from scientific research where the dancers are urged to explore their physicality to the limits. "*Entity* makes use of the dancers' whole body, from the face to the fingertips and feet, and certainly most of the vertebrae" (May 2010). This is not the manner in which we usually see human beings move. Even though the movements are unfamiliar, I can find no evidence of *Entity* being condemned as obscene or vulgar. Arguably, from a Western perspective it would be hard to see it as a sexually stimulating piece even though the dancers exhibit various forms of physical exposure and contact. How can one establish and achieve recognition of such art in Islamic nations?

One answer could be to develop a dance community that is more Arabic than foreign. This is proposed by Nicolas Rowe, a dance practitioner and researcher who spent a significant amount of time in the Middle East (Rowe 2009). Because of the reliance on foreign help in dance education and development, and the cultural difference between teacher and student, the transmission of dance culture is difficult to maintain and develop. Rowe wonders where and how a dance culture can develop in the first place if people are being taught to do something that is foreign to their sensibilities in the first place. Rowe suggests that using dance to maintain or develop a social connection has to begin from the viewpoint of the artistic producer and he argues persuasively that the imposition of Western dance culture on the Middle East works to the detriment of both.

So where does this leave artists who wish to communicate across cultures? Their need to express themselves is no less pressing than any culture's need to preserve their own customs and traditions. Appreciation and acceptance are of equal significance and must exist if any culture is to thrive. An attempt at such a cultural exchange and its results are described in the subsequent section.

An Attempted Cultural Exchange

The Background

Bahrain Spring of Culture first took place in March 2007. The opening was a musical performance entitled *Majnoun Layla,* based on a poem of the same name, and was an amalgamation of musicians, singers, dancers and poets. Marcel Khalife, an internationally acclaimed figure in Middle Eastern music, was the director/composer. The musicians and singers came from Lebanon and Paris. Qassim Haddad, a well-known Bahraini poet, wrote the poem on which the work was based. The 14 dancers were members of the Al-Sarab Dance Company from Lebanon. I was the choreographer and worked in collaboration with the composer and poet on maintaining the story and following the composition. I did not put any extensive thought into how the movement might or might not be perceived because I was simply following the lines of the narrative.

The theatre, which housed the event, seated only 600 people; however, both nights of the performance were heavily over-booked. On the second night people were seated on the floor and up the stairway aisles leading to the seats which made one of the dances impossible to execute: the dancers were supposed to run up the stairs but were unable to. Prior to opening the second night, I went to the theatre entrance and observed crowds of people pressing up against the glass trying to get in. The doors were barred by the security guards and theatre employees who were struggling to prevent additional people from entering. I later described this scene to the cast as "something akin to a rock concert! I felt as if we were suddenly turned into some rock stars and the people were pushing and shoving just to get a glimpse of us". The fact that the dancers would later question the moral indignation of the leaders' response further highlights the divide in the Arab world between the people and those in power.

The Dispute

As previously mentioned, I attempted to create a physical representation of the poem in a similar cadence to the music. Nonetheless, the choreography led to a lengthy dispute among the religious and political leaders of Bahrain. The show was attacked by fundamentalist members of parliament as being in violation of Islamic morals and Sharia laws after an Islamic preacher, Sheikh Ali Matar, complained in a prayer sermon that the Spring of Culture Festival featured a play with scenes that "arouse [sexual] instincts" and "encourage debauchery" (Freemuse 2007). Consequently a committee was formed to investigate allegations that the performance was not only erotically charged, but that it "centered on eroticism". One of the religious elders, Sheikh Mohammed Khalid, commented on the performance: "The actions of the dancers were clearly meant to depict a sexual act between a man and a woman... The female dancer opened the male dancer's shirt and what followed was like a sex movie only without the nudity" (Khonji 2007). See (Figure 3). Parliament's second vice-chairman, Dr Salah Abdulrahman, was quoted as saying the performance included "sleazy dance moves" which were offensive to both Muslims and non-Muslims. So, on March 13th 2007 the Bahraini parliament voted to create an investigative committee to look into the controversy (Freemuse 2007).

In response to the allegations, Marcel Khalife issued a statement that was published in the press:

> When the Bahraini poet, Qassim Haddad, and I turned to the Arab heritage searching for a light to illuminate our present and restore what was forgotten or lost from our lives today, which is Love, we brought back the eternal pearl of love, the torch whose flame never dies out so long as two lovers breath in love. We brought back the tale of a man whose heart melted away (and, it is said, whose mind perished) in love. We dressed up this tale with lyrics and music, song and dance, and scenes of drama. We had only one ambition: to foment joy, not indifference; life, not nihility. Our goal was to give expression to human emotion in its purest, most glorious form; to exult what is worthy of exultation – Love.
>
> Never did we aim to titillate the lower senses of our audience, who attended our work with innocence, confidence, and intelligence. Seeking at once to be edified and entertained, our audience received our work with a wide-open heart, free of preconceived notions, prejudice, and judgment. With our audience, we have a covenant of mutual respect and solemn commitment: we never insult our audience by presenting anything that is trite, trivial, or gratuitous. (*Al-Nahr*, October 2007)

When questioned by S. J. Fowler about the intention and achievement of his adapted poem, Qassim Haddad said: "When the Lebanese composer Marcel Khalife wanted to adapt the text, he incorporated poetry, music, songs and dance in one show. The show caused a shock to some of the conservative mentality [sic] and religious circles, who reacted ferociously, attacking both the show and the text" (2012).

According to Mohammed Al-A'ali, the Bahraini Parliament was accused by fifty-three societies and twenty-five Shura Councillors of taking the country "back to the Middle Ages" by its decision to hold an investigation of the *Bahrain Spring of Culture* festival due to its alleged refutation of Islam. The MPs were asked to back down from their decision and a statement was issued in support of the performance (Al-A'ali 2007a). I (the choreographer) have remained silent until now.

Fig. 3: Photos depicting the scene commented upon by Sheikh Mohammad Khalid

The Dancers and Choreographer Respond

In the preceding sections there are several references to the alleged sexual explicitness of the performance. As the choreographer, I confess that I did not intend to be sexually explicit. I also did not intend to insult or shock anyone. I took measures to ensure that the dancers were dressed both adequately and appropriately; and I took care in how much physical contact occurred between male and female dancers.

However, I was restricted by the poem. I could not delete the sensual love scenes as they were the emphasis of the story begin portrayed. After the fact, I will admit that my naiveté stemmed from my knowledge that the poem had been accepted in the Bahraini Cultural Studies program and the proposal to physically portray this poem had been approved by the Ministry of Culture.

As for the dancers, though they were all Lebanese, none was Muslim; thus none of them dressed according to Islamic codes. The women all were scarf-less as they were told that Hijab in Bahrain was not required of non-Muslims. As the week progressed, however, they had all purchased scarves and were wearing them in different ways but not as they would have used them in Lebanon. The dancers felt comfortable wearing sleeveless shirts in Lebanon, yet felt the need to put on long-sleeved jackets even in the heat of Bahrain. Physical conformity is what dancers are trained to do. For the most part they watch their teachers/choreographers and emulate what they see (kinaesthetic-visual comprehension). Their acquired sense of focus allows for them to move and situate their physicality in a conforming manner. In this case, while out in public, they felt eyes staring at them and this made them feel slightly out of place; they conformed to certain expectations by wearing more modest clothing and scarves in order to feel more in tune with the culture. However, they all reported that did not feel disconnected from the audience during the performances.

During a focus group interview with the dancers, the cultural dichotomy became a central point. When asked whether any situation during their stay in Bahrain made them feel different or unusual, the male dancers' answers comprised a range of opinions from a simple 'no' to pointing out an apparent contradiction in the local custom that as tourists the dancers had "access to a Cabaret Show; while a local wasn't recommended to attend an artistic show", (meaning the performance of *Majnoun Layla*). On the other hand, the female dancers' reactions to this experience of cultural communication and exchange was different. One dancer commented on the feeling of inclusion that came from working alongside artists from different artistic backgrounds and genres, different traditions of theatre, music and dance while another added: "Every work has its ups and downs; however, both of these made me aware of things I didn't take notice of before... the whole work was a blend of different arts (body, words, and music) which gave a volcanic feeling on stage like never before".

Theatre, music and dance had come together to create a performance that was not only unified artistically, but codified to the extent that the dancer and audience seemed in sync. An act of 'artistic communication' had occurred between them, a communicative exchange in which dancers and audience members shared a common code of gesture and movement that transcended cultural differences. The dancers reported feeling that the audience responded genuinely, even viscerally to the performance. They felt that in the performance in Bahrain they had connected with the audience in a way they had not previously experienced. Since dancers viewed the performance as a positive experience from both a cultural and social perspective, they were disappointed when they later found out that there were objections to the performance on social and religious grounds.

On the other hand, the religious community led by the Members of Parliament began a media outcry concerning what they termed the "vulgar and lewd" performance in *Majnoun Layla*. Several Bahraini MPs (few of whom had attended the performance) began referring to the Spring of Culture Festival as the 'Spring of Sex' (Al-A'ali, 2007b). Even after an official request by the Minister of State for Parliament and Shura Council Affairs, Abdulaziz Al Fadhel, for the MPs to abandon the enquiry, the parliamentary members voted 36:3 in favour of its continuation (Al-A'ali, 2007b). One is left to ponder whether the insistence was based on a true concern for a violation or a lack of cultural understanding and awareness of dance and the dancers. One of them commented on this Bahraini official Sheikh Adel Al Maawada mentioned that people were coming to his office protesting that the performance was improper (Al-A'ali, 2007a). The press was also attacked by Al Menbar MP Sheikh Nasser Al Fadhala for its biased coverage of the issue. Fadhala remarked that the press should not be biased: "We are not against singing or dancing, we are against practicing sex in public" (Al-A'ali, 2007b). The dancers argued that they did not have sex in public, nor were their performances erotic, sleazy, or immoral. The female lead in the performance said:

> *Some people could not accept the sight of two bodies of opposite sexes interacting together. This gave me a different insight and feeling about the Arab culture since it killed the joy of being in 'paradise' and pulled me back to the sad truth of the immobile un-evolving Arab world.*

Bahraini official Sheikh Adel Al Maawada mentioned that people were coming to his office protesting that the performance was improper (Al-A'ali, 2007a). The press was also attacked by Al Menbar MP Sheikh Nasser Al Fadhala for its biased coverage of the issue. Fadhala remarked that the press should not be biased: "We are not against singing or dancing, we are against practicing sex in public" (Al-A'ali, 2007b). The dancers argued that they did not have sex in public, nor were their performances erotic, sleazy, or immoral. The female lead in the performance said:

> *People there saw our means of expression in a different way than we did. They did not get our message. They only saw physical movement and related it to sexual ideas! This is what I got from the newspapers and their investigation but when we were on stage I thought everybody was so happy and they were watching and observing and clapping. They even cheered for us and told us "good job" at the end.*

Thus the dance company felt they had not violated any canons of decency. This further exemplifies the culture dichotomy.

The dancers were all from Lebanon, an Arab country. Although globalisation and especially globalised 'media' mean cultural boundaries are disappearing, because Lebanon is ostensibly a democratic country not a theocracy, it receives criticism from neighbouring Arab countries for being somewhat 'excessive'. Such criticisms exist in the West as well: for example, former New York City mayor Rudolph Giuliani once denounced erotic dancing as "a dirty vicious business" and linked it to "the deterioration of New York and places throughout the US" (Ross, B. L. 2000). Judith Lynne Hanna has argued "the exotic dancing body" functions in milieus of power and knowledge. She also argues that American culture is one in which the body in general is highly repressed (1998), thus advancing the 'erotic body' into an unfathomable category. But was what happened in Bahrain unfathomable? Was it erotic? Those involved in the production, not surprisingly, say no, and maintain that the play was a simple and straightforward representation of the poem. The verbal language was embodied in an unpretentious and aesthetic manner as one of the dancers said:

"The play represented a love story and the minimum expected from the movement base was physical contact between the leading roles, in a choreographed and tasteful manner". Since I am the one who created the movement, I agree, but the Bahraini religious leaders did not.

The Body Living in the Middle East Today

Decency norms vary individually as well as culturally. One of the issues that arose during the interview with the dancers about their Bahrain experience was whether or not art has boundaries. According to J.L. Hanna, dance is an art and accordingly falls into the category of expression and is thus protected in the USA by the First Amendment (1998). The dancers of *Majnoun Layla* recognise what everyone knows: freedom of expression has its limits. They accept that their freedom ends where any direct harm to the audience begins. For the dancers, the audience is the ultimate arbiter of the performance and they feel that art in general allows for freedom of expression in ways other communicative genres do not. One of the dancers commented, "What I might consider as unacceptable others may consider differently. For me personally, boundaries are crossed through the audience's mind not through the performer's body".

From a communication perspective, social, cultural, and religious factors all affect how a receiver interprets a message or how an audience member responds to a dance. Understanding and reciprocity have to be present in any social/cultural situation, or, in Victor Turner's terms, a *social drama*, where meanings are exchanged (1974). J. L. Hanna's drama starts with a *breach* and ends with a *reintegration* (1998). Both of these are beyond our control. In Bahrain, the breach occurred when the dance was performed; when the dancers violated religious social norms. The crisis came when what happened on stage was condemned as obscene. The redressive action was when the religious authorities turned their complaints into an edict. The reintegration was the resigned acceptance by the dance company of the assertion of social norms counter to their own. The dancers accepted the invitation to perform in Bahrain in good faith. They were led to believe they would perform in a social setting as open and tolerant as their own. But that was not the case.

Dancers in the Middle East (as elsewhere) are living, breathing, moving bodies: bodies existing in a culture where most are veiled and hidden. Helen Thomas says that we get to know our societies through "rules and rituals surrounding the body" (2003). If this is the case, what can dancers in the Middle East do? They need to adopt as a mantra the words of Farnell: "I move therefore I am". As a dancer/choreographer in the Middle East my answer to the question posed earlier– *Can the Middle Eastern socio-political-religious regions continue to keep the body under wraps?*– is a simple NO.

References

Al-A'ali, M. (2007a) '"Spring of Sex" revolt', *Gulf Daily News*, http://bit.ly/tpMove37

_______ (2007b) 'Row rages over "Spring of Sex"', *Gulf Daily News*, 21 March 2007

Berlo, D. K. (1960) *The Process of Communication*, Holt, Rinehart and Winston

Blakeslee, S. B. & Blakeslee, M. (2008) *The Body Has A Mind Of Its Own*, Random House

Brodie, J. A. & Lobel, E. E. (2012) *Dance and Somatics: Mind-Body Principles of Teaching and Performance*, McFarland

Celebrityfix (2010) 'Too sexy: Beyoncé's ad banned from daytime TV', http://bit.ly/tpMove40
Clark, A. (1997) *Being There: Putting Brain, Body, and World Together Again*, MIT Press
Descartes, R. (1637/1998) *Discourse on the Method* (trans. D.A. Cress) 3rd ed. Hackett
Douglas, M. (1986) *How Institutions Think*, New York University Press
Dox, D. (2006) Dancing Around Orientalism. *TDR: The Drama Review*, 50-4 (T 192), pp. 52-57
Eddy, M. (2002) 'Somatic practices and dance: Global influences', *Dance Research Journal* 34:46-62
_______ (2009) 'A brief history of somatic practices and dance: historical development of the field of somatic education and its relationship to dance', *Journal of Dance and Somatic Practices* Vol. 1 No. 1. doi: 10.1386/jdsp.1.1.5/1
Farnell, B. (1999) Moving Bodies, Acting Selves. *Annual Review of Anthropology* 28: 34173
_______ (2012) *Dynamic Embodiment for Social Theory: "I move therefore I am" (Ontological Explorations)*, Routledge
Foster, S. L. (1986) *Reading Dancing: Bodies and Subjects in Contemporary American Dance*, University of California Press
_______ (1997) 'Dancing Bodies' in *Meaning in Motion* (ed. J. C. Desmond) Duke University Press
_______ (2011) *Choreographing Empathy: Kinesthesia in Performance*, Routledge
Foucault, M. (1980), 'Body/Power' in *Power/Knowledge: Selected Interviews and Other Writings, 1972–1977* (ed. C. Gordon), Pantheon Books
Fowler, S. J. (2012) *S.J. Fowler interviews Qassim Haddad for Poetry Parnassus* http://bit.ly/tpMove36
Frank, A. (1991) 'The Body: Social Process and Cultural Theory', in *For A Sociology of the Body: An Analytic Review* (eds. M. Featherstone, B. S. Turner & M. Hepworth) pp. 36-96, Sage
Freemuse (2007) 'Marcel Khalife and Qassim Haddad cause fury in Bahrain's parliament' http://bit.ly/tpMove96
Gallagher, S. (2003) *How the Body Shapes the Mind*, Oxford University Press
Gardner, H. (1985) *Frames of Mind: The Theory of Multiple Intelligences*, Basic Books
_______ (1993) *Creating Minds*, Basic Books
Gee, P. (1996) *Social Linguistics and Literacies: Ideology in Discourses*, 2nd ed. Routledge
Hahn, T. (2007) *Sensational Knowledge: Embodying Culture Through Japanese Dance*, Wesleyan University Press
Halprin, D. (2003) *The Expressive Body in Life, Art and Therapy*, Jessica Kingsley
Hanna, J. L. (1983) *The Performance Audience Connection: Emotion to Metaphor in Dance and Society*, University of Texas Press
---------------. (1998) *Undressing the First Amendment and Corseting the Striptease Dancer, TDR* 42-2. pp. 38-69, The MIT Press
Hanna, T. (1970) *Bodies in Revolt: A Primer in Somatic Thinking*, Holt Reinhart
_______ (1979) *The Body of Life*, Healing Arts Press
_______ (1993) *Body of Life: Creating New Pathways for Sensory Awareness and Fluid Movement*, Healing Arts Press
Hartley, L. (2004) *Somatic Psychology*, Whurr Publishers
Heidegger, M. (1927/1962) *Being and Time* (trans. J. Macquarrie & E. Robinson) Harper & Row
Hymes, D. (1968) 'The Ethnography of Speaking', in *Readings in the Sociology of Language* (ed. J. Fishman) pp. 99-138, Mouton
Jakobson, R. (1981) *Linguistics and Poetics from Selected Writings III: Poetry of Grammar and Grammar of Poetry*, Mouton
Johnson, D.H. (1993) *Body: Recovering our Sensual Wisdom*, North Atlantic Books
_______ (1995) *Bone, Breath, & Gesture: Practices of Embodiment*, North Atlantic Books.
Johnson, M. (1987) *The Body In The Mind: The Bodily Basis of Meaning, Imagination, and Reason*. Chicago: University of Chicago Press

_______ (2007) *The Meaning of the Body: Aesthetics of Human Understanding*, University of Chicago Press

Kassam, T. R. (2006) 'Response', *Journal of Feminist Studies in Religion*, 22- 1 Spring, pp. 59-67

Khalife, M. (2007) 'Rothko Chapel' http://bit.ly/tpMove99

Khonji, T. (2007) '"Spring of Sex" fury at show', *The Voice of Bahrain Gulf Daily News*, 9th March 2007

Knaster M. (1996) *Discovering the Body's Wisdom*, Bantam Books

Mangione, M. (1993) 'The origins and evolution of somatics: interviews with five significant contributors to the field'. Doctoral Dissertation, The Ohio State University

May, J. (2010) *Dance that's written in the body*. December 28. http://bit.ly/tpMove35

McHose, C. & Frank, K. (2006) *How Life Moves: Explorations in Meaning and Body Awareness*, North Atlantic Books

Merleau-Ponty, M. (1945/1962/2002) *Phenomenology of perception*, Routledge Classics

Mohammed, M. (2008) '"Spring of Sex" Report on Way', *The Gulf Daily News*, http://bit.ly/tpMove41

Olsen, A. (2014) *The Place Of Dance: A Somatic Guide To Dancing And Making Dance*, Wesleyan University Press

Polanyi, M. (2009) *The Tacit Dimension*, University of Chicago Press

Press, C. (2002) *The Dancing Self: Creativity, Modern Dance, Self Psychology and Transformative Education*, Hampton Press

Ross, B. L. (2000) 'Bumping and Grinding on the Line: Making Nudity Pay'. *Labour / Le Travail*, Vol. 46, Special Millennium Issue. 2000. pp. 221-250. Canadian Committee on Labour History and Athabasca University Press Stable

Ross, J. (2007) *Anna Halprin: Experience as Dance*, University of California Press

Rowe, N. (2009) 'Post-Salvagism: Choreography and Its Discontents in the Occupied Palestinian Territories'. *Dance Research Journal*, 41–1, Summer, pp. 45-68

Salamah, S. A. (2009) *Islam on Line*. Dean of the Faculty of Usul Ad-Deen at the Islamic University in Gaza http://bit.ly/tpMove72

Salih, S. (2009) *Islam on Line*. Professor of Islamic Jurisprudence at Al-Azhar University http://bit.ly/tpMove72

Schifter, R. (2004) 'The Clash of Ideologies'. *Mediterranean Quarterly*, 15-3, Summer, pp. 12-23

Sellers-Young, B. (1998) 'Somatic Processes: Convergence of Theory and Practice', *Theatre Topics* 82: 173-187

Schusterman, R. (2008) *Body Consciousness: A Philosophy of Mindfulness and Somaesthetics*, Cambridge University Press

Stinson, S. W. (1995) 'Body of Knowledge'. *Educational Theory* 45- 1. Winter pp. 43-54. http://bit.ly/tpMove42

Thomas, H. (2003) *The Body, Dance and Cultural Theory*, Palgrave Macmillan

Turner, B. S. (2008) *The Body and Society*, Sage

Turner, V. (1974) *Dramas, Fields, and Metaphor Symbolic Action in Human Society*, Cornell University Press

Varela F, Thompson E & Rosch E. (1992) *The Embodied Mind: Cognitive Science and Human Experience*, MIT Press

Weiss, G. (1999) *Body Images: Embodiment and Intercorporeality*, Routledge

JUAN MANUEL ALDAPE MUÑOZ

Choreographic Mobilities

Embodied Migratory Acts Across the USA-Mexico Border

Introduction

In this chapter I engage the concept 'choreographic mobility': how bodies in migration perform choreographic acts in their travels. Central to this research is an interest in the journeys of 'undocumented' Mexican migrants to the USA who are motivated by socioeconomic factors. Importantly, I focus specifically on the extended migration that includes a subsequent return migration to the sending community after a significant time abroad. Research findings are the outcome of the creative practice-led investigation carried out in La Estación – a rural migrant sending community outside of León, Guanajuato, Mexico – from June through September 2012. This chapter intertwines the development of a choreographic project and ethnographic fieldwork.

In order to build this choreographic mobility framework, the examination begins by considering theoretical and practical choreographic ideas used in the creation of the site-specific performance *Los Tres Peligros* (The Three Dangers). I utilise Maurice Merleau-Ponty's ideas of 'embodiment' and Gilles Deleuze and Felix Guattari's notions of 'becoming' to underlie choreographic endeavours. This underlying theoretical optic provides the appropriate perspective to create a production in which the bodily senses and an unfolding experience are vital to understanding mobility.

These performative elements are considered in tandem with the Mexican migrant processes documented from a series of conversations with migrants in La Estación[1], specifically with those who enter the USA without inspection. I incorporate observations of changing bi-national economic and political relationships impacting community-specific phenomena. Concentrating on the effects, I hope to demonstrate how the migrant chooses to take action, choreographically, moving in response to external pressures.

1 To protect confidentiality, all names of interviewees have been replaced with pseudonyms.

Ultimately, this bi-lateral approach reveals that migrants employ the whole of the body to fulfill their immaterial aims, akin to choreographers navigating spaces for creative ambitions. As a consequence of having an embodied abstraction of personal, communal and national spaces, the migrant can imagine a desired alternative possibility. S/he is constantly projecting, reflecting and transmediating, to create better opportunities in a strained environment. Through this tripartite approach, I reach a new lens for observing migrant acts as choreographic acts.

Likewise, viewing artistic endeavours alongside migrant experiences, I see salient migratory attributes in performance practices. As a consequence of the embodied sense of uncertainty, the choreographer pursues creative aims with the belief that it is possible to return to an initially imagined, singular idea.

I would like to acknowledge that this chapter, developed as part of a larger research project for a Master's degree at the University of Warwick, is not an attempt at representational sampling. Instead, the rationale for using choreographic models to observe migrant phenomena is twofold: first, to provide a new sensory lens for understanding the position of the body in transnational socioeconomic spheres; and, second, as a method to expand the understanding of choreographic processes. While not explicitly the focus of this chapter, my own subject position as an undocumented immigrant and independent choreographer informs the framing of this research endeavour. To ignore such key elements would negate the manner in which I see the connection between migrant and choreographic processes.

Choreographic Processes and Corporeal Abstraction

Choreography is more than just a set of dance steps, it is also about embodied thought processes in formulating ideas and making choices. Etymologically, 'choreograph' is divided into two key notions: 'graph', a combining form meaning drawn or written, and 'choreo', a sequenced composition of steps or moves. Through this combination of learning and defining unfolding steps, a tracing is happening across space that renders boundaries, pathways, layers and relationships which were not there before the initial act. Moreover, William Forsythe's elucidation contends (2012) that the choreographic is dissociated strictly from dance itself. Forsythe, a US-born and Frankfurt-based choreographer, is keenly interested in physical thinking and the organisation of motion. In an interview with Diane Solway, entitled 'Is It Dance? Maybe. Political? Sure.' published in *The New York Times*, 18 February 2007, Forsythe asserts, "I keep trying to test the limits of what the word choreography means." Though he comes through a classical ballet lineage, he utilises his 2005-founded troupe, Forsythe Company, to experiment with ideas that range from choreographic objects, synchronous objects and choreographic relationships which are not necessarily dance or that do not follow concert-dance models. At times, his movement investigations fittingly fall into an aesthetics of neoclassical ballet. At other moments, he is frequently penalised for relying too much on poststructuralist concepts and philosophical paradigms to inform his productions. Nonetheless, it is Forsythe's tenacious inquisition into the corporeal-cognitive relationship that has illuminated much current understanding of choreography in expanded areas. For Forsythe, choreographing is the process of observing, reflecting and taking into action an experience to execute an idea. While there are varying directions in contemporary thought towards choreography, Forsythe's observation is particularly revealing because it exposes the intricate relationship between physical and cognitive subjectivities wherein agency is enacted in decision-making processes. To crystalise these choreographic discussions, I now invite the reader to consider the production *Los Tres Peligros*, the performance resulting from embodied workshops, environmental explorations and community interviews in the rural community of La Estación.

La Estación, situated 5km outside of San Francisco Del Rincón, comprises an estimated 985 residents whose primary employment is in shoe-production. The average weekly salary in this sector is $1,100 Mexican pesos (£50, €61, US$77), the majority of inhabitants work long factory hours to earn a sufficient wage. Most leave home before sunrise and return home at sunset – six days per week.The initial design of the performance project called for recruiting a quota of fifteen to twenty heads of household who migrated to the United States in adulthood, spent an accumulated minimum of five years abroad and have since returned and lived in Mexico for five or more years. However, given the living and working conditions of the community, recruiting within a rural community proved more difficult than expected. Ultimately, the number of interviewees sought out was six individuals.

A substantial portion of the research period, from mid-June to late-September, was comprised of conducting environmental observations and explorations using the whole of the body. Beatrice Jarvis's (2012) "practicing space" concept provides significant insight for establishing several methods in which the body in any given space interacts with the components in that space and, as a result, carries out a training of that space.Although Jarvis' primary foci are urban spaces, the idea proves useful across different contexts, such as La Estación.

Walking each day, for a minimum of two hours, I viewed, felt and contemplated both geographical terrain and communal activity.After each exploration, I sketched a quick cartographic map on a sheet of paper.The task offered a material expression to the internal, immaterial, spatial-cognitive references and bodily sensations occurring during environmental explorations.The purpose of these creative cartographies is to establish an emerging map that ultimately informs the trajectory of the choreographic piece *Los Tres Peligros* and serves as the path for the site-specific production. The maps undergo a series of iterative manifestations, evolving over time, based on my transforming understanding of the community.

In order to have a concentrated practising area in La Estación, I established a provisional spatial limit of 800 by 400 metres. The immaterial parameter creates a symbolic border between the performance and the non-performance space. Furthermore, it contributes to a critical parameter for enacting movement as if it were contained within the limits of socio-symbolic demarcations akin to a national border.

Over the span of two months, the sketches progress from recognisable locations in the community to expressive abstract diagrams. Each location – a half-built home; an open field; a dilapidated granary by the train tracks; the rail-road; a bridge of the canal and an alley – begins taking form in relation to the other locations. As I repeatedly journey through these emerging spatial connections, I establish a route that provides similar parameters to those described in the personal interviews, designating particular locations that have a pronounced resonance with locations synonymous with the various phases of a migrant's journey. These stages include: 1) Departure and Travel 2) Arrival, Settlement and Displacement 3) Returning and Travel 4) Return and Re-Placement.[2] For example, a half-built home carries with it the symbolic dimensions of a desire to build a home for the family.The chief aim of the

2 This migration cycle is formulated as a result of personal experience and builds on Douglas Massey's four phases of migration (Massey 1987).

travelling production subsequently becomes to bring these varied elements together into a forty-minute movement sequence, travelling four hundred and seventy meters to induce the experience and decision-making that leads one to migrate.

Fig. 1: Aerial view of the travelling route for the performance *Los Tres Peligros*. Google Maps 2009

Concurrently, under the title 'Migración, Movimiento y Mi Hogar' (Migration, Movement and My Home), a series of facilitated workshops were organised to give participants a space for reflection about personal travel narratives through the whole of the body, addressing motivations for migrating and the social and economic contexts associated with their decisions. The workshops, while initially intended to occur in open public spaces, occurred in personal residences. The structure of the workshops is a combination of sit-down conversations and 'marking' observations. Edward Warburton's (2012: 69) poignant analysis of marking suggests how this dance tool is a "memory device that dancers employ to mark particular moments in the dance". Marking is a process where dancers gesticulate to reference movements or a sequence of movements learned. Utilising 'marking', Warburton says, dancers compress movements in space and wedge sections in time to "commit to memory long passages of choreography". However, I argue it is not just dancers by profession who mark their movements, events, memories and histories. During the home workshops, close attention is given to the interviewee's use of gesture and gesticulation to recount and enact stories related to space. Participants were asked to recount activities performed in different contexts. Examples of events described include memorable episodes in crossing the border and uncomfortable situations in which language is a barrier to ordering hamburgers in fast-food restaurants.

Fig 2: Borja, C. (2012) 'Lejos'. Choreographer: Juan M Aldape. La Estación, Mexico

Returning to Forsythe's contribution about choreographic processes, I want to highlight again how choreographing is the process of observing, reflecting and taking into action an experience to execute an idea. While the realisation of *Los Tres Peligros* occurred on 8–9 September 2012, it is of great importance to know that the actual arrangements and contours of the production were not pre-determined from the beginning. The trajectory of the production was based on the developmental understanding or sense of the potentiality of the project as the research was gathered. The reader can begin to see the composite manner in which this multiplicity of elements began to intertwine and realise a set of ideas beyond an immediate materiality.

Developing the associations within *Los Tres Peligros* is made possible by allowing myself, and the development process, to be shaped by the corporeal abstraction of the felt sense of geographical and social dimensions in space and their relationship to each other. For instance, I make my way to a protective arboreal area via train tracks, passing the shrine of a local man who committed suicide. I later find out he was dismembered across the rails after standing in front of the elephantine locomotive. At that moment, recognising the precarious nature of my walk, I felt and understood that incorporating the railroad into my piece related to elements of danger present in migrant journeys. I also knew that lack of knowledge of the train timetable – it could come through up to ten times a day – required an awareness of the frequent danger present in each exploration and performance, bringing symbolic and concrete elements together. Surely this attests to Moore and Yamamoto's claim, "Through personal movement experience and observation, we develop concepts about the world and the people in it" (2011: 97). Through this embodied processing of external data, we gather that sensitivity to the space around the choreographer prompts action to search for differences in the landscape. In fact, this embodied processing of external data underlies the kinetic awareness and possibility of subsequent decision making.

Key to processing information corporeally, which informs decision making, is the ability and willingness to be affected by external factors while separating oneself from the immediate experience, resulting in an embodied displacement. Sociologist

Bruno Latour (2004) perceptively maintains that learning to be affected results from individuals developing the capacity to articulate previously unrecorded variances in their surroundings; this enables them to observe new layers and unearth critical information for navigating ideas and space. In creative development, for example, as long as I allowed myself to be influenced by external material factors in the community (e.g. the arid climate, half-built homes and loud sonicscapes) I was able to start to formulate a trajectory of the production. The combined and constantly recombining information being revealed about the spatial conditions and my bodily relation to them unearthed a choreographic potential. I constantly oscillated between initiating actions related to the objectives I set out to investigate, subsequently acting on new critical information and being compelled to follow and articulate the unearthing information. Choreographic thinking, then, is a decision-making process where one attempts to combine an unfurling cognitive understanding of space with a willing and displaced corporeal abstraction related to it.

To summarise, a combination of ethnographic field work, movement-based explorations and a performance are employed as part of the research process to achieve a corporeal understanding of the community where the production takes place. I will now provide the subjective context, out of the interviewees' narratives, from which we can perceive migration as an incarnation of choreography.

Reconceptualising Migration

First, I want to devote some time to the term 'migrant'. Customarily, the term is understood to mean a person who travels from place to place. However, this perspective fails to encompass transition periods and varied qualitative attributes before, during and after the actual act. Rather than just arriving at a static position on the Earth's surface (Placemarks), bodies migrating perform embodied acts. The subjective, ontological state of a migrating body is one defined by being in the continual process of change and transformation. Therefore, the purely topological notion of migrant is misleading. I propose that a reconceptualisation is essential, aided by considering migration through choreographic discourse. Accordingly, I assert that bodies migrating perform choreographic acts and never really become a static migrant in the traditional sense.

Referring back to the observation that the interviewees in this project 'mark' as they recall stories, we can ascertain that they are tuned into references to space. In recounting their migrating experience, their present body becomes a reflective mechanism for past experiences of the body in an extended sense of mobility. Under the lens of corporeal abstraction, it is observable that migrants must learn to be affected through the coupling of cognitive and corporeal sensitivities of space, so that with information gained about previously unrecognised variations they may make decisions and learn to articulate the process of navigating inherent dangers crossing the border safely.

Interviewee Cuactemoc seasonally migrated to the United States for work and in the process of going and coming between the two countries, he observed that by learning to be affected he unearthed valuable information for achieving his aims. He explains, "La primera vez vas con los ojos cerrados y no sabes nada y la segunda vez ya sabes a lo que vas a ir" [The first time you go with your eyes closed and don't know anything, but the second time you already know what you are going to do] (Cuactemoc). Developing this understanding can only be carried out when the subject committing a migratory act allows their body to join cognitive and felt experiences of space and time; he or she must see, feel, taste, hear and smell the surrounding changes.

Both migrant and choreographer formalise the experience of understanding the transformation of space and time through the senses. A fundamental commonality in my choreographic endeavours and the migrant stories about strategies to achieve the respective aims is a basic reliance on kinetic corporeality – which Edmund Husserl pinpointed with the term 'kinaesthesis' (Sheets-Johnstone 1999: 226). Crucial to the phenomenon of kinaesthesis is the role that the senses play in bodily movement – in the body doing – and, consequently, how sensing and moving practices are modes of thinking that lead to decision making. Much like my endeavour to produce *Los Tres Peligros*, interviewee Joaquin's migrant undertaking involves the action of the whole of the body to develop significant knowledge and understanding of his experience. While it is easy to observe a choreographer's creative practice maintained by an accordance to movement, what does kinaesthestic awareness look like for a migrant?

As mentioned at the beginning of this chapter, Maurice Merleau-Ponty's ideas of embodiment underlie both my choreographic endeavours and ethnographic fieldwork. Elaborating on these embodied subjective experiences, informed by the senses and activated by social conditions, is critical to unpacking the reconceptualisation of migration.

Reflection and Projection

Joaquin's decision to leave for the United States is preceded by him reflecting on conditions and experiences of his body doing and acting in La Estación. At the surface layer, Joaquin's focus on his family – a symbolic and conceptual paradigm – is extremely important. In deciding to emigrate, he considers a multiplicity of existing conditions, e.g. communal value of self-actualising, life-bettering systems, his own objective circumstances and his subjective bodily satisfaction. Yet, his decision to depart directly results from experiencing poverty around him. He reveals, "No teníamos nada" (We had nothing). As a result of having no physical home, he feels as though he and his family are "rodando mucho de aquí para allá" (rolling around from here to there). This unified sensory experience of rolling takes possession of his motivations. While appearing to be solely initiated by a set of symbolic preoccupations, e.g. family and home, Joaquin is equivalently affected by an embodied tactility, the accumulated unsettling feelings of destitution occupying his body, which lead to his understanding of, and attaching significance to, the need to migrate to find a better situation.

For migrants, vital to decision-making is an elasticity of perspective on the body's potential abilities. The primary condition for Joaquin's felt need to migrate intensifies when elements outside his body cause an activation of his senses, resulting in an embodied projection of a future activity. Living in a "casa de tabiques pegados" (house made of mud and bricks), Joaquin aspires to find a good situation to make more money and "alivianar" (fix or heal) his house with the ultimate goal of having things feel better. He states that his cousin is "allá" (over there), and so, he begins to organise himself "aquí" (here), in Mexico, to meet with him over there, across the border of Tijuana. The 'futurecasting' experience between here and there is one resultant in the creation of a tempo-corporeal synthesis: his eyes look for a stable future he does not currently have – chiefly a house not made of bricks and mud – and his ears long to hear a joyous future not yet materialised. Sensing his condition and being able to project future activity, Joaquin makes attainable the perceptive potentiality of enacting this migration.

Fig. 3 Aldape, M. (2012) 'Recording El Tren'. La Estación, Mexico.

Transmediation

Alongside the experience of projection-reflection, the embodied process which I term 'transmediation', is occurring to inform decision making. Transmediation encapsulates the subjective occurrence of an ongoing recalibration between past and present corporeal experience and the carrying forward of that adjustment.

In performance development, a clear account of transmediation is observed in my environmental investigations of La Estación. During one spatial expedition, while attempting to meet an interviewee in the neighbourhood's periphery, a pack of dogs unexpectedly began to bark alarmingly. Jolted, I sprinted away seeking safety. Essentialised and now corporeally carried, the past-now-present felt experience of running away from the ferocious animals displaces the value of the actual historical event. The essential form of my unsettled feelings and physical reaction became a sequence of movements for one final section in the performance. Consequently, upon generating the various movements, I start to create a now-removed significance of running away from danger. Enacting the corporeal expression of my encounter is an embodied, referential marker of space and time. Again, transmediation is a reconciliation carried forward in the body of the real experience and idea of an experience, in their elemental forms. Though the barking dogs are absent, in their absence they are present.

It is important to note that Merleau-Ponty's term 'repression' (2005: 96), which characterises the embodied action described above, fails accurately to capture the felt sensation of changing and unstable conditions. As such, 'transmediation' better frames Joaquin's situation as he moves from one location to another. Joaquin establishes and carries forward a corporeal imprint of a particular moment which, though physically gone and irreplicable, is nonetheless temporally, spatially and sensorially existent. As illustration, calling multiple times a week to hear his family's voices, Joaquin declares that he needs sensory satisfaction. "Estando allá" (being over there), he asserts, "me imaginaba que estaba con la familia con los hijos ... se siente uno muy solo" (I would imagine being with my family and the kids ... I feel very lonely) (Joaquin 2012). At this moment, a past experience becomes part of Joaquin's body. He keeps his sense of home, and its derivatively associated sensations, in his body, refusing physical displacement in the United States. "Being over there", he corporeally conserves images and feelings of his family, anticipating that they will wait for him while he is abroad. While appearing to be solely faculties which mediate external information, his senses provide an avenue for mediating the fact of physical separation from desired sensorial conditions. Ultimately, by process of transmediation, Joaquin handles the difficult situation of loneliness, a rendering of a bifurcated sensorial circumstance where important elements, once present, are now absent.

Projection, reflection and transmediation expose the intersection of both the migrant and choreographer's principal reliance on the senses as the impetus for knowledge formation and decision making. Across a panorama of these subjective experiences, the senses and embodied sense of movement contribute to a sensorial understanding of space and time. More important, it is possible to discern, extract and maintain that from these subjective experiences bodily and cognitive awareness does not, indeed, end at the point when these tactical agents leave the sending community or arrive at the sought after creative destination. Instead, in an indeterminate state, the migrant's body continuously inhabits space and time saturated with a dilated corporeality. Similarly, the agent producing choreographic acts is attuned to a transforming perceptual synthesis and unity of felt experiences of past, present and future creative encounters.

I now suggest these subjective experiences illustrate how these bodies are in a constant state of becoming something else, thus requiring spatial expertise. I will observe this 'becoming' process in my creative practice and subsequently apply it as an optic in migrant behaviour.

Becoming in the Choreographic

Having established that bodies learn to be affected in choreographic endeavours – resulting in continuously unfolding experiences informed by both subjective and objective elements – choreographic processes change and transform; final productions are only a temporary amalgamation of a developing idea. Deleuze and Guattari's (2005) 'becoming' conceptual paradigm advocates that there is no definite beginning or end; a thought or being is always in the middle of things – nomadic. This prism is particularly useful given the multiplicity of activities, both material and immaterial, which an individual attends to during the development of a choreographic production. Therefore, when we observe bodies performing, we see only a snapshot of other ongoing choreographic processes. The performance is a brief frame of congealed events, motivations and actions (Lepecki 2006).

Integral to constructing *Los Tres Peligros* is acknowledging and attending to undefined and developing heterogeneous clusters of information which overlap and become one element and then another. As illustration, consider my attempt to understand one aspect of a provisional movement section. I use the dance improvisational tool 'mapping' – wherein I use various parts of the body to trace a myriad geometrical aspects and qualitative textures of the immediate space – to develop a relationship in the environment. I stand by a large cactus and outline the prickly, balloon-shaped plant with my knees. Once again, through this corporeal informatics process, my improvisational experiences give attention to a complex, dynamic connection to the space. Subsequently, upon assembling these movement sequences I consider adding other layers of significance, such as being affected thus far by varying elements (e.g. train-tracks, the canal, an ant's sting and an immobilising heat stroke) coagulating with themes of home, departure and return.

Observable in the emerging piece is a reconfiguration and blurring relationship between me and the space. I travel on a daily basis through various sites in the community and am challenged by encounters with different human bodies, as well as topographies such as ravines and rolling hills. In thinking spatially and temporally, being porous to subjective and objective elements, I enter both real and corporeally abstract liminal spaces where I suspend and carry forward varied and imagined future desires for the project. For example, early on I knew I wanted the performance to travel across the unpaved and dusty neighbourhood, but I did not yet know where or how. Similarly, being impacted by the tragedy of the dismembered body on the train tracks, I felt compelled to incorporate the locomotive's pathway in the production. Again, I only had a hunch about the potential use of the space. However, I do not immediately situate the sections' arrangements and sequences. This reciprocity and morphing-sense prompts a kinaesthetic modality that transforms the boundaries between choreographer and the choreography, resulting in the space between the two being constantly blurred.

This process eventuates new possibilities with the compounding elements of the entire research project, resulting in what Maxine Sheets-Johnstone describes as being attentive to the phenomenon of emergence to "engender new relationships among all constituents of the whole" (1999: xxv). Whether it was the train, the ravines or the heat stroke, these elements were introduced into my project and became part of an unfurling vocabulary of the production space. Sheets-Johnstone's observations of a continuous bodily participation – congruous with the earlier Latourian discussion about learning to be affected – captures a horizon of boundless potentialities where associations form and reform. The ideas and concepts, and my references to these elements, were constantly in search of a node where they could attach to other not yet connected themes. Eventually, I fuse the physical elements of the dusty neighbourhood roads, large cactus, and railroad with the immaterial themes of arduous journey, wounds and bodily trauma, and the real potentiality of death, respectively. The compounding multiplicity of spaces, layers, and community participation add to the complexity of the piece as a whole.

Becoming in the Migrant

Now I hope to demonstrate how temporarily established yet constantly changing larger social and political issues between Mexico and the United States have an unfolding corporeal effect on the migrating body and result in the phenomenon of the becoming-migrant. In particular, navigating this unfurling condition requires an attuned sense of national spatial expertise: the migrant is actively in a transitory and nomadic political and social state. I will discuss how this spatial expertise is acutely visible before the emigrating act, at the point where an exilic return is imagined as a possibility.

At the time of writing, the USA-Mexico relationship is undergoing a process of pronounced and emerging economic, political and social change. The financial sector has yet to see a full recovery from its turbulent collapse. There is current political debate about immigration reform for an estimated eleven million 'undocumented' immigrants currently residing in the USA. Additionally, it is forecast that by the year 2050, 51% of the US population will be comprised of minorities, of which 19% will be foreign born (Passel 2008). In this context, Damien Cave maintains, in an article entitled 'Mexicans Looking North, a New Calculus Favors Home' published in *The New York Times*, 6 July 2011, that some Mexican immigrants in the USA are holding in abeyance their decision to return to Mexico. They are waiting until the economic slump and political tensions abate, hoping for the return of pre-militarised borders, a time when travelling between countries was a matter of walking across streets, irrespective of establishing legal authority. The 'waiting' sentiment carries a sense of momentum, pulling forward to an undetermined possibility where 'something' is going to happen. Cave's observation captures the manner in which the migrant's choice to stay is not mere suspension of activity, it is sensing a transforming space around the body. Conversely, my conversations with migrants from La Estación who chose to return to Mexico, revealed that the political and economic climate might not change soon enough. Similarly, both my interviews and Cave's conversations with migrants reveal that these tactical agents sense the potential for a transforming political and economic climate.

In the case of interviewee Joaquin, being poor without viable options for work in Mexico, he left Guanajuato at the age of twenty, his first border-crossing occurred in Tijuana. After a stint of three years, he returned to Mexico. He shares, "No la hallaba aquí, ni allá" (I could not find it here nor there). Meeting the same situation as when he first left, he again returned North. He shares, "Me enseñe a pasar. Yo pasaba solo la línea y por todo el cerro y por donde se pudiera [sic]" (I taught myself how to cross. I would cross the line right through the desert or from anywhere that I could get across). Joaquin's intention and illusion of returning home are there before and after the emigrating decision. Before, during and after his migrant travels of thirty years, he carries the understanding of his complex subjective situation all the while maintaining a desire to, and belief in the possibility that he can, return home.

The corporeal experience of sensing the potentiality of a transforming national space is an emergent bodily experience. Similar to a choreographer's perpetually unfolding artistic sense of a production, a body migrating demonstrates the phenomenon of emergence. As interviewees in this research attest, embedded in the migrating imaginary to the United States is the foundational belief in social and economic mobility, one which includes an eventual return home – even if only temporarily (Massey and Akresh 2006). Douglas Massey contends (2004: 211) that US border enforcement policies from the 1990s contradicted what was otherwise a circular movement between the North American Free Trade Act (NAFTA)-signing countries – leading to a lower probability of returning to Mexico. Likewise, recent data from the Pew Hispanic Center suggests net migration from Mexico has fallen to zero, meaning, more Mexican migrants are leaving the USA than entering (Passel 2006). This recent survey reveals profound political and social effects on both sides of the border. In one aspect, despite what politicians would suggest, it reveals that Mexican migrants are not necessarily an economic threat to the residents of the USA. Also, more importantly, it confirms that the phenomenon of Mexican return-migration indicates an existent imaginary that can be described as the exilic return.

I define the exilic return as the expected and pre-articulated spatial-temporal-embodied imaginary of the migrant returning from the USA while still in Mexico. The conjunctive frame between exile and return is useful for understanding the deep reliance on embodied subjectivities before a migrant's initial act, highlighting the spatial expertise of migrant subjects. The exilic return, as conceptual optic, is based and builds upon the poignant analysis of the exile experience in America conducted by performance studies scholars Silvijia Jestrovic and Yana Meerzon (2011). They invoke the concept of 'exilic imaginary' to account for the pre-existing suppositions, judgements and expectations before an émigré arrives in the USA. By way of the play 'Hunting Cockroaches', the work of Polish émigré Janusz Glowacki, Jestrovic and Meerzon draw out the complexities of exile. They establish that (im)migrants develop an imaginary of America in their home country before leaving it. While being internally exiled in the sending country, Jestrovic and Meerzon propose, émigrés originate "an almost pleasurable dream of the remote and happier place" (2011:1). They posit that the 'exilic imaginary' is one of two key aspects of an exilic paradigm; the other is the incongruous and discordant US reality of marginalisation upon arrival, and most likely ongoing thereafter. While Mexican immigrants are not usually considered 'exiles' in the legal sense, the potential for exile in the USA, due to dangerous border-crossing conditions, labour market shortages and stringent legal purviews, results in the possibility of not being able to return. Interestingly, at least when looking at the (im)migration relationship between the USA and Mexico, the illusion and reality spectrum is not limited to a static binary of before and after moving to the USA. The relationship is imbued with a preconceived idea that it is still possible to return to an initially imagined reality. Although the two countries have agreed on greater cross-border movement of peoples, the symbolic border line between them establishes an imaginary demarcation that limits people travelling for labour purposes – to overcome missing, failed or incomplete markets at home (Massey 2004: 208). This imagined reality resolves in a conjured space and embodied sensation of looking forward to returning home.

Joaquin's strategy of coordinating with his cousin while still in Mexico with the objective of eventually returning is evidence of an exilic return negotiation. As mentioned above, he left his family at the age of twenty. He left while his wife and children stayed behind in Mexico, believing that he would be able to return. Because of the representative demarcation, an imaginary of negotiations – leaving, arriving, returning – exists on a personal level for the Joaquin. This belief is made evident by continuously coming and going, all the while risking his life, until finding his way out of a destitute situation. Fascinatingly, Joaquin's decision to come and go complicates our current understanding of what type of legal structures would satisfy a cyclical relationship between sending and receiving countries where subjects have no intention of staying and are willing to spend the majority of their lives in transition. It is impressive to consider that their intention, as is highlighted by Joaquin's experience and observed in Cave's report, is to come and go intermittently across borders for decades at a time. Ultimately, although each migrant family's decision varies, it is clear that situations like Joaquin's cannot be divided into beginnings and endings. Migrants like Joaquin come and go with an embodied referential marker; they experientially teach themselves and others how to cross through the desert (or anywhere they can) for decades. This dedication is built on a migrant's incipient experience of longing for and having an imaginary home, in time and space, before initiating any actual migration. Surely, migrants are spatial experts tuned into the transformative dimensions of national space.

Common to these intersecting migratory aims is the process of maintaining multiple spatial and individual perceptions of becoming something else: becoming-country, becoming-future, becoming-success, becoming-transit, becoming-stability, becoming-undocumented… quite simply, becoming-migrant.

Migrancy as Choreographic Act and Vice Versa

To reach a temporary end – it would be incomplete to say the chapter comes to a finite end – it is important to summarise and emphasise the possibility of approaching migration discourse through choreographic models and notions of becoming and embodiment. By coupling migrant narratives, environmental explorations, movement and choreographic practices, we gain insights into the corporeal and spatial aspects of bodies in migration. Indeed, connecting diverse yet dialectical methods of investigation generates new appreciation for the role that sense plays for bodies migrating. Particularly, we critically observe how performance aims rely heavily on the experience of acute sensitivity to a felt displacement akin to migration. Simultaneously, we establish that the act of migration is a choreographic act, resulting in the term choreographic mobilities.

In creating the production *Los Tres Peligros*, I submerge myself in an unpredictable liminal state where I am sensitive to the abstract experience of the surrounding space and people, incorporating an understanding of spatial explorations and interviews as part of my daily routine. On a cognitive level, my explorations involve early mapping, photographing and sketching of various sites in La Estación with symbolic dimensions or resemblance to themes or landscapes described by interviewees. The objective is to capture specific attributes and moments which prompt a feeling of choreographic potentiality – meaning that I sought the manner in which space, time and textures around me could be creatively transformed to reflect a singular idea. This aim was attained through the process I call corporeal informatics, the method of developing a cognitive and corporeal understanding of immediate and extended experience, through whole-body movement and observation. The uncertainty of outcomes necessitates a moment-by-moment calibration between subjective state and objective desires. In this unfolding experience, ideas take form and various tentacles of inquiry fuse to carry out the idea of the emerging choreographic act.

In deciding to journey, the return migrants in La Estación willingly enter precarious spaces with an embodied sensitivity to their changing conditions. This sensitivity manifests in reflecting on the penury in which they find themselves, projection of future employment possibilities, and transmediating the ambivalent unease of leaving home and family. The objective is to establish a sense of economic stability by creating a flow of embodied desires between their current situation and their imagined alternative. Migrants like Cuactemoc and Joaquin utilise kin networks, devise tactical strategies to move across the national border and communicate regularly via phone to alleviate the emotional displacement of the internalised, embodied border. The transforming social and political climate requires an ongoing embodied spatial (re)action to become something else, chiefly, becoming-migrant.

As a recommendation for future analysis, we should seriously consider the durational force that is set in motion by the utility of a new sensory lens and rhetoric that focuses on migrating bodies as spatial experts. This alternative approach is uniquely important because it challenges and reroutes established migrant discourse that solely advocates for migrants on an economic basis. Intensifying the focus on the corporeality, the fleshiness and living act of bodies in migration, we might provide an emergent model for a new geopolitical praxis where the USA-Mexico border might be set in motion (Rivera-Servera and Young 2010: 14). We could conceive an emergent political model by asking return migrants, like Cuactemoc and Joaquin – who are bodies of and in motion – to outline an economic and political model based on their kinaesthetic sense of space rather than a fear of movement between nations.

Acknowledgements

This chapter is developed from the dissertation *Choreographic Mobilities: Embodied, Clandestine, and Relational Migratory Acts Across the US-Mexico Border... And Back*. It was in part fulfilment of the Master of Arts in International Performance Research from the University of Warwick, UK, July 2013. I am heartedly indebted to Professor James Harding for his invaluable feedback throughout the development of these evolving ideas.

References

Aldape, J.M. (2012) *Los Tres Peligros* (La Estación, Mexico. 8-9 September 2012)

Choreograph (2005) *New Oxford American Dictionary*, 2nd ed. Oxford University Press

Cuatecmoc (2012) Personal Interview, 10 August, 2012

Deleuze, G. & Guattari, F. (2005) *A Thousand Plateaus: Capitalism and Schizophrenia*, (trans. B. Massumi) University of Minnesota Press

Forsythe, W. (2012) 'Choreographic Objects' in *Dance* (ed. A. Lepecki) pp. 201-203

Jarvis, B. (2012) 'Urban Research Forum. Performance Research', http://bit.ly/tpMove43

Jestrovic, S. and Meerzon, Y. (2011) 'Framing 'America' – Between Exilic Imaginary and Exilic Collective', in *Performance, Exile and 'America'*, pp. 1-19, Palgrave Macmillan

Joaquin (2012) Personal Interview. 10 August 2012

Kershaw, B. and Nicholson, H. (2011) 'Introduction: Doing Methods Creatively' in *Research Methods in Theatre and Performance* pp. 1-16, Edinburgh University Press

LaMothe, K.L. (2012) '"Can They Dance?" Towards a Philosophy of Bodily Becoming', *Journal of Dance and Somatic Practices* 4.1: 93-107

Latour, B. (2004) 'How to Talk About the Body? The Normative Dimension of Science Studies', *Body & Society* 10.2-3: 205-229

Lepecki, A. (2006) 'The Political Ontology of Movement', *Exhausting Dance*, pp. 1-18, Routledge

Massey, D.S. (2004) 'Social and Economic Aspects of Immigration', *Annals of the New York Academy of Sciences* 1038.1: 206-212

Massey, D.S. (1987) 'Understanding Mexican Migration to the United States', *The American Journal of Sociology* 92: 1372-1403

Massey, D.S. & Akresh, I.R. (2006) 'Immigrant Intentions and Mobility in a Global Economy: The Attitudes and Behavior of Recently Arrived US Immigrants', *Social Science Quarterly* 87: 954-972

Merleau-Ponty, M. (2005) *Phenomenology of Perception*, (trans. C. Smith), Taylor and Francis e-Library Edition, Routledge

Migrant (2005) *New Oxford American Dictionary*, 2nd ed. (eds. A. Stevenson & C.A. Lindberg) Oxford University Press

Moore, C. & Yamamoto, K. (2011) *Beyond Words: Movement Observation and Analysis* 2nd ed. Routledge

Passel, J. S. (2006) 'The Size and Characteristics of the Unauthorised Migration Population in the U.S.: Estimates Based on the March 2005 Current Population Survey', Pew Hispanic Center

Passel, J.S. & Cohn, D. (2008) 'U.S. Population Projections: 2005-2050', Pew Research Center

Placemarks (2012) *Google Earth API*, http://bit.ly/tpMove73

Redlich, J. (2010). 'Reading Skin Signs: Decoding Skin as the Fluid Boundary Between Self and Other in Yoko Tawada', *Critical Studies* 33: 75-88

Rivera-Servera, R.H. & Young, H. (2010) 'Border Moves', in *Performance in the Borderlands* (eds. R.H. Rivera-Servera & H. Young), pp. 1-16, Palgrave Macmillan

Sheets-Johnstone, M. (1999) *The Primacy of Movement*, John Benjamins Publishing

Warburton, E.C. (2012) 'Of Meanings and Movements: Re-Languaging Embodiment in Dance Phenomenology and Cognition', *Dance Research Journal* 43: 1–20

PART TWO

Somatics in a Wider Social Context

THOMAS KAMPE

The Art of Making Choices

The Feldenkrais Method as a soma-critique

Introduction

This chapter sets out to position the Feldenkrais Method, a key 20th-century practice of somatic movement education, as a critical practice. Drawing on Feldenkrais-informed choreographic research, on practice and writings by Moshe Feldenkrais (1904-1984), and on writings by contemporaries of Moshe Feldenkrais – Theodore Adorno, Aharon Katzir and Herbert Marcuse, I argue that the Feldenkrais Method uses *choreographic* means to empower the participant to question habitual behaviour. I suggest that Feldenkrais offers the learner tools for self-reflection, empathy and embodied criticality through inter-subjective de-conditioning processes, forming a praxis that echoes ethical positions formulated in Theodore Adorno's seminal essay *Education after Auschwitz* (1966). I examine how modes of facilitation of such processes of de-patterning and re-patterning inherent in the Feldenkrais Method can form a practice of embodied questioning. I discuss the development of non-corrective, Feldenkrais-informed performance pedagogies through practice-led artistic research, and their application in Higher Education contexts as a means to provide the conditions for inquiry, un-knowing and embodied self-examination.

In line with contemporary writers on somatic-informed dance practices (Brown 2011; Fortin 2009; Ginot 2011; Münker 2010), I aim to show that the Feldenkrais Method is an emancipatory bio-psycho-social process – a *soma-critique*. I propose that Moshe Feldenkrais designed his dialogic somatic practice as an emancipatory pedagogy from its inception as an "education towards maturity" (Adorno 1966), providing the conditions for a learning of "fundamentally different existential relations" between multi-dimensional individuals and world (Marcuse 1987).

Context

This chapter emerges from my experience as a practitioner ofThe Feldenkrais Method (FM) working as an educator in the field of"somatic-informed dance practice" (Brown 2011), and from my own practice-led choreographic research undertaken between 2003 and 2011 under the title, 'The Art of Making Choices:The Feldenkrais Method® as a Choreographic Resource'. This trans-disciplinary, practice-led research project explored applications and resonances of FM within performance-making contexts.

My research was initially driven by curiosity and necessity – as a dance-practitioner whose work emerged within the critical frameworks of the UK New Dance and Independent Dance landscape, and who has worked in culturally diverse and inclusive contexts, I needed accessible and non-normative tools for critical and collaborative choreographic practice. My initial research was concerned with questions aboutthe generation and development of choreographic vocabulary and the development of collaborative processes.

Dance-maker Karla Shacklock (2010) suggests that "the [Feldenkrais] method may be used by dancers to improve or enhance awareness of their bodies and the way their bodies move, but it has yet to be integrated into choreography or performance" (2010: 101). My research, consisting of two internationally presented performance works and four laboratory projects, aimed to meet the need for such integration into choreography and performance. It proposes that the method offers more than a training of the awareness of the performers' 'bodies', or quality of 'movement', but constructs an embodied, critical, and inter-subjective process of discovery and *choreographic thinking*. Within a performance-making context it supports the self-organisation of a dance-ecology through placing an uncertain somatic process-of-enquiry within an artistic process-of-enquiry, both concerned with embodied questioning and co-creation.

Feedback by research participants as choreographic peers, co-directors and performers suggested that the integration of principles and ethos inherent in FM into performance-making processes supports the conditions needed for enhanced psycho-physical connectivity, agency, empathy and collaboration skills in process participants. Actor Stefan Karsberg in the project *The Dybbuk* (2010) identified the integration of FM into improvisational performance-making processes as "liberating for the ensemble ... and the individual" (Karsberg 2010). Co-director Julia Pascal (2010) proposed that such a somatic-informed creative process, where performers are "examining sensation, using emotional and intellectual parts of the self at the same time", enhances the quality of ensemble interaction and performance:

> It's because there is no fear. What I think you have done is eradicated fear from the rehearsal process, through the FM and play ... The speed with which [the performers] have absorbed [the acting process], has translated into performance in ways I would not have thought possible. It's as if they have worked together for a year, in fact they have worked together for three weeks (Pascal, interview 08/08/2010).

The Feldenkrais Method

The Feldenkrais Method was developed by physicist and Judo black-belt Dr Moshe Feldenkrais between the 1940s and 1980s as "an approach to working with people, which expands their repertoire of movements, enhances awareness, improves function and enables people to express themselves more fully" (IFF). It is applied within contexts of rehabilitation, sports, and increasingly within Performing Arts education and training. Feldenkrais developed his work in response to Freud and Pavlov in dialogue with leading 20th-century body-learning pioneers and systems scientists. His work, which places learning at the heart of the human condition, is recognised in current research on neuroplasticity (Merzenich 2012), and enactive cognition (Varela 1995; Noë 2009).

Modalities

FM makes use of two interrelated approaches, 'Awareness through Movement' (ATM) and 'Functional Integration' (FI), both social interactions between learner and facilitator which use movement as a vehicle for knowledge creation, learning and enhanced awareness. Feldenkrais defined awareness as the ability to realise "what is going on inside of ourselves while we are conscious" (1990: 50). While ATM lessons are facilitated in groups, FI hands-on interventions happen on a one-to-one, non-verbal level. ATM lessons are led through verbal instruction and questions. FI is an empathetic, touch-based dialogue which allows the learner to discover new and pleasurable sensory experiences and movement possibilities. Through feedback-loops, haptic listening and guiding, the practitioner and student explore a finding of new movement patterns and an improved sense of organisation and coordination. In both ATM and FI, conditions for learning and self-experiment are achieved through non-corrective, pleasurable and structured inquiry, facilitated by the practitioner in empathetic, improvisational dialogue with the learner.

Embodied Thinking

Feldenkrais clarifies his use of verbal instruction within ATM as a mode of facilitating an embodied reflective practice: "In my lessons the student learns to listen to the instruction while he is actually carrying out an exercise and to make the necessary adjustments without stopping the movement itself. In this way he learns to act while he thinks and to think while he acts" (1990: 60). His concerns were with an embodied thinking, organically linked to sensing, feeling and action: "Thought that is not connected to feeling at all is not connected to reality" (1990: 44).

Choreographic Thinking

The title of my practice-led research 'The Art of Making Choices – The Feldenkrais Method as Choreographic Resource' was inspired by Modernist choreographer Doris Humphrey's book *The Art of Making Dances* (1959/1987), and plays through ideas of applying notions of reversibility and variation – key compositional principles within FM – with re-patterning the situatedness of the choreographic.

Feldenkrais dis-places notions of the choreographic from a high-art field, where "choreographers are special people", (Humphrey 1987: 20) into an educational practice designed to improve the functional wellbeing of "the average person" (Feldenkrais 2010: 116). He defined function as "'the interaction of the person with the outside world'", which includes social, sexual and cultural environment (IFF). I argue that the practices developed by Feldenkrais, who likened his works to musical compositions, are distinctly choreographic. When choreographer Michael Kliën (2009) proposes choreography itself as an aesthetics – "a sensitive knowing" (2009: 99) – then the facilitation of such sensitive knowing, at the heart of Feldenkrais's concerns, can be understood as choreographic process. Feldenkrais claimed to provide learners with "conditions where they can learn to think. They have to think without words, with images, patterns and connections. That sort of thinking always leads to a new way of action" (2010: 88).

He referred to this as "thinking with the elements of thinking" (*ibid*). Such embodied, patterned, imaged, connective and divergent thinking, can be posited as *choreographic thinking*, or as the choreographic per se, understood by Kliën (2009) as "the very source of knowledge". Kliën argues, in line with a Feldenkraisian epistemology, that "the perception of patterns, relations and their dynamics, the integration to existing knowledge, and the creative application to a wider reality, all together constitute the choreographic act" (2009: 100).

Self-Imaging

Feldenkrais was influenced by the work of neuro-psychiatrist Paul Schilder (1935/1999). Feldenkrais's interpretations of Schilder's concept of 'self-image' begin with the premise[1]: "We act in accordance to our self-image. This self-image – which, in turn, governs our every act – is conditioned by varying degrees by three factors, heritage, education and self-education" (1990:3).

Feldenkrais saw self-education as key for intervention for personal and social change. FM is not concerned with 'bodies', but with accessing a 'self-image', understood as a unity divided into four components: movement, sensing, thinking and feeling. It aims to foster a capacity for "self-imaging" (Beringer 2001) in the learner through movement.

Self-Image and World Making

There are two major interpretations of FM: one highlighting it as an "approach to changing and improving motor behaviour" (Buchanan and Ulrich 2001). The other, highlighting emancipatory dimensions, asserts that "by developing a better self-image, individuals will evolve towards more autonomy, self-reliance and freedom, and this is the path to social change" (Ginot 2011:155). My work echoes Ginot's call to "construct somatic practice as a practice of empowerment" (*ibid*). In his post-Holocaust anti-totalitarian thinking Feldenkrais posits a holographic relationship between the aware individual and society:

> A society in which its members are only so many units composing it is not the final form of society. A society of men and women with greater awareness of themselves will, I believe, be one that will work for the human dignity of its members rather than primarily for the abstract collective notion of human society (1978/2010: 68).

I suggest that the embodied self-imaging processes developed by Moshe Feldenkrais, form an act of cultural resistance and world-making, part of what Herbert Marcuse

1 For a critical perspective on Feldenkrais' use of Schilder's terminology see Ginsburg (1999) and Ginot (2011).

(2007) called "The Great Refusal" to affirm one-dimensional, totalitarian, and authoritarian traditions dominant in Western culture. Feldenkrais's inward-looking and awareness-forming practices towards "self-education" (1990) echo Marcuse's call for a subversive practice towards a non-conformist subjectivity:

> With the affirmation of the inwardness of subjectivity, the individual steps out of the network of exchange relationships and exchange values, withdraws from the reality of bourgeois society, and enters another dimension of existence ... as a counterforce against aggressive and exploitative socialization. (2007: 69)

Post-Holocaust Education

In his seminal essay *Education after Auschwitz* (1966), Theodore W. Adorno suggests that the only education of any relevance must be an education towards self-reflection, criticality and empathy. Adorno sees a barbarism historically inscribed in civilisatory processes. Its explosive potential can only be *de-fused* through a critical *refusing* of traditional authoritarian and totalitarian psycho-social structures and habitus. Adorno calls for a "turn to the subject" (1966: 2) and directs us to cultivate a self-awareness that includes a capacity of the autonomous individual to make informed critical choices as a necessary form of cultural resistance. Feldenkrais aimed to provide the participant with practical tools for developing such awareness, autonomy and critical facility through embodied educational processes. He believed that aggressive impulses are part of human nature and must not be suppressed through repressive education, but can find their self-regulatory, evolutionary counterpart through the cultivation of awareness.

Embodied Questioning: Education towards Maturity

> The single genuine power standing against the principle of Auschwitz is autonomy ... the power of reflection, of self-determination, of not cooperating. (Adorno 1966: 4)

There are striking similarities between Adorno's quest for an education towards the reflective and self-determined individual and Feldenkrais's somatic educational practices. Adorno's research (1950) on 'the authoritarian personality' was published in the same post-Holocaust zeitgeist as Feldenkrais's first major book *Body and Mature Behaviour* (1949/2005) which defines key aspects of his method. Here, Feldenkrais sets out his anti-totalitarian 'Theory of Reversibility', positing that any truth, as cultural construction, must be questioned and tested: "the first principle of the Feldenkrais Method being no principle" (Hanna 1980). Such critical position and readiness to question the given at any time underpins most strategies and modes of embodiment inherent in the Feldenkrais Method; it provides a context for a somatic criticality.

Fear, Punishment, Liberation and Un-Conditioning

Adorno argued that the authoritarian structures emerging in the early 20th century reached such destructive dimensions because "the people psychologically were not yet ready for self-determination"(1966: 3). He speculated that culturally destructive behaviour is rooted in unconscious, repressed and displaced anxiety. For him education must allow for uncertainty, ambiguity and anxiety. Feldenkrais titled his first major publication *Body and Mature Behaviour – A Study of Anxiety, Sex, Gravitation and Learning*. Like Adorno, he drew on Freud's thesis on discontent in culture, arguing that many problems in physiological functioning in the adult person are the result of "faulty learning" enhanced through repressive cultural conditions. For Feldenkrais, traditional education based on "the promise of great reward or intense punishment" (2010: xvi) leads to a distortion of a well-functioning dialogue of the human organism with the environment. Such repressive education must be counterpointed through embodied processes of re-education. The emancipatory dimensions of FM are articulated most clearly in a conversation sometime around 1970 between the late Dynamic-Systems thinker Aharon Katzir and Moshe Feldenkrais (Feldenkrais 2010). Katzir sums up aspects of their conversation: "We discussed the topic of developing a free awareness that enables the critical and free operation, which results from the needs of self-awareness ... we can think of this as a process of de-conditioning – that is to say, 'un-conditioning'. And then we talked about culture, which is stipulated by the possibility of conditioning" (2010: 173). Katzir argues that an awareness-forming education supports the development of a "self-active part which liberates the individual from his subjective enslavement" (*ibid*).

Facilitating Criticality: Self-Reflection, Learning, Autonomy and Empathy

The International Feldenkrais Federation places "a state of mind that fosters a process of inquiry rather than one that seeks to define solutions" (IFF) at the core of its standards of practice. Dance practitioner and Feldenkrais practitioner Scott Clark comments on the ethos of such education, saying that Feldenkrais "looked for a way that our learning could be directed first and foremost by our inner sensation, and by our own pleasure and judgement. For him, this was the most important step toward becoming a truly capable and free human being" (Clark 2008).

Clark, founder-member of seminal, UK-based Siobhan Davies Company (SDC), taught the dance company for six years. Little is documented on the distinct impact of his work on the choreographic practice within SDC. The late co-founder member and dancer Gill Clarke referred to the emerging practice at SDC as a "laboratory of self as ground for testing ... letting experience be the driver" (Clarke 2011). Such thinking beyond movement, notions of 'testing', 'self' and 'experience' within Clarke's reflections link a choreographic ethos emerging from the SDC artistic community to the work of Moshe Feldenkrais. In the next section I identify a series of modalities inherent in FM that promote an emerging embodied criticality.

Sensory Insight: Action as Reflection

As an overarching strategy to facilitate reflexivity, improved function and self-knowledge in the participant, FM utilises regular "Action-Reflection-Cycles" (Stringer 1999) in both ATM and FI.

We move, then we pause to reflect, often through eyes-closed practice to gather "sensory insight" (Rywerant 2001), then we move again with enhanced sensory insight. This process might also be reversed by beginning with the reflective process of "body scanning" (Feldenkrais 2010:39), before we start to move.

De-Familiarisation: Reduction of Stimuli

Referring to the 'Webern-Fechner Law', which suggests that a lowering of stimuli increases perception, Feldenkrais uses de-familiarisation strategies such as slowing movements down, varying and often reducing effort, size and scale, to foster a reflective position of the participant.

Disorientation as Tool for Inquiry

For Feldenkrais an awareness of one's spatio-temporal orientation is key to self-knowledge. He uses the term orientation to describe our relationship to gravity and space, and between self and other. Most Feldenkrais lessons are also designed to suspend habitual environmental contexts, which will allow habitual thinking/behaviour to become de-stabilised. Lessons which prepare the function of upright walking might be taught lying semi-supine, or on one's side. By using processes of disorientation, Feldenkrais facilitates conditions which "divorce the aim to be achieved from the learning process itself" (*ibid*: 67). Such seemingly aimless practice leads the learner into a non-goal-oriented enquiry, a "learning to learn" (ibid) that guides the participant to engage with a fluid and changing world of sensation.

Asymmetrical Action to Create and Discern Differences

In both ATM and FI, learners are asked to engage over a long period with one side of the body to disrupt habitual self-perception and to guide the learner towards a discerning of differences between the two body-halves through a process of body-scanning. Feldenkrais' preference for asymmetrical body-coding to stimulate curiosity and to enhance self-reflexivity in the learner, offers another similarity to Doris Humphrey's choreographic quest to "stimulate the senses" (1987).

Maturity as Criticality: Refusing/De-fusing/Re-fusing

Feldenkrais lessons are concerned with de-patterning and re-patterning the relationship of parts to the whole. For Feldenkrais, maturity is the human capacity for an embodied questioning, to refuse the given, and to form the capacity to de-fuse unreflective, potentially aggressive behaviour:

> What I understand by maturity, is the capacity of the individual to break up total situations of previous experience into parts, to reform them into a pattern most suitable to the present circumstances; maturity, in that sense is an ideal state where the uniqueness of man, his capacity to form new responses, or to learn, has reached its ultimate perfection (1949/2005: 196).

Guiding the learner towards a dialogic feedback loop – *a zooming in and out* – between detailed embodied inquiries, and a connecting to a broader contexualisation of an awareness of the 'whole self' in relation to its social environment is at the heart of FM.

Structural and Compositional Devices

Feldenkrais lessons are built around compositional devices that enhance self-reflexivity and curiosity, and which offer choice for process participants. These include the use of repetition, variation and reversal of movement patterns, the gradual increase of difficulty of tasks, and the creation of perturbations through the setting of constraints and problems to stimulate pattern change.

The Questions

ATM lessons are taught through verbal instruction, which includes a use of suggestion, imagery and metaphor, reframing, pacing and modelling, and the use of questioning. The Feldenkrais practitioner consistently encourages the learner to ask questions which are of ecological, anti-totalitarian, anti-authoritarian inflection and concerned with relationships, feedback-loops and non-linear causalities:

- Intra-psychic: between sensing, feeling, thinking and action
- Intra-organismic: questions regarding functional relationships between different body areas – how do my ribs begin to open when I reach up with my arm? How does this impact on my breathing?
- Environmental: questions regarding relationships between organism and environment. How does my relationship to the ground change when I let both knees gently fall over to the right while lying on my back?

Through notions of *'What if? How can I find another movement solution or change the quality of my actions?'* the method avoids proposing reductionist, 'correct' solutions. The role of facilitator in FM is to provide conditions that enable participants to differentiate and realign relationships between cultural efficacy, physiological efficiency and "self-efficacy" (Bandura 1994) through felt subjective experience. Hence the title of a 1981 talk by Moshe Feldenkrais: 'To Correct is Incorrect: Conditions for Feedback, Play and Empathy'.

> The inability to identify with others was unquestionably the most important psychological condition for the fact that something like Auschwitz could have occurred in the midst of more or less civilized and innocent people (Adorno 1966: 8).

Doidge (2007) and other trans-disciplinary neuro-scientists (Damasio 1999; Freeman 2011; Hüther 2012) suggest that neuroplasticity (Feldenkrais's aim for *flexible brains*), openness for adaptation and change in behaviour depends largely on a "fertilization" (Hüther 2012) of newly-wired synaptic patterns and neuro-modulators through our affective and inter-subjective perception of pleasure, passion and compassionate love. A key role of the FM practitioner is to consistently 'fertilise' conditions for: learning, discovery and absorption of new behaviour for the individual and between participants. Such fertilisation acknowledges feeling – pleasure, curiosity, fear, pain and desire – in the inter-subjective process of performance making. The non-corrective and playful mode of interaction through touch and aural listening between practitioner and learner disrupts dominant modes of social interaction based on fear and reward, and places the cultivation of an empathetic dialogue at the core of FM-based somatic learning modes.

Body Coding

> Whoever is hard with himself earns the right to be hard with others as well ... an education must be promoted that no longer sets a premium on pain and the ability to endure pain. (Adorno 1966: 6)

Feldenkrais lessons privilege softness, ease and lightness in joint articulation and a core-mobility of the axial skeleton, including a recovering of a "culture of pelvis and hip joints" (Feldenkrais 2005). Lessons allow for complexity, poly-centricity and omni-directionality in body coding. While FM focuses on neuro-muscular-skeletal organisation, the body-coding proposed has no fixed centre, but is part of an ecological system that is reflected in Feldenkrais' concept of a "functional unity between body, mind, and environment" (2005:149). Feldenkrais offers a "relational body" (Batson 2008) that places a dialogic exchange between awareness, curiosity and adaptability as its potent core. It challenges and de-fuses dominant patriarchal Western modes of body-coding and reductionist body-instrumentalisation. Such modes privilege core-stability and verticality of alignment where the axial-skeleton is understood as a centralising anchor supporting the actions of distal areas of the human body (Batson 2008).Feldenkrais disrupts this Cartesian model of alignment by asking the mover to constantly shift the place of movement initiation, and by offering movement explorations where 'joint-order' relationships of stability and mobility are varied and reversed.This proximal-distal-reversal strategy is embedded in both ATM and FI practices.

The spatiality of movement organisation within FM-lessons is self-referential – linked to an intentional relationship between mover and environment – rather than concerned with external theatrical codes of presentation. FM privileges a 'yielding' or 'indulging' of dynamic qualities by encouraging participants to reduce speed, resistance to gravity and force, and scale of movement, while allowing for connectivity with the ground. Such slowing-down and yielding allows participants to align heightened perception with fine-tuned action. Consequently movers are invited to connect intentionality with action.

Crisis and Self-Questioning

Processes of de-patterning, though introduced through play and possibilities for reintegration of new knowledge into enworlded functions, must provoke crises of self-image and of "knowledge and skills" (Martin 2009). Allowing for a space for crisis and creating varying conditions for questioning were part of the emerging methodology within my research. It raised issues regarding the transition from facilitator-led questioning to participant-led questioning where the performance-maker becomes autonomous self-questioner. Seeking an un-knowing as working-position is not always immediately acceptable to process participants, creating an ambiguity towards the process and own direction.

> *Initially, there was a resistance because I felt: 'Can't you tell us what to do?' That's like a deformation of however we'd been taught directively (Dante 2010).*

> *I really could not let go in ATM sessions ... but the sessions took me to some mental space where I don't go normally (Isobe, in Kampe 2010: 49).*

> *Although I am confused and undecided in my own research, I am somehow calm and relaxed due to Feldenkrais (Herman, ibid: 42).*

Inhabiting such a position of un-knowing was described by participants as:

> *... less rational ... although I was aware of every movement.*

... very open and soft, it felt more organic ... (Herman, ibid).

... encouraged ... to listen to our intuition, and that was the crucial approach we took for our artistic practice.

... less fear towards the unknown (Isobe, ibid).

Integration

I refused be wired-in like everybody else
(Feldenkrais 2010: 199)

Feldenkrais (1990) proposed a utopian – and naïve – perspective on human evolution which promises social progress through a growth in self-awareness on the part of the socially embedded individual. He understood his practice as simply enhancing an evolutionary step such as that where "humanoids can develop into Homo sapiens, human beings with intelligence, knowledge and awareness" (1976/2010: 181). Claiming that the 20th century was in need of a change of crippling social structures (2002) and was also a century of constant rebellion by younger generations, Feldenkrais suggested that an embodied de-conditioning towards an "increase of awareness will help them to find a way out of confusion and free their energies for creative work" (1990: 173).

Education in Western society has changed considerably since Feldenkrais and Adorno envisaged their education towards a mature individual. The repressive ,authoritarian and totalitarian psycho-social structures that both referred to have changed, becoming far more disguised. A "dominant social imaginary" (Castoriadis 1998) that determines culturally affirmative behaviour has become all-encompassing through complex, mediatised cultural conditioning. Drawing on Adorno's educational writings, cultural theorist Chris Hedges (2010) suggests that the Higher Education sector has become part of an aggressive corporate system replacing a critical, value-based education with reductionist training towards a skills development that affirms the cultural status quo. The development towards a corporate university setting, where high student fees are charged in exchange for an environment that encourages students to self-identify as customers, demands a tightly modularised provision of employability skills often facilitated through digital media-learning tools. Can somatic processes that foster an "awared learning" (Feldenkrais 2010: 34) and non-linear, uncertain and critical processes of "self-examination" (ibid: 175) offer necessary acts of refusal within a corporate, competitive and increasingly one-dimensional educational environment? Does FM, with its non-corrective and questioning stance, its slow-attending, yielding and environmentally embedded systemic body-coding, provide learners with a timely education and meaningful cultural survival skills?

As a Feldenkrais practitioner and academic working in Higher Education I am engaged in a daily balancing act. As dance co-ordinator at London Metropolitan University I designed a curriculum that successfully integrated somatic processes into a three-year programme catering for students from non-traditional backgrounds with a diverse range of abilities. I was able to draw on a team of educators who facilitated somatic- and Feldenkrais-informed dance pedagogies in accessible ways. More so, London Met supported my PhD research on the application of FM within performance-making contexts, which informed and questioned my praxis as educator greatly. I was awarded a University Teaching Fellowship in 2010 and Associate

Professorship in 2011 for developing a somatic-informed dance syllabus that bridged the gap between reflective learning, dance making practice and professional contextualisation. Performer and ex-student Catarina Moreno commented on the effects of a Feldenkrais-informed dance pedagogy:

> I acquired a deep sense of body awareness and I felt simultaneously challenged and supported, which allowed me to progress in a surprisingly fast and solid manner. Rather than being given answers, I was encouraged to ask the right questions; I feel I was injected with the right amount of tools and curiosity to be able to train myself from now on, both physically and creatively (Catarina Moreno, Performer; BA Performing Arts 2007–2010).

In my current workplace in the Department of Performing Arts at Bath Spa University, management welcomes the input of somatic-informed pedagogies into the professional training ethos of the BA Acting programme. Still, my pedagogical practices are challenged by time constraints, assessment instruments and a grading system based on surveillance, reward and punishment. While I am happy and able to facilitate the development of alignment, communication and expressive skills necessary for professional dexterity, it is clear to me that as a Feldenkrais practitioner I not only teach movement, but facilitate conditions for a non-corrective learning 'through movement'. Such learning includes giving students time to enter a trans-subjective world of sensation, touch and feeling, and taking time for reflection and debate where students learn to find their own modes of re-translating enacted knowledge into verbal and written language and to share internal realities with their peers. Equally, I attempt to provide the conditions to facilitate the development of skills for inquiry, unknowing and embodied self-examination. These include improvisational practices, which use ATM processes as kinaesthetic-tuning process and touch-interaction based on FI principles as resources for creative inquiry. The use of verbal instruction through questioning and a commitment to a non-corrective approach to process facilitation support the psycho-social learning climate of my lessons.

Powerful Modalities

Maria Molofski, who reviewed the performance of my choreographic research project *The Dybbuk* in 2010, identified the modes of embodiment emerging in performance as an "extremely powerful modality" where performers "do not act, but move and become" (Molofski 2010). As a Feldenkrais-informed pedagogue I continuously attend to the dialogic exchange between moving and becoming, and am interested in students developing an awareness of such fluid and emergent process. The late dance-maker and pedagogue Gill Clarke (2007) envisioned the role of the dancer as "facilitating experiences rather than delivering consumable goods". I understand my role as Feldenkrais-based pedagogue primarily as a facilitator of experiences. These experiences are not arbitrary but understood as a critical process – a being in question: facilitating a growing ability to interact critically with the world through embodied sensitivity and agency.

~

A version of this chapter was published under the title 'Moving After Auschwitz: The Feldenkrais Method as a Soma-Critique' in *The Journal of The Korean Dance Society for Documentation & History* (vol.33), in June 2014.

References

Adorno, T.W. (1966) *Education After Auschwitz* http://bit.ly/tpMove44

Adorno, T.W., Frenkel-Brunswik, E., Levinson, D. J. & Sanford, R. N. (1950) *The Authoritarian Personality*, Harper and Row

Bandura, A. (1994) 'Self-efficacy' in *Encyclopedia of Human Behavior* (ed. V. S. Ramachaudran) (Vol. 4, pp. 71-81) Academic Press

Batson, G. (2008) 'Teaching Alignment' in *The Body Eclectic- Evolving Practices in Dance Training* (eds. M. Bales & R. Nettl-Fiol) University of Illinois Press

Beringer, E. (2001) 'Self Imaging', *Feldenkrais Journal* 13; pp. 33-38

Brown, N. G. (2011), 'Disorientation and Emergent Subjectivity: The political potentiality of embodied encounter', *Journal of Dance & Somatic Practices* 3: 1+2, pp. 61-73, doi: 10.1386/jdsp.3.1-2.61_1

Buchanan, P. & Ulrich, B. (2001) 'The Feldenkrais Method: A Dynamic Approach to Changing Motor Behavior', *Research Quarterly for Exercise and Sport* Vol. 72, No. 4, pp. 315-323

Castoriadis, C. (1998) *The Imaginary Institution of Society*, MIT Press

Clark, S. (2008) *About Feldenkrais*, http://bit.ly/tpMove45

Clarke, G. (2007) 'Mind is as in Motion', *Animated*: Foundation for Community Dance (Spring 2007)

_______ (2011) *Crossing Borders*, talk; Siobhan Davies Studios London 25 Oct. 2011

Doidge, N. (2007) *The Brain That Changes Itself: Stories of Personal Triumph from the Frontiers of Brain Science*, Penguin

Feldenkrais, M. (1990) *Awareness Through Movement: Health Exercises for Personal Growth*, Harper Collins (Second edition)

_______ (2002) *The Potent Self*, Somatic Resources (Second edition)

_______ (1949/2005) *Body and Mature Behaviour: A Study of Anxiety, Sex, Gravitation and Learning*, 2nd ed. International Universities Press

_______ (1978/2010) *Embodied Wisdom: The Collected Papers of Moshe Feldenkrais* with E. Beringer (ed), North Atlantic Books

Fortin, S., Vieyra, A. & Tremblay, M. (2009) 'The experience of discourses in dance and somatics', *Journal of Dance and Somatic Practices* 1: 1, pp. 47–64, doi: 10.1386/jdsp.1.1.47/1

Freeman, W.F. (2011) *How Brains make up their Minds*, Columbia University Press

Ginot, I. (2011) 'Body schema and body image: At the crossroads of somatics and social work', *Journal of Dance & Somatic Practices* 3:1+2, pp. 151-165 doi: 10.1386/jdsp.3.1-2.151_1

Ginsburg C. (1999) 'Body-Image, Movement and Consciousness: Examples from a Somatic Practice in the Feldenkrais Method'. *Journal of Consciousness Studies*. 6(2-3): 79-91

_______ (2010) *The Intelligence of Moving Bodies: A Somatic View of Life and its Consequences*; Awareing Press

Hanna, T. (1980) *The Body of Life*, Alfred A. Knopf

Hedges, C. (2010) *The Empire of Illusion: The End of Literacy and The Triumph of the Spectacle*, Nation Books

Hüther, G. (2012) *Was wir sind und was wir sein könnten*, Fischer

Humphrey, D. (1959/1987) *The Art of Making Dances*, 2nd ed. Dance Horizons

IFF (International Feldenkrais Federation) Standards of Practice http://bit.ly/tpMove46

Keleman, S.(2011) 'Slow Attending', *USA Body Psychology Journal Vol. 10, No.2, 2011*

Klein, G. & Noeth, S. (eds.) (2011) *Emerging Bodies: The Performance of Worldmaking in Dance and Choreography*, Transcript

Kampe, T. (2010) 'Weave: The Feldenkrais Method as Choreographic Process'; *Perfformio Vol*: 1, No: 2 (Spring 2010)

_______ (2011) 'Recreating Histories: Transdisciplinarity and Transcultural Perspectives on Performance Making', *The Korean Journal for Dance 2011*, 6.Vol 67

Kliën, M. (2009) 'Choreography as an Aesthetics of Change', Unpublished PhD thesis, University of Edinburgh, UK

Marcuse, H. (1987) *Eros and Civilization*, 2nd ed. Routledge

_______ (2007) *Art and Liberation: Collected Papers of Herbert Marcuse*, Routledge

Martin, R. (2009) Between Utopia and Intervention; talk; German Tanzkongress Hamburg; Nov 8th 2009

Merzenich, M.(2012) Neuroscience, Learning and the Feldenkrais Method http://bit.ly/tpMove74

Molofsky, M.(2010) *Review of "The Dybbuk"* http://bit.ly/tpMove75

Münker, K. (2010) 'A continuous experiment and a continuous finding: A reflection on choreography, somatic practice and the aesthetics of change and conditions, written from practice', *Journal of Dance & Somatic Practices* 2: 2, pp. 163-176

Noë, A. (2009) *Out of Our Heads: Why You Are Not Your Brain, and Other Lessons from the Biology of Consciousness*, Hill and Wang

Rywerant, Y. (2001) *Acquiring The Feldenkrais Profession*, El Or

Schilder P. (1935/1999) *The Image and Appearance of the Human Body*, 2nd ed. Routledge

Shacklock, K. (2010) *Dance Consciousness*, Lambert Academic

Spatscheck, Christian (2010). 'Theodor W. Adorno on Education' *The Encyclopaedia of Informal Education* http://bit.ly/tpMove47

Stringer, E.T. (1999) *Action Research*, Sage Publications

Varela, F. (1995) *Large Scale integration in the Nervous System and Embodied Experience;* in *Report -1st European Feldenkrais Conference;* pp.12-14 ; International Feldenkrais Federation

Interviews

Dante, J. & Perlin, S. in conversation with T. Kampe 10 Aug. 2010

Karsberg, S. & Sykes, K. in conversation with T. Kampe 10 Aug. 2010

Pascal, J. in conversation with T. Kampe 08 Aug. 2010

LIZZY LE QUESNE

An Intricate Field

In search of freedom and togetherness: a tangible meditation on inter-subjectivity and materiality in shared space

An Intricate Field, my participatory durational performance-ritual presented at Coventry University on Saturday 13th July 2013, proposed possibilities of dance as self, as society, as lived experience and as dynamic act: dance as being in the world. After years of research and evolution through changing performance forms, it asked afresh: What/where is the distinction between performing and doing? What insight has dance for citizenship, and vice versa? What is and what facilitates agency and responsiveness in my body, in space and in community?

In this chapter I will describe how the performance grew out of a score-based group piece first presented in Prague in 2002, and in the light of ongoing research. This has included: profound immersion in the practice and teaching of somatic movement, primarily Skinner Releasing Technique; social psychology; politicised thinking around inter-subjectivity; phenomenologies of self and space; theories of perception; dance theories and notions of 'social choreography' and my experiences as a dancer in works by Wally Cardona, Rosemary Lee, Tino Sehgal and (after the performance at Coventry) Michael Kliën. Each of these fields and experiences has fed into my thinking/sensing around the resonance of creative embodied being, through and beyond the world of the art object or event, towards notions of individual emancipation, engaged citizenship and mindful co-existence. I will introduce these interconnected concepts, looking at how somatic dance is a compelling medium in which to develop them, and then explore how they materialised through the evolution of, and reflection on, the performance of *An Intricate Field*. I shall argue that to recognise and negotiate one's own state and position in relation to others in the moment is a political act, and that this has significant impact upon how we live together in this world.

The Strength of 'Feeling'

In *Fear of Freedom*, social psychologist Erich Fromm defines human freedom not only in terms of 'freedom *from'* external controlling forces,[1] but equally importantly, and yet to be achieved, as 'freedom *to'* take personal action. Fromm writes "...we have to gain a new kind of freedom, one which enables us to realise our own individual self; to have faith in this self, and in life" (1942: 91). Fromm asserts that in order to unfurl into our own fullness and thus into being active participants in life we must also have 'faith'; and that trust and love are fundamental tools to recognise and to loosen "... inner constraints, compulsions and fears" (1942: 91). Trust and love are integral to being free.

Fromm's aim of 'freedom to ...' is for people to have the ability *spontaneously* and *creatively* to engage with the world. This requires, he contends, that we express and act from all aspects of the self. Amongst these aspects he includes 'feeling', both as emotion and as sensory perception. Fromm criticises the way that feeling has been repressed in Western culture: maligned as irrational and primitive; he argues that this cultural stance has led to the destructive repudiation of a vitally perceptive and eloquent aspect of the self. Fromm also acknowledges Freud's assertion of the relationship between somatic symptoms and psychological states: between physical experience (e.g. of feeding and defecating in infancy) and the way an individual fundamentally perceives and relates to the world.

Writing in 1942, Fromm did not refer to the processes of somatic attentiveness in the way that we understand them today but I believe that this field of activity offers a way to access, foster and expound his powerful, elusive 'feeling' and effectively develops and extends Fromm's call for the promotion of awareness, assertion and nudging into action of a more integrated, embodied self. Several somatic processes practise awareness of – and giving space to – feeling in its nebulous physical and emotional configuration. In philosopher-turned-psychologist Eugene Gendlin's Focusing Technique for example, the pre-verbal 'felt-sense' is the active focus of attention, with the express aim of engaging feeling, rooted in the physical, in a process of self-realisation, emancipation and personal development.

In our age of supposed equality and freedoms (defined in rational, though not experienced in material, terms) somatic awareness allows us to perceive and express deep inner (bodily) realities while remaining in relationship with context and outer (world) realities, and to cultivate a tangible sense of presence within them. Lepecki writes of "the gap between body and presence in the history of modern Western subjectivity and modern Western dance" (2004: 3). I would argue that with the emergence of somatic practice facilitating new depths and fluency of awareness, we gain a new measure of presence, and of arrival, in the self/moment/world. With this comes new potential for original impulse, for agency and the kind of spontaneous action that Fromm envisaged. One of the principles around which Joan Skinner developed her Skinner Releasing Technique (SRT) is the notion that "Awareness is the first step to change" (2006: 1) SRT classes constantly practise both awareness and spontaneity.

---

1 This is chiefly represented in Fromm's writing by 20th-century resistance to Fascism.

Fig. 1: *An Intricate Field*, Lanchester Gallery, Coventry 2013.
Dancers: Hannah Greyson-Gaito, Ella Tighe. Photo: Lizzy Le Quesne

Selves and Others: Disparate or Dancing

How do personal emancipation, and a capacity for agency, sit in terms of our relationships with other people, and with the world we share? If, as for Sartre's existentialist free man, "Hell is other people" (1944), then being together, sharing space, is not necessarily simple or snug. In *Violence* Slavoj Žižek (2008) outlines his theory of the violence of the neighbour:"a neighbor … is primarily a thing, a traumatic intruder" (2008: 50) in which our terror of the other (all around us in the modern world) formulates an intolerable onslaught on our personal space, and thus hatred. The unknown or unacknowledged is distressing, dangerous. Žižek's neat, mischievous phrase "fear thy neighbour as thyself", suggests that not only are our fellow citizens terrifying and offensive, but that we are all unstable and unfathomed, even to ourselves (Žižek 2008: 34). Fear, he writes, is "a basic constituent of today's subjectivity" (2008: 34) and our chosen solution to this is to isolate ourselves from one another. He complains that "we exist in a social space which is increasingly worldless" (2008: 67) – i.e. the virtual – and that we have established a "code of discretion", (2008: 50) which allows us to avoid authentic exposure to, or genuine contact with, other selves. We habitually present to the world, and thus to our own consciousness, only certain edited aspects of ourselves, in a vicious cycle of otherness and fear.

Žižek argues that in having proclaimed language (diplomacy) and a language-based rationality as the favoured peace-making response to distrust, conflict or difference, we cannot properly tackle, and in fact only reinforce, this distance. Language, he claims, essentially contains and reframes aggression because it "dismembers the thing, destroying its organic unity" (2008: 52) and places it in a culturally constructed field of meanings and associations. In phenomenological tone he writes "When we name gold 'gold' we violently extract a metal from its natural texture, investing into it our dreams of wealth, power, spiritual purity etc, which have nothing to do with the natural reality of gold" (2008: 52). Following Lacan, Žižek writes "discourse is ultimately grounded in a violent imposition of the Master-Signifier ... *It is so because I say it is so*" (2008: 53). Discourse alone cannot effectively dispel fear. Somatic practices, operating on a pre-verbal level of sensation, offer a wealth of resources to address a state of 'othered-ness' or fear.

Emotions are physical. Fear is physical. It is tension. If we replace, or supplement and enhance, discourse with sensitive attention to the physical, and actuate more bodily slack, elasticity and roominess for ourselves, we could become less vulnerable, and less threatening, to the other. SRT addresses this directly. Releasing or 'letting go' is the fundamental process of the technique, activated in the service of discovery, of cultivating ease and articulacy, and ultimately freedom and power of the integrated self or "whole self" (2006: class 1). Through softening and relinquishing holding in both mind and body and in practising stillness and economy in motion, SRT actively disperses states of compression or constraint and creates new possibilities of movement or of action. SRT classes cultivate trust and practise the disarming of inner fears and compulsions (which Fromm says prevent us from acting spontaneously), by enacting a sense in which we surrender ourselves to a kinaesthetic image, allowing it to "move us" (2006: class 2). In Joan Skinner's radical proposition that "'it' dances us" (2006) we are engaged in an active process of allowing our creative and sense-based imaginations to take possession of our minds and bodies in such a way that we can both discover new layers of ourselves and move beyond our expectations, our existing understanding of ourselves. SRT and other somatic or psycho-physically based movement processes such as Authentic Movement effectively evade Žižek's language trap and provide real ways to explore Fromm's 'freedom to...'.

Furthermore, if we can disarm and modify our sense of fear, community can not only be endured but can be a productive space for growth and life. SRT is practised in groups, enacting community, with people opening themselves up to deep, personal kinaesthetic discovery in the presence of others. People, at different stages of skill or experience, dance alongside one another in mutual discovery and play. These elements, intentionally and sensitively framed, generate warmth and openness, a sense of common yet individual journeys and a state of trust and respect for ourselves, for one another and for the space we share. A softening self has less impact on, is less in collision with, others and with the environment. Joan Skinner reminds us to "have our radar out" (2006: class 1) so as not to crash into, or insensitively through, the space of others, to sense and respect the presence of others while attending to our own inner states. Skinner reminds us literally to reduce jarring as our feet meet the floor; to "soften into moving" (2006: class 1) and "soften into stopping" (2006: class 1); and to minimise the vibrations that we emit and that we cause. In this, SRT aims not to forbid our physical and energetic resonances in the world, but sensitively and responsibly to acknowledge their existence and their power. In so doing, dissolving somehow/somewhat into our world, we open possibilities for greater presence, spontaneity, and expression both for ourselves and for those around us.

Dancers have always had a fundamental understanding of the state of inter-subjectivity: that while we each exist at the sentient centre of our own world, we are also objects, energetic entities, with weight and mass, in the space and activities of others. We affect and are affected by one another and we fundamentally depend upon material cooperation. Add to this instinctive knowledge, the new depths of reflection and discovery within somatic explorations for the wider self and its potential in the world, and you have a powerful force of emergent knowledge and proficiency. Working with the moving body, dancers have a natural connection to the somatic field and can make perhaps greater use of it than many. My own encounter with somatic practice has met and quenched a lifelong thirst I hadn't been able to name but which simply 'dancing', previously, had not. Delving deeply into Skinner Releasing Technique, The Feldenkrais Method, Authentic Movement, Focusing and Body-Mind Centering returned to me a curiosity, a passion and, most crucially, a *use* for moving. It drew together disparate awarenesses that I knew through words, image or memory. It gave me effective tools to tackle inner constrictions and to practise instinct and impulse. It made dancing more personal and political: because it was somehow newly 'me' doing it. Thinking, feeling and dancing from a place of somatic inquiry has enlivened my ability to feel present in, and to contribute originally and meaningfully to, the world around me.

The meaning inherent in physical states and in movement is felt, or sensed. I contend that this is a three-dimensional, material event, sedately ambiguous, and it circulates in ways that are yet to be established in scientific terms. We can transform ourselves and affect the spaces that we inhabit, through sensitive attention to material realities. The tools for this are active openness and receptivity, involving the relinquishing of rationality. Playfulness and gentleness replace habits of anticipation or intent. In our culture it is still acutely radical to waive anticipation, classification or critique in favour of really open perception, whether in the experience of art or of one another in the world. Authentic Movement's notion of witnessing as opposed to watching one's partner move is for example a freshly participatory, empathic and engaged way of experiencing someone moving. It allows and acknowledges inter-subjective difference and relationship.

SRT classes sometimes involve apparently obscure exercises that are not explained in logical terms, but which practise sensing in new ways. This involves a letting go of anticipation to allow for more active perception of the unknown. It encourages actual experiencing rather than a kind of trying or intending to experience something externally given. Fromm writes of growth into one's potential self as an organic unfolding, unique to each person, as opposed to a 'growth' by the super-imposition of given selves, which develops not individuals but automata. SRT and other somatic approaches consciously develop an organic, dynamic process of self-discovery.

The Making of a Dance: Resurrections and Reformations

With personal and political interest in active, embodied presence, and the potential for spontaneous action in the presence of others, I decided to readdress an earlier work. First made and presented in 2002 during my year-long British Council residency at the Academy of Performing Arts, Prague, *Life Forms* had since unfolded through various evolutions in the Czech Republic, Russia, and the UK, becoming *Games*

Without Frontiers (film), then *Life Forms Interactive*, then *people Moving people Moving people* before re-emerging in Coventry as *An Intricate Field*. *Life Forms* was performed by professional dancers, on the stage, although I almost immediately instinctively felt the problematic of the stage. A series of felt action-states that held enigmatic meaning for me – based largely around the experience of moving and being moved through space – were arranged in defined spatial plans. There was a live, improvised sound-score played on everyday objects. *Life Forms* was performed in theatres across the Czech Republic and in Russia, accompanied by my growing frustration that the 'feeling' of the work – that which had inspired it and which we worked so hard to define in the movement states – was not served by this format, which contained, flattened and dramatised it. The theatre stage highlighted a symbolic function of the material rather than becoming a set of vital kinaesthetic awarenesses of event, space and people. This was in some way inappropriate, too easy, indeed grotesquely artificial, to me. The first development beyond the theatre setting was a film version, where the camera moved around and amongst the dancers in an attempt to help the viewer reach into the spaces and activities of the piece. It was shot on a tennis court, overlaid with sounds of tennis and football spectators. The court's lines of 'in' and 'out' suggested to me rules and structures, which could be transgressed.

The next and bolder progression some months later took the live work out of the theatre and into an art gallery (Futura, Prague), where both body and space are more palpable and material, and where space is shared with the viewer. The piece became participatory, with the audience invited to join in the game. Added sound was removed. The states became fewer and simpler, focused on the heat of spatial proximity and the physical negotiation of the bulk of bodies. I engaged an actor, older people, and children in the pre-rehearsed cast. A new playfulness emerged as audiences enjoyed the dual role of doing and being done to, watching and being watched. At TAP gallery, UK for the exhibition PLEASE TOUCH this was re-developed through workshops with dancers and local artists, involving enjoyable philosophical exchange. Seven-year-old participant Lily Freeman observed brilliantly: "Over there looks weird, but when you get there it is lovely". Focusing on leading one another through the group by the hand to take up a new position elsewhere, it became with the public a very English game of eccentric social awkwardness, reminiscent of a skewed mediaeval court dance.

Still I wanted to take the material further, to get closer to the felt essences of some of the original movement states, and to the potential transformation and political awareness within it. My research had begun to gel around the notion of the somatically enlivened self as a dynamic agent, capable of attending to the moment and of creating societies that respect, support and interact with one another. Hence another evolution and outing at Coventry.

New Intricacies, New Fields

I returned to dancers as cast, to refine the movement and go deeper into the feeling states, while slackening restraints on time and space. We moved in and out between the art cocoon of the gallery space and the city, becoming interactive with the general as well as with the 'art going' public. I gave participants (both 'performers' and 'audience') more time, space and freedom to be present in it, more access to the inner awarenesses, and more quiet contemplation of the forms. As the process became increasingly unquantifiable, if not vague, I had to trust my own kinaesthetic and spatial fascinations and the rich, alive engagement of the dancers that I worked with.

Fig. 2: *Games Without Frontiers,* Art of Movement Festival Russia 2003. Dancers: Sandrine Harris, Lucie Klosová, Pierre Nadaud, Teresa Ondrová, Jana Sykorová. Photo: Alexandra Lerman

I almost lost my way with it when I realised that some of the original states were concerned with psycho-physical awarenesses that had already moved on for me and that my interest was turning away from states of activity and passivity to a more nebulous and complex sense of inter-subjective negotiation: less push and pull, more autonomous sensing. But the deliberate non-specificity and conscious approach towards fresh happening offered by much of the material within SRT was a useful background to this process and I strove to create a safe and welcoming space for embodied playing. I aimed to offer an invitation into a framed but undefined process and experience. In Coventry, performance gave way to ritual.

Propositions: to Dance Differently (2012) by Michael Kliën was a crucial discovery at a late stage in the new form of the work. Kliën's propositions, boldly written, preacher style, make an impassioned call for dance to be "re-sensed" as something natural, meaningful and unbounded. They resonate profoundly with my sense that art, that dance, is an act of becoming. They call for dance to be liberated from the constraints, not just of the theatre but of the rarefied art object and industry, and to demarcate a radical new framing of the process of becoming alive amidst the world and in society. They tally closely with many of the principles and practices found within Skinner Releasing Technique, whereby dance becomes a poetic experience of newness: a simultaneous discovery and expression of personal truth. Highlighting the sections of the propositions that especially resonated with *An Intricate Field*, I used them in rehearsal (as much as anything to prop up the wondering, wandering hearts of my trusting dancers) and displayed them in the performance space and on the windows to be read both by viewers inside the gallery and by those watching from the street. The propositions open with the encouraging statement that "everyone has a sense of how to dance" (2013) – close to Skinner's principle that "every living being can move with a natural, primal grace" (Skinner 2006: 1) – and calls for dance to be "the spirited suspension of normal life, untouched by rationality" (Kliën 2012).

Available for browsing in the performance space were a handful of books that had also informed me in the areas of somatics, spatial theory, social science, psychoanalysis and politics. Assuming that most people would do little more than glance at them, I felt that the titles and cover images could nevertheless elucidate and contextualise proceedings in useful ways. Just as a Skinner class ends with free drawing and writing to support the creative integration of deeply felt experiences, so words and images can go usefully along with experiential process.

In our exchanges since the project, Kliën has spoken of "dance being 'sheltered' by philosophy" (2013). I love this image. Not defining, containing or justifying, shelter suggests vulnerability, and the offering of essential protection, within which repose or change, or simply life, might occur. This resonates with Fromm's call for love and faith, and Joan Skinner's for gentleness, in the service of emancipation and empowerment. I had felt Kliën's *Propositions* doing that for this work, providing shelter for the nebulous thing – part demonstration, part experience, part experiment – that we were engaged in.

Fig 3: *An Intricate Field*, Lanchester Gallery Coventry 2013. Dancer: Ella Tighe. Photo: Lizzy Le Quesne

The event was centred in the large contemporary space of Coventry University's Lanchester Gallery, situated on a corner with street level windows – two vast glass walls – looking onto busy, city centre roads. "Dance spaces will have windows..." Kliën's propositions assented, "Human imagination without constant connection to its contextual surroundings is perilous" (Kliën 2013). And, in marvellous accordance with my earlier discomfort around theatrical presentation, they denounced the "artificial hell of the black box" (*ibid*). The glass created a soundproof and reflective interface, revealing the contrast, and allowing mutual awareness, between the smooth, silent, warm and meditative interior and the grit, the breezy air, activity and dissonance of the city surrounding it. In *The Poetics of Space* phenomenologist Gaston Bachelard describes the "dialectics of outside and inside" (1969: 211) as saddled with a crudely delineated oppositionality and challenges us to "follow the daring of poets" towards an imaginative perception of intimate encounter between worlds. The outside always visible from within the dance and vice versa, we sensed the jostling fields of 'inner' and 'outer' and renegotiated our presence with them as we met them. We ventured in and out, as did our audiences and fellow movers. We encountered one another directly or indirectly through the glass, in the reflections in it, pressed ourselves against the edges of worlds, the glass echoing our own invisible boundaries. As Bachelard puts it, "the dialectics of outside and inside multiply with countless diversified nuances" (1969: 216).

The 'performers' in *An Intricate Field* were myself and seven young women, current and former dance students of Coventry University. They were mature, somatically cognisant and skilled. We worked easily and deeply, in mutual trust, despite the apparent vagaries of the project. I had expected not to participate myself, eager to experience the event as a visitor might, but – as indeed some visitors were – I was instinctively drawn in, and moved for several hours with and amongst the cast and those audience members who joined us. It was a strange, warm, thick, soup that we created amongst us, with much communication of more or less conscious kinds. Little direct eye contact was needed, more a scanning of the space and peripheral vision, from a grounding and expanding physical self. Kliën writes, "If we encounter others in the moment of dance, relations are naked: a primal, communal site is substantiated in its embryonic state. A third body is born, made of all dancers in continuous exchange: the invisible assimilation of one body to another" (2013). Moving both in some kind of union, and in the strangeness of ourselves, we practised our own somatic perceptiveness within repeated looping through the various undertakings of the choreography. Members of the audience, and public, watched, rested, read or drew in the softened space we created, or joined us in movement and participated in our playful, indeterminate sniffing out of the reality of the space and moment.

The score outlined an instinctive journey, in repeated cyclical or spiralling structure; from a state of attachment with matter we flowed towards states of autonomy and fluidity, of interaction and inter-relationship across the sheltered space of the gallery, and beyond into the city before returning as a softened mass, melting together before we separated to begin again. From each of us alone, sensing through the midline via the crown of the head, the surfaces of the inside edges of the space (walls, windows, pillars), we progressed to moving across and into space, leading and being led by invitation of the touch of hands and a sense of mutual drift. The gesture of gently offering one's hand, of taking someone by the hand, or of being taken by the hand, is loaded with the gravity and openness of trust. It is a gesture of relating, of connecting. It crucially does not directly involve the core – which I increasingly sense as the spine, the central nervous system, linking brain to gut and sex. It is not an embrace; it is not a pressing of selves together, but a linking, across a gulf, leaving the border intact. The core of the physical self may not be engaged in touches of the hands, but there are causal, tactile links to that core, at a graceful distance, providing a filtering, receptive, protective portal to the physical self. Like looking through glass into a different space, touching hands acknowledges difference, while making connections. We were patient, gentle and deliberately unhurried in offering this gesture to one another and to visitors, allowing stages of recognition to establish. We waited, invited, followed or declined. We joined hands in lines of motion, stillness, in mutual rest, mutual support and mutual shifts. The transmutation from being attached to a solid material at the edge of a space to traversing it, through space, is massive on a kinaesthetic level, and joining forces seems a natural way to face the unknown. New territories may be entered more easily in the company of others. It enabled one partner to keep their eyes closed and to sense the shift internally, and created a way to 'travel' while in a state of reciprocal sustenance.

We dragged into this the objects that we found around us, and other people, adding sound and different shapes and weights and energies to the shifting environment. We dragged them with us round the space... a desk, a desk chair, hammer, podia, step-ladders. A desk on wheels made a weighty, swerving end to our line of human selves. A spindly wooden stool came with us, rasping, scraping on the ground, announcing its own inertia, friction and physical resistance. A knotted coil of lengthy electric cable got involved – I don't remember how, grabbed instinctively in passing, or hitched accidentally around an ankle – and was drawn along with the tide, its plastic plug-head swinging and clacking on the concrete floor. Bringing objects with us, we confronted space as active creators, shapers of our world, while we too were directed, shifted and affected by their weight and form. I became entangled, slowly, with the cable: gravity and friction acting on us both in different, surprising ways, as we both consented to our own indeterminate journeys. I held myself back from the acting out or moving on that I would once have felt compelled towards as a 'performer'. I remained instead enthralled by the convoluted mingling of my body with the wall and with the wire in the richness of the moment.

We went outside, bringing our meditative openness, our togetherness and acquiescence, our sensing, with us, and hung out in the open air and in the pitching, volatile movement of the city. On re-entering the silent interior of the gallery we climbed and piled over one another, merging into something soft and dense: a pile of people, giving and receiving support en masse.

And throughout there was a crucial caveat, a wholly new addition to the choreography. This was that at any time, any one of us could go 'off piste', as it were, from the main score, and pursue a solo investigation, spontaneously following a personal awareness or desire (hence my curious duet with electric cable). It could take any form and last as long as it required. Fromm says that: "Spontaneous activity is the one way in which man can overcome the terror of aloneness without sacrificing the integrity of his self; for in the spontaneous realization of the self man unites himself anew with the world – with man, nature, and himself." (1942: 224). When the 'solo' resolved itself we re-joined the main score.

Within the structure, timings were unfixed, emerged naturally, allowing different kinds of interactions to occur with visitors. We relied on depth of concentration and openness as a core structural configuration. We completed two and a half cycles on that afternoon. Stillness, and real waiting, are a crucial part of this work ... of dropping in and opening up to sensual indicators. Moments of perceptive being emerge with attention. They are *allowed*. This isn't stuff that you can 'make happen'. It requires having the time to let reality emerge via the sensing body-mind. It requires the viewer/witness/audience/participant to have the opportunity to investigate or organise his or her own presence in relation to it. And the stretching of time often found in somatically based work or processes challenges our expectations. (I have professionally been advised to avoid the word 'somatic' in making applications for dance funding as it is likely to be seen negatively.) Somatic live-ness is not perhaps considered compelling or accessible enough. But I would argue that it facilitates genuine perceptions and discoveries that are exhilarating, dramatic and progressive, and offers an art of dance that is of real, resonant use to people. Joan Skinner said: "All kinds of moving can be dance, even stillness" (2006: 1) and her technique practises how spirited action might slip unexpectedly, easefully, suddenly, in and out of stillness. Attentiveness, lack of anticipation, and allowing are the building blocks of presence, growth and life and can stand dynamically within dance and within choreographic form. These, consciously practised in SRT, directly facilitate the whole-self spontaneity that Fromm is convinced forms real agency or emancipation.

Fig. 4: *An Intricate Field*, Lanchester Gallery, Coventry 2013. Dancers: Stephanie Dagnall, Hannah Greyson-Gaito, Jade Griffin, Abbie Hannaby, Leanne Holder, Lizzy Le Quesne, Hannah McBride, Ella Tighe, with members of the public. Photo: Fresh@CU and C-DaRE

The Dance as Emancipatory, Political Act

The complexity of sensory attentiveness and the inter-relations between physical form, energy, persons and power, is invigoratingly clear to me… it keeps me dancing and thinking about dancing, through the world, through history. It empowers me and embeds me amongst my fellow beings. It stimulates me and it supports me. But a concern prevails: how can being so subtle, so open ended and nebulous, so, indeed, 'somatic'… how can this depth of information hope to be apparent to an audience? Is therefore dance, fundamentally, something that you need to do in order to experience? I don't know if it can function as a spectator sport in the way that dance has been doing: with people herded into darkened rows, tacitly to wonder at the rarefied litheness of others. The capacity for objectification to lie implicit in this model is violent. And it misses the potential of active, poetic, transformative engagement with one another and with the world, which dance has to offer. Fromm's "We must replace manipulation of men by active and intelligent co-operation" (1942: 235) sounds like a call in choreographic terms for participatory, engaged or improvisatory dances.

An Intricate Field posited a way in which choreography may be shifted from designing events to be watched, to making frames for nurturing embodied perception, and from objectifying bodies to arousing a live inter-subjectivity. We acted as exemplars of the structures of the piece, rather than as 'performers'. Our role was to enter, for our own purposes, into the processes of the work, to guide/invite participants into the process and to explore it with them. It is complicated to find ways of doing this that do not leave visitors feeling exposed, but rather as equal players. The depth of concentration and courageous unselfconsciousness of some supports others in being there. Able to 'just watch' from outside through the windows, on entering the space people were somehow participants, even if only in a state of quiet contemplation, or associated musing, using the materials provided. An usher was present to try to help people feel comfortable to participate, or not. The notorious "or not" offered after many an instruction in SRT classes I have found radically permissive, welcoming and inclusive, and, in its potent release of expectation, capable of facilitating a more insightful, more spontaneous level of active engagement than may at first present itself.

In *What is Social Choreography?* dance artist and writer Jeffrey Gormly writes, "Social choreography is performed by citizens rather than 'performers'" (2013). This doesn't mean that trained or professional dancers are not welcome, but that they are treated, and expected to behave, as real people in real societies, while using their particular skills. "There is a special role for dancer/performers to act as models, insiders or exemplars of how to inhabit the specific choreographic procedures at play" (*ibid*). As much as empowering the citizen as dancer, the notion of social choreography, more radically I would argue, empowers the dancer as citizen!

Choreographic experiments with open structures and participation can make advances towards addressing the essential problematic of how the political value of embodied freedom can be experienced. In *Social Choreography: Ideology as Performance in Dance and Everyday Movement*, Andrew Hewitt describes dance as "an enactment of a social order" (2005: 3). He puts forward a notion of dance and choreography as a model for society: a living together and alongside one another of emancipated selves, based on embodied awareness and creativity, and complains of dance's failure to, or failure to be understood to, function in this way: "What I will call social choreography has been dehistoricised and depoliticised by a prevailing modernist understanding of choreography as an essentially metaphysical phenomenon organised around questions of transcendental subjectivity rather than social and political inter-subjectivity" (Hewitt 2005: 3).

Seeming to address the concerns of Fromm and Žižek around the immateriality, impotence and isolation of contemporary life, Hewitt places dance as potentially pivotal in terms of making a real difference. Embodied, responsive and creative activity can activate more of our human agency and potential. Hewitt calls for "a more radical understanding of the aesthetic as something rooted in bodily experience" and, with this in place, predicts that "The aesthetic will function … as a space in which social possibilities are both rehearsed and performed." (2005: 4). Creative, poetic activity offers a space for real change that can resonate into lives and wider contexts. SRT once again addresses this precisely. It consciously nurtures the idiosyncrasy of poetic resonance, through its use of imagery as opposed to prescribed movements, and of cultivating kinaesthetic awareness not only in service of physical freedom but also creative process.

The act of moving… to another place (even minimally to a few feet away, or simply turning to face in a new direction), into a different relationship with space, a new encounter with surroundings, structures, light, temperature, with moving objects, or (heaven forbid!) with other life forms… is immense. Not just an idea of change, of newness: physical change is experienced bodily, through the senses. To experience a new perspective with reality, and to be sentient to such developments, represents significant adventure. It is an overtly courageous and political act to enter into and to change relationships. To negotiate one's own energy, will, and power in a way which has resonance in the world is to enact agency and contributes to the formation of the world in which we live. As Fromm says: "The only criterion for the realization of freedom is whether or not an individual actively participates in determining his life and that of society … in his daily activity, in his work, and in his relations to others" (1942: 235).

Affecting, making an impact upon, the state of affairs in the world around us is an inevitable part of living in a material world. We move, and the world moves. Each sentient body must collude with, resist or negotiate multiple influences. We are confronted with the scent of our own will, and that of others, written in skeletal and muscular configurations, as well as with the forces of materiality and energy, of physical laws, of social rules, animal drives, of personal and cultural histories, and all the unseen structures that shape our movings and our doings. This dense and knotty territory of possibility and impossibility is what I called the 'Intricate Field' of shared human space.

Somatic practice offers us new and creative ways of entering and negotiating that vibrant field: of playing in it, charting and affecting it. "The state of dance realigns the dancer with her surroundings. For a fleeting moment, attuned with the oceanic that holds this world together she enacts a personal and collective life upon her experience", states Kliën's tenth proposition (2013) The privileging of the felt, the sensory and the aesthetic provides vital, semi-conscious insight and access to realities. We can relate to spaces and to one another in ways other than our culture and customs have constructed for us. We do not have to 'understand' or rationalise exactly what we're doing. We can explore possibilities other than the reactive. We can allow ourselves to be led, to flow, to drift. We can cultivate new possibilities of trust and community, of equality, and play.

To enact an awareness of, and the opportunities for, participation in such a field was my intention with the event that was my presentation in the Dance and Somatic Practices Conference, 2013. I see it as sculpture, as performance, as dreamspace, as experiential practice, as meditation, as game, as political exercise, as ritual, as an experiment in personal and collective power… in vital confrontation with the present. This is all fundamentally concerned with considerations of how and why we dance and make art, and beyond that, how we register and negotiate the intricate field of embodied energy, both personal and collective, and how we might establish the capacity to act courageously, joyfully and creatively within it, of how we might arrive, as active subjects, amongst others, in and of our world.

Performers

An Intricate Field: Stephanie Dagnall, Hannah Greyson-Gaito, Jade Griffin, Abbie Hannaby, Leanne Holder, Lizzy Le Quesne, Hannah McBride, Ella Tighe, with spontaneous participation from Rees Archibald, Andrea Barzey, Katye Coe, Hilary Kneale, Rahel Vonmoos, Sarah Whatley and members of the public.

Life Forms: Sandrine Harris, Lucie Klosová, Klara Lidová, Andrea Miltnerová, Pierre Nadaud, Teresa Ondrová, Mirka Eliašová, Veronika Šimková, Jana Sykorová. Music: Pavel Macák. Light: Daniel Tesář. (Performed at Divadlo NoD, Prague 2002; Divadlo Ponec, Prague 2002; Divadlo Barka, Brno 2002; Art of Movement and Dance on the Volga, Russia 2002.)

Games Without Frontiers: Sandrine Harris, Lucie Klosová, Pierre Nadaud, Teresa Ondrová, Jana Sykorová. Camera: Alexandra Lerman. Edit: Dalibor Janda. (Screened at South London Shorts 2010.)

Life Forms Interactive: Lizzy Le Quesne, Philipp Schenker, Patricia Woltmann, Gabriela Zaičková. (Performed at Futura Gallery, Prague 2003)

people Moving people Moving people: Lily Freeman, Anna Gunnason, Ann Harvey, Agnese Lanza, Colin McClean, Brian Parker, Susana Recchia. Curator: Michaela Freeman. (Performed within the group exhibition PLEASE TOUCH at TAP Gallery, Southend 2010.)

References

Bachelard, G. (1969) *The Poetics of Space*, Beacon Press

Canetti, E. (1962) *Crowds and Power*, Phoenix Press

Fraleigh, S. (1987) *Dance and the Lived Body, A Descriptive Aesthetics*, University of Pittsburg Press

Fromm, E. (1942) *The Fear of Freedom*, Routledge & Kegan Paul

Gormly, J. (2013) *What is Social Choreography?* http://bit.ly/tpMove76

Heller-Roazen, D. (2007) *The Inner Touch, Archaeology of Sensation*, Zone Books

Hewitt, A. (2005) *Social Choreography: Ideology as Performance in Dance and Everyday Movement*: Duke University Press

Kliën, M. (2013a) *Propositions: To Dance Differently* http://bit.ly/tpMove77

_______ (2013b) Conversations and unpublished diagrams, RICE on Hydra, Greece

Lepecki, A. (2004) *Of The Presence of the Body*, Wesleyan University Press

Perec, G. (1997) *Species of Spaces and Other Pieces*, Penguin

Rose, J. (2003) *On Not Being Able to Sleep*, Chatto & Windus

Surowiecki, J. (2004) *The Wisdom of Crowds*, Little, Brown

Thompson, G. (2005) *Phenomenology of Inter-Subjectivity*, J. Aronson

Skinner, J. (2006a) *Introductory Pedagogy*, Seattle: unpublished

_______ (2006b) *The Principles of Skinner Releasing*, Seattle: unpublished

Skinner, J. and Davidson, R. (2011) *Introductory Pedagogy*, Seattle, unpublished

Žižek, S. (2008) *Violence*, Profile Books

Embodied Adventures in and out of the Irish Countryside

Wild Geese
You do not have to be good.
You do not have to walk on your knees
for a hundred miles through the desert repenting.
You only have to let the soft animal of your body
love what it loves.
(Mary Oliver)

Prelude

This chapter weaves the embodied voices of three of the four women who make up the Somaticats – four women who meet regularly in the southern Irish city of Cork to muse about our embodiment with no agenda, much playfulness and some Nina Simone[1]. Beginning in the autumn of 2012 we spent the better part of a year in an open-ended research framework focused on the somatic perceptions underpinning performance practices. For reasons we've now forgotten we started researching the pelvis. We traced its various structures, paying attention to its movements, intensities,

1 See the Somaticats blog at: http://bit.ly/tpMove80

histories, songs and voices. We somaticats – Bernadette Cronin, Regina Crowley, Jools Gilson and Roisin O'Gorman – weave our shared somatic practice with the charged Irish context in which we are embodied, with the space and place of our own and historical femininities. We are always haunted by the gorgeous interplay of our listening, resistant bodies and our verbal, voicing, articulate selves. Perhaps not surprisingly, the tapestry we weave here is haunted by a mother-thread that persistently re-emerges in one context and/or embodiment or another. This essay then is a glimpse of a year-long pelvic meditation which marked a commitment to get off our knees and connect with the soft animal body and its loves. Here we offer a fragmented conversational snapshot of the threads of our motivations, explorations and tangents as they interweave with our lives and loves as well as a particular case study where the subtleties of somatic practices merge and emerge through performance. We splice our voices at the paper's start, to meet musically the sense in which we braid our embodiments in the studio.

First Movement

Bernadette: Out of the Somatics and Performance Workshop, University College Cork, organised by Róisín O'Gorman in August 2012, Somaticats is born. We resolve to continue to meet throughout the year ahead to foster that sense of a nurturing connection that emerged from the three-day workshop.

Jools: I make seedy bars, fruit bettys, figgy coconut balls and fruit cake for a gaggle of dancers from all over Ireland and the UK who come to Cork when the blackberries should have been in season in 2012. We come to listen to the insides of ourselves altogether. I melt peanut butter with honey and vanilla essence, and stir this into a pile of seeds, so that we might grin together over elevenses. And then, we didn't want it to stop.

***

Róisín: In August 2012 we held a Somatics and Performance workshop at University College Cork attended by 14 practitioners from across somatic fields in the aim of sharing practice, making connections, offering sessions of each other's work and seeing what would happen. After three revitalising days we thought – 'Let's keep a thread going here and see what happens.' And so we become Somaticats. The name is intended to be playful and open, yet it marks a space, a cellular alliance across institutional and disciplinary divides. These 'cats' prowl for the possibilities for what somatics can perform, what an embodied approach can 'do' in the particular socio-cultural setting, which is Ireland in 2012. At this time of global contraction, they are forging potential openings in a conservative culture, which historically severely limited the available or acceptable range of bodily expressivity. They are on the hunt for a language and vocabulary that moves, for the rooted connectivity that gives succulence to voice, power to ideas and surprises us with its creative force.

Jools: Elderflowers: Watching my small daughter playing camogie (Irish hockey for girls) at the local field, my eyes wander to the small trees and shrubbery that border the Gaelic Athletics pitch in Ballymacoda, in East Cork, an area people even a few miles west of here call 'real country'. I've spied elderflowers, lots of them. It's late June, and every time I look at elders I get hungry for the cordial I'm longing to tempt from their blooms. And so I nip back to the car for a bag, and sidle towards the unruly hedgerow, between bouts of cheery encouragement to my daughter on the pitch. I begin to break off creamy umbels of elderflowers. Their fragrance crushes on my fingers, as I drop them one by one into the bag. I know half the village are giving me side glances, wondering what I'm doing raiding the greenery whilst there's a match on, but I'm greedy for what I know these tiny pastures of blossoms will give me. I smile, acknowledge the nods of greeting, and carry on filling my bag. My daughter, adopted from Guatemala eight years ago, is a hearty warrior on the camogie field. There she is below me in her helmet and shin guards, tackling tenaciously with her wide wooden hurley (a sort of Irish hockey stick), battling for pleasure between the pale skins and freckled faces of Father O'Neill's Under-9s. I smile at her, and the musky sweet smell of elderflowers engulfs me.

Bernadette: Four teachers, practitioners, researchers, mothers, wives, partners, daughters… women – each with a long history of doing, preparing, planning, doing – structuring, nurturing, doing, come together and consider non-doing as a possibility for discovery. For a time it is almost as though we have to keep giving ourselves permission not to do, to resist asking the question 'what are we doing?' to afford ourselves the 'guilty pleasure' of booking a studio space in the middle of a hectic working week to engage in nothing particularly planned, and work from intuition.

Róisín: We then begin to gather together, through the winter, through rains and accidents, high temperatures, shifts and separations, growth, forgetting, aging, loss, going on even when we can't go on.

Tea and cake: crucial.

Laughter: as necessary as deodorant.

We share touch and listening, languages of sounds, sighing – breathing – opening, singing together we learn, re-member – if we keep on dancing we'll never ever ever grow old.

Jools: As soon as we're home, we go into production. Water is boiled in great pots by the gallon load, and once the boil is rolling, they are lifted carefully onto the floor (for safety), where we slowly stir in a shocking amount of sugar. We watch melting white crystals turn water into syrup. Bowls of picked-over elderflower heads, thirty in each, with the zest and sliced up flesh of two lemons stand on the table. We move them to the floor, and carefully drench their contents with hot syrup. Then we cover them with clean cotton cloths and leave them to steep overnight in the laundry room. They smell divine, and whilst our hands are sticky and the children running wild, we are glad. In our bodies, we're grinning. The next day after work, we retrieve the steeping buckets and bowls, and strain them through muslin, before bottling them. They stand in elegant groups on the kitchen table, and we taste some – best with cold sparkling water – and it is heavenly, like drinking summer.

Bernadette: And in spite of myriad obstacles, busy work schedules, impromptu meetings, car accidents on icy roads, sick children and hospitalised parents, distressed au pairs, in short, the vicissitudes of life multiplied by four, we manage somehow to keep it going.

***

Jools: When the somaticats come to my house for our summer adventure in July, I greet them with cordial. I give them cordiality, gathered from the ditches of Ireland, spun with sugar and lemons, diluted with bubbly water. They grin, as I have grinned over these elderflowers. And we set about our astonishing feat – to give ourselves time and space to wonder and wander about embodiment. We giggle down the boreen (little Irish lane) in the sunshine. I've packed hard-boiled eggs and salad. We picnic and cat nap and chat ourselves into the Irish sea. We curve and squeal. I am writing this in September beside the same boreen, and hundreds of starlings are up to no good in the trees beside me.

Róisín: We go to the seaside...

Low tide low theory: What happens as the tide goes out and the gurgling dredge gives up its dead but fecund secrets? What can we sniff out, reach for in the sucking ooze – and why would we want to?

Bernadette: What is 'it'? Space to play, to explore, to share elements of the complex of somatic or psychophysical practices that through years of engagement have become part of who we are and how we make work – Body-Mind Centering, tai chi, Linklater voice work, yoga, Alexander technique, reiki, singing, chanting to sound the chakras ... space to just be.

Róisín: Other forms of being emerge at low tide. Those in the half wet and half land world. I think I've always liked those edge zones, and much has been written and discussed on the liminal nature of performance as a site. The tidal zone is a betwixt and between zone too, but unlike the liminal threshold which might promise to take us to another level, the only thing the tide promises is to return and ebb again, a circular undulating that results in an ultimate kind of flatness maybe, an oozing out? What of it? We go for a swim... and then the tide also comes in...

Jools: Elderflowers matter because they connect my body to this place. The alchemy of making them into cordial enchants me. They matter because they are a cypher for embodiment. Think of the word 'umbel', a term which means the gathering of tiny flowers to make a greater flower. I long for the taste of this word in my mouth only a little less than I long for cordial on summer days. And this is a story about four women who had been working with performance and somatics for more summers than they can remember. Four women who found each other because one of them made it happen. Another one made cake. A third brought her heart, and the fourth her voice. And after that we brought whatever we had.

Bernadette: Four women, breathing, sensing, moving together in time and space, dancing to Nina Simone singing 'Feeling Good' on a dark, damp winter's morning, exploring each other's sacrums on a frosty spring morning, tracing the sacroiliac joint, where the sacrum joins with the large bone of the pelvis known as the ileum, toying with ideas over tea and scones that could lead to a performance project, whilst also knowing that that would not in fact be possible in the short-term, sitting together in a country kitchen consuming sumptuous homemade cake and elderflower cordial, swimming in the sea together on a gloriously sunny day in July, scurrying to get our shoes and bags from the rocks as the tide comes in, and laughing, sharing an old rug with an interesting history on a pebbly beach to picnic in the sun, and laughing, and bunching up together in a city garden with a spectacular view to take a group-photo, and laughing, and laughing, and occasionally also crying.

Jools: We joined curiosities. We tangled and entwined. We were absent through illness, elderly parents, black ice, sick children and very important meetings. We were present though. O, we were present. We stole mornings from weeks that exhausted us. We danced to Nina Simone, shared packed lunches, voyaged about our sacrum, became continents and FELT GLAD. Sometimes there are two or three of us, but we work anyway, with what we have, from where we're at. We work deeply. We move, and are moved. There is movement, and it astounds us.

Róisín: We return to the sea – a maybe mother, but I think more of the multitude it offers, the noise, the relentless horizon. This sounding, breathing – what – creature, creaturely energy – not exactly formless yet not exactly formed – offers another beginning, a quiet space, solitude, dropping in and away ...

Second Movement

Bernadette: One might ask, so what? And the answer, I find, is that, through duration in time and a sharing in precious snatched hours of these bodymind-centred activities, through the mindful[2] decision to persist in spite of so many obstacles and 'reasons' not to persist, a heart connection has been established: "heart Hebrew leba, centre of courage, intelligence, feeling – the breast, the mind, pith, marrow, centre, or best part of anything" (Tuffnell and Crickmay: 254). This, together with an awareness arising out of the somatic or psychophysical practices that free us from a dualistic thinking that separates the body from the mind, and learning to give ourselves permission to trust our intuition, makes, in my experience, for a rich seed-bed for creative collaboration.

Róisín: We work slowly, finding the gentle body. I write after an early session:

> *Today we mapped and traced and danced the pelvic joints and wondered at the poetry in motion and the mystery of twists suspending us in and with gravity. Tonight*

2 On page 4, Jon Kabat-Zinn (1994) teaches us about mindfulness meditation for everyday life, how it "wakes us up to the fact that our lives unfold only in moments" and that "if we are not fully present for many of those moments, we may not only miss what is most valuable in our lives but also fail to realize the richness and the depth of our possibilities for growth and transformation".

I sit and find two poems from Mary Oliver that remind me about what it means to take time, to say no to some things which might also be as necessary as finding how the ilium can really roll around the head of the femur, how the acetabulum (which means small cup) can hold and move at the same time, like the call out on the moving line of geese throbbing through the winter, somehow finding their way again and again.[3]

Jools: Writing, like the playful labour of somaticatting, happens best if it's wrought from the lived memory and presence of flesh. Writers who are able to capture our embodied struggles and pleasures are the ones who move us most. And so being moved (such an understated description of powerful emotional moment) can come from writing, but only insomuch as it captures the sweat and ache of living, moving bodies. (I'm talking about writing in books here – novels or poetry). Being moved is always connected to moving, even and perhaps often, in stillness. Somaticatical writing is writing that brings us to our bodies – provocations found in print – that leads us astray or keeps us close, but always moves us. But it is also writing that comes from our body wondering, captured by loosely held and swiftly moving pencils.

Bernadette: Our collective intuition takes us for some reason quite often to

3 The open secret of the approximately 12 women who each day travel outside of Ireland for abortion also somehow finds its way again and again. There is no space here to elaborate on the '12 A Day Project' that I directed in February 2013 which created a performance from testimonial accounts of women's journeys from Ireland to the UK for abortion. However, I must acknowledge it as another rhizome of the pelvic projects of 2013, where the somatic explorations grounded me through the politically and emotionally fraught terrain of this work. This project aimed to give voice to the direct experience of the abortion journey faced by women, their partners and families in Ireland and to open a space to witness the complexity of their choices rather than to rehearse the painful shaming and reductionist politics of the abortion debate. The impetus for the theatre project happened alongside a video based project which has since been launched on Youtube, see: http://bit.ly/tpMove81 and http://bit.ly/tpMove82.

the sacrum as our site of inquiry. *Os sacrum* from the Latin means holy or sacred bone, so-called, anecdotally, because it was the part of an animal offered in sacrifice, being the seat of the organs of procreation, or because the soul resides there. Other translations of *sacrum* from the Latin include: holy thing, sacred vessel, shrine, keystone, offering, victim, rite (Collins Latin Dictionary & Grammar). And in the plural, *sacra* can mean mysteries, secrets, or poems (sacred to the muse). The holy or sacred connotation persists in other modern languages, for example *osso sacro* in Italian or *heiligbeen* in Dutch. In the chakra system – the seven main energy centres that control the flow of energy to a living being – the first, root or base chakra is located at the sacrum, and here in this lowest energy centre, the kundalini or cosmic energy lies sleeping coiled like a serpent. No wonder the holy, sacred, secret, mysterious connections persist...

Róisín: Saucing singing sacra... pelvic pluralities. Weeks later, we find, we are still lingering in the pelvis; the lure of the sacrum and her cohort of singing bones is too strong. We weave together the vocal and physical playfulness of our various experiences.

***

Jools: Here there are sacrums that grow great roots, dark pools within hips, cellular support the size of yoga balls. Print to corpuscle to pencil, and back again. We write out of embodied experience, as many do. But we do it better if I have drugged the cats with cordial first. I'm telling stories. Believe me.

Bernadette: Given that we allow ourselves to work intuitively, it seems appropriate that we are drawn to the sacrum again and again. A junction between upper and lower body, it is at the top of the body when we drop down through the spine and let the head off the hook of that particular responsibility. Jerzy Grotowski used the word *croix* in referring in French to the sacrum, not the official term 'sacrum'. In German the sacrum is *Kreuzbein*, cross-bone: a sacred crossroads between the upper and the lower body.

Róisín: OED online:

> SACRUM Pronunciation: /ˈseɪkrəm/
>
> Forms: Pl. sacrums, sacra.
>
> Etymology: Subst. use of neuter singular of Latin *sacer* sacred.
>
> A composite, symmetrical, triangular bone which articulates laterally with the ilia, forming the dorsal wall of the pelvis and resulting from the ankylosis of two or more vertebræ between the lumbar and coccygeal regions of the spinal column.

We find sacral fans and eagle flight.[4]

4 Following Eric Franklin's Dynamic Alignment Through Imagery (1996)

Bernadette: A few days after a Somaticats session where we explored the sacrum I write the following in a poetry workshop led by poet Matthew Sweeney:

Sacrum-Making

After working with the
Sacrum for an Hour and
a half we Scatter to find
objects to Assemble
something:

A blue umbrella,
A spineless collected works of
Shakespeare, standing upright,
fanned out like a daisy, a rear
bicycle light flashing,
a front bicycle light not flashing,
a broken vase,
a brown velvet cap,
a sequined top,
a biscuit pierced

by two lollipops,
a glass shard,
a shiny black boot, a
silver cycle helmet
its straps spread-eagled on the floor,
some crumbs;

After panning and zooming
To place our objects,
we lie belly down and
gaze
at what the sacrum
moved us
to make.

Róisín: We add Linklater pelvic dances, saucy stirring and butterfly patterns. From the floor we peel and tip and let our voices drop out from our floors through the mouth. We add some Roy Hart puppy panting and then finally, forming a head-belly laughing chain: release, release, release, together, release. Write – we must write ourselves ...

With even more violence than fiction, theatre, which is built according to the dictates of male fantasy, repeats and intensifies the horror of the murder scene which is at the origin of all cultural productions. It is always necessary for a woman to die in order for the play to begin. Only when she has disappeared can the curtain go up; she is relegated to repression, to the grave, the asylum, oblivion and silence. When she does make an appearance, she is doomed, ostracised or in a waiting-room. She is loved only when absent or abused, a phantom or a fascinating abyss. Outside and also beside herself (Cixous, 1984: 546).

Bernadette: Guy Claxton discusses the link between intuition and creativity: "... the truth is that our ideas, and often our best, most ingenious ideas, do not arrive as the result of faultless chains of reasoning. The 'occur to us'. They 'pop into our heads'. They come out of the blue. When we are relaxed we operate very largely by intuition" (Claxton 1999: 49).

Jools: And there is another thing. It isn't writing, but it is to do with the writing into somaticats and writing out of somaticats, and that is the voice that leads an exercise, if there is one. And what that voice has to do with how we meet the invitation to explore internal worlds. Regina teaches Kristin Linklater's voice practice, and she does so by conjuring caverns and depths, pools and waterfalls within our pelvis. (If we searched this internal woodland, I'm sure we'd find elderflowers). Just as the body is moved by poetry outside itself, so we are led by a poetic language rehearsed through training, but improvised in the moment to an internal architecture, and it is this poetic language that makes possible all manner of openings and releases, as we re-imagine what embodiment could be. Our bodies become enchanted spaces of possibility, where we play with possibility through the invitation of voiced suggestion. And we like it. Us somaticats. We do.

Róisín: Sometimes we talk about Ireland. The Celtic Tiger has departed. We talk of laundries where women were sent and their babies taken away, of endemic abuse, of convents and hope and emigration, of the way the push of these bodies shapes the silences in the relentless chatter and detail of cups of tea and children's clothes and birthdays and funerals and all of that while the abortion debate in Ireland and the lack of action by successive governments and their citizenry in the twenty years since the so-called X Case[5] ramps up again.

Jools: I'm the blow-in of 17 years, out in the countryside stirring blackberries. This Ireland buffets me between enchantment and its underbelly.

Róisín: I could tell you now of the anti-abortion posters on the street where I live, that deface and defame the city I now call home, but I don't want to repeat any more of their nonsense and propaganda. I just want the simple sovereignty of dignity, of choice and voice, the right to decide what happens to my body. We voice these ideas as we share time and tea. We move and sound to shed the impact, the shapes that silenced bodies, ours and our ancestors', there are patterns that need expression, lineages that need some dusting off and re-animating, but we work quietly, gently...

Bernadette: I find this Somaticats club, or coven, or pack, has become a sort of rhizome, a subterranean stem that builds up and stores important nutrients. I like rhizomes, like ginger and turmeric; they are warming and healing, have numerous medicinal properties. A yoga teacher told me recently that his Indian grandmother used to make a milky drink with turmeric and honey every day to keep the doctor away – in fact, on principle she never went to a doctor, but used turmeric in all different kinds of blends and pastes to heal her body on the outside and the inside. A rhizome sends out new shoots from its nodes, and if it is separated into different pieces, each piece can individually give rise to new plants. We somaticats decided that it would not be possible to plan a Somaticats performance project in the short term. A project I was involved in last April, as part of another collective, involved a series of site-specific performances of Beckett's *Footfalls* and I would like to reflect here on this process, contextualising within the work we had been doing in Somaticats, and the theme of attending to movement in the context of the psychophysical practices I have been engaging with over many years. I would like also to consider it in the light of a piece of the rhizome that broke away giving rise to a new plant.

5 The 'X Case' refers to a pivotal moment in Irish abortion law in 1992 when the Supreme Court ruled that the threat to a woman's life (not health) meant she could terminate her pregnancy. The case appealed a High court injunction granted to the Attorney General to prevent a 14-year-old rape victim from travelling to the UK to have an abortion.

Although the X Case ruling technically made abortion legal in Ireland when the mother's life was at risk, including the risk of suicide, it was July 2013 before the Irish government finally passed legislation (called the 'Protection of Life during Pregnancy Act') that legalises abortion under very limited circumstances.

This bill was passed in part as a result of the international attention following the death of Savita Halappanavar (who was refused a termination that might have saved her life) and the result of the European Court of Human Rights case – ABC v Ireland – which ruled that Ireland had breached Human Rights Conventions in its sustained ambiguity around the right to an abortion in Ireland. See http://bit.ly/tpMove83.

Third Movement

Bernadette's case study

Attending to the Footfalls

M: Mother. [Pause, no louder.] Mother

V: Yes, May.

M: Were you asleep?

V: Deep asleep. [Pause.] I heard you in my deep sleep. [Pause.] There is no sleep so deep I would not hear you there.
(From *Footfalls*, by Samuel Beckett)

My 85-year-old mother has recently been ill, a heart problem. Somehow life has ordained that of her six offspring I am the one who spends most time with her in this late phase of her life – a precious gift, at times a strain. Sometimes my shoulders are full of tension, my diaphragm is constricted, and my sacrum aches. As my feet hurry to and from hospitals I find myself leaning forward, efforting, hollowing my upper body – an old defence mechanism – trapping my worries in that hollow of my heart centre and my solar plexus, being absent from many moments. In Philosophy of Hatha Yoga, Swami Veda Bharati writes: "when a person actually places his body in a certain position, what he is doing is making the mind experience that position ... the mind experiences that shape in thought" (Bharati 1985: 13). Bharati is referring to hatha yoga positions and training the mind through the body in a beneficial way, but equally we can apply this to training the mind through the body in positions that are not beneficial, habitual positions that keep us trapped in thought/behavioural patterns. Or, as Abbot John Daido Loori expresses it in his DVD *The Still Point* (2007), "how you posture your body creates a state of consciousness".

And somewhere between choice and ordinance, in the midst of this phase of worry and deep connection with my mother, I find myself performing *Footfalls* – in an attic room of the deserted upper floors of a pub called Mr Bradley's on Barrack Street in Cork city.

When clearing the room, we find a walking stick and a wooden cross with the name of the elderly woman engraved on it who had lived in the house until her death. Presumably, the cross had stood on her grave until the headstone was erected. She was also a mother. Across the hallway in the other attic room of this building the actress playing 'V', whom I address as 'Mother', sits at her microphone surrounded by a dusty jumble of the residue of family life, toys, blankets, crockery, posters of football teams, rugs, hairbrushes... Mairin is also a mother. I too am a mother. I pushed through my mother's sacroiliac complex to come into the world and my daughters pushed through mine. The birth of my first daughter takes two days: my sacroiliac joints cannot seem to give way; perhaps I am holding something in my holy bone that I do not know how to release. I wonder does my baby girl sense that her mother's sacroiliac complex resists shifting to let her out. Does she feel trapped? I know she's a girl because the midwife tells me my baby's so strong she must be a girl. I accept inducement and an epidural to help me give birth. Sometimes now, many years later, my sacrum still aches, especially when I don't attend to my learned habit of leaning forward, when I don't remember to re-pattern, allow my spine to straighten and become erect, the muscles in my shoulders relax, my shoulder blades drop, my sternum rest gently in the vertical, rather than tilt down and inwards compressing my diaphragm, when I don't let my skeleton do the walking, from my centre. When I don't remember... to let go.

Samuel Beckett was recorded as having said there was only one theme in his life: "To and fro in shadow, from outer shadow to inner shadow. To and fro between unattainable self and unattainable non-self" (Knowlson 1997: 631). Beckett explores his theme in the inexorable pacing to and fro in shadow of May/Amy in *Footfalls*. May obsessively paces to and fro on her strip of floor revolving some indeterminate "it all" in her "poor mind", "it all ... it all". We learn from Freud that we address repetition to what we cannot comprehend – the repetition compulsion. For Beckett the most important element of the piece is the movement, the walk: "if it is full of repetitions, then it is because of these life-long stretches of walking. The walk is the centre of the play, everything else is secondary" (Ibid: 628). He apparently spent much time in rehearsal with Billie Whitelaw for the first production getting May's posture "exactly right": "a stooping, twisted figure, her hands clutching her upper arms across her body. As the lights fade from section to section, so the figure stoops lower and lower" (Ibid: 628). For Beckett the trauma externalised in May's stooping, twisted figure went back to his experience of being *in utero*, as Martin Esslin tells us:

> Sam told me that he remembers being in his mother's womb at a dinner party, where, under the table, he could remember the voices talking. And when I asked him once, 'What motivates you to write?' he said. 'The only obligation I feel is towards that enclosed poor embryo ... That is the most terrible situation you can imagine, because you know you're in distress but you don't know that there is anything outside this distress or any possibility of getting out of that distress'. (Knowlson 2007: 151)

Esslin observes that we find confirmed over and over again in Beckett's work what he calls Beckett's "mystical obligation towards that poor, suffering, enclosed being that doesn't know there is a way out" (ibid.). He says that Beckett "had this terrific imagination or dream or reality of this memory of being enclosed. And that self is self-enclosed. You can't really get to the others."

May's inexorable pacing is not just a reflection of the psychologically disturbed young women Beckett had encountered in his life, such as Lucia Joyce, or of himself and his "complex and highly emotional relationship" with his mother, whom he

had nursed before she died and who was called May, but rather it assumes mythic status "harking back to Ixion on his wheel, Tantalus tortured by hunger and thirst, or Sisyphus pushing his stone forever uphill" (Knowlson 1997: 616). As Julie Salverson writes, "personal narratives of crisis are never merely personal" (Salverson 1996: 182).

Pacing

In the stage directions to Footfalls May (M) is seen pacing towards the left of the performing area as the lights fade up on the strip. The pattern for the figure's pacing is as follows:

> **Pacing:** starting with right foot (r), from right (R) to left (L), with left foot (l) from L to R.
>
> **Turn:** rightabout at L, leftabout at R. Steps: clearly audible rhythmic tread.

For my first production of Footfalls I was directed by Phillip Zarrilli as part of "The Beckett Project in Ireland" at the Granary Theatre, Cork, in 2004. I had trained in Zarrilli's pre-performative actor training method, which encompasses a combination of the Indian martial art form kalarippayattu, taiqiquan and yoga. Of his training method Zarrilli writes the following:

> The practice of yoga, kalarippayattu, and taiqiquan is one means by which the primary empirical, material elements of the psychophysical actor's art are discovered and then attuned. The psychophysical exercises begin with the body and move both inward toward subtle realms of experience and feeling, and outward to meet the environment. They are a form of empirical as well as (meta)physical (re)search. This (re)search is not undertaken by the side of our brain which engages propositional, analytical thought, but by the bodymind together as they become one in and through daily practice. (Zarrilli 2009: 63)

The kind of directions I was given by Zarrilli in rehearsing *Footfalls* had nothing to do with psychological motivation or character work. According to Zarrilli, a different kind of dramaturgical approach is required for the theatre of Samuel Beckett: as in much of his work, in this piece Beckett is exploring a particular state of being or condition as opposed to delivering meaning. The question, therefore, for the actor is how to embody May/Amy's state of abjection and afford the audience an experience of it. In rehearsal Zarrilli focused on aspects such as the connecting of one moment to the next psychophysically rather than motivationally. For instance, just as May endlessly revolves an indeterminate "it all" in her "poor mind", after taking nine steps in each direction her feet "revolve" at each end of her strip as her stooping twisted figure paces to and fro. I was instructed to maintain a residual awareness of my last point of focus as I shifted to the next – so I worked on extending my back awareness as a line of energy in one direction as my front awareness extended as another in the opposite direction.

He encouraged me to work on the relationship of my feet to the floor using the practice of lion steps from the kalarippayattu martial art form to cultivate this relationship. When practising lion steps Zarrilli instructs the performer, apart from sensing into the feet and their relationship with the floor, to also maintain a sense of energy in the palms of the hands, out through the top of the head, and a sense of awareness out through the back of the head and the body when going forward and through the front of the body when going backwards. He uses the translation of the malayalam phrase "making the body all eyes" as an image to work with to cultivate an activation of energy awareness in the actor's entire bodymind. This gives the actor rehearsing May/Amy a great deal to work with for the very slow walk, for the sculptural quality of the shaping of the hands clutching her twisted upper body and maintaining an aliveness in the hands, for the purposes of establishing a relationship with the space and the audience in the space.

As described above, the practice of kalarippayattu, like yoga and taiqichuan, cultivates our awareness of energy circulating in the body and of how to direct that energy in performance, in order to create and inhabit in the moment the particular environment and experience that is being described in the text. Since I first performed *Footfalls* in 2004, in the intervening period I have also been practising zazen – a seated meditation practice – along with the kinhin walk as part of this meditation practice, and have found that this work further builds on the pre-performative psychophysical training and rehearsal work I experienced with Zarrilli. Coordinating breath with movement, this very slow kinhin walking meditation teaches us to attend to each step in the moment, as Ven. Shikai Zuiko o-sensei writes:

> When we step forward, present in this moment, feeling the left foot lift from the floor, feeling this change in the temperature as the skin of the foot is raised higher from the floor, as we notice the knee joint bending and the space around the bones, as we feel the breath rising and falling, as the foot steps forward and the air rushes between the toes, as we feel the contact of the heel on the floor about half to three quarters of the way down the length of the other foot, as we feel the heat of the skin of the left foot reaching out to the skin of the right foot, we are feeling into this moment... "It is not mindfulness of walking, stepping, or even of a step. It is mindfulness of this step, and this step, and this step" (Zazen-ji, 7 June 1996).

What taiqi allows the individual to achieve, as discussed by Zarrilli, is also in part applicable to the zen (walking) meditation practice:

> Yuasa Yasuo explains that this state of "no-mind" (Japanese mushin) is "a state of self-forgetfulness, in which consciousness of oneself as the subject of bodily movement disappears and becomes the movement itself". (Yasuo cited in Zarrilli 2009: 74)

The practice of kinhin assists me the actor in transcending duality and thus me the walker in becoming the walk.

Finally, in kinhin the posture is similar to the seated zazen posture in that the spine is erect, shoulders relaxed and down, chin slightly tucked under to maximise the lengthening of the spine as the head pulls away from the sacrum, which, as we Somaticats read in A Widening Field is ideal as to "find the essential length of the spine, sacrum and head must be able to move away from each other" (Tuffnell and Crickmay 2004: 218). In this position the bodymind is balanced, in alignment in relation to the world and other living beings, and therefore a minimum of muscular tension is required to sustain this posture. May/Amy in Footfalls, on the other hand – "a stooping, twisted figure, her hands clutching her upper arms across her body" – is out of balance in herself and with the world around her, literally holding herself and her trauma, addressing repetition to what she cannot comprehend, as V asks her, "will you never have done ... revolving it all?" (Beckett 1984: 240). As I am working psychophysically and not motivationally I can use the awareness I have around my sacrum, the interconnectedness to the upper spine and shoulders, which the Somaticats work gave me space and a supportive environment to explore, to choose a physicalisation to embody May's abject state – to create a state of consciousness that will communicate to the audience while also working not with muscular tension but rather with an awareness of the circulation of energy in my body and an attentiveness to the breath.

Coda

Somaticats on the prowl for a performance project...

Along the way we Somaticats got interested in old well saints and traditions, which took us westwards one misty autumn day to St. Gobnait's holy well in Ballyvourney. As the story goes, Gobnait fled a family feud to one of the Aran Islands only to be told by an angel who appeared to her there that she should go to a place where she would find nine white deer grazing. Here she built her monastery, kept bees and healed the local people with her honey. Celtic lore has it that the soul leaves the body as a bee or a butterfly. The cats are on to something and they want to know what kind of dance the bees and butterflies will lead them on..

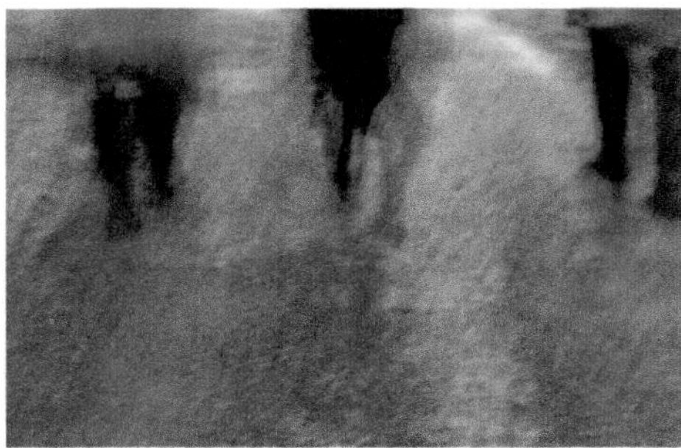

Gathering mists, 14 October, 2013

The mist is down for the day but we head out along the western roadways to places of honeyed secrets and mossy circles, graveyard maintenance means dipping plastic angels in rusty buckets and strimming in the rain. Even Sheela na Gig is well dressed here. We wander and wonder and know there's more to it. Off track, we know something else now.

References

Beckett, S. (1984) *Collected Shorter Plays*, Faber and Faber

Bharati, S.V. (1985) *Philosophy of Hatha Yoga*, The Himalayan Institute Press

Cixous, H. and Kerslake, B. (1984) "Aller à la mer." *Modern Drama* 27.4: 546-548. Project MUSE. Web. 4 Jul. 2013_http://bit.ly/tpMove85

Claxton, G. (1999) *Hare Brain, Tortoise Mind: Why Intelligence Increases When You Think Less*, Harper Perennial

Daido Loori, J. (2007) *The Still Point, Introduction to Zen Meditation*, Dharma Communications (DVD)

Franklin, E. (1996) *Dynamic Alignment Through Imagery*, Human Kinetics Europe

Hodge, A. (2010) *Actor Training*, Routledge

Kabat-Zinn, J. (1994) *Wherever You Go, There You Are, Mindfulness Meditation for Everyday Life*, Piatkus

Knowlson, J. (1997) *Damned to Fame, The Life of Samuel Beckett*, Bloomsbury

Knowlson, J., and Knowlson, E. (2007) *Beckett Remembering / Remembering Beckett*, Bloomsbury

Oliver, M. (2005) *Dream Work*, Grove Press

Salverson, J. (1996) 'Performing emergency: Witnessing, popular theatre, and the lie of the literal', *Theatre Topics*, vol. 6, no. 2, pp. 181-191 http://bit.ly/tpMove59

Tuffnell, M. and Crickmay, C. (1999) *Body Space Image*, Dance Books

_______ (2004) *A Widening Field*, Dance Books

Ven. Shikai Zuiko o-sensei Zazen-ji (1996) *Kinhin: The Dignity of the Buddha* http://bit.ly/tpMove58

Zarrilli, P.B. (2009) *Psychophysical Acting: An Intercultural Approach after Stanislavski*, Routledge

PART THREE

Interplay of practice and writing

ADAM BENJAMIN

The Fool's Journey and Poisonous Mushrooms

Introduction

This chapter has arisen out of a pleasure in the abundance and unexpectedness of the lived experience and its connectivity with the performative experience. It is written in a spirit that acknowledges the need to reflect while accepting the inherent impossibility of language to adequately capture the immediacy of the improviser's world. In this world, acausal connections subvert the seriousness of the research imperative: "There is no way to really understand play without also remembering the feeling of play" (Brown and Vaughan 2009: 20). We might trace this ideology back to J. Huizinga: "You can deny, if you like, nearly all abstractions: justice, beauty, truth, goodness, mind, God. You can deny seriousness, but not play" (Huizinga 1970: 21). I have chosen to embrace this paradox, and enfold myself into this writing in a way that, I hope, resists dissection, neat conclusions or a singular perspective. Instead I position myself in the midst of my research and allow it to "open up to me" (Pernille Østern 2009: 44). A play of ideas is present to a degree in all research, artistic or otherwise, even if that playfulness is necessarily subsumed by the time a paper is submitted, and the often chance and errant moments of discovery are revised and ordered for academic consumption, leaving us with a collection of words that have long forgotten the fluidity of ink; a hermetic rather than hermeneutic seal.

Getting home

> A beginning is an artifice, and what recommends one over another is how much sense it makes of what follows.
> (McEwan 1997:18)

I'd been bringing wild mushroms back to my mother-in-law's house on Ariake Mountain on a regular basis that autumn, and my mother-in-law had, on an equally regular basis, been tipping them surreptitiously into the compost bin. The argument being, He's English, what can he possibly know about Japanese mushrooms?

Fig. 1: Etsuko Tanaka. Photo: Adam Benjamin

Driving home along the mountain road early one evening we passed a very old man with a basket full of assorted fungi. "Let's ask him," I urged, hoping we could get a definitive answer as to whether or not my mushrooms were edible. We stopped the car and my wife, Tamami, got out and began talking with the old man. It was soon evident that something was wrong; he seemed distraught, his grief almost palpable, and his distress rendered him all the more fragile than his 90-something years.

It transpired that he had come up the mountain on his moped and then, after a very successful mushrooming expedition, had become disorientated, confused and was now unable to find his way back to his bike.

"Get him in the car" I called. "We'll find it!" What happened next is something I can't quite explain other than, after threading my way through the forest, I stopped the car, got out, walked along a path and found the moped, effortlessly, as if I had always known where it would be. Now, it's fair to say I knew that part of the forest quite well, so it was a bit of an inspired guess, and I could have been as completely wrong as I happened to be completely right. What is more difficult to factor is that we unknowingly and effortlessly positioned ourselves to serve someone who was in great need of assistance.

In the past few years I have improvised with many different performers in a many different settings and countries, with the companies 'Five Men Dancing' and 'Neat Timothy', with Kirstie Simson, Russell Maliphant, Susanne Martin and Gabi Reuter, and with Chieko Matsumura and Takuya Oyamada in Japan. Each performance has been entirely unique in terms of its content and outcomes, each has followed its own particular pathway, its own unique trajectory. How then does this body of work constitute a research practice, and what does it have to do with mushrooms?

Analogies

So to un-pick the mushroom analogy a little further: these are wild mushrooms – unusual flavours, hard to find, not for those who prefer their consumables ready wrapped, labelled and uniformly presented.

The old man analogy: experience, he knows the mountain, he knows his mushrooms, he knows where to look, but along with his experience comes frailty, fallibility, (foolishness.?).You could see the possible homecoming:

"You lost your moped? Again! This is the fourth moped you've lost! You know we can buy those mushrooms now at Juscos[1] for bupkes, but no, for you they're not fresh enough; at 98 you still have to go up the mountain... on your moped! With these mushrooms you're killing me! Next year I swear I'll tie you to the moped, god forbid you don't kill yourself first. I married such a meshugener!"

(*long pause*)

"So where are the mushrooms?"

Ah, you weren't expecting the Jewish wife. Lots of things I wasn't expecting, I could write a book about it. Actually I have written a book about it.[2] My father, Joe Benjamin, wrote a book about it too – well not actually about improvisation, but about the nature of children's play (*In Search Of Adventure*, 1966), and my uncle (on my mother's side) wrote books, lots of them, that I'd never read, mainly due to the complexity of the ideas contained therein, until my colleague John Matthews wrote an article about a workshop led by myself and fellow improviser Kirstie Simson.

On showing me the draft I pointed out that he had quoted the philosopher Max Black. "He was my uncle," I said. "You're kidding," said Matthews. "No, he was my mother Rivka Black's brother, he died in 1988." Now the fact that uncle Max had written about dead metaphors and that Matthews should cite him when talking about an improv workshop I was co-leading would constitute an interesting coincidence, as would the minor fact that Black and Simson both left the UK to teach at Urbana-Champaign University in Illinois. Indeed, there was a trail of coincidental events that surrounded my teaching/performing partnership with Simson, too numerous to list, but significant in their clustering.

As a researcher, whose field of investigation exists solely within the elements of time and space, I should consider myself neglectful if I were not at least to note these fetching agglomerations, even if, after due consideration, they were destined for the compost bin. It is at this point that I stop the metaphorical car, get out, and ask an old man for advice.

Unearthing patterns, C. G. Jung

It is apt that I wrote much of this article while teaching in Vienna, where Jung had contested Freud before proposing his own theory of the unconscious. An event that proved to be pivotal in Jung's thinking is his now famous encounter with a scarab beetle. In brief, a patient who was caught in an overly logical and controlling mental state was relating a dream to Jung in which she was handed an ornament in the shape of a golden scarab; at the same instant a real scarab beetle banged against

1 For Jusco read Tesco.

2 Benjamin, A. (2001), *Making an Entrance. Theory and Practice for Disabled and Non-Disabled Dancers*, London: Routledge.

Jung's office window. Jung brought it in and offered it to his patient. The coincidence caused a dramatic and remedial shift both in her overly rigid personality, and in Jung's understanding of how the world is structured. For Jung the experience helped formalise a psycho-physical understanding of the world that allows for a meaningful interface between psychological and physical phenomena, something he termed *synchronicity*.

It would of course be possible to give rational explanations for these events: Jung was familiar with biology, he was able to identify the beetle, which was actually a rose-chafer (closely related to the scarab), Zurich is close by Rapperswil, known as 'the town of roses', so both Jung and his patient may have been seeing these beetles in numbers. Actually we saw one of these impressive creatures in our garden in Cornwall this spring, and my son Kodai was amazed later that morning, when a friend brought what he thought was the same beetle to school in a match box. There's essentially nothing remarkable about that; it was the time of year when you see them, and boys like collecting beetles. What is harder to explain is how Jung was positioned in that moment to effortlessly help someone who was in great need of assistance, or to put it slightly differently, how, because of a certain receptivity, plus a combination of knowledge and skills, he was able to draw on an unforeseen and unplanned event to affect a significant and positive outcome.

It seems to me at this point that there are two evident classes of coincidence: things that seem to cluster together with no causal connection, and things that cluster together with no causal connection that are associated with fortuitous, beneficial or altruistic outcomes. One could then surmise that there might be another category of things that seem to cluster together with no causal connection that are associated with unfortunate outcomes, all of which leaves us effectively wandering around the forest looking for a moped or a mushroom or both.

Do the events we have considered constitute synchronicity or simple coincidence? While Jung's writing is reassuring, it doesn't constitute scientific data, the kind of thing we expect from objective research. It doesn't offer us any certainty into the ordering of the events in the physical world or what their relationship might be to our inner, felt, embodied world. Despite his interest in and engagement with one of the leading physicists of his day (Wolfgang Pauli), Jung's work is still viewed with suspicion by many in the scientific community. While there are still those within the scientific (and psychiatric) communities who strongly resist Jung's psycho-physical connection, they have nonetheless had to acknowledge a far less rational/causal underpinning to reality, and this has included accepting the existence of what Einstein termed 'spukhafte fernwirkung' or 'Spooky action at a distance'; the ability of particles separated by enormous distances to behave as though they are intimately connected, indeed, to behave as though they inhabit the same space (Greene 2011). Interestingly, Uncle Max had a lot to say on this subject (Black 1952), but before I reveal the paucity of my knowledge of mathematical philosophy or physics (quantum or otherwise), and do both them and my own field of study a disservice by leaping to unfounded and unsupportable conclusions I shall try to find my way back through the forest to my metaphorical moped, mushroom, car, and see if I can determine the basis on which I make my own decisions and how this shapes my understanding of my research-led practice and my teaching. Something I am sure uncle Max would be relieved to hear.

Choosing to be lost

While I am not a scientist, there is nonetheless a rigorous praxis that shapes my understanding of human bodies moving in time and space and the choices and pathways we choose, a praxis that might shed light on why my embodied experience resonates so strongly with an old man lost in the woods, not to mention the ideas expressed in Chaos and Entanglement theory… and mushrooms.

To paraphrase Wittgenstein:

> Almost in the way a man who is not used to searching in the forest for mushrooms will not find any because his eyes are not trained to see them and he does not know where you have to be particularly on the lookout for them, similarly, someone unpracticed in improvisation passes by all the spots where patterns are hidden in the grass, whereas someone who has had practice will pause and sense that there is a pattern close by even though he cannot see it yet. (See [1946] 2001: 29 for the original)

Given that we have so far failed to come up with a reliable explanation for finding mopeds, perhaps we can consider Wittgenstein's analogy in the light of Matthews' workshop observations.

> The knowledge can be … contingent and apparently contradictory almost to the point of being self-negating but, by doing the exercise over and over we extend, develop and refine these principles and add new principles and we perhaps also acquire the expertise to choose which principle to apply in any given situation on stage. (2012: 351–52)

What principles?

Improvisation is a research into unknowns (etymologically from the Latin *im - pro - visere,* not - before - seen) and so our methodologies or practices may be described but are only the recipes. Elsa Gindler points to this dilemma in her article 'Coming to Our Senses',

> It is difficult for me to talk about *Gymnastik* because the aim of my work is not the learning of certain movements, but rather the achievement of concentration. (Gindler in Johnson 1995: 5)

We can practice to refine the senses and sensibilities with regard to time, sound, sight, memory, touch (smell, taste)… the list is as apposite for cooking as it is for improvising, but they (the exercises) do not constitute the meal. It is true to say that there are innumerable approaches to training in improvisation: the physical skills of Contact Improvisation following Steve Paxton and Lisa Nelson, the text based word play of Keith Johnstone, the movement, text interplay of Julyen Hamilton to name a few. It would also be fair to say that, to the trained eye, it is possible to recognise techniques used in performance and identify where (and even with whom) students have studied. A few years ago in a workshop in Norway a dancer complained that I was not doing Improv 'right'. What she meant was that I was not doing it according to the tenets laid down by her teacher with whom she had diligently studied for some years. I was breaking too many of her (his) rules, and she was feeling, if not out of her depth, then certainly out of her comfort zone. So while much training seeks to equip students with the tools or principles with which to deal with unknown circumstances, a student who has been trained only with a specific skill set may reject the possibilities offered by unknowns and prefer to tread only familiar territory in order to verify to themselves the efficacy of the method they have been trained in. The training of improvisation must therefore encourage (however gently) a journey into self-doubt, and different teachers have evoked different strategies to take their students and themselves to this point. Anne Bogart describes this precarious, self-disturbance:

> If speaking does not threaten your own stability, your ability to stand, then you probably do not have a good enough reason to speak. (2007: 22)

While the old man on the mountain did not choose to be lost – and though we might get into analytically deep water if we said the same of Jung's patient – they nonetheless share certain features. Both were in moments of crisis or impasse; both were unable to see a way forward, and both were unexpectedly assisted in ways that they could not possibly have foreseen as their pathway inadvertently crossed with, well with Jung and a beetle, and me and my wife and a small car (what I would not give for it to have been a VW… it was a Suzuki). I mention my wife here, because without her Japanese language, this story would have been as inconsequential as Jung's without his knowledge of entomology. In addition to these intermediary elements, both stories involve openings: a window that Jung opens to bring in the beetle and the door we open to let the old man into the car; both stories involve loss and 'help without effort' and both stories involve compost. I would like you to hold onto the compost idea while I attempt to get my bearings.

As a performer, with a history of training in dance, in bodywork, in tai chi and fine art, I am still forced, in the end, to admit that I often do not know exactly what it is I am doing, until I am *in the doing of it*. I refer again to T. Pernille Østern:

> For me, a hermeneutic-phenomenological spiralling means positioning myself in the midst of my questions and research material and letting it open up to me. (2009: 44)

I am trusting that I am on the right path, I am trusting a pattern will emerge and that I will be part of that pattern, but I cannot predict, direct or determine what the pattern or the final destination (outcomes) will be, nor can I claim any ownership of them. I am perhaps more of a soul searcher than a sole researcher. This is not *my* choreography and it is my fallibility, my ability to be lost that enables new and unexpected solutions/resolutions/connections/ideas to arise. As D. A. Schön argues convincingly of his pedagogic approach,

> I am presumed to know, but I am not the only one in the situation to have relevant and important knowledge. My uncertainties may be a source of learning for me and for them. (1983: 300)

At the same time if I am too hands off as a teacher, or too conceptual I risk under-preparing students for a praxis that is highly reliant on a combination of very particular skills: physical, vocal, musical, spatial, temporal, kinaesthetic, haptic. Enabling students to identify the skills that help them progress is part and parcel of the journey, one that allows them to build the path along which they are travelling. It is what Biggs (1999) terms constructive alignment and what Karen Schupp (2011) utilises to develop informed decision making in her improvisation students.

If I become overly convinced of my singular perspective as a teacher or performer of improvisation, I increasingly filter out other possibilities. Like the student in Norway, I become unable to engage and play with ideas beyond a certain set of known rules or parameters. In my own practice I counter this tendency by performing without scores and often with minimal lead-in time: for example as a guest in Susanne Martin and Gabriele Reuter's *Salon* (2011), with Neat Timothy in *Unsettled Scores* (2009), and with the musician John Matthias in Plymouth (2013). Sometimes, I encounter artists in performance with no preparation: Andrew Moorish in a performance of *Five Men Dancing* at The Place, London (2008) and Takuya Oyamada in the Jazz Café, Nagoya, Japan (2010). Team teaching and performing with practitioners like Kirstie Simson also ensures that my practice and practices are scrutinised and tested.

I have somehow to balance the acquisition of skills or knowledge with a state of 'not knowing', or to imbue knowing with a kind of 'volitional fallibility', an acceptance of, and willingness to embrace, error. Humility is not often a word associated with education and far less with research, but one that we might consider in this context. The old man, despite his profound knowledge of fungi, is reliant on a 'gaijin' (a rather uncomplimentary term for a foreigner) to help him find his bike. Jung, the founder of analytical psychology, is dependent on a bug to help undo the complexities of his patient's trapped mind. This is humility again: a word that etymologically connects us with the earth, from the Latin *humus*. Time we looked more closely at the compost you have been holding on to.

Compost, which for many evokes images of decay (or entropy) has its origins in the Latin *componere* 'to put together', and is from the same root as 'composition', which we take to be the essential component of choreography. The choreographer is the mapper of human movement in time and space, but her or his work is *written*, it is a map, not a field of discovery. The putting together has already been done by the time we view it, the artist's (research) journey already accomplished. The stage is largely void of substantive choices or decisions; what we witness is obedience. As a result, countless highly skilled dancers still emerge from the experience of training (and then working with choreographers) expert in following directions, but terrified, incapable or dismissive of improvisation. As Celeste Snowber puts it, "So schooled in persisting in a linear fashion that even a spiral interruption is troubling at times" (Richmond & Snowber 2009:123).

The improviser on the other hand is in the process of putting things together, trying and testing, succeeding and failing in the knowledge that all these experiences are equally important, that the fruits of our creative process are bound inextricably to a wider field of exploration that may only become apparent if we are able to divest ourselves of the hubris of 'knowing'. I am aware that in the doing, in the praxis, patterns emerge, and these patterns or this 'order' may be felt and responded to by those who witness the performance… sometimes with surprise, sometimes with laughter, sometimes with moments of profound recognition, silence, even tears. To engage in this particular practice the improviser must learn to co-exist with the possibility of public failure, and in an equivalent to Paxton's physical surrender to gravity, be emotionally willing to fall to earth – *hum*iliation. To some extent this might be considered an ecological imperative as well as an artistic one, which Paxton, as an organic farmer, as well as dancer, would seem to exemplify. I am putting things together here as I write, unearthing connections, breathing life into dead metaphors – I'm researching when I'm supposed to be performing, performing when I'm supposed to be teaching, playing with words when I'm supposed to be writing.

Playing with words – the lead-in to the performance

Unsettled Scores, Plymouth (2009)

There is no connection.
Time is passing I am still running about trying to gather biogs and get programme notes printed. I feel ill. I don't know if it is just nerves or the bug that has prevented Tam from coming in with the kids to watch.
I feel alone.
The dancers somehow seem foreign and unapproachable.
I manage a brief warm up and find a duet with Bryony (Perkins) –
some kindred-ness, a shared language and room for some hope.
Remember there is no preparation, why fight the emptiness?

'*Whatever you're feeling is the right thing*'. Trust where you are, always.
Yes, but where is that just now?
A long, long, way from my body,
These are good folk, something will happen, something always happens.

I am about to be exposed, my art form found wanting and I will walk this building a failure – the lecturer whose work doesn't stand up
No proper warm up
Still not everyone here
I am getting the notes together, running them down to Jane
PC not a Mac, doing the wrong things, Jane patient thankfully
Dancers and musician arrive an hour before we start
Can't connect. I feel even more ill, am more than likely coming down with Tam's bug.
Can't feel myself in my body, can't feel any connection to impro
Why am I doing this?
Seems a completely foolish venture.

Force myself onto dance floor and into movement, seek my voice
Bounce, wriggle, stretch, still avoiding other dancers
Much rather be anywhere than here now. Doors open in 10 minutes.

Jamie McCarthy plays fiddle, brilliantly
I find my voice, harmonies
I sense something other than fear for the first time today; some small flicker of courage and defiance.
The house is open.
I am in. I am on. Everything else is in the hunt.
I am hunted and hunting.
Shhhhhh!

Fig. 2: Adam Benjamin & Naho Matsumoto improvisation, Japan 2013. Photo: Omi Toshihiro

Hunting mushrooms and chaotic conditions

> We were all nomads once, and crossed the deserts and the seas on tracks that could not be detected, but were clear to those who knew the way.
> (Winterston 1989:43)

So are the mushroom and the scarab beetle complicit in this pattern or imposters? Both beautiful in their own ways, both replete with imagery from Alice to the Ancient Egyptians, and both saprotrophs; you weren't expecting biology? There were many things I wasn't expecting when I started writing. The scarab beetle larvae and the rhizomorphs, or root system of mushrooms, both feed on decaying organic matter. They are not *im*posters in this context but *com*posters albeit in different parts of their life cycle. Whatever falls to the floor, be it leaves from the trees or dung from a cow, is recycled, nothing is wasted, nothing is extraneous to this particular ecology, and this is exactly or metaphorically the mindset of the improviser, nourished by whatever is in the space, generating order and pattern as we re-search.

While, as dancers and dance audiences, we continue to place our faith in the choreographer as the imposer of order on bodies moving in time and space (a tradition in the West we can trace to Louis XIV of France), Chaos Theory threatens the succession, suggesting that order may arise un-beckoned from random conditions, like composters, undirected and unnoticed, ignorant of state sanctioned directives, busily putting things together.

The classic choreographer's skill is the demonstration of a singular, but limited perspective (no matter how extraordinary); a movement highway if you like, replete with speed limits, traffic lights and road signs, and it is difficult, as we all know, to stop and offer help, let alone stop and ask for it when travelling at such speed. If we bend this analogy to encompass the modern technological superhighway we are within that territory that Ronald Barnett (2004) describes as the "radically unknowable world", and like him we will confront the ever more pressing need to find a pedagogy (and accompanying dance) that will help students locate themselves within an increasingly changing and uncertain environment.

Review

> Intelligent choice might well be thought of as the exercise of an informal, practical art, rather than the application of a mathematical calculus.
> (Black 1985:34)
>
> ***Isogeba maware*** when in a hurry, take the long route. (Japanese proverb)

All of this brings us full circle to the very human question posed at the outset when we first stopped our little Suzuki on the mountain road: how is it that we find ourselves 'inexplicably positioned to offer service to others'? Perhaps it is only when we no longer 'know' with certainty, that inexplicably a tree (*ki* in Japanese) rings a bell (*suzu*) if we have eyes and ears and a mind to perceive. 'Suzuki', used in this translation, is reaching somewhat, but patterns do metaphorically ring bells or 'resonate', leading us forward to new understanding and interpretations. Patterns for most of us serve as a means to make sense of our journey through life. That we live in a time when our steadfast refusal to acknowledge and respect nature's patterns has brought us to the brink of ecological disaster might suggest that pattern recognition has an essential role to play in our future survival. The isolation and alienation that is evident in so many students (and researchers) is a reminder that our culture imposes a disconnection from nature and from the natural world that might accurately be described as 'a loss'. A few days before completing this chapter I happened upon these words from Julian Barnes: "Grief seems at first to destroy not just all patterns, but also to destroy a belief that a pattern exists" (*Guardian*, Saturday Review, 30 March 2013, p.2).

Conclusions are an unsatisfactory state for an improviser. There is a mathematical finality to the word that sits uneasily with those who know that each ending is merely an opportunity for a new beginning. Being '*i*nexplicably *p*ositioned to be of *s*ervice to *o*thers' (i.p.s.o.) is not something we can manufacture any more than '*f*inding our *a*ctions *c*ontribute *t*o *o*rder' (f.a.c.t.o.). Given the right conditions, it is perhaps just a consequence of being fully human. Here we might reference Barnett's (2004) list of dispositions: "carefulness, thoughtfulness, humility, receptiveness, resilience, courage and stillness" which, allied to a sense of direction and a sense of humour (from the improviser's tool bag), may indicate the kind of students, performers and people we might hope to meet when navigating our way through the unknowable, and hence the kind of pedagogy and performance we might begin to explore and value. In terms of what might serve as compass to our peregrinations, I turn again to Bogart: "In order to engage in effective action you must first find something that you value and put it at the centre of your life" (2007: 1).

Perhaps, in the end, it is the absence of the 'ipso facto' pattern that might provide grounds for reflection, the question being not so much, 'How do these opportunities or openings to help others arise?' as 'Why are they so rare?' and perhaps, 'What is it about my research/worldview/pedagogic practice that isolates me from this particularly human experience?' Or to put it more succinctly, 'What was it I lost along the way?'

***

The largest living organism on the planet is an Armillaria ostoyae fungus that grows in the Malheur National Forest in Oregon, USA. Connected by an underground and unseen network of filaments or rhizomorphs, it is 3.5 miles across and covers an area of 2200 acres. This means that if you pick a honey mushroom on one side of the forest, and walk for an hour or so and pick another honey mushroom, you would essentially be eating the same fungus when you get home. Mother-in-law permitting.

References

Aziz, R. (1990) *C.G. Jung's Psychology of Religion and Synchronicity*, State University of New York Press

Barnett, R. (2004) 'Learning for an unknown future', *Higher Education Research and Development*, 23:3. pp. 247-260

Benjamin, A. (2001) *Making an Entrance. Theory and Practice for Disabled and Non-Disabled Dancers*, Routledge

Benjamin, A., Alessandri, S., Halls, R., Nodine, R. & Watson, D. (2013) 'We'll See What Happens, You'll See What Happens', an improvised performance with music by John Matthias and Dustan Belcher, Theatre 1, Plymouth University, 20 Feb. 2013

Benjamin, A., Nodine, R., Reuter, G., Leaney, J., Chimutengwende, S. & Perkins, B. (2009) *Unsettled Scores*, an improvised performance with the collective 'Neat Timothy', music by Jamie McCarthy and Alexis Kirk, Theatre 1, Plymouth University, 1 Oct. 2013

Benjamin, A. & Oyamada, T. (2010) *Untitled*, an entirely unforeseen improvised performance at Jazz Café, Nagoya City, Japan, 18 April

Benjamin, J. (1966) *In Search of Adventure*, London: National Council of Social Service on behalf of The Nuffield Foundation

Biggs, J. (1999) *Teaching for Quality Learning at University*, Open University Press/SRHE

Black, M. (1952) *The identity of indiscernibles*, Mind, 61:242, pp. 153-164

_______ (1985) *Making Intelligent choices. How useful is decision theory*, Dialectica Vol. 3, pp. 19-34

Bogart, A. (2007) *And Then, You Act: Making Art in an Unpredictable World*, Routledge

Burns, C. (2011), Wolfgang Pauli, *Carl Jung, and the acausal connecting principle: A case study in transdisciplinarity* http://bit.ly/tpMove16

Brown, S. and Vaughan, C. (2009) *Play: How It Shapes the Brain, Opens the Imagination, and Invigorates the Soul*, Avery

Five Men Dancing (2008) *Five Men Dancing an improvised performance* at The Place, London, 3 May, http://bit.ly/tpMove18

Gleick, J. (1998), *Chaos: The Amazing Science of the Unpredictable*, Vintage

Greene, B. (2011), *Spooky Action at a Distance* http://bit.ly/tpMove17

Huizinga, J. (1949/1970) *Homo Ludens*, Maurice Temple Smith

Johnson, D.H. (1995) *Bone, Breath and Gesture*: Practices of Embodiment, North Atlantic Books

Martin, S., Reuter, G. & Benjamin, A. (2011), *Salon*, in dialogue with invited guest (Benjamin) and audience, this evening revolves around the Improvisation as performance, choreography and research, Theatre 1, Plymouth University, Plymouth, 29 Nov. 2011

Matthews, J. (2012) 'What is a workshop?' *Theatre, Dance and Performance Training Journal*, 3:3, pp. 349-361

McEwan, I. (1997) *Enduring Love*, Jonathan Cape

Pernille Østern, T. (2009), *Meaning-making in the Dance Laboratory. Exploring dance improvisation with differently bodied dancers*, Acta Scenica

Richmond, S. & Snowber, C. (2009) *Landscapes of Aesthetic Education*, Cambridge Scholars Publishing

Schön, D.A. (1983) *The Reflective Practitioner: How Professionals Think in Action*, Basic Books

Schupp, K. (2011), 'Informed decisions, dance improvisation and responsible citizenship', *Journal of Dance Education*, 11:1, pp. 22-29

Simson, K. & Benjamin, A. (2012) *About Time* improvisation performed at the MultiPlié dansefestival, Trondheim, Norway, 21 April

Winterston, J. (1989) *Sexing The Cherry*, Vintage

Wittgenstein (1946/2001) *Philosophical Investigations*, Blackwell

CATH CULLINANE, NATALIE GARRETT BROWN,
CHRISTIAN KIPP and AMY VORIS

At Dusk, the Collaborative Spills and Cycles of L219

Introduction

This viewpoint seeks to articulate the choreographic and performative strategies of the work *L219*, framed by the work of practitioner-scholars who explore the relationship between collaborative writing and making processes. Text and image are arranged to reconsider the practices that have given rise to the work, shown as part of the Dance and Somatic Practices Conference 2013. This collaboratively authored chapter considers the resources that have enabled previous versions, suggesting that this writing is perhaps another incarnation of the work. The poetic approach to experiential anatomy within Body-Mind Centering, the witnessing practice of Authentic Movement and the RSVP cycles following Halprin and Poynor are discussed for their contribution to the work's emergence.

This writing is offered as a viewpoint on artistic practice. It seeks to articulate the choreographic and performative strategies of the work *L219* using image and text to constellate the practices and ideas that have given rise to it. In doing so, it 'wrestles the slippery fish' of collaborative and *re-collective* writing in order to develop our conscious understanding of a nascent project (Poynor & Worth in Pitches *et al.* 2012: 148).

It is intended that the relationship between text and images be poetic rather than directly illustrative[1]. This dialogic relationship between image and language extends the collaborative character of *L219* which, in its most recent incarnation at the Dance and Somatic Practices Conference in July 2013, encompassed nine artists experimenting with the adjacent spillover of their materially-oriented making processes. Those artists were lighting designer Cath Cullinane, jewellery designer Zoe Robertson, photographer Christian Kipp, two filmmakers Stephen Snell and Steve Chamberlain, two sound artists Daren Pickles and Nicholas Peters and two dancers Natalie Garrett Brown and Amy Voris. Within this configuration of artists, the repeated 'multiples of two' points to the pre-existing collaborations brought to bear on the project. All of the artists involved were curious about how their existing practices would permeate each other in this souped-up rendition of the work.

The words in this chapter were written by Garrett Brown and Voris and are focused around the dance/movement dimensions of the work. The images, which feature all of the artists involved in the project, are Kipp's. Lighting designer Cullinane is the 'artistic engine' of the work, responsible for originating the project and coordinating those involved. Thus, for the reasons just named, Garrett Brown, Voris, Kipp and Cullinane are named as official authors of this chapter. However, we (Garrett Brown and Voris) feel uneasy about officially naming only half of the team as authors in a project that is so collectively driven. Therefore special acknowledgement is given here to the distinctive artistic practices of Robertson, Snell & Chamberlain and Pickles & Peters.

L219 began with lighting designer Cath Cullinane's desire to fill the Lanchester Gallery with its blue-green tones projected through nine humming slide projectors at dusk. About the colour, Cullinane says: "L219 is not a pretty colour. In fact it is very artificial. If electricity could be seen I think, in my mind this is the colour it would be. I am interested in how this colour can sculpt energy, whether it be potential or kinetic, a body or a space."

The Lanchester Gallery, Coventry is marvellously porous and its surrounding pavements are marvellously peopled. Owing to its slightly shaded glass walls, during the day the interior of the space is somewhat invisible. At night the space reverses its identity and, when lit, becomes intensely visible. During the work, the colour L219 slices, diversifies and spills out of the gallery while, on the inside, the very human activities of *artists making and doing* becomes evident.

As dancers, we (Garrett Brown and Voris) share a site-responsive practice[2] with particular influence from Anna and Lawrence Halprin's RSVP cycle (1969) and from the environmental dance-maker Helen Poynor. An overarching concern of our practice is to reveal a site through the offering of our danced-relationship to it. Informed by the RSVP cycle, we follow a pattern of generating scores that are called up or 'resourced' by direct relationship with the site. Through practice and reflection, the score develops and changes.

---

1 Here, "poetic" refers to the adjacency of materials which, through their relationship, generate meaning and resonance.

2 enter inhabit project: http://bit.ly/tpMove70

The particular site of this project, the Lanchester Gallery, holds many identities. It was originally intended as a retail space that has since become an art gallery, sitting inside a brand new university building ('the Hub') directly next to an office called 'The Centre for Applied Entrepreneurship'. The interior of the space has a concrete industrial feel; it is literally unfinished, the intended floor never completed. Directly outside there is a constant stream of pedestrians and cars. The artistry of skateboarders often occupies the neighbouring ramps. We came to consider the shifting light, the duration of time and the wealth of companion activities like another landscape. As movers, the site conjured up in us the desire to dwell and daydream alongside the urge for mischievous and sometimes intensely physical outbursts.

In order to deal with the expanses of the site and of time, we felt we needed a very 'open' score that at the same time would ground us in the materiality and connectedness of the body. So we turned to body-based resources that would enable us to meet the conditions of the work. Such physical resources are "somatically-informed" (Garrett Brown 2011) – inspired by the poetic approach to experiential anatomy and developmental movement in the practice of Body-Mind Centering. The score from the 11th July 2013 performance read:

During dusk

Playing with changes from
empty to full
inside to outside

the contents and container of the body
from centre to periphery
webs of interior connection
fluid & solid
the layers of the midline

composing
intervals of space

'witnessing' potential
sitting in the membrane

forming and dissolving
practicing the ability to invest or to drop
scenes, coming and going

a laboratory of live composition
spillage between artists
in the moment of making

practicing 'seamlessness'
between being, doing and performing

The dancing body revealing and intervening with
a site of constant construction.

In *Job's Body*, Deane Juhan writes:

> Touch is the chronological and psychological Mother of the Senses. In the evolution of sensation, it was undoubtedly the first to come into being. It is, for instance, rather well developed in the ancient single cell amoeba. All the other special senses are actually exquisite sensitizations of particular neural cells to particular kinds of touch: compressions of air upon the ear drum, chemicals on the nasal membrane and taste buds, photons on the retina. (2003: 29)

As part of our practice, we exchange hands-on work that then leads into moving, witnessing and dancing together. Typically such hands-on work is focused around a certain system or coordination of the body. The quality of contact stirs a certain awareness from which movement emerges. One of our artistic curiosities, in a general sense, has been how to direct such qualitative awareness into live composition. How does this felt sense of the body – awakened through touch – extend into what we do when we 'touch' the site with our dancing? Juhan writes:

> Every time that I touch something, I am as aware of the part of me that is touching as I am of the thing I touched … at the moment of contact, two simultaneous streams of information begin to flow: information about an object announced by my senses, and information about my body announced by the interaction with the object. Thus I learn that I am more cohesive than water, softer than iron, harder than cotton balls, warmer than ice, smoother than tree bark, coarser than fine silk, more moist than flour, and so on … By rubbing up against the world, I define myself to myself. (2003: 34)

Amidst the sea of collaborative activities, we wondered what resources in the body would be called up or 'touched upon' by the environment?

In order to deal with the multiplicities of this particular site, we were drawn toward physical-poetic resources that cultivated a sense of substance and coherence in the body alongside a sense of inner readiness and flexibility. For example this led us to explore the sense of the body as container and contents – the 'container' being the skeleton and the 'contents' being the organs and soft tissues of the interior (Bainbridge Cohen 1993: 28-53). We also explored the "navel radiation pattern"[3] which, according to Bonnie Bainbridge Cohen, is the second basic neurological pattern to emerge in utero. Linda Hartley writes:

> The 'mind' of this [the navel radiation] pattern ... involves openness, spaciousness, receptivity, communication – these interchange and merge with boundaries, limitations of space, enfoldment, and self-containment. There is an experience of integration, wholeness, oneness, and unmanifest but infinite possibility. (1995: 40)

We have found that consciously working with this pattern supports a sense of self-coherence in meeting the environment.

We also explored the presence of connective tissue. Juhan describes connective tissue as a kind of 'meta-membrane' that binds the body together:

> Connective tissue ... forms a continuous net throughout the entire body and constitutes the immediate environment of every cell in the body, wrapping and uniting all structures with its moist, fibrous, cohering sheets and strands ... from scalp to soles and from skin to marrow. (2003: 75-76)
>
> From jellyfish to human beings, connective tissue is the primary organ of structure, gluing cells into discrete colonies, defining their shapes, forming them into functional units, and suspending them together in the correct relationships within the organism. (*ibid*: 87)

We have found that connective tissue supports a sense of the body's own intricate interweave and inner volume.

In the wider and roaming reality of *L219*, we (as dance-artists) have been asking ourselves: 'What holds this work together and what is it that we (as dancers) are offering to the space?'

We are still figuring this out, but *our work in the work* seems to be about opening to the different currents of the space and of ourselves, allowing something to emerge and then following that something through to discover its particularity until it dissolves. In the context of the improvised, durational, shifting and disparate activities of *L219*, we have felt in our bodies a 'call' for containment and coherence that the aforementioned physical resources seem to offer. Perhaps we have felt this call most deeply when something isn't 'working' or when we are lost.

But, what else could we call upon to cooperate with this open practice? What might help us 'hold the tension' of entering the unknown?

---

3 Linda Hartley describes this pattern as "facilitating the differentiation of the limbs of the body, and their integration through the navel centre into a whole body pattern" (2004: 107).

Voris's personal movement practice is heavily influenced by the practice of Authentic Movement[4]. This practice involves establishing boundaries of time and space, then closing one's eyes and responding to the movement of attention in the presence of a witness. There is no intended focus to the practice but rather an intention toward 'opening' to what is present (however mundane and unappealing that may be). Key to the practice is reflection afterwards in equal proportion to the moving.

The notion of 'witnessing' underlies the practice of Authentic Movement. As Janet Adler (2002), Hartley (2004) and others have explored: witnessing intends toward non-judgemental and compassionate presence usually practised in relationship between a mover and a witness. This witnessing presence is internalised by the mover as "the inner witness" (Adler 2002: xvi) Cultivating an inner witness is the work of Voris's regular practice. Borrowing a term from Arnold Mindell, Hartley (2004) describes witnessing as a "meta-skill" or an "embracing attitude which both guides and contains" (Hartley 2004: 66)

Intending toward witnessing while moving supports noticing how we notice, which, in turn, affects the choices that are subsequently made, like 'revving up' receptivity prior to activity. In addition to the physical resources named earlier, we began to turn consciously to the notion of witnessing while dealing with the shifting weather systems of *L219*.

4 See Pallaro *et al.* (1999, 2007) for collections of writings tracing the development and various applications of Authentic Movement. Voris's research is concerned with Authentic Movement as a "container" for the fluidities and complexities of emergent choreographic process and takes its cues from a number of practitioner-researchers named here. Janet Adler (2002), Linda Hartley (2004), Tina Stromsted (2008) among others have written about Authentic Movement as a spiritual practice.

The potential links between Authentic Movement and performance practice are well articulated by Penny Collinson (2005) and by Jane Bacon (2007). See also the artistic work and writings of Joan Davis (2007a and 2007b) and Emma Meehan's research (2011, 2012) concerned with Davis' work.

Contact Quarterly dedicated an edition to Authentic Movement in 2002 (Volume 27, No.2). Bacon (2010) proposes Authentic Movement as a creative research methodology.

Adler, Hartley and others in the realm of Authentic Movement sometimes refer to different modes of attention when moving, or 'being moved'. In her teaching, Hartley (2010/2011) differentiates these modes into the realms of tracking/proprioception, sensation, emotion and image – an artificial separation of intertwined phenomena – which nevertheless allows for the recognition of patterns, of preferences and of what layers of experience are being foregrounded. Garrett Brown and Voris began to use light awareness of these modes of attention as potential entry points and as ways to deepen engagement with material.

In *L219*, the meta-awareness of witnessing supports the capacity for zooming out and zooming in, for dwelling with the moment prior to action and for feeling the contingent creativity of live composition. This was succinctly expressed by Garrett Brown in the shorthand advice for us as performers: *Don't push it out too soon.*

As a piece of work, *L219* is fluid and sprawling. It spills across spaces and media revealing cycles of making and un-making. As dancers we have been wondering how to engage with the multiplicities of the site, of the collaboration and of our own moment-to-moment condition. The image and feeling of connective tissue, of the navel radiation pattern and the attentional quality of witnessing arouse in us a feeling of fluid holding which supports the step 'into the unknown' without abandoning the sense of self-coherence and agency necessary for live composition. As resources, they also seem to allow for spells of ambivalence and failure that belong to any good experiment.

As part of the emerging identity of *L219*, we have begun to notice certain sets of dualities in the work, such as:

light / dark
surface / depth
yielding / pushing
movement / stillness
everyday activity / specialised activity
industrial / human
togetherness / separation

Awareness of these dualities and movement across and between them seems to reveal processes of construction. A time-generous approach to generating material calls forth the durational identity of the work. We have come to see the movement of our attention and, moreover, the witnessing of the movement of our attention as a key resource or 'modulator' of the work across time.

However, all of this language feels speculative and strange – akin to what Jane Bacon and Vida Midgelow (2012) describe as "the double vision" of being reflexive (p. 4). Nevertheless, the process of assembling this writing has helped us to articulate our emergent working process and to get to know the work, or as Rosemary Lee and Niki Pollard (2010) put it "to grow" the work (p. 34), which maybe also means getting to know the work differently through language. This writing functions, in Halprin's (1969) language, as a form of "valuaction"[5] in preparation for the work's next rendering. As Bacon and Midgelow suggest "the forming of language informs the moving body, and in a cyclic process, each forms and then re-(in)forms the other" (2011: 6). Writing from, about and alongside one's practice can be both "disruptive" and "purposeful" (*ibid*).

5 "'Valuaction' is a neologism that encapsulates the combination of reflection on / evaluation of performance and the action that results from these responses" (Poynor & Worth in Pitches *et al.* 2012: 151).

Likewise, the very process of selecting images has informed us about how we would like the work to continue to emerge.

For example, the visual nature of photography has reinforced a choreographic interest in generating imagery which comes from an embodied engagement with site and which also seeks to have a visual impact within its environment. This writing is perhaps another incarnation or 'offshoot' of the work, which makes use of photographic imagery and language to activate memory of the live event while also germinating the work's next iteration.

Artists

Zoe Robertson, jewellery designer: http://bit.ly/tpMove68
Steve Chamerlain and **Stephen Snell** are sellotapecinema: http://bit.ly/tpMove49, http://bit.ly/tpMove22 and http://bit.ly/tpMove20
Daren Pickles, sound artist: http://bit.ly/tpMove21 and http://bit.ly/TPmove19
Nicholas Peters, musician: http://bit.ly/tpMove69

References

Adler, J. (2002) *Offering from the Conscious Body*, Inner Traditions
Bacon, J. (2007) 'Psyche moving: "Active Imagination" and "focusing" in movement-based performance and psychotherapy', *Body, Movement and Dance in Psychotherapy* 2: 1: 17-28
_______ (2010) 'The voice of her body', *Journal of Dance and Somatic Practices* 2: 1: 63-74
Bacon, M.J. & Midgelow, V.L. (2010) 'Articulating choreographic practices, locating the field: An introduction', *Choreographic Practices* 1: 3-19
_______ (2011) 'Writing the self, writing the choreographic', *Choreographic Practices* 2: 3-7
_______ (2012) 'Editorial', *Choreographic Practices* 3: 3-5
Bainbridge Cohen, B. (1993) *Sensing, Feeling, and Action: The Experiential Anatomy of Body-Mind Centering*, Contact Editions
Collinson, P. (2005) 'See and Be Seen: A Quality of Presence, An investigation of Authentic Movement in Creative Process and Performance', Unpublished MPhil thesis, Manchester Metropolitan University, UK
Davis, J. (2007a) *Maya Lila: Bringing Authentic Movement into Performance, The Process*, Elmdon
_______ (2007b) *Maya Lila: Bringing Authentic Movement into the World, The Offering*, Elmdon
Enter & Inhabit (2013) http://bit.ly/tpMove70
Garrett Brown, N. (2011) 'Disorientation and emergent subjectivity: The political potentiality of embodied encounter', *Journal of Dance & Somatic Practices* 3: 1+2: 61-73
Halprin, L. (1969) *The RSVP Cycles: Creative Processes in the Human Environment*, George Brazillier
Hartley, L. (1989) *Wisdom of the Body Moving: An Introduction to Body-Mind Centering*, North Atlantic Books
_______ (2004) *Somatic Psychology: Body, Mind and Meaning*, Whurr Publishers
_______ (2010/2011) *Authentic Movement and Therapeutic Presence* [workshops] module 2, Kelling, Norfolk: Institute for Integrative Body Work and Movement Therapy.
Institute for Integrative Body Work and Movement Therapy (2013) http://bit.ly/tpMove71
Juhan, D. (2003) *Job's Body*, Station Hill Press
Meehan, E. (2010), 'Visuality, discipline and somatic practices: The "Maya Lila" performance project of Joan Davis', *Journal of Dance and Somatic Practices* 2: 2, pp. 219-232
_______ (2011) 'Somatic Practice in Performance: The Maya Lila Project of Joan Davis', Unpublished PhD thesis. University of Dublin, Trinity College, Ireland
Lee, R. & Pollard, N. (2010) 'Writing with a choreographer's notebook', *Choreographic Practices* 1: 21-41
Pallaro, P. (ed.) (1999) *Authentic Movement: Essays by Mary Starks Whitehouse, Janet Adler and Joan Chodorow*, Jessica Kingsley Publishers
_______ (2007) *Authentic Movement: Moving the Body, Moving the Self, Being Moved, Volume 2*, Jessica Kingsley Publishers
Pitches *et al* (2012) 'Performer Training: Researching Practice in the Theatre Laboratory', in *Research Methods in Theatre and Performance* (eds. B. Kershaw & H. Nicholson) pp. 137-161, Edinburgh University Press
Poynor, H. & Worth, L. (2004) *Anna Halprin*, Routledge
Poynor, H. (2013) http://bit.ly/tpMove51
Stromsted, T. (2009) 'Authentic Movement: A dance with the divine', *Body, Movement and Dance in Psychotherapy* 4: 3: 201-213

CAROLYN ROY

As My Attention is Wandering

A score for somatic enquiry

> If my thoughts have wandred, I must intreat the wel-bred Reader to remember I have wandred through many deserts.
> (Sir Thomas Herbert (1634) cited in the OED)

This is an enquiry into the nature of wandering. It gathers reflections by practitioners on their experience of walking and dancing, together with philosophical and theoretical speculations. First person narratives drawn from my teaching scores and research journals invite the reader to enter the experience of a wanderer. Through the process of writing and ordering this assemblage the potential of wandering in the world unfurls. It becomes apparent that wandering is a quality of attention to being in the world. How does this matter in somatic dance practice? Sir Thomas Herbert, a 17th-century traveller, offers us a clue. In acknowledging the influence of desert journeys on his thought process he alludes to the inextricable relationship of physical experience and thinking. He recognised that wandering is not simply an activity or way of being in the world, but an undercurrent to living.

16th September 2013

> *As we arrive in this space, allowing our attention to wander lightly through our bodies. Noticing pathways of attention, leaps and skips. Where our attention alights, and moves on. What draws our attention beyond our bodies, to the sounds, scents, vibrations of the space. Our attention may wander lightly between perceptions of our internal and external worlds.*

What do I mean by wandering? Meandering, roaming, nomadism, drifting, itinerance, strolling, straying, diverging, deviating, walking, or all of these? Each of these words provokes an image of moving, travelling or making a journey and none of them implies an urge to arrive at a destination. I accept the inherent mobility of wandering, yet feel uncertain that wandering is specifically physical rather than a concept, sensation or perhaps a quality. Further, how would I bring wandering to dance? By walking?

16th May 2012

> *So we walked without a map along a path without destination. Moving through an open landscape with the river Severn constantly on one side. Although it imposes a physical parameter, the river opens space for our gaze to travel to the limits of seeing – the horizon, or vanishing point. A space to explore wandering. By which I mean moving through our environment open to its potential. But already we have questions. And by having questions to answer we subvert the state of wandering. But perhaps the questions can be considered as provocations, merely to frame experience, rather than requiring an answer. What would the question be? Rhythm, response, agency, desire, choice, orientation? We need to start simply. So, let's move through this vast space. Let's observe our bodies being as we meet this environment, bringing attention to the shifts and structural adaptations in the body as we are walking.*

Yes, let's start by walking. Walking is moving practised without question several times a day by the majority of people, primarily as a means of locomotion from A to B, but it can be for pleasure. Long practised by philosophers and writers as a means of generating clarity of thought, anthropologist Tim Ingold (2011: 17) goes as far as to state "locomotion and cognition are inseparable, and an account of the mind must be as much concerned with the work of the feet as that of the head", suggesting that walking is a process of knowledge production. While walking we generate understanding of our world and, by implication, of our place in the world.

Since 1960 arts practitioners have engaged in walking as art, simultaneously re-orienting perception of practice and re-contextualising work. For visual artists such as Richard Long and Hamish Fulton walking was often an epic, solitary process of ephemeral art production, challenging conventions of 'object art' in a climate of dematerialisation and the situation of art in life beyond the gallery. Their work existed beyond the moment of its making only as a trace in photographic or written form. Long cited in Heddon & Klein (2012: 97) emphasises that walking is a tool for making: "To walk a line is the simplest thing a man can do to put a mark on a place." Fulton argues that his work responds to landscape through walking rather than inscribing on landscape with an action. Nevertheless it is an act that produces art. Dancers who walk have different concerns. Although various issues might be embodied in walking, for dancers their 'work' is the physical act of the body walking. Walking is movement pared away to the limits of what is dancing, allowing attention to focus on the body's engagement with the world. In 1967, choreographer Steve Paxton made *Satisfyin' Lover*, a walking performance for 34 to 84 people. Working with untrained performers and using recognisable movements of sitting, standing and walking, it proposed dance as a universal language, accessible by and to anybody. It scrutinised human beings as they walked, with traits, habits, differences all revealed through close attention to this everyday activity. It presented life. As dancers' bodies challenged gravity by walking on the surface of a vertical plane in Trisha Brown's *Walking on the Wall* (1971), the familiarity of the movement allowed spectators to make a kinaesthetic[1] identification with the material and experience a shift in perception of their relationship with the world. In a personal communication, (27 February, 2014) dancer Simone Kenyon, whose own walking practice ranges from long treks to attending to the detail of the smallest step, understands this experience as a physical connection to the rhythmical and time-based nature of walking as dance that is absent in walking as art. The familiar, routine, embodied state of walking continues to evolve in dance as an engagement with life's realities: politics, collectivity, the body, duration, endurance, form, perception, the landscape, the urban condition – walking as dancing is an open-ended question, and one that concerns the body and the body as a conduit of knowledge. Christine Quoiraud walked and danced pilgrim routes and old rights of passage[2] around the globe, engaging with writers, scientists and artists in an investigation of place. She observed: "Walking, like dance, belongs to the instant, welcoming the circumstances and the unexpected, letting the formulations emerge" (cited in Perrin 2009). Walking engages the moment, knowledge emerges in these encounters. In a personal communication, (11 May, 2014) Simon Whitehead similarly sees walking as an extension of his practice of somatic dance. His is an essential, physical meeting with the land he travels; its seasons, people and places. Walking opens up to chance encounter and participation. Dancers who walk are open to meeting with the world. They give their attention to how their bodies touch the environment, the knowledge emerging from that experience and how to open that experience to others. All the while they tread the border of dance / not dance.

In *Relationscapes* (2009) Erin Manning argues that walking is an act of mutual engagement with our environment, and that through walking we perceive our environment relationally. She suggests that in walking we are always 'moving-with' as well as within our environment. We are walking and our perceived world is changing as we walk. A horizon shifts, a wall moves closer; the texture of the ground alters beneath our feet. Whilst we perceive our world changing as we are moving, we also sense the kinaesthetic experience of our body responding, adapting and participating in these changes. 'Walking-with' we are intricately bound in an unfolding engagement with our world.

16th May 2012

> *Striding out along a path, the attempt to import my habitual urban walking rhythm to this location fails as an imposition, a dislocation from another environment. This ground demands to be met. The rough terrain destabilises our steps, interrupting any attempt to impose a rhythm to walking. Gradually we become aware of other influences in this destabilisation. The sight and sound of a lark ascending, hovering and descending, its anxiety transmitted to my breath as I halt. A courtesy hello to strangers. Physical obstacles, gates and fences. Grasses and more weighty vegetation in our path. The pace of our companions. The wind is most dominant, its sound and force isolating each of us in our senses and self. It stimulates our skin, disturbs our hair and clothes and as we lean into it, imposes on the weight and direction of our movement.*

---

1 I use kinaesthetic throughout this text to mean a simultaneous awareness of our body's position and organisation in space and sense of our body moving in a relational field. Referencing personal training in Skinner Releasing Technique I understand kinaesthetic awareness as simultaneous attention to our inner and outer worlds and a fundamental of somatic practice.

2 Following rights of way.

> *All around, vegetation is moving in its eddies. Birds glide on its waves. Although we are continually moving through this landscape, we cannot avoid adapting to its conditions, changing in each present moment. We keep moving through, as if there has been no beginning and will be no end.*

Artist Francis Alys (Johnstone 2008) points out that walking is a physical engagement with place and one that frees you to process thoughts whilst simultaneously attending to a wide range of sensory experience in changing environments. He also hints at a call and response, or mutual relationship with the environment when he refers to the city as an 'interlocutor'. Alys's walks unravel through their environment like story lines, initiating and gathering a succession of incidents, meetings, and revelations. Constantly moving, they generate references, interpretations and associations, but do not set out to 'construct' a specific narrative, instead allowing the spectator to read their own meaning in the journey. He refers to walking as "one of the last private spaces", a notion that resonates with Simone Kenyon's observation that "we all have our own way of walking and so we have our own personal walking signature dance", (personal communication, 27 February, 2014) but also alludes to the walker's luxury of being simultaneously contained in a personal experience whilst fully engaged in the public realm. Each step is an encounter that brings into being our own discreet[3] alliance between interior and exterior worlds.

Philosopher Michel de Certeau (1925–1986) also proposed the practice of walking as a narrative enquiry that could generate infinite experiences through each walker's particular relationship with their unfolding world, as they are walking. He read the city as a language, with walking the way of understanding, speaking or even writing it.

> Walking affirms, suspects, tries out, transgresses, respects, etc., the trajectories it "speaks." All the modalities sing a part in this chorus, changing from step to step, stepping in through proportions, sequences, and intensities that vary according to the time, the path taken and the walker. These enunciatory operations are of an unlimited diversity. (1984: 99)

'Walking speaks a trajectory', unveils its potential, lives and articulates its transient existence. Walking creates, interrogates and affords experience of our world in an eternally negotiable relationship of unlimited diversity. I sense De Certeau's need to grasp and hold on to the physical, pedestrian experience of walking so as not to dissipate in the chaos of an incessantly mutating world. Somehow our movement makes the world matter. Within the eternal bustle of individuals 'worlding' as they are walking he proposes walking as an act of attending to and describing what is. Walking integrates us in our space and time – our 'private space'. It gives us our ground whilst we are alive to the simultaneous perceptions of ourselves walking, the world we are walking-with and the infinity of change evolving in that alliance. In its simplest terms, to paraphrase Jan Masschelein, who proposes walking as a pedagogic process, walking opens up the world, allowing us to be present in the present (2010: 282).

Does wandering offer us anything beyond the being present in the present of walking, and indeed what more would we want? The OED (1989) consistently uses wandering to define nomadic behaviour: "moves from place to place without readily apparent purpose. Travelling by uncertain and devious routes. Having no fixed abode or station …" In *Walkscapes* (2002) Francesco Careri contests this interchangeability, proposing instead that, in evolutionary terms, wandering was the precursor of

3 Discreet in the context of privacy.

nomadism. He sees nomadic life, the continual movement by a community with the aim of nourishing that community, as a cultural development of the erratic movement of hunting and gathering for the purpose of finding food. He suggests wandering as an essential or primal ingredient of both.

In the chapter '1227: Treatise on Nomadology – the war machine', (1987: 387-467) Deleuze and Guattari briefly introduce a nomadic protagonist, the warrior player of Go. An agent of nomos, the law of living, and without properties except those emerging from the present situation, the warrior is perpetually mobile yet waiting, moving "without aim or destination, without departure or arrival", (1987: 389) unaffiliated, an outsider to convention, unconstrained by any boundaries but the parameters of the present: an embodiment of pure strategy. This anonymous warrior exemplifies the nomad specifically in the manner by which it generates, moves and shatters territories. It creates and holds territory purely through spatial alliance, but it does not hold on, being continually open to the potential for new alliances, moving and relinquishing territory.

Thus Deleuze and Guattari identify a nomad as: having territory, albeit one that is an un-bordered field of activity, giving ground to another as the nomad moves on; moving from one point to another; following customary paths. He travels between points: water points, dwelling points, assembly points, etc. They emphasise that the nomadic life is not living these points but rather the paths between, the points merely servicing the paths, existing to be moved from, not settled. The paths may connect points, but they are lived as trajectories not links. "The life of the nomad is the intermezzo" (1987: 419). Even visiting and returning to the same points is seen as movement of factual necessity, as relays or pauses rather than as settlement. The nomad is perpetually in motion, not putting down roots. At the same time he is intricately bound in relation with his unfolding world. "The nomads make the desert no less than they are made by it" (1987: 421). The territory of the nomad does not exist, but rather it is created in these moments of encounter. The nomadic way of being creates and lives the territory of the in-between. Nomadic travel moves through vast but known spaces, from useful point to useful point. It is life as it is being lived, a journey as it is being travelled on a shifting path, creating and abandoning territory, yet still it is a movement of progression toward a specific aim. By contrast, wandering is processual rather than progressive. It may adopt pathways, but does not take them to a particular destination. A subtle distinction, but one to investigate. Further, if wandering is understood as moving-with the world rather than from or to place, as in relationship with a place albeit one that gives ground to another, as restless, located in the unknown, perhaps, it too could be considered as a mode of being rather than a physical activity.

7th January, 2014

> *As we are moving, noticing where our skin touches or is touched by the air. Where our body touches or is touched by the ground. And as our attention wanders through these points and planes we might notice the possibility of expanding into meeting the air, or the ground. Perhaps in this space between, this space of meeting, we dance an alliance.*

As concepts, wandering and nomadism seem increasingly aligned. But if we accept wandering as pre-nomadic, a way of being in the world that precedes aim or intention,

there must be a divergence. "Wandering happens in an empty space that has not yet been mapped, without any defined destination" Careri (2002: 48). If we translate this to practice, could wandering have equivalence with drifting, the derive, or drift, used by Guy Debord (1931–1994) and fellow Lettrist and Situationalist Internationals as a technique for accumulating and analysing collective ambient experiences of liminal, urban environments? A form of mapping based on rapid transit from place to place guided by encounters and the terrain itself, vividly described by Vincent Kaufmann as a "technique of transience, devoted to places themselves transient" (2008: 100), "the emblem of lost children who drift, who abandon themselves to a principle of pure mobility" (2008: 96).

The state of pure mobility, incessant movement without beginning or end, is resonant of nomadism. But I question whether the derive really could be considered 'pure' mobility. It may have been moving from place to place, drifting from void to void, but always with the intention of creating a psychogeography. It had an aim beyond the act, a mappable beginning and end. Taking place in areas of transient populations, marginal places or areas in danger of imminent demolition, it may even be considered a form of nostalgia, clinging to a disappearing world, but always with the goal of re-appropriating social space in a modernising city. As a journey with a start and an end point and further, an intention, drifting cannot be pure mobility. Pure mobility must be without aim or roots. And though wandering drifts, is aimless, it is not being adrift. Not all at sea. It relies on a relationship with ground.

Is a relationship with the ground possible without sacrificing the state of pure mobility? Can one be grounded, yet rootless? Perhaps this depends on our understanding of ground.

Ingold (2011: 130-133), argues that ground should not be understood as a stable surface but as a dynamic interplay of materials that constantly mutates in relation to weather, human or geological action. Seen in this light it is easy to conceive that rather than something that anchors, supports or roots us, ground could be our partner in a mutual relationship. To return to the notion of walking-with our world, in walking we place one foot after the other on the ground, and new ground influences our kinaesthetic experience of stepping, opening the possibilities or potential of each step, changing our perception of world, and so on. When Steve Paxton observes, "Solo dancing does not exist. The dancer dances with the floor" (Nelson & Stark Smith 1997: 103), he is referring to exactly this dynamic relationship. We dance in a continually shifting alliance with our changing ground.

But we are still in the realm of nomadism. How do we access the specifically pre-nomadic, and wander? Erin Manning (2009: 13–28) devotes a chapter to examining the concept of incipient movement through the kinaesthetic detail of preacceleration. Preacceleration is experienced prior to displacement, before stepping out into movement or even before consciousness of movement. She suggests it is a palpable sensation, without beginning or end. It does not determine or prescribe form to the movement to come, but rather holds the possibility that movement might emerge. The not-yet of moving. As a development Manning proposes that preacceleration initiates 'the interval', which is not an absence or space but rather the quality of in-between or alliance through which incipient movement is experienced. Here there is a conceptual echo of nomadism but also something deeper, an undercurrent that resonates with wandering. It is important to note that Manning is articulating the kinaesthetic experience that nourishes her conceptual enquiry. She has accessed the 'pre' of movement through somatic awareness, perceiving that it is not something that comes before, or as part of a sequence but a continual state of not-yet. She taps into a discernible sensation that allies all movement. Perhaps wandering as pre-nomadic operates in a similar relation. We could then understand wandering as an eternal current or vibration that underscores nomadism. And if wandering is a vibration, a wanderer, rather than somebody who acts, is somebody who attends to that vibration. And further, through our attention in wandering, we initiate the in-between, access the intermezzo and its limitless potential.

In his essay 'Berlin Chronicle', Walter Benjamin proposes that "not to find one's way in a city may well be uninteresting and banal. It requires ignorance – nothing more. But to lose oneself in a city – as one loses oneself in a forest – this calls for quite a different schooling. Then, signboards and streetnames, passersby, roofs, kiosks, and bars must speak to the wanderer like a twig snapping under his feet in the forest" (Benjamin 1955-72/1978: 8). There is a precision in his use of the word "wanderer" to describe a person losing herself. The twig snapping underfoot resonates with possibility. It suggests the vigilance essential to survival in the wild. Synapses, reflexes, interpretation, assessment and movement response are all activated, bringing an alertness underemployed in the urban environment where food can be bought and danger takes other forms. The wanderer is privileged in this alertness. Not reliant on it to survive, the wanderer can tune it to pure attention, immersing in signals and their potential in the moment of their emerging rather than speculating on the events they might cause. The wanderer is lost, removed from past and future, attentive to the potential that is in the moment.

Rebecca Solnit cites Benjamin in support of her proposal that intense attention is requisite for being lost. She suggests that "to be lost is to be fully present, and to be fully present is to be capable of being in uncertainty" (Solnit 2005: 6), proffering a compound of attention, being present in the present, and not knowing as an exquisitely alive state of not-yet.[4] To dance improvisers the not-yet is familiar as the place of not knowing or disorientation. It can be a micro-moment in a specific movement or a perceived pause or cessation of movement. We feel suspended; being, but not doing. We might respond by covering it over, filling it or ignoring it. Alternatively we could resist this first impulse, wait[5] for the next and prolong the interval. Or, as Nancy Stark Smith suggests, simply allow its potential to emerge, "bring attention and charge to a moment that would have passed without remark: ... Where you are when you don't know where you are is one of the most precious spots offered by improvisation. It is a place from which more directions are possible than anywhere else. I call this place 'the Gap'" (Nelson & Stark Smith 1997: 113). Stark Smith's 'Gap' could be seen as a crystallisation of the state of being lost and as such, is the territory of the wanderer. She describes it as a momentary suspension of reference point. It is not one specific

4 In the summer of 2012 there were posters on London streets stating, "Not all those who wander are lost", using a quotation from J.R.R. Tolkein's *The Fellowship of the Ring* that implies there may be something undesirable about being lost. Each time I saw one I felt confronted, as not only was I convinced by Solnit that being lost is fundamental to being alive to our world, but also had begun to suspect that wandering might be the route to being lost, that being present is a condition of being lost, rather than a strategy to avoid being lost. Continually wandering we are lost, and further, only in wandering are we living with attention to our present.

5 Jan Masschelein reminds us that the French root of attention is 'attendre', that is, to wait, thus attention entails a suspension of judgement and implies a kind of waiting (2010: 282). And the nomad: "he who does not move", "knows how to wait" (Deleuze & Guattari 1987: 420).

place, or sensation, or thing, or duration. Rather it is incorporeal, infinite and vibrating with potential.

Steve Paxton's *Small Dance of Standing Still* offers us somatic access to 'the Gap', by enabling us to allow our attention to wander and to follow our wandering attention. His early movement explorations were of gravity and falling, revealing a gap in consciousness as we are physically suspended or falling. He suggested that this gap occurs during unexpected movement, when the movement happens too fast for consciousness, and the reflexes step in. Through Contact Improvisation[6] he sought to construct a working model that would encourage being alive to the experience of moving, even in moments of disorientation. Analytic, rationalising perhaps, but his observations and methodologies foreground the role of intense attention to moving whilst moving. The video *'Fall after Newton'* (1979) was made in part as a tool to examine the gap, its nature, and patterns of occurrence. To an extent Paxton was working to eliminate the gap in order to integrate full consciousness with the body's movement and utilise its full potential, to harness disorientation, but in the process eradicate it. For Nancy Stark Smith on the other hand, 'the Gap' became something to embrace. She recognised 'the Gap' as a space of potential, and bringing full attention to 'the Gap' a means of moving in that potential. She found that in the disorientation of 'the Gap' something unpredictable, non-habitual could appear. 'The Gap' itself brings forth change.

16th September 2013

> *A dance of attending the small reflexive movements of the body as it is standing still, relaxed. Eyes closed, attending the experience of a body as with the least possible effort it responds to the force of gravity yet remains upright. It opens to the world as the world opens, changing with the world as it is changing. As attention flickers through the body there is a sense of its substance fragmenting, micro-movements magnified, a feeling of disorientation. Sensing the small movements of tissues around the skeleton in a search for equilibrium. Relax, breathe, sense the length of your spine, the skull in suspension, the direction of your fingers falling. What could be the smallest fall? The smallest stretch, the smallest release. And for a moment imagine you are taking a step with your right foot. Don't take it, just imagine. Take another with your left, with your right. Still standing. Outside the studio, in a park, small dance tunes attention equally to the air on skin, sounds, scents, motion around us. We merge, meet our environment. And for moments, wandering through this experience, oscillating between internal and external sensation, our attention straying, deviating, retracing, we are suspended, uncertain, precarious, waiting, in 'the Gap'.*

'The Gap' between moment and moment, experience and experience, internal external, between, suspended, waiting, pre-aim, incipient, still, moving. And in the exquisite experience of the 'not yet' in the tension between the past and the possible, in the disorientation of 'the Gap', something unpredictable, non-habitual will appear.

Early in this enquiry, before I began writing, I searched for a concept of wandering, not as a metaphor for dance improvisation or a choreographic structure, but as an

6 "Contact Improvisation is a dance form, originated by American choreographer Steve Paxton in 1972, based on the communication between two or more moving bodies that are in physical contact and their combined relationship to the physical laws that govern their motion – gravity, momentum, inertia." (Contact Improvisation UK) - see website for more information.

image to resonate with the experience of dancers who wander and who write. In the world of plants, wandering is considered to be the sending out of adventitious roots. It is an opportunistic, variable, expansive process. Unexpected roots are generated through alliance with the specific conditions of the environment, moving and extending in the in-between.A rhizome is an underground stem that does exactly this. A rhizome is a living system of processes. It doesn't have a specific form, but manifests as bulbs, tubers or mats. Nor is rhizomatic manifestation pre-determined. It will develop in response to the opportunities and setbacks of its environment. It exists through relationship. Yet in itself it has the potential for continual movement and growth. If you rupture or break it apart, a rhizome will offshoot, not grow back into its previous form. Although subterranean, it is not a root, but rather a stem, hence 'middle'. Things flow through it as it moves through the earth. Not itself an organ of reproduction, it generates spurs, stems and filaments, forming a mesh of relating segments spreading through their environment. The rhizome nourishes and is nourished by its offshoots. It is multi-directional, multilayered and alive with potential. It is nomadic, but is it a wanderer? Conceptually the rhizome emerges from the collective thinking of Gilles Deleuze and Felix Guattarri as an image of multiplicity, movement, relationship, not-yet, potential and transformation, based on a life process.

> A rhizome has no beginning or end; it is always in the middle, interbeing, intermezzo...the rhizome is alliance, uniquely alliance ... the fabric of the rhizome is the conjunction, 'and ... and ... and ...' This conjunction carries enough force to shake and uproot the verb 'to be'. Where are you going? Where are you coming from? What are you heading for? These are totally useless questions. (Deleuze & Guattari 1987: 28)

Rhizome is an image that resonates with somatic enquiry, but rather than becoming a way of conceptualising or mapping wandering, it seems that the assemblage of written thoughts and physical experience of wandering has offered insight to the concept of rhizome. I have found that wandering is not a mode of moving but may be understood as a continual and palpable underscore to movement; wandering attention allows us to experience the not-yet of 'the Gap'; the quality of wandering initiates the gap, bringing attention to the generative possibilities of incipient movement. Through wandering I perceive rhizome not as a fixed concept but a living quality that brings attention to the generative potential of incipient concept. Maybe. But how does rhizome matter in the context of somatic practice?

Perhaps it opens the possibility that in wandering, in attending the gap, we are not solely generating movement but generating concepts. Perhaps it opens us to the possibility that, like dance improvisation, concepts are moving, in process, are relational and transient. And maybe through the lived experience of dancing we might understand the rhizome and its implications for what thinking dance might be. I imagine a score of concepts generated and departing through performance; a score of the gap, not knowing and not yet, no starting or ending, no time frames for tasks, and no hierarchy of material or performer. Dancers moving-with their world. Waiting, attentive to the potential of the present. Movement becoming. A dance not defined by points or positions or links between them, but composed only of lines, lines of "segmentation" and "stratification" and "lines of flight", leaking, flowing, seeping into the world – movement in itself, or lines of becoming (Deleuze & Guattari 1987).

My attention is wandering and my wandering attends to my body's attention as it wanders.

References

Benjamin, W. (1955-72/1978) *Reflections: Essays, Aphorisms, Autobiographical Writings,* (ed. P. Demetz; trans. E. Jephcott), Schocken Books

Careri, F. (2002) *Walkscapes. Walking as an aesthetic Practice,* Editorial Gustavo Gili

Certeau, M. de (1984) *The Practice of Everyday Life,* University of California Press

Contact Improvisation UK (n.d.) http://bit.ly/tpMove86

Deleuze, G. & Guattari, F. (1987) *A Thousand Plateaus: Capitalism and Schizophrenia.* (trans. B. Massumi) Athlone Press

_______ (1994) *What is Philosophy?* (trans. Columbia University Press) Verso

Heddon, D., & Klein, J. (eds.) (2012) *Histories and Practices of Live Art,* Palgrave Macmillan

Herbert, T. (1634) *A relation of some yeares travaile, begunne anno 1626 : Into Afrique and the greater Asia,* William Stansby and Jacob Bloome

Ingold, T. (2011) *Being Alive: Essays on Movement, Knowledge and Description,* Routledge

Johnstone, S. (ed.)(2008) *The Everyday: Documents of Contemporary Art,* Whitechapel and MIT Press

Kaufmann, V. (2008) 'The Poetics of the Dérive' in *The Everyday: Documents of Contemporary Art* (ed. S. Johnstone) pp. 95-102 Whitechapel and MIT Press

Manning, E. (2009) *Relationscapes: Movement, Art, Philosophy,* MIT Press

Masschelein, J. (2010) 'The idea of critical e-ducational research: e-ducating the gaze and inviting to go walking' in *The Possibility/Impossibility of a New Critical Language in Education* (ed. I. Gurzeev) pp. 275-291, Sense Publishers

Nelson, L. & Stark Smith, N. (eds.) (1997), *Contact Improvisation Sourcebook,* Contact Editions

Oxford English Dictionary, 2nd ed. (1989) Clarendon Press

Perrin, J. 'Against the Erosion of Gesture and Gaze', *Cairon – Revista de estudios de danza – Journal of dance studies, n° 12 Cuerpo y arquitectura / Body and Architecture* (2009) pp. 272-282 http://bit.ly/tpMove23

Solnit, R. (2005) *A Field Guide to Getting Lost,* Canongate Books

SALLY E. DEAN

Amerta Movement and Somatic Costume

Gateways into Environment

The approach and the methodologies of the *Somatic Movement and Costume Project* led by me, Sally E. Dean, in collaboration with founding costume designers/visual artists Sandra Arróniz Lacunza and Carolina Rieckhof (2011-2015), has been influenced by Suprapto Suryodarmo's Amerta Movement practice. In this chapter, I begin with an overview of the *Somatic Movement and Costume Project*, to include its ongoing developments, with reference to the importance of positioning it in a social-cultural context. A social-cultural 'framing' of clothing, body and senses is briefly discussed, along with our reasons for taking a multi-sensorial and haptic approach. The value of this social-cultural lens comes from the Amerta Movement practice itself – an approach inspired by Suprapto's Central Javanese roots and his work with Westerners for over 25 years. Next, I focus on one key influence of Amerta Movement on the project: its relationship to environment;[1] in particular Suprapto's approach called 'Fact/Fiction' or 'Reality-world/Dream-world' and his 'state of flux' attitude. Examples from my Middlesex University Artist Residency in 2012 and the 'Here and There' participatory performance at the Dance and Somatic Practices Conference in 2013 demonstrate how somatic costumes act as gateways into new embodied relationships to the environment.

The Somatic Movement and Costume Project

How does what we wear affect how we move and perceive and what we create and perform?

The aim of the project is to create a process, practice, methodology – to include

1 I use 'environment' to refer to the surroundings (the place) as well as the conditions (in-flux, changing circumstances operating in the environment, such as weather, temperature, etc. with reference to 'time'). In this chapter I include 'geographical location', 'site' and 'nature' in the term 'environment'. Our 'environment' is part of and influenced by our social-cultural context.

approach and attitude – whereby costumes act as a somatic resource into multi-sensorial experiences for moving, creating, teaching, performing and being.

Following Thomas Hanna (1988), I use the term 'somatic' to refer to bodily practices and perspectives on embodiment that give attention and value to the subjective experiencing of the whole self and its perceptions, and that emphasise the role of the body in that experiencing. My somatic movement approach adds to this definition by giving attention and value not only to the subjective experiences of participants, but also the objective experiences – following the Amerta Movement methodology of 'Fact/Fiction' or 'Reality-world/Dream-world', to be discussed later in this chapter.

The original key research questions were: How can we create, design and choose costumes that generate specific body-mind experiences and support new and enhanced kinaesthetic awareness? How can these 'somatic costumes' shed new light on socio-culturally informed psycho-physical habits, to offer new ways of moving, being and performing? Although all senses are important, we typically start with the sense of touch or the haptic sense[2] (to include the tactile, the kinaesthetic[3] or kinaesthetic body consciousness'[4] and proprioceptive senses).

Fig. 1: 'Pointy Hats' worn by Kate Pyper, Carolina Rieckhof, Shantala Melody Sacco, and Rachel Gildea. Still from *You're Not Supposed To Be Here 2*, filmed and edited by Sergio M. Villar, directed by Sally E. Dean, with idea and concept in collaboration with Sandra Arróniz Lacunza and Carolina Rieckhof.

2 The haptic sense is our sense of touch and implies a participant's active engagement in the experience (Grunwald 2008: vii). The haptic sense receives sensory information from two sensory receptors: our mechanoreceptors (responding to mechanical pressure or distortion) and thermoreceptors (responding to changes in temperature). These receptors can be found both on the skin (cutaneous inputs) as well as in our muscles, tendons and joints (kinaesthetic inputs) (Lederman & Klatsky 2009: 1).

3 The kinaesthetic sense is our perception of the body and its movements. The material, texture, weight, form, movement of the somatic costume itself typically creates a direct and tactile kinaesthetic experience for the wearer. For example, if the costume is heavy, the person will experience a 'heaviness' in their body.

4 "'Kinesthetic body consciousness' is awareness of the body's movement, position, and level of muscular tension. It is achieved through perception of muscle and joint movements and through the senses, primarily the tactual; the auditory is also frequently involved, and all of the senses can play a part" (Storm 1987: 306).

Over the past three years, the *Somatic Movement and Costume Project* has included a series of workshops, performances, lecture/demonstrations, a film and published articles. Twelve prototype costumes were created and performances have often been site-specific with the audience becoming active participants through wearing the costumes themselves.

Significance of the Research

Although costume has been incorporated in performance for centuries, this research argues for a critical social-cultural 'paradigm shift': the aesthetic and movement of the performance work comes from the somatic experiences (haptic and sensorial) of the costume, rather than the costumes being designed to enhance an aesthetic already established in advance. The visually dominated performance approach to costume is replaced by an experience of costume as a multi-sensorial experience. My research aims to shift Western ocular-centrism and re-balance our 'sensorial hierarchy' (Classen 1993) by starting with the multi-sensorial experiences and the haptic sense – the experience that the costume generates while wearing it. In doing so, I aim to shift the value of costume beyond the 'aesthetic' to utilise its resource for body-mind awareness and social-cultural understanding – reprogramming our body schema[5] and body image[6]. Somatic costumes have the potential to change our relationships to ourselves, others and to the world around us – our environment.

Costume has been underutilised as a resource for somatic practices, performance making, performance training, fashion and therapeutic/health research. My research aims to create bridges and new knowledge in all of these fields. I aim to create new methodological approaches for somatic movement education and performance making; to shed new light on socio-culturally informed psycho-physical habits; and to offer new ways of moving, being and performing.

Somatic Movement and Costume Project: Background

The initial impetus for this project came from my experience of living in Java in 2007-08, practising Amerta Movement and witnessing and learning traditional Javanese dance forms. I noticed a quality of 'containment' in the movement of many Javanese people, both in daily life and in dancing and performing, which I could clearly see and sense, but found I was unable to embody for myself – until I tried on the traditional Javanese dance costume. The costume itself created a kinaesthetic experience of 'containment' in the mid to lower body: a *kain*, a long cloth tightly wrapped around

5 Gallagher defines *body schema* as "a system of sensory-motor capacities that function without awareness or the necessity of perceptual monitoring" (2005: 24). Blakeslee & Blakeslee define body schema as the physiological construct that your brain creates "from the interaction of touch, vision, proprioception, balance, and hearing. It even extends it out into the space around your body. You use it to help locate objects in space or on your body" (2007: 32).

6 Gallagher defines body image as follows: "A *body image* consists of a system of perceptions, attitudes, and beliefs pertaining to one's own body" (2005: 24). Body image includes the terms of body percept, body concept and body affect. Blakeslee & Blakeslee define body image as "the psychological construct that includes learned attitudes, expectations, assumptions and beliefs about yourself, your body, others, the environment and the world" (2007: 42). Body image is also highly influenced by the social and cultural context from which you came: "It is about your attitudes toward those traits in yourself, your emotional response to how you experience your body, including how you dress, pose, move, and believe others see you" (*Ibid*: 39).

the lower body, held in place by a *stagen,* a cloth wrapped around the lower half of the torso. The costume helped me to find an experiential understanding of the feeling state of 'containment' inherent in the movement I was seeing around me (Dean 2011).

Suprapto also uses the term 'Clothing' as part of his movement practice – as both a functional and symbolic element in his work. This planted seeds, in my own practice, of how one's clothing affects one's movement.

This experience inspired new reflections on the role of costume in work as a performer, dance/theatre-maker and teacher. I began to wonder how costumes could act as 'portals of perception' supporting people to find gestures and movement qualities that might otherwise be missing from their repertoire.

What is a 'Somatic Costume'?

'Somatic costumes' offer intentional sensorial experiences. They are designed to bring awareness to different areas of, and qualities in, the body, as well as to support the understanding of certain movement principles in relationship to self, other and the environment. For example, we created two prototype somatic costumes for the pelvis: the Hula Hoop Skirt and the Bin Bag Skirt. For these costumes, the theme was weight – the Hula Hoop Skirt is designed to give a sense of weight and orientation towards the ground, while the Bin Bag Skirt is intended to create experiences of lightness and orientation towards space and sky.

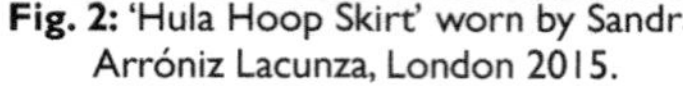

Fig. 2: 'Hula Hoop Skirt' worn by Sandra Arróniz Lacunza, London 2015.

Fig. 3: 'Bin Bag Skirt' worn by Iris Chan in London, photo shoot, June 2014.

Somatic Movement and Costume exercises support the experience of these costumes in relationship not only to self, but also to others and the environment: "Follow your Pointy Hat or Balloon Hat to a moment of interaction with the environment – perhaps your Hat touches the wall, or the floor, or even another person. What can you sense through your hat? ... How do you greet your partner from afar in this costume?" (*Somatic Movement and Costume Workshop* notes, 2011).

The somatic costumes are embedded with multi-sensorial experiences which interweave and feed the perceptions of the participants. Although we often start with the haptic sense, which is experienced primarily through the tactual, all senses may participate. We have 'multi-sensory neurons' which allow sensations to overlap: "What you feel with your body literally shapes what you hear" (Blakeslee & Blakeslee 2007: 117) and "You will see something faster if it also makes a noise ... What you hear influences what you feel" (*Ibid*: 116).

This project both incorporates the multi-sensorial experiences involved in wearing different kinds of costumes, and also intentionally influences and enhances these experiences by the use of selected somatic exercises.[7] Somatic costumes are worn before, during, and after somatic exercises.

The experience of wearing somatic costumes is intentionally influenced and enhanced through three different sensorial capacities:

- working with the inherent multi-sensorial experiences that come from the costume itself
- removing a sense (e.g. vision – especially important in the West to remove because the visual sense often leads or dominates the experience of other senses)
- adding multi-sensorial stimulation (sensations not coming from the original costume itself, but from outside).

Experiences in Relationship to Self, Others and Environment

These somatic costumes and their multi-sensorial experiences change our relationship to the self, others and the environment. For example, we added multi-sensorial stimulation to direct and heighten the experience of the participants' sense of sound (both inside and outside the body) in one of the *Somatic Movement and Costume Workshops* (Independent Dance, Siobhan Davies Dance Studio, 2011). We also wanted to experiment with the concept of 'multi-sensorial neurons' – how sensory experiences overlap and support each other. Could the kinaesthetic experience we aimed to facilitate through the somatic costume be heightened or clarified with the sense of sound? How does adding sound to the somatic costumes change our relationship to ourselves, others and the environment? We experimented with adding materials that create sound to our original prototype somatic costumes, as well as adding a live musician to the environment of the workshop.

For example, the aim of the Pointy Hat was to give the experience of the "direction of the skull in space as a development of the spine as an axis" (Dean 2011: 173).

With this costume, although many participants experience their sense of verticality, participants often spoke about not knowing where the end of the hat was located in

7 Somatic exercises, applied to *The Somatic Movement and Costume Project*, are put together from my background in some of the following somatic practices: Skinner Releasing Technique (to include the teachings of Stephanie Skura), Amerta Movement (to include the teachings of Helen Poynor) and Scaravelli Yoga (as taught by Giovanni Felicioni). For example, I use an adaptation of the Skinner Releasing partner exercise of 'cradling the skull' from class 6 to bring into awareness the weight and buoyancy of the skull and its connection to the spine before putting on the Balloon Hats.

the space above them, except when it made contact with others and the environment. We added a bell to the top of the Pointy Hat to support participants in sensing the location of the end of the hat, without touch or contact, but through sound. Interestingly, this bell also added another layer of potential interaction between those wearing Pointy Hats – they could respond and communicate with each other at different locations in the space through ringing their bell by moving their head, and this created many playful movement exchanges. The added bell changed participants' relationships with each other – before the bells were added, the Pointy Hat created more of an isolated, lonely experience for participants, and when interaction was initiated, it had typically been combative – poking each other with the Pointy Hats, etc (Participants' notes Workshop 2, 2011 and my notes 2011 and 2014).

Live musician Esbjörn Wettermark also played music inspired from his sensorial experience of wearing the somatic costumes in the workshop (Siobhan Davies Dance Studios 2011). For example, we began with such questions as: what musical instruments and sounds shall I use to translate my experience of wearing Lentil Socks? How can sound support the experience of awakening "the sensitivity and responsiveness of the feet, and through them the whole body, to the texture of the ground"? (Dean 2011: 173). Wettermark chose a variety of wind instruments to play while wearing Lentil Socks, creating cyclical, spiralling sounds that added a somewhat meditative and grounding quality to the atmosphere and to the participants' movements. As a teacher, although participants continued to follow the sensorial experiences coming from the somatic costume – many began to follow the sound coming from Wettermark's music more than the sensorial experiences generated by the somatic costume.

Sensorial experiences generated by the costume are powerful – if we change one element, such as by adding a bell, the experience of the somatic costume can drastically change one's experience of oneself, others and the environment. The environment itself also changes the experience of the somatic costumes – as we saw above with Wettermark's music. Somatic costumes are always in relationship to, and experienced through, a changing context.

Although I often choose to direct and enhance certain multi-sensorial experiences through specific somatic costumes, somatic exercises and sensorial capacities, no two participants' experiences are exactly alike. Participants' experiences are costume-specific, person-specific, site-specific and social-culture-specific.

Context of Clothing – Social Cultural

Numerous theories of the functions of 'dress' range from addressing intrinsic, communicative, psychological, physiological and social-cultural factors. From adornment to utility and protection, to status and roles, to social class, economics and group dynamics, clothing is an integral, intrinsic, inseparable element in our lives. As Penny Storm says, clothing is the "key to the individual and his or her society" (1987: 335) – revealing the essential beliefs, values and attitudes of both. What we wear is part of our "social construction of reality" (Berger & Luckmann 1967).

Mass societal values are represented and revealed in the clothing and costumes worn. The long skirts and dresses of Martha Graham, the simple shirts and trousers worn by Trisha Brown Company, and the mechanistic costumes of Schlemmer all reveal the values of a specific time and culture. Even today in dance training in universities, the type of clothing worn by students is influenced by the fashion of the day.

By emphasising the social-cultural influence on clothing, I open an alternative approach to costume: choosing costumes based on the awareness of 'value' (attitudes, beliefs, principles) and context. Does my value reflect a mainstream or 'counter-cultural' approach?

The Multi-Sensorial Body

I approach the body as multi-sensorial, i.e. through the lens of the somatic, cultural and ecological body, as defined by Sandra Reeve in *Nine Ways of Seeing A Body*.

The senses are a gateway for meaning and knowledge. Starting from the "somatic body" (Reeve 2011: 17–22), the senses are key to experiencing and accessing the "materiality of the body" as well as an "interface between body and mind" (Grau 2011: 8) and an interface between the interiority of the body and the external world. Sensation, the basis of the somatic body, implies a relationship between an organism and its environment (Schiffman 1996: 2). Sensation leads to perception of ourselves, others, and the world around us.

Scholars in the field of the anthropology of the senses, such as Constance Classen (1993), Paul Stoller (1997), David Howes (2005), Tim Ingold, Kathyrn Geurts, Michael Jackson and Caroline Potter (2008) have reasserted the primacy of the senses and have emphasised their potential as a resource in researching and understanding other cultures: "Senses are both the shapers and bearers of culture" (Howes 2005: 17). *The Somatic Movement and Costume Project* comes from the view of the "cultural and ecological body" (Reeve 2011) which approaches the body in relationship to its environment and context – "situated in flux, participation and change" (*Ibid*: 51) – connecting body, movement, environment and others through "embodied states of 'interbeing'" (*Ibid*: 51).

Sensory models are not universal in different cultures and throughout history. The number of senses, how senses are ranked and prioritised – even the definition of 'sense' – is dependent upon history and culture. Although Western society today typically follows the Aristotelian sensory model of five senses (touch, smell, taste, hearing, vision), with a prioritisation of vision, historically there were other classifications.[8]

Sensory categories, models and ranking affect how we value and perceive the world. For instance, in Buddhist cultures the mind is classified as a sixth sense. In other cultures, each sense is not linked necessarily to a specific organ in the body. For example, for Suprapto, there were at least two ways of experiencing sound: the sense of 'hearing' with the ears and the sense of 'listening' with the whole body (my Indonesia Journal, 2007).

Sensorial ranking is also culturally specific. Anthropologist Constance Classen found that the Ongee of the Andaman Islands in the South Pacific live in a world ordered by smell. For the Ongee, "odour is the vital force of the universe and the

8 For example, Plato did not separate senses from feelings; in "one enumeration of perceptions he begins with sight, hearing and smell, leaves out taste, instead of touch mentions perceptions of hot and cold, and adds sensations of pleasure, discomfort, desire, and fear" (Classen 1993: 2).

basis of personal and social identity. Therefore, when an Ongee wishes to refer to 'me,' he or she points to his or her nose, the organ of smell" (Classen 1993: 1). A culture's sensory ordering is not just a theoretical construction, but affects how its people live, how they see their world, and what they value: "The sensory order, in fact, is not just something one sees or hears about; it is something one *lives*" (Howes 2005: 3).

The effects of a culture's relationship with, and social-cultural construction of, sensation cannot be underestimated. It frames the social and intellectual aspects of culture – including how we make and experience movement, performance and art. In the West today the visual, in dance, theatre and the visual arts, still dominates. As Classen says: "It would never occur to the ordinary Westerner ... in a museum that meaning might lie not only in its form and function, but also in its texture, taste, and smell" (1993: 136). The term multi-sensorial body then implies that all sensory experiences, categories, rankings, descriptions in the great variety of historical and cultural landscapes are included.

Sense of Touch – the Haptic System

The Somatic Movement and Costume Project begins with the sense of touch – the haptic system. At the same time, we are coming from a multi-sensorial body and the perspective that all senses are interconnected and interrelated. Although we start with the sense of touch, in the process of the somatic costume experience (from designing the costumes, to teaching, to moving, to performing), we are simultaneously attending to and open to other senses – to include other sense organs, sensory modalities, sensory rankings and sensory classifications.

I start with the sense of touch, the haptic system, for many reasons. First, because in dance and physical performance, touch is central to experiences, learning, knowledge and the creation process. Second, the haptic sense has an inherent relational and multi-sensorial approach; its multi-sensorial modes enable us to perceive "weight, pressure, balance, temperature, vibration and presence" (Fisher 1997: 2). Third, the haptic sense also implicates the body's proximal and distal sense – linking in our experience both the interiority of the body and the environment around us. Fourth, the haptic system, in the visually dominated Western culture, has been the least researched. This lack of research is also due to the complex role that touch plays as a result of being inherently multi-sensorial, with various theories about how the nervous system makes sense of the information arising from touch (Scharf 1975: 178). Scholars tend to approach touch from a visual framework although visual versus touch sensorial processes can be quite different. Finally, 'haptic' implies intentionality, engagement, action and movement – where the body is active in its explorations and experiences in the world. An active changing participant is responding to an active changing environment/context. I apply this 'haptic' approach directly to the somatic costume performances and to the workshop experience – where participants become active in their engagement with the work, as opposed to passive receivers.

Haptic, active touch is the doorway into how we become aware of our surroundings and our sense of self. In "this way, the sense of touch is sine qua non for thought, action, and consciousness" (Grunwald 2008: vii). It is through touch that we come to understand ourselves, others and the world around us.

Body Schema and Body Image

My view of body image and body schema also comes from viewing the body as multi-sensorial. To define the terms body image and body schema, I incorporate definitions derived from Gallagher's phenomenological approach (2005) along with the functional neuro-scientific/neuro-psychological approach of Blakeslee & Blakeslee (2007) – see footnotes 5 and 6 in this chapter. My view is that body image is in interaction with its social-cultural environment, and cannot be separate from space and its surroundings. The body's "[interactional] intentionality" (Gendlin 1992: 343) is always with us. This approach is different from Gallagher's definition of body image, where: body image "is distinguished from the environment" (de Vignemont 2006: 2) and as Isabelle Gionot further emphasises in her analysis of Gallagher's work, "body image is only concerned with one's own body, and therefore separates itself from space and surroundings" (Gionot 2011: 157).

By including the social-cultural environment within the definition of body image, we allow knowledge to arise, not simply about our bodies, but also about others and the environment. As somatic practitioners, do we typically propose creating a somatic practice that helps us understand the experiences of others or of another culture? Not all, but many, somatic practices focus on self-awareness of our bodies as a starting point. But costume, embedded as it is with social-cultural values, and if approached as a multi-sensorial experience with a multi-sensorial body, has the potential for social-cultural awareness. For example, as one participant in a somatic movement and costume workshop described, "Wearing the wrap-around skirt and belt finally I understood why many Japanese, Indonesian, women move in the way that I have so often seen. Of course, so much is a part of the clothing! I noticed with the skirt it helped me pay more attention to the vertical space/length, especially from my hips to my feet and how the movement when walking travels through the leg [*sic*]." (*Somatic Movement and Costume Workshop 2014*). This participant was reflecting both on her own body awareness and that of another culture.

Functionally, the experience of our bodies is integrated – body image and body schema are interacting and overlapping all the time. Body schema responds to body image and vice-versa. Even before we move, a "pre-movement" (Frank 2003) occurs, during which we respond to our past experiences and our social-cultural beliefs and contexts about our bodies, ourselves, the world, and each other. For example, a person from Indonesia who sees a dog might see food and feel hungry, but a European might see a pet and feel love. Someone who has been attacked by a dog might see danger and feel fear. Our body schema will prepare itself to move and act physically according to our individual beliefs and context.

What is Amerta Movement?

Amerta Movement was first developed in the 1970s by Javanese movement artist Suprapto Suryodarmo. Amerta Movement is a form of non-stylised movement practice that draws on Vipassanā meditation, Javanese Sumarah meditation, Javanese Theravada Buddhism and the basic movements of daily life: of walking, sitting, standing, etc. The environment, to include nature and site, are key elements in the creation and the practice of Amerta Movement.

The Approach: *Designing and Selecting Sites for Somatic Experiences*

In Suprapto's approach the choice of site depends not only on the intent of the course, but also on the needs of the group and its individuals.

Movement practice is conducted in the workshops in relationship to the environment and nature and takes place in historic Javanese sites and temples around Central Java and Bali (e.g. Borobudur, Candi Sukuh, Candi Cetho, Boko Palace and Goa Gajah), as well as Suprapto's movement-practice garden called Lemah Putih. Lemah Putih has specific practice-areas designed by Suprapto, each with a different feel and function, often inspired by the land itself or by sacred sites in the region (e.g. the Buddhist temple of Borobudur) or by Suprapto's own cultural heritage (e.g. the pendopo).

> "For example, the 'Mandala' site is an unroofed octagonal, concrete stage, with tall white trees standing at each corner, rising into the air where they seem to open to the sky. He calls this site 'nature's stage', and relates it to prayer, healing and purification". (Dean 2009)

Fig. 4: 'Lemah Putih' - Suprapto Suryodarmo's movement practice garden in Plesungan village, Central Java, Indonesia.

Although 'site-specific' was not an unfamiliar term to me, the concept of selecting and designing intentional sites to learn from was new. This led me to question how I could create intentional costumes to learn from, and how the costume itself could invite and inhabit certain movement practices and experiences.

Fig. 5: 'Mandala Site' at Lemah Putih - Suprapto Suryodarmo's movement practice garden in Plesungan village, Central Java, Indonesia.

The Attitude...

Environment as collaborator: One attitude inherent in Amerta movement is that sites and nature are not just locations, destinations or dead matter – they have lives of their own. Similar to animistic cultures, the environment exists both in the material and spiritual realm. The environment is a collaborator, guide, and co-creator in my movement practice and experience. This attitude is reflected in my somatic movement and costume workshops. In one of the exercises the costume itself becomes the 'Invisible Director' and we follow it as guide, allowing it to move and direct us.

Environment 'in flux': Amerta movement gives value to the body in a 'state of flux' or change – what Sandra Reeve refers to as an aspect of the 'ecological body' – a body that "experiences its changing self as a changing system among other environmental systems" (2011: 2). As with an ecological body, *The Somatic Movement and Costume Project* has begun cultivating this way of perceiving and interacting with the costume as an 'ecological costume'.[9] The *In Flux Costume Creation Exercise*,[10] for workshops, includes the practice of working with a moving, changing body in relationship to a moving/changing costume.

9 The 'ecological body' is defined by Reeve (2011: 2) as a 'body-in-movement-in-a-changing-environment' (*Ibid*: 48). I apply this terminology to my definition of 'ecological costume' - where the costume is a 'costume-in-movement-in-a-changing-environment'. The costume is viewed and approached as being in a 'state of flux' and in relationship to (and interaction with) the wider environmental context.

10 In the *In Flux Costume Creation Exercise*: Person A moves and now and then has moments of stillness. Person B creates a costume with simple materials (e.g. trash bags, tape) on A as well as having moments of stillness witnessing or 'reflecting' A's movement. B is encouraged to create the costume in response to A's moving body. A is encouraged to move in response to the changes of the costume and the effects they have on their body and their relationship to their environment.

Environment as body: Another attitude of Amerta is that we embody the sites that we live in and come from. During my time in Java in 2007–2008, my journal reveals this experience: Suprapto asked me when I was moving, "Why do you take the box with you?" Having lived and moved most of my life in 'square-shaped' spaces, I unconsciously took this way of responding to site with me – even if in an oval or circular space. Site was like a body – with its own body-image and body schema inherent in it. When site and body move together our body-images and body schemas meet, and a dialogue unfolds. This led me to the *Somatic Movement and Costume Project* question: How does our own clothing, in the same way as site, reveal our own body-images and body schemas, as well as invite us into new physical gestures, body attitudes and new places of embodiment?

The Methodology: *The World of Fact/Fiction or Reality/Dream*

One of Amerta movement's key methodologies in working within an environment is what Suprapto calls: the world of Fact/Fiction or Reality-world/Dream-world. 'Fiction' refers to "the imagination, the symbol" while 'Fact' refers to "the concrete". Fact typically encompasses objective experiences while Fiction does not mean that the experiences are untrue, but instead enter the terrain of the subjective (my Indonesia Journal, 2008).

In general, when approaching a site (or even an object or person), we can consider both its Facts (the function, colours, texture, orientation, location, structure, weight, size, shape, time, etc.) as well as its Fictions (associations, meanings, imagery, metaphors, feelings, stories, characters, etc.).

Suprapto's work with environment and site embodies both approaches of Fact and Fiction. The Amerta Movement practices might direct a functional relationship to site or a metaphorical relationship to site often influenced by Suprapto's Central Javanese cultural heritage. For example, one of Suprapto's practice sites in Lemah Putih is the 'pendopo'. A pendopo is an architectural structure that has a roof but no walls, held up by pillars running from floor to roof.

Fig. 6: 'Pendopo' site, Java, Indonesia.

They are common ritual spaces in Solo, Java, and many of the classical Javanese dances are performed in pendopos. In one of Suprapto's movement exercises, we simply move from pillar to pillar in the pendopo – a seemingly functional exercise. But within the exercise, layers of meaning arise from the symbols and metaphors from Suprapto's cultural heritage. The centre of the pendopo is called the 'Saka[11] Guru'. 'Guru' means 'teacher' in the Indonesian language. The Saka Guru typically has four pillars. A pillar[12] is also referred to as a 'brother'[13]. In the centre of the pillars is the 'axis' – also referred to as 'the fifth brother' or what Suprapto calls "The source ... the nectar" (Interview with Suprapto, 2008). Pillars and the spaces between them exist in a state of flux and may be interpreted literally or metaphorically.

Somatic Costume as 'Site' – Fact and Fiction

Somatic costume is also a 'site' – a place where both Facts and Fictions are embedded, and either can be followed. The costume affects the wearer directly through the kinaesthetic sense – the material, texture, weight, form, and movement of the costume itself typically creates a direct and tactile experience. The multi-sensorial sensations from the costume are Facts because they result in the same sensations for each person who wears the costume (affecting our body schema). But the subjective experiences and associations are different and unique for each person – the Fictions (affecting our body image). For example, one person associates the Bin Bag skirt[14] with "wings flapping" and feels a sense of freedom, while another associates the Bin Bag skirt with the feeling of "suffocation" (Dean 2011: 179).

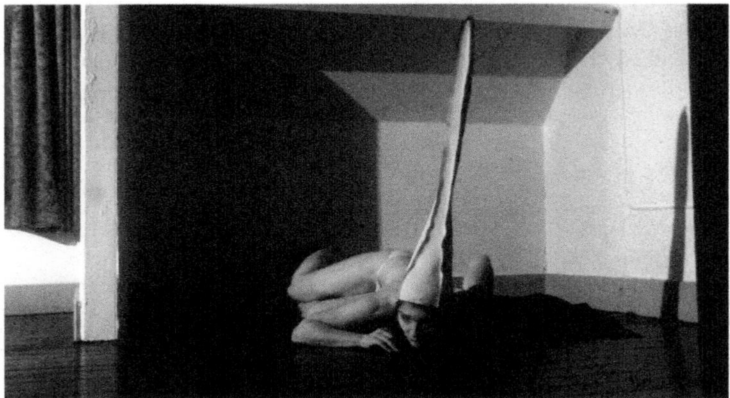

Fig. 7: 'Pointy Hat' worn by Sally E. Dean in *The Myth of the Porter's Mess Room* at Battersea Arts Centre, London, Oct. 2011.

11 'Saka' means 'wood vertical' and 'coming from' in the Javanese language (Suprapto, pers. comm., 7 Nov. 2013).

12 The 'pillar' is made from a tree. The tree is 'wit' in Javanese and 'begin' is 'wiwit'. Suprapto says it's like 'the tree of life' concept shared by many cultures (pers. comm., 7 Nov. 2013).

13 'Brother' is interchangeable with the word 'sister' (Suprapto, pers. comm., 7 Nov. 2013).

14 Bin Bag Skirt was a layered skirt composed of twelve to fifteen large black inflated bin bags attached with string to an elastic band wrapped around the pelvis at the hips (see Fig. 3, p.158).

In working with costume in the framework of Fact and Fiction, we can literally create a meeting or a dance between body schema and body image. In creating and performing 'The Myth of the Porter's Mess Room' (Battersea Arts Centre, London, 2011), a *Somatic Movement and Costume* performance, both approaches of Fact and Fiction were applied. For example, if I move with the Tall Pointy Hat costume following its sense of weight and direction in space, I am following the Fact. However, if I move with the costume of the Tall Pointy Hat, beginning by following my associations with it of the Ku Klux Klan or Dunce Cap, I am following the Fiction.

Somatic Costume and Relationship to Environment

As collaborators in our experiences, somatic costumes can change not only our relationship to ourselves and to others, but also our relationship to our environment. Neuroscientists reveal the important relationship that clothing has with the sense of self and the world around us through the body-mind. The discovery of "'peripersonal body space'[15] mapping" (Blakeslee 2007: 5) shows how the brain not only creates maps of your body, but also maps the space around you, to include other people and objects that you are in contact with. The self does not end where the skin ends – but blends with the world, others and objects.

One of the principles of Amerta Movement practice is that an unfamiliar or complex environment can evoke a new vocabulary of non-habitual movement, as compared to the way in which we may move in a familiar studio. In the participatory performance of 'Here and There' at the Dance and Somatic Practices Conference in 2013, the audience was taken through a journey of indoor and outdoor environments whilst wearing Pointy Hats. As the participants passed through corridors and stairways, their Pointy Hats would run into the indoor environment, creating an immediate relationship and interaction through restriction: the participants needed to adapt the movement of their bodies to fit the tall size of the hat to the relatively low ceilings of the Ellen Terry Building in which they were working.

Similarly, a new costume can turn a familiar environment into a strange one, changing one's embodied relationship with it and the way one moves in it. In the 'Here and There' participatory performance, some of the participants found that the verticality of the Pointy Hat supported them, sensing the verticality not only inside themselves, but also of the tall trees and the church spire in the surrounding environment:

> the word that came to my mind watching the cathedral tower was 'kinship' ... interesting also the reference to architecture in my senses, not just about the tower, but generally speaking about verticality. even this short amount of time changed the alignment of my cervical spine ... i was in awe on where 'vertical' actually is ...(really somewhere else than i thought!). the feeling stayed with me for several days ... [*sic*] (Note of participant Kerstin Kussmaul, 2013)

15 Peripersonal body space is the invisible, changing volume of space around the body that expands and contracts, depending upon one's actions and perceptions (Blakeslee 2007: 3-4).

This experience of verticality in the environment was an intentional choice. As the 'guide' of the indoor and outdoor expedition, I led participants to places outside with strong verticality (e.g. a park with tall trees). I repeatedly stopped and paused to look at the church spire, and concluded by taking the participants indoors to watch a film of other participants, wearing Pointy Hats, who travel to a vertical obelisk before disappearing. The Pointy Hat became a 'gateway' into understanding and connecting with the outdoor environment.

Fig. 8: 'Pointy Hat' worn by Sally E. Dean and Carolina Riekhof, Middlesex University Artist Residency, Trent Park Campus, London. Photo: Sandra Arróniz Lacunza. April 2012.

Somatic Costume as Gateway

I first began to explore the potential for costumes to act as gateways into natural environments during my artist residency at Middlesex University in 2012. Starting with the kinaesthetic sense of the body and the movement that the costumes evoke, how do we relate to the environment? Relationships of belonging and disjunction emerged.

On the first day we walked through the Trent Park campus wearing Pointy Hats, asking ourselves the following question, "where do these costumes belong in this natural environment?" We searched for places where the kinaesthetic experiences from the Pointy Hat seemed to parallel the experiences of the natural environment.

Fig. 9: 'Pointy Hat' worn by Sally E. Dean and Carolina Riekhof, Middlesex University Artist Residency, Trent Park Campus, London. Photo: Sandra Arróniz Lacunza. April 2012.

When we entered the forest we began to have the kinaesthetic sense that we were merging with the environment. Our movements became quite minimal – walking, standing, or kneeling, often with a sense of reverence, or making simple movements to reflect the direction of the tree limbs. We had a similar experience around some reed beds near water.

Fig. 10: 'Pointy Hat' worn by Sally E. Dean,
Middlesex University Artist Residency, Trent Park Campus, London.
Photo: Sandra Arróniz Lacunza. April 2012.

The most striking example was with the Pointy Hats and the obelisk (Figures 8 and 11). Moving with the Hats around the obelisk, a palpable physical sense of kinship with the monument emerged. Even the journey to the obelisk was similar to the Hat itself.

We followed a direct, straight path to the obelisk with a specific end point, similar to the form of the hat. I created a film from this experience and presented it as part of the 'Here and There' participatory performance at the Dance and Somatic Practices Conference in 2013.

Different costumes created different relationships and movements when worn in different environments. With the Balloon Hats, we found a feeling of disjunction from an environment full of daffodils (Figure 12). They are delicate flowers and I had to be careful not to step on the them – evoking a more delicate and minimal movement quality in the body – while the Balloon Hat itself, in contrast, evoked a bouncy quality. The environment that was more experientially like the Balloon Hat was the bouncy soft green grass (Figure 13).

Fig. 11: 'Pointy Hat' worn by Sandra Arróniz Lacunza, Middlesex University Artist Residency, Trent Park Campus, London. Photo: Carolina Rieckhof. April 2012.

Fig. 12: 'Balloon Hat' worn by Sally E. Dean,
Middlesex University Artist Residency, Trent Park Campus, London.
Photo: Sandra Arróniz Lacunza. April 2012.

The second discovery was made whilst we were creating site-specific costumes from the environment itself. We took the frame of the Hula Hoop skirt and covered it with tree branches that we had found lying on the ground. (Figure 14.) Wearing this Tree Skirt shifted the mover's sense of embodied relationship to the forest environment and stimulated new movement qualities that reflected this new relationship. The tree branches that we attached to the costume had a shaking and shuddering quality, which translated to the moving body. The somatic costume was mediating a two-way dialogue of influence and exchange between body and environment.

Another unexpected experience was that of having a new, embodied relationship to time and to change, i.e. to a state of flux. One day we worked with a see-through net as a costume covering my entire body (illustrated in Figure 15). This net costume was then used to mediate a collaborative relationship with an old umbrella that was half-sunken into the mud at the edge of the lake where we were working.

The sense of my feet sinking into the mud created an embodied resonance with the half-submerged, abandoned umbrella, and from there a palpable sense of the nature of appearance and disappearance, both in the body and the environment. This was enhanced by the awareness of my own semi-disappearance from the environment within the spider-web-like costume.

Fig. 13: 'Balloon Hat' worn by Sandra Arróniz Lacunza, Middlesex University Artist Residency, Trent Park Campus, London. Photo: Sally E. Dean. April 2012.

Fig. 14: 'Tree Skirt' worn by Sally E. Dean,
Middlesex University Artist Residency, Trent Park Campus, London.
Photo: Sandra Arróniz Lacunza. May 2012.

Fig. 15: 'Net' costume worn by Sally E. Dean, Middlesex University Artist Residency, Trent Park Campus, London. Photo: Carolina Rieckhof. May 2012.

More broadly, during the weeks we worked on the site we found that our heightened kinaesthetic relationship to the site, as mediated by the somatic costumes, gave us a deeper awareness of how the site was changing. When we returned to the umbrella after rain, it had completely submerged in water except for its outermost tip. The daffodils that were in the height of bloom when we began working had disappeared by the time we finished. Bare trees had come into bloom, or even begun to shed their pink plumage.

Fig. 16: 'Balloon Hat' worn by Sally E. Dean, Middlesex University Artist Residency, Trent Park Campus, London. Photo: Sandra Arróniz Lacunza. May 2012.

Fig. 17: 'Pointy Hats' on blossoming tree
at Middlesex University Artist Residency, Trent Park Campus, London.
Photo: Sandra Arróniz Lacunza. May 2012.

My experiences of time and flux in relationship to environment as mediated by the somatic costumes during my Middlesex Artist Residency were further developed in the 'Here and There' performance at Coventry University (Dance and Somatic Practice Conference 2013). In this participatory performance, the role of the somatic costume was to act as a gateway into two worlds: 'here' and 'there'.'

'Here' is a live moment where the audience follows a guided walk through the outdoor sites of Coventry. The intent is to cultivate 'the ecological lens', where participants are experiencing their relationship to themselves, others and the environment in a state of flux. The aim is that the perception of time will live in the present moment.

This contrasted with 'there' – a 'film moment'. After the walk, participants were invited into an enclosed indoor space where they stood and watched a film with Pointy Hats on. The intent was for participants to experience their relationship to themselves, others and the environment, in response to something fixed, i.e. the film. At the same time, the film became a portal into experiencing other living worlds or environments beyond the Coventry campus. The effect of exploring such experiences is that the perception of time refers to past and future. The film also acted as a bridge between 'here' and 'there' in that it continued the walking journey, but through the lens of a camera, with other individuals wearing the Pointy Hats on screen.

Fig. 18: 'Pointy Hats' worn by Kate Pyper, Carolina Rieckhof, Shantala Melody Sacco, and Rachel Gildea. Still from *You're Not Supposed To Be Here 2,* filmed and edited by Sergio M. Villar, directed by Sally E. Dean, with idea and concept in collaboration with Sandra Arróniz Lacunza and Carolina Rieckhof.

Conclusion

Amerta Movement has re-shifted the value I attach to clothing and my relationship to the environment. It has made me question and reflect upon the social-cultural values embedded in both. This new awareness instigated the need to re-evaluate the role of costume in performance and to find a way of integrating the 'somatic perspective' to include the in-flux attitude and the Fact/Fiction methodology of Amerta Movement. These approaches have the potential to reconnect us to our environment and site, creating new embodied ways of relating to ourselves, others and the environment – shifting the way we act and live in the world. *The Somatic Movement and Costume Project* will continue to integrate the practices and approaches of Suprapto Suryodarmo through future performances, workshops and the creation of new somatic costumes – exploring further both site-specific costumes and the values inherent in an 'ecological costume'.

Notes

This chapter includes excerpts from my contribution (Dean 2014) 'Amerta Movement and Somatic Costume: Sourcing the Ecological Image' to the book *Embodied Lives.* With thanks to Triarchy Press and the editors. This chapter also refers to and develops ideas first published in 'Somatic movement and costume: a practical investigative project', which appeared in the *Journal of Dance and Somatic Practices* (2011). With thanks to the editors and publishers.

Thanks to costumer designer/visual artist Marta Jiménez Salcedo, who participated in the project from February to May, 2014.

References

Berger, P. & Luckmann T. (1967) *The Social Construction of Reality: A Treatise in the Sociology of Knowledge*, Anchor Books

Blakeslee, S. & Blakeslee, M. (2007) *The Body Has a Mind of its Own*, Random House

Classen, C. (1993) *Worlds of Sense: Exploring the Senses in History and Across Cultures*, Routledge

Dean S. E. (2009) 'Departing from Tradition: Insights from Java', *In Dance*, Jan./Feb., p. 3

_______ (2011), 'Somatic movement and costume: A practical, investigative project', *Journal of Dance and Somatic Practices* 3: 1+2, pp. 167-182

_______ (2014), 'Amerta Movement & Somatic Costume: Sourcing the Ecological Image', in K. Bloom, M. Galanter, and S. Reeve (eds), *Embodied Lives: Reflections on the influence of Suprapto Suryodarmo and Amerta Movement*, Triarchy Press, pp. 113-126.

de Vignemont, F. (2006), 'A Review of Shaun Gallagher, How the Body Shapes the Mind', PSYCHE 12:1 http://bit.ly/tpMove60

Fisher, J. (1997) 'Relational Sense: Towards a Haptic Aesthetics', *Parachute 87*, Summer, pp. 4-11

Frank, K. (2003) 'Seeing the Ground of a Movement: Tonic Function and the Fencing Bear'. n.p.

Gallagher, S. (2005), *How the Body Shapes the Mind*, Oxford University Press

Gendlin, E.T. (1992), 'The primacy of the body, not the primacy of perception', *Man and World*, 25 (3-4), pp. 341-353.

Ginot, I. (2011) 'Body schema and body image: At the crossroad of somatics and social work', *Journal of Dance & Somatic Practices* 3: 1+2, pp. 151-165

Grau, A. (2011), 'Dancing bodies, spaces/places and the senses: A cross-cultural investigation', *Journal of Dance & Somatic Practices* 3: 1+2. pp. 5-24

Grunwald, M. (ed.) (2008) *Human Haptic Perception*, Birkhäuser Verlag

Hanna, T. (1988) *Somatics*, Addison-Wesley

Howes, D. (ed.) (2005) *Empire of the Senses: The Sensual Culture Reader*, Berg

Lederman & Klatzky (2009), 'Haptic perception: A tutorial', *Attention, Perception & Psychophysics*, 71(7). pp. 1439-1459

Levine, M. (2000) *Fundamentals of Sensation and Perception*, Oxford University Press

Potter, C. (2008) 'Sense of Motion, Senses of Self: Becoming a Dancer', *Ethnos*, Volume 73, Number 4, December 2008, pp. 444-465

Merleau-Ponty, M. (2002) *Phenomenology of Perception*, Routledge

Reeve, S. (2011) *Nine Ways of Seeing a Body*, Triarchy Press

Scharf, B. (1975) *Experimental Sensory Psychology*, Scott, Foresman

Schiffman, H. R. (1996) *Sensation and Perception: An Integrated Approach*, John Wiley

Stoller, P. (1997) *Sensuous Scholarship (Contemporary Ethnography)*, University of Pennsylvania Press.

Storm, P. (1987), *Functions of Dress*, Prentice-Hall

Trisha Brown Dance Company (n.d.), *Repertory/Early work*, http://bit.ly/tpMove52

Sally E. Dean Performance Work with Somatic Costume:

Something's In The Living Room: Somatic costume performance in site-specific and traditional theatre spaces. Taman Budaya Jawa Tengah, Theater Arena, Solo, Java (July 2014), Edinburgh Fringe Festival, UK (August 2014), private home, Helsinki, Finland (September 2014).

Here and There: Site-specific, participatory performance indoors and outdoors to include film and costume. Coventry University: Part of the 'Dance & Somatic Practices Conference', Coventry, UK (July 2013), Counterpulse in San Francisco (June 2014) and IDOCDE teach me (not)! symposium 2014 in Vienna, Austria (July 2014).

You're Not Supposed To Be Here 2: Site-specific, costumed performance for film, in response to the outdoor environment at Trent Park, Middlesex University (May 2011).

Experiential Costume, Movement & Performance: Middlesex University: Part of the 'Symposium on Collaboration'. Included an artist residency, London, UK (April-May 2012).

The Myth Of The Porter's Mess Room: Battersea Arts Centre (BAC): Site-specific, costume and participatory performance, part of 'Freshly Scratched', London, UK (October 2011).

The Clan Of The Tall Pointy Hat People: Coventry University: Improvisational, participatory and costumed performance, part of the 'Dance & Somatic Practices Conference', Coventry, UK (July 2011); supported by the Rebecca Skelton Fund. Siobhan Davies Dance Studio: Part of 'Stranger Than Fiction', London, UK (May 2011). The Centre for Creative Collaboration: Part of the 'Participatory Research & Learning in the Performing Arts – Symposium', London, UK (May 2011).

HILARY KNEALE

'The Daily Round, The Common Task'

Embodied Practice and the Dance of the Everyday

> *She sits high on a tall black chair surrounded by earth-coated potatoes. Over her clothing she wears a long canvas apron stitched with a low-set marsupial pocket. She sits quiet and still; only breath moves.*

With a clear focus, she stands, bends forwards and down and begins to fill the low-slung pocket of the apron with potatoes from the wide spread mound about her feet. When she has filled the pocket, she seats herself upon the tall black chair again. Once more she bends forward from the high seat, doubling over to retrieve the potatoes from the low-slung pocket by her feet, one at a time. Potato in hand, she selects a peeling tool from the collection on the low stool beside her; she is ready for the task at hand.

Fig. 1: Peel (2013) Lanchester Gallery, Coventry. Photo: Christian Kipp

One by one by one by one she peels, peelings tumble to the floor in an age-old journey back to the earth. Silently, to the sound of repetitive peeling, she begins working her way through a seemingly never-ending continuum of potatoes, 'one potato, two potato…' 'the daily round, the common task', her grandmother's words whisper in her ears and sing through her heart.

Skimming the surface of each potato she reveals the wetted whiteness of the earth-grown harvest. She fills and empties, fills and empties, fills and empties the marsupial pocket of the apron. Her hands become painted with the starchy juice of the root crop as she peels. The lifelong stories of the creases on the palms of her hands become ingrained and enriched with the pigments of the earth. The earth colours now fill her life-line that had been scored around the base of her thumb even before her birth; her fate is now highlighted by the paint of the soil.

The mound of potatoes shifts about her as the white, new peeled potatoes replace the earth-covered and the pile of peelings grows between the two. She adjusts her weight and position on the chair, in order to balance the repetitive movement of peeling throughout the length of her body. She calls the movement up through the centre of her spine with her breath and out along her arms and into her busy hands and fingers.

Viewers come and go. Some stay for a while; they take what they find and leave with the murmurings of their thoughts and some stirrings of ancient memories. Still she peels, and still she peels, and sometimes as she peels she sings with a deep low sound turning from somewhere within her or far beneath her, the sound of a familiar song. The endless turning of an ordinary action, a meditation, an old, old story, a song, a prayer, a life, 'a daily round, a common task.'

Fig.2: *Peel* (2013) Lanchester Gallery, Coventry. Photo: Christian Kipp.

> Since to follow a trail is to remember how it goes, making one's way in the present is itself a recollection of the past, onward movement is itself a return.
> (Tim Ingold & Jo Lee Vergunst, *Ways of Walking*, 2008)

I first performed *Peel*[1] seated amongst museum cabinets in an upper gallery of MoDA (Museum of Domestic Design & Architecture). The cabinets were filled with domestic gadgets and objects that were predominately made since 1900. These were mostly hand-held tools, powered by the movement of the body. During the performance, the tools I used to peel the potatoes were also many and varied, both in design and efficiency. Some were new and some had been handed down through generations of family. As I handled and worked with the tools, there were moments when I had a sense that I had called them out of the vitrines around me and back into life. I could see similar tools locked away within the cabinets as I peeled. The domestic detritus surrounding me, in the upper museum gallery, was closed off from life while encased inside the cabinets. As I unpeeled potatoes amongst the vitrines, the wet and the heat of life began oozing, moving through my hands and out and all around me. The life force contained in the vegetables was accentuated by the domestic objects that were held as though in a distant dream inside containers.

I chose to create the installation in a way that, because of the physical size of the components, meant that the structure and movement of my body might be accentuated or diminished in relation to the scale of installation and surrounding environment. Movement arose and was accentuated through the considered construction of the installation and props: a too high chair and too long apron and a large mound of potatoes, always a pile too large to be peeled within the allotted time span.

Susan Stewart, in her work *On Longing*, also investigates the scale of the miniature and the gigantic as reflections of body and space. She writes,

> When the body is the primary mode of perceiving scale, exaggeration must take place in relation to the balance of measurement offered as the body extends into the space of the immediate experience. But paradoxically, the body itself is necessarily exaggerated as soon as we have an image of the body, an image which is a projection or objectification of the body onto the world. Thus the problems of imagining the body are symptomatic of the problems in imagining the self as place, object, and agent at once. (Stewart 1993 132:5)

I have a sense as I read Stewart's words, of the body extending beyond its physical confines, like a shadow that is grown or shrunk by the movement of the earth in relation to the sun. It is this fluidity of form and perception of form that interests me. I have opened an enquiry into this through my work, questioning the fixed relationship between object, form, body and landscape to create the opening.

I continue to peel potatoes. The high black chair was out of kilter with the

1 Peel was devised and first performed in 2006, it was created and developed as a solo performance as part of a larger body of work made during a residency at MoDA undertaken by Kitchen Antics and Appliances (KAA), (Barbara Dean, Hilary Kneale and Ann Rapstoff), supported by ACE and the Museum of Domestic Design & Architecture (MoDA), Middlesex University, London.

domestic objects and furniture that were 'on show' within the museum. From the height of the chair's seat my feet did not touch the floor, the long apron ran out beyond my feet and in amongst the potatoes.'Domestic, not domestic, something other'. I specifically chose to wear black clothing under the long apron; the clothing I chose was neither overtly masculine nor overtly feminine: androgyny, timelessness amongst a growing pile of peeled potatoes. On and on my hands work, they lead the wave of movement through my arms and deep into the back of my body, calling breath to expand my lungs wide and low, opening into ribs and pelvis.The performance is held within a cycle of continuous motion, breath, organs, bones, muscle, skin and thought; I am present to the continuum of the work and the spaces between.The inside and the outside of both the work and the body moving in united rhythm.

Over the period of the performance, the 'uncontaminated' museum environment was filled with living vegetables covered in earth.A combination of site, environment and installation, creating a paradoxical and surreal quality within both the museum gallery and the installation, there was a sense of life unfolding in amongst a locked up past. I performed the durational piece over a six-hour period. During this time, I was periodically alone; I performed in the silent upper gallery, while the other 'Kitchen Antics and Appliances' artists were showing work in different parts of the museum.The absences and the presence of viewers, due to this, felt in harmony with a greater unfolding of the piece.

Absorbed in the task at hand and soothed by the rhythm of my body, the quiet timeless repetition allowed my thoughts to move with the pulse as I peeled potatoes alone. I awoke to new layers within the language of body awareness, the phenomenology of strangeness: 'It is happening, it is not happening, I am peeling, I am not peeling. I continue to peel... 'If a tree falls in a forest and no-one is around to hear it, does it make a sound?' a philosophical thought experiment that raises questions regarding observation and knowledge of reality, posed by philosopher George Berkley (1710), catches my thoughts. I continue to peel.

As I peel, other dream-like images move through my mind, some coming into clear focus.A particular and strong memory of the work, both painting and sculpture, by artist of the Surreal, Dorothea Tanning comes into focus. I turn my thoughts to Tanning and other practitioners who work in the realms of the everyday made surreal. Female surrealists attempting to name the hidden and the unseen, in order to bring them to light so that polarities they were experiencing in life might dissolve and move back into balance through expression in their work. I wonder to what extent women are still identified with the domestic environment as a logical space for the female body? I conclude, as I continue to peel, that the question is still open as the boundaries between male and female roles continue to shift in the 21st century.

Where does the action of peeling potatoes within an embodied practice lie in relation to the ordinary, to the feminine and to notions of the surreal? I am aware that much of the work of Dorothea Tanning, both painting and sculpture, was concerned with essences and relational qualities within the field of the feminine and the female body even though she was not physically present within her work. Examples of her work that I consider hold the dual map of body and installation within the field of the feminine and the surreal are *Rainy Day Canape* (1970) and *Tragic Table* (1970-3); these are works in which body and furniture are morphed, they are works from which I feel an impulse move forward to the more contemporary work of Sarah Lucas. The work, *Pauline Bunny* (1997) for example, which I find strongly reminiscent of Tanning's earlier works, at the same time brings in a more edgy and flagrantly sexual twist. Tanning's images and forms were often placed and given context within the domestic environments of house and garden. Although these works are not performed and do not have a 'live' component, they have a close relationship to body and to the domestic, I see these works as part of my lineage. The body inspired aspect of Tanning's work and that of other women Surrealists – Lee Miller, Remedios Varo, and Francesca Woodman, for example – has been critiqued by Katherine Conley (2010). Conley writes:

> Long identified with their bodies and familiar with the use of the female body as a symbol for everything from motherhood, to beauty and Justice, women artists connected to surrealism embraced this cultural trope by representing women's bodies in multiple ways. Representations of women in houses, women as houses, allowed women artists to question a woman's relation to a house as a safe haven and the inevitably of a woman's confinement to it. (Conley 2010: 46:1)

Looking back over my work, I can recognise the subtle influences of the art of women Surrealists returning my gaze. I see that the re-working of the familiar in order to make 'strange', unsettling or the Freudian term 'uncanny' is interesting to me. Aspects of the subtle disorder of my work can make room for each piece to reflect back on itself and in turn the viewer, creating a change in perception, a shift in 'seeing'. *Peel* embraces the unsettled edge, making a call out beyond it in order to highlight the familiar within its new container. As the work emerges through repetition and continuum of the motion of the body, the actions begin to 'travel' back through the ancestral line to become story or fantasy. It is these pivotal moments of disorder that call for a re-seeing; the familiar then drops its 'name' and becomes renewed once more and nameless.

In her essay to accompany the exhibition *Angels of Anarchy, Women Artists and Surrealism* (2010) at the Manchester Art Gallery, Patricia Allmer states that, "The everyday, domestic interior is emptied out and returns as a space full of haunting and nightmarish potentials or potentials for transformation and becoming" (Allmer 2010: 21).

The otherness that she calls forward resonates with me, calling beyond that which we so easily take for granted or subtly accept in domestic spaces and structures. These are environments that are so close to us that we may not recognise our own condition within them. Art can become a mirror or a magnifying glass to reveal a mythological quality through the reflection or magnification of what has already been recognised on a subtle level.

According to Witney Chadwick, quoted by Almer within the same essay,

> Fantastic scenarios play a significant role in the women surrealist artists' works allowing the exploration of alternative social orders and personae, exploring the identification with moments prior to historical time. However, still more interestingly, a number of artists draw on this genre to rework and appropriate fairy-tales and classic myths which are strongly anchored in patriarchy. (Allmer 2010: 24-5)

Artists have a strong call to abstract objects from the everyday, to render the ordinary 'uncanny' or to create simulacra of life as art and in so doing have given weight or 'other' value to the everyday. To include the body within this field of attention is to create a further opening into the space of the 'real'. I call myself present to the 'practice' of living in a body while inviting in a 're-enchantment' of living in this world, through each breath, heartbeat, moving bone and muscle, within each and every experience including, from time to time, the peeling of potatoes. I refer here to the quotidian; I see its representation within art and literature and its move out again through the body and into relationship with object, environment and ritual. I am concerned with everyday actions that through a turn of attention moves into the realm of art can be touched by magic. I am drawn to the idea of making art out of nothing or at least the making of art through small shifts and the no-thing of that holding everything. Through my practices I transmit stories. Through my body I open to the day, to the land, to the earth, to ideas and transmit the stories that I find. I choose to include my body as part of my work and to be as present as I am able. I am interested in work that comes through the vehicle of the body and the sensory field and into the physical realm, stories and ritual, both once known and unknown.

Over the years, I have performed within landscapes of self-made, surreal environments, ordinary domestic spaces and in open landscapes of hill, moor and littoral zone. Some of the stories that I perceive during the unfolding of my work have had a deep-seated familiarity about them, others holding an almost pre-cognitive quality, 'I know the story, I remember the story, I do not know the story'. As I perform *Peel* once more, amongst a large gathering of potatoes, I peel them whilst unpeeling myself once more into the work. As I peel, the story of Rumpelstiltskin and his alchemical spinning of straw into gold to enable the princess to marry the prince comes to mind. The price of the choice she made, to give her power away to the imp in return for spinning straw into gold, was the life of her firstborn child which, the imp later returned to claim. The princess took back her power and her child, by finding and speaking the true name of the imp. When in the story the princess finally names the imp Rumpelstiltskin, he falls away and falls apart and is swallowed by the earth. As echoes of these known old stories come through my work, so, tripping on their coat tails, unknown others come.

Story and writing have found their way into my practice and completed works as I have absorbed visual and physical stories from the outside. The natures of the landscapes I move amongst have intertwined themselves through my body and as I move; they have remerged through writing. As I have sensed stories arising I have had a stronger and stronger call to record them and bring them out of the sensory field within which they arise. Writing has become closer and closer to the making of my work, to the point where movement spawns writing and stories spawn work. Mostly the physical arises before the written, and the written clarifies the physical. The writing that emerges often feels as though it has been present all along, locked away, the key to its emergence has been to move a wrist, a limb, a roll, a peel, a heave, a breath of movement. As I inhabit my body, each cell responds and wakes into the work and the story of the work flows from my body as it wakes.

I write in response to movement with the intention to call the work, to receive the work, to know the work and to expand the work as it emerges. Without its written element my work would be far less, it might be closer to a black and white image in contrast to the colour that I see comes through with the act of writing. There are a number of aspects and functions to my written work. I write in response to movement practice that I undertake, both in studio settlings and in the natural landscape. Writing is a way of accessing that which is set free as a result of moving, it is the 'under story' of the movement that emerges. I often write in prose that is poetic, rather than in poetry, working with words to weave a sense of the physical and of sensation. I also write in order to call forward the unseen stories from the land itself, ancient stories that I sense exist under the surface of things. I call the stories out as though they are a truth and invest the words that come with that quality of 'truth'. It is an exciting and challenging way to enrich work.

I actively began to work with the written word as art during my residency at MoDA (2006). I have since developed writing as part of my general practice and art. I have written *Silent Vessel* (Kneale 2012), an artist book inspired by the performance and installation *Silent Vessel*. The book of the work is composed of photographs, poetry and writing that was created during the ten years that I worked with *Silent Vessel*. At other times, I have written stories to accompany performances as a way of casting a wider essence over the whole.

Over the last five years I have worked in collaboration with photographer Christian Kipp within environments that have a strong physical relationship to the action of water. We 'inhabit' the places, take time to strip a layer of ourselves away as we enter the landscape, while we slowly move closer to what we consider the core essence of the places we inhabit. The work emerges through inhabiting place over time, the results are both photographic and written. Christian Kipp and I have completed a book of images and text for each of the parts of the series that we have undertaken thus far. However, our preferred form for showing *With Water* (2010–14) is through installation, whereby the photographic images and the accompanying written text are shown in a gallery or other large space. The work is installed in a way that creates a need for the viewer to physically engage with the work: bending, handling, moving, sitting with the work. We are also present during the showing of the work, our presence within the installation is a part of the work. I continue to write and we re-work the installation as the time unfolds; it is a live process.

Most recently I have re-worked the written narrative of *Coat* for a short film, where parts of the text have become the whispered narrative for the film *Coat: The Turning and Returning of the Tide* (2014), first shown at Decoda Summer Dancing in Coventry, June 2014.

Coat is an evolving work. It is a story that began to emerge in 2012 from the shape of a coat with a long, long tail. It is a story with an ancient echo, a story of a magical garment which, when worn outside in the landscape, collects the forgotten stories of the land and its creatures into the warp and weft of its fabric. *Coat* has emerged as a performance in amongst an installation of curious objects and at other times in 'real time' when I walk alone wearing the coat, collecting the ancient 'stories' of the land through its tail. I have called the stories as I have walked through trees in wooded lands and by the edges of the ocean and while sitting within the tidal zone of the River Thames within the city of London.

Fig. 3: Coat. Connemara (2012) Photo: Christian Kipp

Until last year, any recording of this work had been made through still photograph and written word. *Coat: The Turning and the Returning of the Tide* (2014) is a new chapter of the story made as film through collaboration with artist/filmmaker Vicky Vergou and director Helen Poynor. The making of the film *Coat* (2014) within a tidal landscape in the south of England has opened up a new layer of the work. During the short film, the essence of the coat emerges as the wearer inhabits the littoral zone and mingles with the ancient forgotten stories of the land and its inhabitants. Phrases of the written story are whispered over the images and environmental sounds and add depth to what is seen.

From time to time my written work takes on a further variation of form, as I write alongside artists and dancers at work. As I witness, my intention is to write from the centre of the work, in the hope that the words I write will assist the artist to see and receive their own work. Writing has become, through these different forms, an integral part of my practice.

> I am not separate in my work, to the self that inhabits any other part of my life. What I find in physical exploration, I find everywhere else. I teach myself, through experience, allowing my internal weather to unfold through the layers of my physical, emotional and sensory landscape within this weather filled land. I unfold myself into and onto the physical land, into woodlands, at the base of cliffs, over pebbles, onto the edge of the ocean, into streams and between rock pools. I unfold into the field of the hidden within the physicality of my body and the land. (Kneale 2010: 213:3)

Over this chapter, I have written around the work *Peel* with the intention to focus on the work as a meeting point of myriad practices. *Peel*, as with all my work, is supported by body-based practice and through the meeting place of ritual within the physical and the everyday. It is concerned with a shifting shape within perceptions of time and space and in between actions. The work may at times come close to meditation and at others times it is as familiar as breathing. Somatic practice and indeed art, in this context, might be considered a perspective on living in this world, a perspective that I have contemplated and cultivated within the spectrum of my work. The work is a ground for story, the written word, both new and ancient. The story of *Peel* itself has changed over the years between the first and last performance; the work has evolved from inside itself. There is a further chapter of the work in development, beginning: "Imagine a farm barn in Scotland in early autumn, filled to the roof with newly harvested main crop potatoes. Imagine a woman, sitting on a high black chair in the barn, surrounded by potatoes. She seems very, very small at the base of the mountain of potatoes. See the woman sitting, she is wearing a long, long apron, she has a potato peeler in her hand, she begins to peel, one potato, two potato..."

> But an endless activity could also be decided upon, which would apparently transcend palpable time... The common function of these alternatives is to release the artist from conventional notions of a detached, close arrangement of time-space. A picture, a piece of music, a poem, a drama, each confined within its respective frame, fixed number of measures, stanzas, stages, however great they may be in their own right, simply will not allow for breaking the barrier between art and life. And this is what the objective is. (Kaprow 1956: 263:33)

Allan Kaprow, maker of assemblages, environments and happenings was interested in the intersection between art and life, the fluidity of the unfolding moment in life put under the spotlight, an ordinary task in repetition becoming the moment or a series of moments in which the barrier between art and life could be broken. Although I am interested in and inspired by Kaprow's perspective, to break this barrier is not my perceived intention; it is rather to work inside the extraordinary of the ordinary, inside an ordinary mythology, and so it is with this intention that I often work within a continuum. This is work that takes some years to unfold as I dig towards that which I finally perceive as the true essence of the piece.

I frame my wider practice within what I have described as a 'physical philosophy', meaning that I can experience art as moments of presence while living. I have discussed this approach in the article, 'A field guide to a physical philosophy' (Kneale 2010). As I work, I move through the interstices of many disciplines, gathering them together, breathing life into them and then letting them go into the work while perhaps never fully inhabiting a single one of them on its own. I also carry the parcel of the practices with me into life. In making performance work with the support of movement practices, I have developed a range of work, the constant across which remains a relationship with a consciously inhabited body. I can, if I choose, bring the same quality of attention to what may appear as the mundane within the everyday: 'I sit here on a chair, legs crossed, arms bent, hands and fingers typing keys, breath inhaling filling and exhaling emptying my lungs, eyes attending, pelvis, back, neck resting in position'. In this moment, I am filled and moved beyond the mundane.

Work that I have made since I first devised *Peel* (since 2006) has taken me in twists and turns away from the domestic environment and out into the natural landscape. I am supported in my work by practices, which I undertake with regularity. Over the last ten years I have studied closely with movement teacher, director and performer, Helen Poynor. Through the support of her 'Walk of Life' programme, her trainings and mentorship I am now committed to a regular personal physical practice, and this in turn has supported the evolution of working through my body as artist. Poynor describes her work in her year workshop schedule as *grounded in an experiential understanding of the structure of the body, an awareness of the relationship between the moving body and the self, and of the responsive inter-relationship between body, earth, self and environment.* I am also supported in my work by a commitment to practising raised levels of awareness through the awaking of a shamanic sensibility, as I study and practise ancient indigenous teachings concerning the relationship between spirit and 'all relations': earth, plant, animal and element. Without these ongoing practices, my work would undoubtedly have taken a very different form.

As I practise and as I make work, I feel kindred spirits in other artists, who work closely with the land, in particular in Richard Long, who walks the land in continuums and repetitions. He measures the land in words and recordings of moments, lists of sounds heard and distances of land passed over. He also makes work by moving stones from here to there to make lines and circles to create absences and presences. Long has made much of his work alone, unseen by the 'viewer'. He has made his work with the land, his art has evolved out of the everyday action of walking, and many people 'know' his art as walking. I am interested in Long's subtle approach to falling into dialogue with his surroundings.

> The structure of Long's sculpture is based in part on the living reality of the situation in which it is created (the earth itself or substances derived from it) in all its complexity and detail. (Ann Seymour in Long, R. [2002])

As I observe his work, I sense the strength of his presence, even though he is not present within the photographs, or the writing and maps that often go on to become the 'seen' aspect of his work. I sense his presence in his absence. Other of Long's works are great and vibrant mud circles, made of river silt collected from their watery edges and then painted directly onto gallery walls through the fast, dynamic movement of hands, the physical action of the body present in the energetic drips and splats around the circle and below the work, on the floor. These works are created in situ by the sheer velocity of his fast moving limbs and hands. I see the depth and simplicity of his work meeting like the in-breath and the out-breath. The work excites me and I feel my response to it calls me deeper into living. Long's work often emerges from that which already exists, it has a sense of nothing added or taken away; these are subtle shifts and recordings that measure the monumental. He refers to making "art out of nothing", (O'Hagen 2009) which, from my perspective, could look like simply being alongside what exists. As he states,

> The idea of making art out of nothing, I've got a lot of time for that. (O'Hagen, 16:12 2009)

Long began working with the whole world as his studio fairly early on in the evolution of his work. He stepped into the vast studio of everywhere and has since made interventions into and comments upon the natural order of things through physical intervention. His interventions are close to the action of frost or of water moving through the land, or the ordering of objects by weight by movement of the ocean as seen on the high tide line, and the movement of in-breath and then out-breath returning to the whole, just as '*touch is a gesture of exchange with the world*', (O'Hagen 2009). I identify strongly with this notion of exchange with the world in relation to art, to site and to presence. Long's work seems to me to sit in its own field, outside definition, even though the physical residues of his actions are shown in art galleries.

Artists are often asked where it is that they place their work in the wide fields of practice. I have a background in Fine Art; the theories I understand are those that sit within what is described as 'art', and the history with which I am familiar is art history. As I move more and more deeply into movement and I inhabit my body with a growing consciousness that serves the work I make, the further I feel that I move from the fields of 'art' and closer to the practitioners who work within the field of 'dance'. I have conversations with 'dancers' concerning overlapping practices; over these conversations we have considered whether dancers are dancers, and when they might also be described as artists. And if artists are artists, when might I describe them as dancers? Over the last few years I have become more closely connected to the field of dance, and to dancers. Some of the work I experience within the field of dance has a recognisable quality about it: I have come to a similar place along a different route. It is now these colleagues that I exchange references with, our backgrounds are different, our rootstock is different, but the flowers of our practice belong in the same bed and our different colours enhance each other. This excites me, this is a rich place to work, a land across disciplines, where art through the body holds sway.

I continue to hold many thoughts and further questions, which I now leave outside the work, as I sit on a tall black chair surrounded by potatoes. I breathe deeply into my back and through to the base of my spine, as I prepare to perform over a period of six hours. I quietly contemplate the potatoes around me, potatoes that have grown under the surface of the earth, that are filled with minerals of the earth and of the stars. I call myself present to the form and tone and sensations of my body, a body born through a body, also filled with the minerals of the earth and the stars, here present in the same work, as I begin to peel potatoes, an unpeeling is arising, something akin to prayer.

References

Allmer, P. (ed.) (2010) *Women Artists and Surrealism. Of Fallen Angels and Angels of Anarchy*, Prestel

Berry, P. & Wernick, A. (eds.) (1992) *Shadow of Spirit. Postmodernism and Religion*, 250-262: 19, Routledge

Conley, K. (2010) 'Safe as Houses: Anamorphic Bodies in Ordinary Spaces: Miller, Varo, Tanning, Woodman' in Allmer (2010)

Gablik, S. (1991), *The Reenchantment of Art*, Thames & Hudson

_______ (1995), *Conversations Before the End of Time*, London: Thames & Hudson

Huxley, M. & Witts, N. (eds.) (2002) *The Twentieth Century Performance Reader*, Routledge

Ingold, T. & Vergunst, J.L. (2008) *Ways of Walking: Ethnography and Practice on Foot*, Ashgate

Kaprow, A. (1956) *Assemblages, Environments and Happenings*, Harry N. Abrams.

Kneale, H. (2006), *The Manual of Domestic Incidents*, Pelinore Press

_______ (2010), 'A field guide to a physical philosophy', *Journal of Dance and Somatic Practices* 2: 2. pp, 205-217, doi 10. 1386/jdsp.2.2.205_1

_______ (2012), *Silent Vessel*, Pelinore Press

Kotik, C. *et al.* (1994) *Louise Bourgeois: the locus of memory, works 1982-1993*, Harry N. Abrams

Long, R. (2002), *Richard Long, Walking the Line*, Thames & Hudson

Macfarlane, R. (2012) *The Old Ways: A Journey on Foot*, Hamish Hamilton

O'Hagen, S. (2009), 'One step beyond. Interview with Richard Long', *Observer* Magazine, 10 May 2009

Perec, G. (1974) *Species of Spaces and Other Pieces*, Edition Galilée

Pink, S. (2004) *Home Truths. Gender, domestic objects and everyday life*, Berg

Stewart, S. (1993) *On Longing: Narratives of the Minature, the Gigantic, the Souvenir, the Collection*, Duke University Press

Tanning, D. (2001) *Between Lives: An artist and her world*, W.W. Norton

Artworks referenced

Tanning, D. *Rainy Day Canape* (1970) mixed media. 820x1740x1100mm, Philadelphia Museum of Art

Tanning, D. *Tragic Table* (1970-73) mixed media. 1100x1220x850mm, Gallery of Modern Art, Centre Pompidou. Paris

Lucas, S. *Pauline Bunny* (1997) mixed media. 950x640x900mm, Tate Gallery, London

SARAH WHATLEY

Motion Capture and The Dancer

Visuality, Temporality and the Dancing Image

Introduction

Image plays an important role in how dancers source and make movement, and how audiences make sense of the fleeting nature of dance. Image can also provide dancers with a way of visualising the 'felt' sense of movement, offering a bridge between self and other. Motion capture is a technology that can participate in what might be termed the poetics of the moving, sensing body in dance. It can also be a tool that offers another way of bridging between 'self' and 'other', between the visual and the kinaesthetic, to generate visualisations that provide sensory feedback to the dancer. But how do dancers experience their re-mediation through the technological process of motion capture, particularly when there is an understandable resistance to 'capturing' what is an embodied practice, and which then may be reused and rendered into new forms of expression? This chapter will explore this question in relation to dancer/performer/subject agency, to argue that the visualising of data using motion capture technology opens up space to examine the ways in which temporality intervenes or interacts with the visual, and generates new modes of creating, documenting and analysing dance.

Importantly, what I am focusing on is very much connected to the work of dance and visual artist Ruth Gibson and her project exploring the intersections between the technological process of motion capture and a somatic body-based movement practice, Skinner Releasing Technique (SRT), to create visualisations for different kinds of art outputs[1]. I am writing from my perspective as observer of the ways in which motion capture intervenes in, supports or constructs the artist's making processes rather than as a practitioner who works with motion capture as a creative or analytical

1 The research is the focus of an Arts and Humanities Research Council Creative Fellowship at Coventry University; 2010-13; see http://bit.ly/tpMove53

tool. My aim is thus to offer an interplay between practice and writing through a form of *dancing with* Gibson's practice in my articulation and theorising of her work. But my writing will draw on the voices of some of the dance artists who have been directly involved in Gibson's research and reflect on their comments to say more about a *techno-poetic* process of dance. I borrow this term, *techno-poetic*, from Kevin Williams's discussion of the communicative possibilities of music video but here I use it to suggest that technology, and in this case motion capture, can contribute to experiencing dance as a poetic process (for its making, aesthetic and rhythmic properties) and also in reference to Heidegger's observation that "as a 'bringing-forth', technology is less a tool than an act of poetics" (1977, cited in Williams 2000: 105). Heidegger's conception that the relationship between human, technology and world is a communicative inter-relationship still seems relevant today when looking closely at the work of artists who are using motion capture to do things to the world, but Heidegger was less positive about modern technology, claiming that modern technology performs an 'enframing' in the way that it "demands that nature supply it with materials which can be extracted and stored" (1977: 329). I hope to join with other scholars and artist practitioners to show that motion capture is a technology that can be used by artists to reveal fresh perceptual possibilities, somatic connections and new cultural, creative expressions by doing what Salter argues for in relation to the human/technology interface in performance, by "conjuring forth environments that emerge simultaneously with the individuation of the technical or living being" (Salter 2009: 35), thereby avoiding Heidegger's understandable accusation of the enframing tendency of modern technology that produces a 'standing-reserve' of the actual. Poetics is also important because writing that draws upon somatically informed movement practice tends to call upon poetic structures of metaphor, rhythmic and textual play to encourage the reader into a poetic engagement with the writing and in turn some flavour or taste of the poetry of the dancing body in the practice/art, which again calls forth an *inter*-play between practice and writing. However, I acknowledge that motion capture is a technological process that might appear to diminish the individual agency of the dancer. Moreover, motion capture and a body-centric practice such as SRT might seem uncomfortable partners in a creative process but it is this apparent disjunction that is at the core of Gibson's investigation, has proved surprising in its discoveries, and which informs the observations that follow.

Imagery and dance

A brief, perhaps even cursory review of some of the thinking around imagery in dance is valuable for providing some context for this exploration. The use of imagery in the training of dance has been the subject of many dance research studies with a pedagogical focus, primarily to demonstrate the way in which imagery participates in and supports different teaching strategies (e.g. Franklin [1996] and numerous articles in the broad area of Dance Science[2]). It has a long history in dance training, reaching back to Mabel Ellsworth Todd's influential text *The Thinking Body* (1937/1968), which introduced to dance pedagogues at the time, and ever since, the way in which image supports the biomechanical principles of dance movement. This was followed by Lulu Sweigard's work, amongst others[3], on the role of imagery in a dancer's understanding

2 See for example the various publications connected with the International Association for Dance Medicine and Science; http://bit.ly/tpMove87.

3 For example, Barbara Clark (1889-1982) and Sally Swift (1913-2009).

of anatomical structure and function, which she termed 'ideokinesis' (1974). Subsequent generations of dance practitioners have continued to draw from these methods, incorporating metaphorical images to enhance learning and performance. Joan Skinner, who was a pupil of dance teacher Cora Belle Hunter, who was herself a student of Todd, is one of several to have evolved her own method, in her case Skinner Releasing Technique (SRT) using guided poetic imagery, which she describes as 'image clusters' that are core to her work (cited in Neuhaus 2010).

Writing by dancers themselves is replete with the imagery that has inspired movement or which provides a language for description and reflection. More recently, imagery has played a central role in research that has brought dance scholars and professional practitioners together with cognitive and behavioural scientists to explore the experiential and neural attributes of imagery in dance to understand more about 'choreographic thinking'. The work for example of a team led by psychologist Jon May, working in collaboration with Wayne McGregor|Random Dance in the UK, set out to "record dancers' *awareness* of their use of forms of imagery during movement creation, and to relate these measures to evidence of patterns of brain activity from neuroimaging studies" (May *et al* 2011: 405; original emphasis). Their work, which has benefitted from spending time with highly experienced dance practitioners, conducted over an extended period, has contributed to the growing recognition that imagery is not only concerned with the visual but can, and does, relate to different sense modalities. As deLahunta *et al* observed in relation to their own work with Wayne McGregor and his dancers, "it can be aural as in imagining sounds or voice, sensorial as in imagining a texture and kinesthetic as in imagining movement without moving" (2011: 245)[4]. The team discussed how their research set out to move the "focus of attention around *points in mental space* and across the interconnected imagery spectrum" (*ibid*) to show how innovative movement creation can start from both mental as well as physical processes. Whilst May *et al's* research indicated that the dancers they were studying believed in the main part that they were creating movement intuitively, they were also able to separate for the purpose of the research task the two phases of movement creation and imagery creation. This in itself demonstrated the expertise of the dancer involved in the creative choreographic process.

There is perhaps an understandable anxiety about the implied hierarchy of knowledge when science and the arts meet for collaborative research. Dance can appear to defer to the positivist methodologies that science wields, particularly when it involves measurement and evidence gathering to support particular hypotheses, but the growing relationship with psychologists situated within the broad domain of embodied cognition means that dancers and scientists stand to gain from the dialogue, which acknowledges the complexity of dance and the expert knowledge of dance artists. Thus the meeting between dance and science provides a bridge that reflects the bridging relationship between 'self' and 'other' offered by the use of imagery in dance practice.

The imagination is a particularly fascinating aspect of the human experience and whilst research such as that of May and deLahunta *et al* is telling us more about

---

4 The Wellcome Collection exhibition, Thinking with the body: Mind and movement in the work of Wayne McGregor|Random Dance (2013) tracked the interdisciplinary activities of Wayne McGregor|Random Dance, which through a series of projects have investigated aspects of creativity in dance with researchers from other fields such as cognitive and social science; see http://bit.ly/tpMove54.

the physical and cognitive processes involved in imagination, the fluency with which dancers draw upon and source image as part of their practice suggests that dancers are particularly expert in moving between different sense modalities. It is also probably the case that dancers relate to imagery in ways that are specific to different dance practices. In the field of somatic dance and movement practices[5], dancers are attuned to imagery in particular ways and draw on imagery for its transformative potential rather than what the science community might see as the generative possibilities of imagery. So whilst many contemporary dance training systems are increasingly informed by somatic principles, specific practices such as SRT foreground the image as fundamental to the development of personal autonomy, in terms of encouraging freedom from habitual dominances of one thing over another, by deepening sensory awareness and relationship with the environment. In SRT, 'image actions' are given, which individuals can choose to move with, or not. As metaphors to stimulate the imagination and kinaesthetic experiences, such as 'breath transforming into a white mist', the use of image allows the dancer "to experience a personalized version of them so they are relevant to each individual's process and needs as they are situated in that precise moment in time" (Emslie 2009: 173). This reference to what is common to many somatic practices, that of the privileging of intentionality, spontaneity and a process-led movement exploration, is particularly interesting in the context of Gibson's project. This is because SRT, and the images that are so central to SRT, initiates a process that by using motion capture moves through several stages of data collection, rendering and remediation in the production of artefacts that exist in real, virtual and hybrid environments (separate from that in which the dance was first made) for an audience to view and interact with.

Motion capture and the dancer

Motion capture is a technology that appears to *extract* movement from a body, and then go on to *abstract* bodies from the site which the animations that are created from motion capture data might eventually inhabit, suggesting a divide between the dancer and the capture that the movement generates. The self and other is on one hand divided – my animation is 'me and not me' – or maybe it is a 'doubling of me'. But the relationship is much more complex. As others have commented, from either (or both) a viewer or practitioner perspective (e.g. Popat [2011], Dils [2002], Kozel [2007]), the data that is captured creates what appears to be what Dils described as a "digital portrait" (2002: 94) of the individual dancer, able to reproduce the essential elements of the dancer's movement. And yet for some there is still something 'missing' in the familiar dots and line drawings of the animation that initially results from the capture.

So just as the use of imagery in dance can provide a bridge between self and other, enabling dancers to visualise self in relation to the kinaesthetic 'felt' sense of movement, when motion capture enters the creative space (of dance) it provides a tool that offers another way of bridging self and other, and between the visual and the

5 The umbrella term 'somatic practices', though not prescriptive, generally refers to body-based movement forms such as SRT, Body-Mind Centering, Alexander Technique and Feldenkrais, amongst others. The term 'somatics' was introduced by Thomas Hanna who argued that the concept of 'soma', which suggests something changeable and adaptable, is preferable to 'body', which suggests something static or solid (1980: 6). Since Hanna, the discourse around somatics has expanded in parallel with the practice, leading to many publications and other modes of dissemination.

kinaesthetic. It does this bridging either by the simultaneous and temporally connected live danc(ing) and projected capture of the dancer or through the visualisations that are created through motion capture data (which is generated by the use of imagery) that motion capture might otherwise seem to separate.

So what I find interesting is how, and the extent to which, an image that is core to the dance action infuses the motion that is captured, and how the temporal properties of the dance/dancing might be reconfigured through the visualisations, which then feed back to the dancer (and viewer) an individual sense of embodiment, place and presence. However, it would seem that not only the temporal properties of the dancing but also the temporal properties of the motion capture process impact on the relationship between the visual and the temporal.

For example, in practical terms, the process of 'capture' means that the dancers are often required to repeat movement patterns or explorations for the captures to succeed in computational terms. The repetition of a movement exploration that exists ostensibly through the dancer's desire to be alive, responsive, open to and concerned with the present moment, that neither emphasises an easy recall of what has gone before, nor is able to predict what may unfold in the future, provides a solution for the technological process but might seem to question the authenticity of the captured moment. In effect, the dancer practises to be 'in process', privileging a state of phenomenal emergence or *becoming* rather than *fixing* in set patterns. And yet the capture holds and gives value to the individual moment, which is then transformed, much in the same way as the initial image is transformed by the mover, who is not concerned by questions of 'how' to move because the (point of the) exploration is one of alignment with the image. What results is thus perhaps a temporal paradox; the image-derived movement exploration is held in time to produce data that transforms to a new image, that reflects back on, recuperates, reiterates the first – the image changes, perhaps even transmogrifies beyond what might be anticipated or intended. This temporal tangle produced by the meeting between motion capture and dancer, in which the dancing body becomes data to be remade (etc.) mirrors the frequent debate about the immediacy and 'liveness' of dance and its resistance to reproduction and documentation in a form other than itself. And yet these visualisations, whether made for screen, installation or live events, though never a facsimile of the dancing body, perhaps add to our knowledge about our historical and contemporary performance practices, and how these practices are inscribed in our bodies and reverberate through the work to transmit something of our individual and collective dance histories, and our sensorial world. But there remains a question: what is lost and what is gained through a process of rendering the dancer into digital code, for the dancer, the practice and our valuing of the living, sensing, changing nature of the moving body?

Gibson, motion capture and the digital image

This is where Gibson's current project enters and asks how the stilling, breathing, image-based motion of SRT can produce animations and visualisations that speak of the individual dancer and the more collective, relational dancing body of SRT, to show the potential of motion capture to reflect back on SRT as pedagogy, and as source for technical and compositional practice[6].

6 See Whatley (2012) for more on this project.

Fig. 1: *Vermilion Lake* part of the VISITOR exhibition, 2011 installation: mixed media, computer game environment, 5.1 channel sound (installation view James Taylor Gallery) Credits: Gibson/Martelli, Photo: David Surman

Fig. 2: *Vermilion Lake* part of the VISITOR exhibition, 2011 installation: mixed media, computer game environment, 5.1 channel sound (installation view Towner Art Gallery).
Credit: Gibson/Martelli

Gibson's project grew out of her work with partner Bruno Martelli as *igloo* that has extended over many years and which has seemed to enjoy defying simple categorisation, which is what makes it so interesting as well as difficult to situate and speak about. Working in extreme physical landscapes and habitats has fed their creative projects, enabling them to explore the transformation from the material to the immaterial, to create hyper real virtual, interactive and intermedial projects that have challenged conventional modes of viewing, participation and analysis and which have been exhibited in various settings.

For example, *VISITOR/Vermillion Lake* (2011) takes the viewer into a log cabin in a gallery, but it is not what it seems; a plywood construction is made 'realistic' by the application of photographic imagery to the outside surface. Inside is half a rowing boat, in which the 'visitor' sits and takes hold of oars to row 'around a lake' that is made *real* through more photographic imagery. The interactive experience of *VISITOR* means that the viewer is the title of the work and thus is what the work becomes – the visitor not only *sees*, but also by being in an embodied connection with the hybrid physical/virtual environment, *feels* the relationship with virtual sky, trees and falling stars. The visitor may find that she reflects back on her own corporeality even if unaware of her own agency in determining how the work unfolds. This blurring between real and artifice, and the play with hyper reality and mixed reality, is hypnotic and dreamlike, and yet edges towards unease and discomfort. This in itself is interesting in the context of a practice, SRT, that is very much about connecting with the environment, the natural, the 'real' of experience, now taken into the "uncanny and thus unsettling" (Birringer 2007: 48) world of *igloo*. But it is this transposition that tells us more about that relationship and also how we source and embody metaphors, which is not always comfortable even if apparently 'organic'. Indeed, as Popat reminds us, the inclusion of technology can actually "heighten and stimulate bodily awareness" (2011: 133). Thus on one hand there is the experience of the viewer/user to consider and on the other the experience of the dancer, or subject.

In her Fellowship project, Gibson has been focusing on the poetic metaphoric imagery cited in Joan Skinner's technique, which has brought attention more firmly back to the materiality of the dancing body: something she has named as a *kinosphir*[7]. As Gibson herself acknowledges, SRT can be a very powerful practice, which taps into different feelings and sensing states, so the imagery is a potentially rich resource for creating visualisations that might awaken the senses through an awareness of orientation, dislocation or displacement. The project further interrogates the relationship between real time and pre-recorded motion capture in performance settings, and the status of the dancer as subject and object of capture, as well as Ruth's own role as artist/engineer/programmer/interlocutor in the creative process. Her project set out to ask a number of questions:

7 Gibson defines ***kinosphir*** as the special attention given to experience generated through a new methodology of giving audiences immersive experiences using a variety of techniques including game engine visualisations, motion capture, haptic interfaces and stereo projections to convey imagery derived from and relating to SRT (Gibson 2013). The link with 'kinesphere' is acknowledged, but whereas 'kinesphere' – first defined by movement theorist Rudolf Laban (1966) as the area around the body, which can be reached by the limbs outstretched and is effectively carried with the dancer wherever she moves – ***kinosphir*** emphasises the experiential rather than the spatial.

- Can motion capture 'map' somatic dance practices to test out how notions of embodiment are 'read', visualised and transmitted to increase understanding of the limits and expansion possibilities of motion capture technology?
- Can avatar behaviour expose more about stillness in performance and first-person sensorial experience to expand kinaesthetic engagement and awareness?
- How might these digitally produced bodies for immersive virtual environments provide new viewing experiences and what kinds of art events unfold?

Earlier outcomes from the project created from captures of SRT produced some beautiful kinetic, poetic and sometimes numinous visualisations that had no overt human avatar presence but appeared to embody the dancing body in the way that they seem to breathe, fold and fly through a virtual landscape, reflecting the metaphoric properties of the image action – such as 'mist'. Sometime later the dancing figure re-entered Gibson's experiments and a motion capture mobile application emerged: MocApp, appearing to strip away some of these more complex and expansive visualisations to reveal the apparent simplicity and immediacy of the dancing image. The 'stick figure' returned but in its visual clarity we find the 'digital portrait' of each highly experienced and skilled SRT practitioner and when collected together, a rich corpus of animations that tell us something about SRT as a practice that is located historically, somatically and culturally. On one level it appears to capture the literal movement but the technology seems to have found its own 'consciousness' by watching and capturing the *why* and *how* of the dancer moving. MocApp is in itself a delightfully intuitive and playful application, available for anyone to experiment with a user-friendly version of motion capture, and which simultaneously documents in a living, changing form the experiments of the SRT experts. Its beauty, from Gibson's point of view, is that MocApp was seeded through her Fellowship project and that the wider community of SRT practitioners, of which Gibson is part, helped to bring it 'into the world'[8].

What seems particularly interesting is that in Gibson's project we are forced to rethink our, or the dancer's, relationship with image, to revisit the idea that the image confines itself to its transformative potential. Image is now simultaneously transformative *and* generative. Moreover, image is both source and output but the image 'leaves' the corporeal body; imagery generates movement that in turn generates another image or visualisation in which the corporeal body is then absent. But does the image remain in some way, does the animation hold the image, or say more about the image to reinforce the centrality of imagery in the dancer's work? Imagery in dance produces individual responses but within a community of practice, such as the community of expert SRT practitioners, dancers become familiar with, and skilled in, the language of the image and it may be that this determines to some extent how images evolve and are carried through the body and become 'understood'. And yet

8 Gibson's intention is for the app to be primarily a tool for those interested in motion capture and for movement educators (not necessarily those interested in SRT). It is not primarily an artistic venture. MocApp is a software, a viewing tool, a general purpose motion capture viewer. When the user downloads the app it comes with eight 'demo' files, which are likely to be deleted so the animator loads it with his/her own 'takes'. There is a very small charge for the app to encourage only the 'serious' user. The dancers who are involved in the project are able to download their own captures using a private link; see http://bit.ly/tpMove55

at the same time, the image travels through various incarnations always touching on something that insists through them all, rather than each new 'version' of the image representing or augmenting in some way the previous one. This apparent conundrum led to my interest in talking to Gibson and to the dancers who participated in her research who are very much part of this expert community of practice to find about more about dancer/performer/subject agency. I asked the dancers[9] a series of questions to find out more about how they experienced their remediation through the technological process of motion capture, to discover if they experienced any resistance to capturing what is an embodied practice, and held any anxiety about how their own data 'bank' might be stored, reused and rendered into new forms of expression, particularly now that their own 'digital portrait' is recorded and is available as a series of 'demo files' for others to view (although it is expected and intended that users will delete these files and use the app to upload their own captures).

Agency, image and the dancer

The dancers confirmed that imagery is very important if not fundamental to them, saying that it is *core to their teaching, making and dancing*. One acknowledged that she was probably drawn to SRT because she had *finally found a technique that made complete sense ... because of its underpinning use of imagery*. She added, *It's just how my mind works, and what my body responds to.*

When asked if they perceived a difference in how they were sourcing or drawing from imagery when working in the motion capture studio the dancers voiced a surprising ease about the process. As the studio can feel like a laboratory in which they are being studied and tested, it is likely to be a result of Gibson's own embodied knowledge of SRT and her own experience of being able to adapt to different environments that promoted this easefulness. It may also reveal a surprising flexibility and fluidity in the practice, and how the practice develops a 'super awareness' in the dancer so that s/he is able to stay with the principles of the work, despite what the dancers described as a potentially 'artificial' environment. One dancer even suggested that the environment was very conducive to her dancing, commenting, *I had expected to feel less involved or immersed in the imagery because of what I assumed would be the artificiality of the situation – but in fact it felt a perfectly natural and comfortable thing to do to work in the motion capture studio and I felt able to source from imagery in a very involved way and could have kept going indefinitely.* Another was able to point to times when it was more testing saying that:

9 I asked Gibson a similar set of questions:

1. *How important is imagery to you in your working with the dancers?*
2. *Did you perceive a difference in how the dancers were sourcing/drawing from imagery when working in the motion capture studio? If so, can you say how/what?*
3. *When working in the motion capture studio did you get a different/new sense of your own subjectivity in relation to how the dancers were embodying, owning and directing their own moving?*
4. *How did you experience the relational nature of working in the motion capture studio, did it have an effect or impact on how you worked with the dancers and dance yourself?*
5. *How do you feel about the 'capture' of motion capture – does it change/affect how you move and what you do in the studio during the motion capture session?*
6. *Has your experience working with the dancers changed your practice in any way – if so, can you say how?*

> *There were some challenges around dropping fully into the image though, because of being aware that it was specifically for the recording and because of the limitations of the motion capture suit (latter recordings were slightly easier in that respect due to the use of trackers that could stick straight onto skin). Not being able to lie on the floor was also challenging, particularly for me as I return to the floor a lot, and because it is a place where I can move into standing in an embodied way.*

But the same dancer noted that *Ruth did take care of that [in some way by] encouraging participants to give images from the work to each other (for example: I gave Moss to xxx).*

Similarly, when asked if working in the motion capture studio led them to a different or new sense of their own subjectivity and sense of how they were embodying, owning and directing their own moving, their responses differed slightly. One acknowledged that she *possibly wasn't as embodied as [she] may be in a different situation* but *due to being experienced at releasing, and at working with image, [I] was able to 'drop in' nonetheless; plus Ruth was supportive and encouraging.* Whereas another commented *I had expected a level of self consciousness to creep in and disrupt the flow of subjective experience but this did not happen.* All remarked upon the *intimate and supportive rather than intrusive* relational environment provided by Gibson, which for at least one dancer was surprising.

Some of the most interesting responses came from being asked how they felt about the 'capture' of motion capture, and whether it changed or affected how they moved and what they did in the studio during the motion capture session. This question is important because the dancers are working from image and not from choreographed or 'set' movement patterns and exercises, which is perhaps the more familiar experience for dancers when part of a research intervention in the motion capture studio. With the watching eye/lens of the camera as well as Gibson and others who may be witnessing the dancers, it is understandable that one dancer felt that *the 'capture' of motion capture injects a performative element to the process – just by knowing one is being captured. So it requires a rigour to stay embodied and present and raises questions of the differences that may occur in performative mode. Ideally one retains the same being state, but this can be a challenge.* Another dancer seemed to find the process more transformative, and also generative for her own moving, commenting that:

> *You need to regularly pause in a particular position (arms outstretched) so that the computer can recalibrate, and actually finding your self in this place from time to time became quite interesting – like revisiting a familiar place but finding a new resonance each time. I had feared that the outcome of 'capture' would encourage me to become over focused on form rather than the process of the image unfolding but this was not the case, and from what Bruno and Ruth have said I think sticking with the process of the image unfolding allowed for a certain clarity of data – i.e. the forms captured are clearer as a result of not predetermining them.*

No dancer thought that the experience of working with Gibson had changed their practice, experiencing it as *more about capturing an aspect of it than changing it.* The questions allowed them to reflect on their relationship to their image in relation to the project, observing their interest in the transformation from an *intimate experience* to the creation of an app, now in the public domain, whilst appreciating that the project enabled them to view their own work in a user-friendly way, without the need for motion capture workstations and specialist software.

In summary, these comments say something about the *techno-poetic* processes involved, showing how spontaneous movement data evoked through sensory imaginings can be captured and visualised to unearth something of the poetics in the SRT pedagogy and the dancers' own philosophies of movement. More particularly, the sensations that Skinner tapped into and expresses through her images seem to persist through these renderings and (re)writings, reflecting back on the way that SRT as a practice expanded. But what does this tell us about the image and the use of imagery in the practice of dancers and in our ways of communicating through the body? Image can easily become associated with a fixed visual form, as icon, created through capturing the body in motion, as proxy for the real, but there are multiple ways in which an image can be transformative, merging with the dancer. As Skinner contends, it becomes so real that one can become the image (in Neuhaus 2010). The intertwining of SRT and dance practice lies in this relationship between the image and the dancer. Each re-generates the other to provide a potent creative force that emerges through a process of mutual becoming rather than a unilateral invention. Imagery is thus fundamental to a dancer's perceptual awareness and for enhancing the communication of kinaesthetic data. When brought into the domain of motion capture, image is both input and output, generating and transforming whilst virtualising the sensory, corporeal world with which it participates. The modern technology that Heidegger was so wary of now produces work that is far from a 'standing reserve' in its generation of interstitial experiments and expressions. Together, the combined effect of spontaneity, remediation and reuse enables us to contemplate how temporality intervenes and interacts with the visual to generate new modes of creating, documenting and analysing dance, which then also reflects back on dance's ongoing and sometimes agonising entanglement with past and present, absence and presence, and the enticing spaces between.

References

Birringer, J. (2007) 'Data Art and Interactive Landscapes', in *SwanQuake the user manual* (ed. S. deLahunta) pp. 37-52, Liquid Press

deLaHunta, S., Clarke, G. & Barnard, P. (2011) 'A Conversation about Choreographic Thinking Tools', *Journal of Dance and Somatic Practices*, 3.1/2: 243-259

Dils, A. (2002) 'The Ghost in the Machine: Merce Cunningham and Bill T. Jones'; *PAJ: A Journal of Performance and Art*, 24.1: 92-104

Emslie, M. (2009) 'Skinner Releasing Technique: Dancing from within', *Journal of Dance and Somatic Practices*, 2.1: 169-175

Franklin, E. (1996) *Dance Imagery for Technique and Performance*, Human Kinetics Publishers

Gibson, R. & Martelli, B. (2013) 'As Yet Impossible presents igloo: Kinosphir – she's lost control'. http://bit.ly/tpMove56

Hanna, T. (1980), *The Body of Life: Creating New Pathways for Sensory Awareness and Fluid Movement*, Healing Arts Press

Heidegger, M. (1977) 'The Question Concerning Technology' (trans. Lovitt, W.) in *Heidegger, M.: Basic Writings* (ed. D. Krell) Harper and Row

Kozel, S. (2007) *Closer: Performance, Technologies, Phenomenology*, MIT Press

Laban, R. (1966) *Choreutics*, MacDonald and Evans

May, J. *et al.* (2011) 'Points in mental space: an interdisciplinary study of imagery in movement creation', *Dance Research*, 29.1: 402-430

Neuhaus, B. (2010) 'The Kinaesthetic Imagination; an interview with Joan Skinner'; *Contact Quarterly Online Journal*, July 2010; http://bit.ly/tpMove57

Overby, L.Y. & Dunn, J. (2011) 'The History and Research of Dance Imagery: Implications for Teachers', *The IADMS Bulletin for Teachers*, 3.2: 9-11

Popat, S. (2011) 'Technology' in Pitches, J. & Popat, S. *Performance Perspectives: a Critical Introduction*, pp. 114-115, Palgrave Macmillan

Salter, C. (2009) 'Environments, Interactions and Beings: The Ecology of Performativity and Technics' in *Interfaces of Performance* (eds. M. Chatzichristodoulou, J. Jefferies & R. Zerihan) pp. 27–42, Ashgate

Sweigard, L. E. (1974) *Human Movement Potential: Its Ideokinetic Facilitation*, University Press of America

Todd, M. E. (1937/1968) *The Thinking Body: A Study Of The Balancing Forces Of Dynamic Man*, Princeton Book Company

Whatley, S. (2012) 'The poetics of motion capture and visualization techniques: the differences between watching real and virtual dancing bodies' in D. Reynolds and M. Reason (eds) *Kinesthetic Empathy in Creative and Cultural Practices*; pp. 263-279, Intellect

Williams, K. (2000) 'Music Video, Technology and the Reversal of Perspective' in Ascott, R. (ed) *Art, Technology, Consciousness; mind@large*, pp. 103-108, Intellect

PART FOUR

Pedagogy/Education

SARA REED

Attending to Movement

The need to make dance that was different from that which went before

Introduction

In this chapter I trace the effects of explorations into somatic practices, the roots of new and postmodern dance and the consequent influence on teaching methodologies within late 20th- and early 21st-century dance higher education and training in the UK. The chapter charts the intertwining histories and interplay of somatic practices, New Dance and dance education in the UK during this period of time. I begin with a contextualisation for this development, including a brief introduction and historical background. Reference is made to a number of seminal UK dance practitioners through using primary interview material. Particularly highlighted is the work and contribution of Gill Clarke, a renowned British dance educator, performer and seminal pedagogue (1954–2011), understood through her own initiation into the relationship between dance and somatic practices and the effects on her own practice.

~

As Adshead-Lansdale notes, "In the UK in the late 1960s and early 1970s, a crucial shift in the art form of dance coincided with an equally crucial acknowledgement of dance in higher education, with far reaching effects" (2001: 65). It was in the late 1960s that it first became possible to study dance at degree level in the UK. From this point on the development of dance degrees within UK higher education flourished. In professional modern dance the Central European methods of dance training, performance and making were seen as the chief driving forces of change and influence through the middle of the 20th century, from the 1940s to the 1960s. However these were not the only influences on the development of modern dance and therefore dance education (Preston-Dunlop 2005). The first visit by the Martha Graham Company from the USA in 1954 precipitated a major change in British dance. The influences from American modern dance techniques affected both professional theatre dance and eventually dance education. The visit was significantly influential because of the support of Robin Howard, philanthropist and dance patron, who then pursued his dream to found a school for the training of British dancers in the Martha Graham technique in London, the London School of Contemporary Dance, thus establishing the first modern dance training in the UK. However this was not the first American dance influence in the UK; American dancer Margaret Barr, who studied with Martha Graham, had made regular visits to Dartington Hall from the 1930s onwards and indeed is credited as the developer of dance at Dartington from this time (Nicholas 2007).

In 1961 Ruth Foster, a key figure in UK dance education in the 1960s, met the American dancer Dorothy Madden. Madden had trained with Wigman, Holm and Horst, seminal European modern dancers of the time, and in 1965 she toured her company of students to some of the key teacher training colleges in the UK. The tour was highly significant and in that same year Madden ran a course for dance teachers at Dartington College of Arts (DCA). By this time Ruth Foster had become vice-principal of DCA (1964–1971) and amongst other things taught a course known as Resources, which was focused around the human body and how it worked. She was later to author the seminal book *Knowing in My Bones* (Foster 1976).

Within the same period of time (1966–1969) Flora Cushman, an American dancer, was teaching Graham-based technique at DCA. Cushman was, apparently, drawn to dancers when she felt that "Their souls were connected to their bodies and this made their movement fascinating in spite of technical deficiencies" (Manor 1996: 126). Mary Fulkerson, who arrived from the USA in 1973 to be head of dance at DCA, referred to her own work as "Anatomical Release Technique". "In Mary's classes we worked with developmental movement ... We studied and practiced rolling, crawling, walking, running, falling, and the transitions between these patterns" (Lepkoff 1999: 2). Fulkerson's influence in the UK can be seen as highly significant in relation to those that she taught, such as Rosemary Butcher, and those that she worked with at Dartington, for example Strider and members of the X6 collective, through the Dartington festivals (Jordan 1992). Undoubtedly she had a substantial impact on the New Dance movement and its development from the 1970s (Early 1978; Jordan 1992; Claid 2006; Nicholas 2007). Fulkerson, along with Cushman, may therefore be seen as one of the first dancers to be drawing together the threads of dance and bodywork practices in UK dance education and training. There were certainly strong resonances in their work with some of the key concepts of somatic practices, which are detailed later in this chapter. Cushman also taught Graham-based dance technique at the London School of Contemporary Dance, further extending the tentacles of connection between what was happening at Dartington and in London during the 1960s and 70s. Therefore these two areas of bodywork and dance technique were beginning to be brought together at both DCA and in London. However this was still an unusual combination of modern dance technique and bodywork that was being developed at DCA within a higher education context; significantly it also produced some talented dancer/makers, as Nicholas (2007) points out. At the same time as this the London School of Contemporary Dance was forging ahead with Robin Howard at its helm, officially opening in May 1966. Thus it was an exceptional time in the development of dance higher education in the UK (Adshead-Lansdale 2001). The challenge to accepted dance practices of the time was therefore beginning and developing a new curiosity and feeling of empowerment which was to be later more fully explored within the New Dance movement at X6. Although postmodernism may have deepened the connection between somatics and dance higher education, I suggest that the seeds were already being sown within the earlier modernist practice of Cushman and others.

In this chapter I therefore locate the emergence of somatic practices alongside dance within a period of time relating to the specific development of a particular style of dance, growing out of the modernist tradition, and recognised as postmodern or, in the UK, New Dance. The role of somatic practices within the evolution of postmodern/New Dance was particular to that time and those places where it grew, which spanned three continents and included not only New York and London but also Melbourne, Australia. The influence of postmodernist thought spread widely and from this, as Stephanie Jordan suggests, "Britain nurtured some of the most vital contemporary dance activity in Europe" in the 1980s (Jordan 1992: 3).

The need to make work that was different from that which went before can, I argue, be seen as the main driver for the development of postmodern dance in both the USA and the UK. Furthermore the introduction of a range of different somatic practices into dance making and education became a key feature of postmodern and New Dance (Banes 1987; Claid 2006; Jordan 1992). The influence of Alexander Technique, the Feldenkrais Method, Skinner Releasing Technique, Sensory Awareness, Ideokinesis and many other practices can be evidenced in the pages of a number of dance specialist journals and in particular *New Dance, Writings on Dance* and *Contact Quarterly*. However somatics in itself was not new in its relationship to dance, as has already been discussed. It was the desire by dancers and dance makers to challenge the past methods of training and performance that led to the exploration of different somatic practices in an attempt to forge new ways of working and of presenting dance performance to an audience. If it wasn't for this desire to deconstruct traditional methods of training, performing and dance making then it is, I suggest, unlikely that somatics would have taken on the more recent prominence that it now, arguably, has within UK dance higher education and training.

The radicalisation of dance practice brought about through postmodernism can be seen as a 20th-century phenomenon. Through their work the American postmodernists deconstructed technical demands and instead experimented with natural and pedestrian movement (Banes 1987). Some British dance artists similarly dealt with many of the same issues (Claid 2006). In particular a group of British dancers may be seen as seminal to the development of that relationship between a new radical dance practice and somatic practices in the UK. The dance collective known as X6 existed for just five years from 1976 and consisted of five artists: Jacky Lansley, Fergus Early, Maedee Dupres, Mary Prestige and Emilyn Claid (Claid 2006). Claid says of the X6 members "we had a question to ask: how had the systems from which we had arrived, or were escaping, ruled our lives?" (2006: 11). These five dance artists and those that joined them at the X6 space were part of a network of experimental artists, including musicians and filmmakers, working in London at that time. X6 had a hugely significant influence on the direction of UK professional contemporary dance and subsequently dance training and education from the mid-1970s onwards; the results of this can be seen in many performance companies, management contexts and performance teaching today (Claid 2006). The subversion by the X6 dancers of previously learnt practices, such as ballet, and the discovery and use of a range of somatic practices instead of and alongside dance technique has been key to the development of dance-somatics in the UK from then on. Emilyn Claid states that X6 provided "the hinge to a door that opens backwards to a view of the past and forwards to a construction of the future" (Claid 2006: 12) and part of that future was a different way of dancing and making dance (Jordan 1992). It should be noted that the term dance-somatics is still a relatively new term mentioned by a number of dance educators who are strongly influenced by and committed to both dance and somatic practices, for example Glenna Batson (1990; 1993; 2007), Martha Eddy (2009) and myself (Reed 2011). However it is a term that is now being more widely used and recognised.

The dance born of the 1960s, 1970s and 1980s therefore resulted in a definite change in the world of contemporary dance practice in the UK during the time of X6. These changes have slowly but surely impacted upon dance pedagogy in UK higher education ever since. From then on many dancers worked independently rather than being part of one company. They would perform with several groups or companies as well as making and performing their own work of solos, duets, etc. in a range of different performance contexts including outdoor spaces and alternative indoor spaces such as railway stations, museums, art galleries and empty buildings. Thus the training they undertook explored a wide range of practices and techniques necessary to provide the body with the versatility needed to perform in these very different places, using a more eclectic range of movement styles.

It can be seen, therefore, that many UK dance practitioners who were training during the post-X6 period experienced a range of training seen as typical of the eclectic style of the late 20th, and now 21st, century and as a direct result of the New Dance influences (Reed 2011, p.53). These practitioners were, on the whole, studying and training whilst still in their twenties, during the early-to-mid-1980s. This was at the time that *New Dance* magazine, the seminal and influential dance magazine published by the X6 collective, was still being produced in the UK (the magazine was published until 1987). The identities of these dancers were considerably shaped by the challenges presented through New Dance. For example Scott Clark, a dancer who performed with the Siobhan Davies Dance Company based in London, discusses the "different world of the intellect" he discovered through dance,

> that was part of that different culture. Dance and even gymnastics ... [these] were the first places I had heard anything in the way of serious discussion about meditation or the value of practices that we might think of as religious practices from other cultures and how they might be useful to people learning about movement. (Reed, interview 2002)

As a scientist who began his dance training at the age of 21, Clark's story was unusual but not untypical of the postmodern/New Dance experience, which often involved untrained dancers and explored non-dance or pedestrian movement: the antithesis, I suggest, of the highly trained technical dancer who had started their career as a child ballet dancer. But postmodern or New Dance was not just for the untrained; far from it: the Judson dancers were an eclectic mix, many of whom had performed with the leading modern dance companies of their times. Similarly in the UK the X6 collective was started by a group of dancers and choreographers, some of whom were professionally trained and experienced ballet dancers. For all of these artists their concerns with movement were very different from what had gone before.

At the same time, in the latter part of the 20th century, dance degrees were becoming well established across the UK and were responding to the changing nature of contemporary dance performance and choreography. UK-based dancers and choreographers, who were themselves influenced by the new ways of working in contemporary dance practice, were teaching within dance higher education and training contexts and, in parallel, they were also teaching dancers, choreographers and teachers in daily classes at professional dance centres across the UK. Many of the participants in these classes were newly graduated from degree courses. Thus these same influences were shaping dance pedagogy and becoming firmly established both in and outside dance higher education courses in the UK from the late 20th century onwards.

As Gill Clarke suggested, the New Dance movement begun at X6 presented an opportunity for those "technical people" to do something else and for her "it was a door she couldn't wait to have opened" (Reed, interview 2002a). During her work with the Siobhan Davies Dance Company, from the 1980s, Clarke experienced a range of practices, such as the Alexander Technique, Klein-influenced work and the Feldenkrais Method. For Clarke, as for many other dancers at the time, the introduction of somatic practices into dance training changed her whole understanding of the dancing body. Alongside these changes in ways of working she also discovered Todd's seminal work *The Thinking Body* (1937) and Sweigard's *Ideokinetic Facilitation* (1974) and consequently awareness training had a huge influence on her development as a dancer, dance maker and in particular as a dance pedagogue (Reed, interview 2002a). A key part of Gill Clarke's work as a dance practitioner, as with many contemporary dance professionals, was, and always had been, as a teacher:

> My teaching has always been a learning place because it's a time for you to explore but also you get so much visual feedback that makes you think about how you could approach things differently; what language and activity seems to work, and what could I say in different words, finding other words. And I think through teaching, which is a sort of passion of mine, I more and more realise that it is not what I do but it's what I say that makes a difference; how I say it maybe, how to come at the same idea differently or how not to do everything all at once. To have patience; at least to be simpler and clearer about the instruction, to refine the quality of attention and therefore the benefit and change. (Reed, interview 2002a)

The connection that Clarke found between her dance training, somatic practices and her teaching has greatly influenced those whom she taught and those courses she developed and led both within a formal higher education context and beyond. As she pointed out, in her own experience and through the exploration of different body practices she became "more technically able and more articulate. I was more aware of what my body was doing" (Reed, interview 2002a). Gill Clarke advised on numerous courses. She was closely aligned to the undergraduate studies at the Laban Centre London (now Trinity Laban) among others, and involved in the development of the MA Programme in Creative Practice for mid-career artists run by Trinity Laban Conservatoire of Music and Dance, Independent Dance and Siobhan Davies Dance. This exemplary MA for experienced dance practitioners includes a module in Embodied Practice which, as the Independent Dance website states, "aims to deepen and extend your embodied understanding of your own movement practice" (Independent Dance 2014).

I suggest that there is a spectrum of teaching styles within dance higher education/ training ranging from pure instruction, regarded as the dominant paradigm, to a more esoteric fluidity of somatic-based dance practices, perhaps perceived as the marginal paradigm. This paradigm, I argue, encourages a greater questioning and critical approach to the development of the dancing body (Fortin, Vieira & Tremblay 2009). Many of those who teach within a dance higher education context have come from the professional dance world and bring with them an eclectic experience of dance and/or somatic practices. There is evidence that many UK contemporary dancers who were training during the late 20th century were strongly influenced by their engagement with different somatic practices (Reed 2011). Much of this influence came from the New Dance Movement, as described by Gill Clarke, and through seminal practitioners such as Mary Fulkerson. These dancers and teachers, in their turn, have influenced the current generation of dancers who demonstrate the eclecticism prevalent in UK dance pedagogy today.

Gill Clarke, for example, discussed the lack of any bodywork practices apart from codified dance technique within her own training. However, once she discovered this 'other' area of movement practice, she was particularly excited about the possibilities it had for her own development as a dancer:

> I couldn't believe that somehow I had been performing for that many years and I wasn't as clear as I had imagined about what my whole body was doing, so that's what I think is really exciting about this work. (Reed, interview 2002a)

Gill Clarke and Scott Clark were both members of the Siobhan Davies Dance Company during the 1980s and 1990s. The majority of the company dancers in the early years were initially trained in Martha Graham technique at the London School of Contemporary Dance (LSCD), as was Siobhan Davies herself. However Gill Clarke and Scott Clark were exceptions to this. The style of training at LSCD was considered the standard contemporary dance training of the time and was greatly sought after by young dancers wishing to train (Reed, interview 2002). Paul Douglas, another dancer with the Siobhan Davies Dance Company, came from an Aikido training as well as a contemporary dance training background, although at this point he hadn't brought these two practices together (Reed, interview 2002). Scott Clark, however, during his time with Siobhan Davies, did bring the Feldenkrais Method into a daily company class by linking it with the dancing that the company were doing at the time. This was an innovative development encouraged by Davies. Clark suggests that the difference between teaching dance technique and teaching a somatic practice is that in dance technique classes, participants expect to be told what to do and to be corrected. He points out that somatic practice is more than learning rules and his particular interest lies in "something which is independent of tradition or physique or one's background" (Reed, interview 2002). Furthermore, he explains that somatic practices do not give the answers but dancers find the answers for themselves. It is this ability for reflection and question that is nurtured through somatics and, it is argued, is central to its value alongside dance. Moni explains this bodily perception as "a way to join the mind and the body in the same place and time. It is also a way of synchronising the fast and boundless mind in action with the experiential, sensory reality" (2004: abstract). In discussing a two-hour session focused on students' breathing and their sensing of the spine, Gill Clarke emphasised the importance of the time needed for such careful, slow work, thus enabling participants to really focus (Reed, interview 2002a).

It is an understanding of the qualities and characteristics of somatic practices, and awareness of those practices, that is most useful to dancers and so crucial to the development of a dance-somatics within dance higher education and training. This method of learning is not about the correct execution of form as in ballet or contemporary dance technique. Learning in and through somatic practices relates to the qualities of those sensations experienced, which dancers may then go on to develop and use in their own practice and technical training. I suggest that key concepts inherent within somatic practices illustrate what it is that might be useful to a dancer's education. These concepts include, though not exclusively: increased sensory awareness, efficiency of movement, functional integration, body-mind integration, re-patterning, addressing habitual movement, breath awareness and use of imagery (Reed 2011; Murphy 1992). A dancer's personal exploration of these and other key concepts through engagement with somatic practices enables them to challenge habitual movement, thereby learning through the practice and thus affecting their creative thinking and originality (Green 1996). Scott Clark refers to the effects of the Feldenkrais Method and he discusses how participants "have sensations that would in some way be different from the usual pattern and that different pattern of sensation would then lead them somewhere new" (Reed, interview 2002). He admits that his explanation sounds rather "amorphous", which may be one of the criticisms sometimes aimed at somatic practices. Clark describes what he means through his own work:

> My job as a Feldenkrais practitioner is to help people make sense out of their sensations; not to tell them how they should sense but to help them find out what they do sense and how that can come together to form patterns that they want to produce. (Reed, interview 2002)

In the case of a choreographer studying the Feldenkrais Method, for example, this may give the opportunity to break away from habitual movement and to develop new movement vocabulary. Moni describes it thus: "non-reaction releases a dancer from the habitual and instrumental patterns of moving and brings her or him into the 'here' moment of body-mind integrity"; in other words, the dancer becomes present in the moment (2004: abstract).

Gill Clarke reflected on her experience of discovering bodywork practices through her work with Scott Clark in the Feldenkrais Method and Jeremy Nelson, who trained in Klein technique:

> An opportunity to work with Scott Clark ... was fabulous and we had a few sessions with an Alexander teacher, who I then kept in contact with. Working with Scott was about sensation, but also about perception and the active engagement of body and mind ... The radically different thing with Jeremy was that he started by talking about the skeleton, and gave very clear directions to move from the bones, rather than a sense of shape or musculature and that, as I sensed it, changed my body and my movement. (Reed, interview 2002a)

This suggests that it was through these and other influences, from the field of somatic practices, that Gill Clarke took a particular path in the development of her own practice as both dancer and teacher. This direction and interest seems to have been critical in her work as Head of Performance at the Laban Centre, London. In addition her partnership there with Kirsty Alexander, Head of Undergraduate Studies, in rewriting the dance undergraduate programme led to the integration of dance and somatics throughout the curriculum. Clarke described the new regime, introduced by her and Alexander, for incoming First Year students. In the first five weeks of the academic year a 'Fundamental Skills' intensive programme was introduced, comprising a 'mini foundation course'. The course included three hours a day of 'experiential anatomy into contemporary dance technique' (Reed, interview 2002a). One of the questions that arose from the introduction of the new course was how best to introduce students to this particular way of working. Clarke's suggestion was that such a course "introduces students to the tools that they need to go forward with and allows them to build on strong foundations of better movement patterning" (Reed, interview 2002a). For some students, particularly those starting their first undergraduate year, dancing means using steps and therefore working more holistically can be very challenging and for some extremely difficult. However, in this example given of the changes made by Clarke and Alexander, dance technique class was always included within the framework of the fundamental skills intensive as a clear reference point for students. As Clarke pointed out:

> there was always bodywork within the course and the students generally understood that what they gained was useful to them and that through this work they learnt to question things they may have previously taken for granted; for example the ways that they moved, how they felt about that and how they got to that point of moving. (Reed, interview 2002a)

Developing a strand of somatic practice alongside dance technique especially within undergraduate programmes can be, and often is, problematic (Reed, interview 2002a; Roubiceck 2009; Weber 2009). I suggest that those who are teaching within the framework of a dance-somatics pedagogy need to have had direct experience of somatic practice that they have integrated into their own dancing and teaching. If this is not the case then, I argue, their understanding of somatics may remain purely abstract and therefore often without meaning and, consequently, potentially confusing to those they teach.

Kirsty Alexander refers to a "continuum of somatic and traditional practices" relating to pre-existing vocabulary through which students explore kinaesthetic experiences and develop their own language, resulting in a cross fertilisation. She argues that "attending to kinaesthetic experience is a dimension of practice that can underscore both somatically focussed or codified techniques and therefore offers students a consistent framework of values" (Alexander 2008). I suggest that this cross fertilisation is becoming the more usual pattern for those dance higher education courses which already, authentically, embrace dance-somatics. However, such a cross fertilisation needs to be handled carefully in terms of sound pedagogical practice to avoid what may be described as a potpourri method whereby students could be unclear about what and how they are learning.

Within a dance-somatics based programme it may be expected that students will develop their own styles and methods of working, which come from their exposure to a range of practices and dance techniques across the curriculum. For example, at Dartington College of Arts (1961–2008) students studying for a BA Choreography degree were timetabled in both dance techniques and bodywork practices across all three years of their degree programme. The range of practices included Body-Mind Centering, Alexander Technique, Feldenkrais, Yoga and Pilates (Reed 2009). They also received theoretical underpinning in somatics and there is evidence through their practical work and writings that they were able to make clear corporeal connections that had an impact on their creative work, which was the focus of their degree. One final year undergraduate student described her experience of somatics and the influence that it had on her developing choreographic practice:

> My experience could be described as a process of re-uniting my body and mind. I realised how alienated I was from my physical being but I hadn't been aware of this. This progressed into an attitude of allowing my body to learn, often giving it time and active concentration to process movement. By listening to my body, I allow it to adjust. In my choreographic work, I often create movement ideas through a process, which includes experiential research on others and myself. (Anonymous, (g) 2008)

Of her experience of the Feldenkrais Method the same student noted, "I found my body learning new ways to move and an ease in the process. I noticed I was automatically becoming more efficient within dance technique classes." Of the dancers she worked with she found that "the more they had been developing new movement functions and patterns, the greater choice there would be to research and play and to then create choreography" (Anonymous, (g) 2008).

Another undergraduate student described her experience of previous training, before arriving at DCA, in Graham technique and the resulting injury she had acquired:

> In our daily Graham and ballet classes, the approach was to stress the body into conforming to a certain shape at a given time. Although I desired to achieve this position my body would not respond. Repeating these failing schemes of movement led to much mental and physical strain. When I had eventually recognised the injury this had caused (a strain in the psoas muscles) there came a time of reflection. I realised I needed to redirect my focus. By trying to imitate another's body, I was misusing mine. Most importantly it had created a feeling of restriction, discouragement and lack of creative impulse. It is through this minor injury that I woke up to a real body awareness: focussing from inside, accepting what my body needed, having a clearer image of anatomy. It opened up a new fascinating site of exploration: body-mind awareness. (Anonymous, (h) 2008)

These examples support my argument that a dance pedagogy and learning style which is research-led, through what Margaret H'Doubler, (1940) so long ago, described as the dancer's laboratory, will be more innovative, critical and challenging; thereby leading to greater creativity in performer/makers, as can be evidenced by the alumni of dance performance training and education departments that use this approach (Jordan 1992; Nicholas 2007).

It may be that it is the privileging of kinaesthetic learning over visual learning which is particularly pertinent to somatics-based work. For example, the ideal of "removing the reliance of visual modelling" as in the dance technique class with its predominately didactic style and use of mirror images and replacing it with the more verbally led somatics (kinaesthetic) teaching as in the Feldenkrais Method (Long 2002: 75). Warwick Long therefore endorses a plurality of approaches, which may be seen to be supported by Howard Gardner's theories of teaching and learning. Gardner suggests that if "we are to encompass adequately the realm of human cognition, it is necessary to include a far wider and more universal set of competencies than has ordinarily been considered" (1993: xiv).

Fortin discusses the appropriateness of somatics within dance training and its potential to "stimulate reflective thinking" and in particular she endorses connections relating to Feldenkrais work, and the necessity to re-educate students in the area of "motor patterns" (1995: 254). She reflects on the usefulness of somatic practices in developing students' "expressive capacities" and this is something that Green (1996) also discusses in some detail. More specifically it can be seen that somatic practitioners pay particular attention to the psychophysical process and encouraging dance students towards a more holistic approach to their training which, I argue, is essential within dance-somatics. These psychophysical processes lead students towards a self-reflexive approach to their work, which is appropriate for both their creativity and dance training. However, students do need guidance on ways of working to avoid the danger of their work becoming too inward-looking and overly self-referential. The delivery of a dance-somatics curriculum with a balance of dance techniques and somatics through theory and practice should, I suggest, avoid this tendency. Natalie Garrett Brown describes the dance university course she leads at Coventry University and the importance of,

> working from a shared understanding of somatic practices within undergraduate education. We have had to address the student's notion of what dance technique is and what somatic practice is. At present it is embedded into what we call 'Movement Studies 1–3'. Year 1 have tasters of somatic practice and healthier dancer studies. Year 2 have Skinner Releasing Technique and Year 3 have Body Mind Centering. But to the students they are all just doing dance technique class. We also introduce key seminar papers and discussions around somatic practices as a way to situate somatics and to further illuminate their histories and principles. (Reed, interview 2010)

Garrett Brown discusses the need to modify the curriculum in order to give a more "integrated approach because students don't like not dancing" (Reed, interview 2010). This is a common complaint from undergraduate students first introduced to somatics (Reed 2011). When dance technique classes are informed by somatics the students are more able to make the link. It is also important for all members of a dance faculty to have experience and training in somatic practices (Reed interview 2010).

In this chapter I have explored the interweaving of somatics and dance. Discussions with experienced dance pedagogues and the influence of somatic practice on their own methods of teaching have informed the writing. Dancers should not have to wait until they have finished their education to be introduced to somatic practices, as Gill Clarke said,

> People sometimes say isn't this (somatics) something that one needs to come to later? And I think they are saying that because what they see out there is dancers who have come to this work later but that is only because it wasn't around before and if we've got knowledge and information then we should pass it on to people as soon as we possibly can. (Reed, interview 2002a)

If somatics is present within UK dance undergraduate programmes, it is, on the whole, fitted within the traditional pedagogic framework and dominant discourse for dance higher education and training (Reed 2011). The dominant discourse of dance "values an ideal body where the aesthetic criteria of beauty, slimness, virtuosity, devotion and asceticism prevail" (Fortin, Vieira & Tremblay 2009: 49). Thus somatics is often squeezed between the seemingly more 'important' aspects of the dance curriculum rather than being allowed to lead through what may be termed a more radical approach to teaching and learning in and through somatics, which is currently considered the more marginal area of dance higher education programmes. However, over the last few years there has been a discernible, though subtle, move towards the inclusion of somatics within dance higher education degree courses in some universities and colleges in the UK, although this movement is currently perceived as relatively modest (Reed 2011).

Late 20th-century dance, in contrast to the modern dance in both Europe and America, freed dancers from codified techniques such as those of Martha Graham, Doris Humphrey and Merce Cunningham. The postmodernists dealt directly with movement ideas allowing a different articulation of issues and thus challenging what was seen as art, rather than conceiving of dance as narrative which, it is argued, the modern dance in fact had rarely departed from despite its challenge to ballet. Consequently the pre-existing vocabulary became inappropriate and inadequate for the expressive needs of the time. The postmodernists challenged the hierarchical nature of the more traditional principles within the modernist modes of choreography, performance and teaching, many of which, I suggest, were borrowed from ballet's authoritative patriarchal style. From this emerged a more democratic form of movement in parallel with a social democracy of gender/politics/lifestyle, now well documented in the UK within the pages of *New Dance* magazine and also by such writers as Banes (1987) and Jordan (1992). This legacy is now having a significant influence on 21st-century dance education and training.

References

Adshead-Lansdale, J. (2001) 'London Contemporary Dance Theatre: its Legacy in 1964, Higher Education in the UK', *Choreography and Dance*, Vol.6, Part 4, pp. 65-89

Alexander, K. (2008) 'Somatic and Creative Practices', Conference held at John Moores University, Liverpool. Reed, S. notes from the conference and unpublished papers 9 Feb. 2008

Anonymous (g) (2008) Final year undergraduate student Dartington College of Arts

Anonymous (h) (2008) Final year undergraduate student Dartington College of Arts

Banes, S. (1987) *Terpsichore in Sneakers, Post Modern Dance*, Wesleyan University Press

Batson, G. (1990) 'Dancing Fully, Safely and Expressively: The Role of Body Therapies in Dance Training', *Journal of Physical Education, Recreation and Dance*. 61(9): pp. 28-31.

_______ (1993) 'The Role of Somatic Education in Dance Medicine and Rehabilitation', *North Carolina Medical Journal*. 54(2) pp.74-77.

_______ (2007) 'Revisiting Overuse Injuries in Dance in View of Motor Learning and Somatic Models of Distributed Practice', *Journal of Dance Medicine and Science*, Vol. 11, No. 3 pp. 70-74

Claid, E. (2006) *Yes? No! Maybe.... Seductive Ambiguity in Dance*, Routledge

Early, F. (1978) 'A Good Year', *New Dance*. No. 5, New Year, pp. 3-5

Eddy, M. (2009) 'A brief history of somatic practices and dance: historical development of the field of somatic education and its relationship to dance', *Journal of Dance and Somatic Practices* Vol 1, No. 1, pp. 5-27

Fortin, S. (1995) 'Toward a New Generation: Somatic Dance Education in Academia', *Impulse*, Vol. 3, pp. 253-262

_______ (2008) 'Somatic and Creative Practices', Conference held at John Moores University,

Liverpool. Reed, S. Notes and unpublished papers 9 Feb. 2008

Fortin, S., Vieira, A. and Tremblay, M. (2009) 'The experience of discourse in dance and somatics', *Journal of Dance and Somatic Practices* Vol. 1, No. 1, pp. 47-64

Foster, R. (1976) *Knowing in My Bones*, A&C Black

Gardner, H. (1993) *Frames of Mind: The Theory of Multiple Intelligences*, Fontana Press

Green, J. (1996) 'Choreographing a Postmodern Turn: The Creative Process and Somatics', *Impulse*. Vol. 4, No 4. Fall, pp.267-275

H'Doubler, M. (1940) *Dance: A Creative Art Experience*, Appleton-Century Crofts

Independent Dance (2014) 'MA Creative Practice' http://bit.ly/tpMove61

Jordan, S. (1992) *Striding Out: Aspects of Contemporary and New Dance in Britain*, Dance Books

Lepkoff, D. (1999) 'What is Release Technique?', *Movement Research Performance Journal*. No 19, Fall/Winter, p. 2

Long, W. (2002) 'Sensing Difference: Student and Teacher Perception on the Integration of the Feldenkrais Method of Somatic Education and Contemporary Dance Technique', Unpublished MA thesis, University of Otago, Dunedin, NZ

Manor, G. '25 Years of Creativity: The Kibbutz Contemporary Dance Company', http://bit.ly/tpMove67

Moni, K. (2004) 'The Poetic Movement of Being: Philosophical Interpretations of the New Paradigm of Dance in the Light of Martin Heidegger's thinking and the Artistic work of in years 1996–1999', Unpublished Doctoral thesis, Theatre Academy of Finland

Murphy, M. (1992) *The Future of the Body: Explorations into the Further Evolution of Human Nature*, Jeremy Tarcher

Nicholas, L. (2007) *Dancing in Utopia: Dartington Hall and its Dancers*, Dance Books

Perazzo Domm, D. (2007) 'Dancing Poetry: Jonathan Burrows reconfiguration of choreography', Unpublished Doctoral thesis, University of Surrey, UK

Preston-Dunlop, V. (2005) *The American Invasion* 1962–72. PAL, UK

Reed, S. (2002) Unpublished interview with Scott Clark

_______ (2002a) Unpublished interview with Gill Clarke

_______ (2009) Choreography timetable and curriculum, Dartington College of Arts. Notes and college papers unpublished

_______ (2010) Unpublished interview with Natalie Garrett Brown

_______ (2011) 'The Articulation of a Dance Somatics for a Twenty-First Century Higher Education', Unpublished PhD thesis, University of Surrey, UK

Roubicek, S. (2009) 'Hara breathing applied to dance practice', *Journal of Dance & Somatic Practices* 1:2, pp. 255-262

Sweigard, L. (1974) *Human Movement Potential: Its Ideokinetic Facilitation*, Harper and Row

Todd, M.E. (1937) *The Thinking Body*, Dance Horizons

Weber, R. (2009) 'Integrating semi-structured somatic practices and contemporary dance technique training', *Journal of Dance & Somatic Practices* 1:2, pp. 237-254

FIONA BANNON and DUNCAN HOLT

Attending to Ethics and Aesthetics in Dance

Introduction

> In the opening solo of Affections (1996), you could almost feel her breath reaching through her limbs or spiralling inside her torso. In contrast to that contained intensity, in Bank (1997) it was the inventiveness and density of detail in the dancing that struck you, and the exactitude of its execution.
>
> ... she upheld her core belief in the body not only as a means of action and expression, but as a source of knowledge and understanding.
> (Roy and Lee, 2011)

We step into the chapter sharing the memories of two people watching 'another', whilst she danced. Through these fragments the irreducible effect of the ways shared moments might forge relations that are at once emotional, kinaesthetic and participatory is made evident. Both quotations are taken from *The Guardian* newspaper obituary for dance artist Gill Clarke. They tell of a person who danced, and who held a clear conviction that the ecology of thinking through motion could facilitate affective and significant personal and cultural growth. It is these threads that we identify as guides for the following discussion where the concern is with what might usefully be identified as an ecology of thinking in the practice of motion found in and through an education in dance.

With the refreshing increase in scholarly attention now being given to sensorial awareness and bodily perception, there are opportunities to revisit and to delve further into 'knowledges' that can be generated as identifying features of dance education. Always crucial in such a debate is an appreciation for the movement of attitudes, across the roles and power structures that are part of the social engagement of teaching and learning. Whilst this remains a complex arena, it is evident that many who teach dance have rich experience engaging students in the design and activation of their own routes to mindful knowledge. The discussion shared in this chapter aims to articulate a dialogic engagement between aesthetics and relational ethics as a vital feature in learning to think in terms of interrelatedness. It can be argued that it is this, embodied, felt, thought that frames learning in dance education as a self-actualising inter-discipline.

The discussion will reference realms of sociality explored in choreography, where makers and movers generate material through the realisation of a shared relational practice. Through these modes of activity, consideration can be given to the ways in which ethics and aesthetics might contribute to the diversified knowledge found through motion. Focus is also given to thinking in terms of improvisation, collaboration and ongoing rehearsals of collective practice where the choices made about how 'we pay and give attention' come to act as precursors to sustaining a diverse range of voices. In bringing aesthetics and relational ethics together the intention is to understand more of how they contribute to our means of existence and resource our power to act. What is perhaps familiar for many of us is, as Bojana Cvejić suggests, the idea that "movement operates in the middle of things" (2004: n.p.). It is not straightforward; we educators are in the business of encouraging those we teach to step beyond their comfort zones and pre-determinations towards expressions of individual potential in moving. Liz Lerman neatly encapsulates the thoughts of many working in the field when she acknowledges:

> how much dancers know and how little we share it with the rest of the world: in how much dancers know and how little the rest of the world knows we know it. (Lerman 2011: xiv)

As dance educators and academics we come to understand something of the features that constitute moving around this world, and appreciate that an extraordinary amount of interconnected 'knowing' takes place in learning to think in terms of the choreography of places. Like any other discipline and by necessity, much of the work undertaken through movement happens in discreet specialist locations, spaces that to the uninitiated appear empty, devoid of the more obvious laboratory equipment. Learning through studio practice, where transmission is reliant on being present, emphasises that this experience of education is about being in negotiation with time, space, self, others and ideas. It is through these corporeal experiences that ethical awareness mingles with aesthetic and cognitive aptitudes. In what are effectively fluid, ongoing relations, students can individually learn to exercise organisation over how they think and what they deem to be important to think about. At the forefront of this endeavour resides a desire on the part of the educator to guide students towards ways in which they might construct coherent meanings from experience and consequently to open routes to ways of making-sense and effecting substantial change.

What we return to again and again in terms of the value inherent in study through motion is that, for each of us, it is our body that is the centre of our existence in the world. It is through this bodily, emplaced self that we "literally are selves expressed" (Schenck 1986: 46). Considered in these terms we can realise that changes in attitudes and in modes of thinking can be understood as something generated through 'bodily-dwelling'. It is through what is effectively a responsive engagement that a situated or adaptive *ethics of practice* might be recognised. What dance education, taught well, can offer is a lively engagement with acts of negotiation. This can be made evident as a form of dynamic interaction with an increasing appreciation of embodied ordering that enables us to generate knowledge effectively as a practical philosophy of our embodiment.

Ways of being in the world

In the following paragraphs we reflect on processes that guided our own development of a dance degree in the UK in the mid-1990s and find reassurance in tracing something of the continuation of similar work and ideas in the current development of programmes. Change, we are reminded, takes time, and is most usefully recognised as a process rather than an event.

At the beginning of discussions about what identifies degree-level study in dance we struggled with the apparent contradictions of supporting individual students in an educational tradition that served many 'masters', whether economic, political or ideological. As the work progressed we endeavoured to bring the required language of the validation documents to a different life. The shared ambition was to present an holistic view of the benefits of education in and through dance (Holt 1997). Eventually our understanding of what constitutes a worthwhile education in dance shifted. We sought a contextualised reading of dance that meant championing a multi-directional curriculum that could engage with responses to movement that were at once culturally, politically and socially aware. Whilst thinking of dance as both multi- and inter-disciplinary by nature, we especially appreciated the values inherent in exploring interconnected intelligence – senses and somas.

Exploring these areas of curriculum development more fully brought us to an 'everyday aesthetics' that stepped beyond traditions of art theory and towards consideration for an expansion of perceptual powers and the cultivation of sensibility as key guides to apprehending the world. Having taught dance in the university sector in Australia we had both been introduced to *Safe Dance Practice*, guided by the work of dancer, lecturer, physiologist and therapist Tony Geeves (1990, 1997, 1999). At the time this included the introduction of somatic awareness as a range of distinct practices into the dance curriculum. This included aspects of Body-Mind Centering, the Alexander Technique, the Feldenkrais Method and some work in a selection of yoga practices. Returning to work in the UK, we were eager to integrate this material into the new programme.

What had informed our desire to do this was the formative educational philosophies of John Dewey (1934) particularly his views of education as a process in continuous formation, of growth, experiment and transaction. These ideas blended with our own experiences of dancing with people who dance for a host of reasons beyond formal educational settings. Looking back we see that at the heart of our project lay an assertion that education should focus on the realisation of the potential of human intelligence. It should enhance each individual's ability to order their experience, and to aid them to make sense of a lived world (Greene 1988).

In terms of the delivery of a dance programme, it meant needing to address how learning happens and examining how learning to think through dance might be put into practice. What became evident was that in order to foster what we saw as an autonomy to think, to trace cause and effect and to consider subjective reality in relation to objective reflection, we needed to access personal growth as something more than fulfilling the requirements of a statutory, fixed, measurable entity. Yes, we were looking for students to succeed in terms of the requirements of the degree but what drove this was a desire that they would recognise the cohesion of interconnected modes of knowing as a significant part of their learning. Eventually, these modes of thinking led to explorations of what we thought of as 'unexpected learning outcomes' rather than the more familiar expectations of delivery. In this endeavour we felt the support of Ivan Illich, who, in prizing a fluidity of the re-creation of self through educational change suggests that,

> It is growth in disciplined dissidence which cannot be measured against a rod, or any curriculum, nor compared to someone else's achievement. In such learning one can emulate others only in imaginative endeavour, and follow in their footsteps rather than mimic their gait. (Illich 1971: 40)

By addressing what we saw as questions concerning ways to identify embodied potential, we drew inspiration from thinkers who themselves championed sensitive perception, and who strove to facilitate versatility rather than to tame it. Eventually, there was a shift towards activity and operation that validated engagement with uncertainty rather than predictability and towards generating self-reflexive knowledge rather than dependence on our ongoing supervisory evaluation. Looking across the range of disciplinary practice in current delivery in the UK context, it is evident that for many the question of how to design meaningful and relevant learning experiences continues to be negotiated. The popular use of modularisation in the academy in the UK continues to fragment programme cohesion and coherence. Programme teams strive to create interconnections in the learning experience for students who arrive already patterned by an education that has trained them into disciplinary division. It is also evident that generative 'meaning making' remains a core intention of many programme designs; priority may be given to knowledge being found through experimentation but there are questions to ask about challenging what has been traditionally taught as dance in terms of identifying history, choreography and practice. In a history curriculum that often chooses to highlight named choreographers and theorists for the challenges they presented to 'tradition', current design of modules and assessments often fail to drive students to generate a similar impetus in their own work.

An education in dance might be understood as a process in which we can learn to hone our ability to address a range of 'propositions', to borrow a term from choreographer, organisational theorist and educator William Forsythe (2008). He argues that when working with a range of differing ideas we need to learn to let them co-exist as contrary threads to be explored and reconsidered for the potential relational connections that they might generate. Such experiments in movement can in turn provide building blocks for further engagements and provoke contemplation in realms of our unknowing. Ultimately, in dealing with areas of uncertainty and trusting that we can each enhance our competence through creatively managing tasks, we can come to recognise that we can orchestrate thinking. This idea draws on a growing appreciation for an ecology of mindful motion that does not recognise disciplinary boundaries or at least is not prohibited by them. William Forsythe speaks in a similar tone, when referencing his personal preference of working to keep things indefinite, learning to cherish the possibilities inherent in a stammer rather than a closed, inflexible text. In what appears to be an emerging awareness of working through multiple modes of disseminating thinking, it is interesting to see that he acknowledges the difficulties inherent in learning to 'not know', to practise being frightened and, in this process, to be in the middle of things (Forsythe 2012). This is certainly a familiar difficulty in terms of developmental practice working with choreography students. The ideas themselves are not new, in that they are reminiscent of *Negative Capability*, referenced by Keats to be,

> when a man is capable of being in uncertainties, mysteries, doubts, without any irritable reaching after fact and reason. (Keats 1817/1970)

However it is difficult to work in this way when the choreography curriculum more easily favours the exploration of traditional structures and form.

Attending to a discipline

What is evident in the design of dance programmes in UK higher education is the variation between dance as a professional practice and dance as a cultural, artistic, philosophic phenomenon. The position is made more complex because dance as a discipline still struggles to secure its 'knowledge base' and relative youthful academic integrity. The desire to be 'taken seriously' in the academy, to thaw cycles of rationalisation in budgets and ideological prohibition are recurring themes in the sector. The named somatic practices incorporated into curricula make evident that there are favoured 'alternative' methods in practice, for example Skinner Release, the Alexander Technique, the Feldenkrais Method, Body-Mind Centering. The tutors involved in the delivery of this curriculum see the habits of thinking and moving as inextricably related (Kovich 1994).

Although there are evident variations in approach, they do reinforce the integration of being physical/intellectual/emotional selves as part of a clear theme advocated in dance academia. This grounding might prove essential in securing the holistic benefits of the discipline in the eyes of those who question the relevance or sustainability of dance. However it is worth considering that whilst the introduction of this somatic work may be seen as commendable for those seeking a particular depth of embodiment, for many others it is as restrictive in its prescriptive dynamic range as the previously dominant, named training techniques, such as ballet, Graham or Cunningham. For students, these 'soft' practices are often perceived as removed from any association with their experience or interest in dance. This in turn makes them question the purpose and relevance of committing to the study of hybrid forms as part of a university dance degree. The trickle-down effect, where changes in content might be thought to reach the high school curriculum, has not yet taken place.

It is also worth noting the evident drive of arguments that frame the need to see 'cultural impact' as a necessary aspect of viability for future planning. Work under the umbrella term 'applied practice' often facilitates projects with the 'hard to reach', 'the disenfranchised' or 'other' than the mainstream communities. Whilst these are positive developments of inclusion, and important work is done in a host of such socially driven projects, they are sometimes used to placate the arguments of a liberal community who call for the instrumental use of arts provision for marginalised groups. It is interesting to acknowledge that this same liberal community appears not to comprehend clearly or acknowledge that our very embodiment is our means to action, our source of knowledge. It is in this that we affectively and effectively integrate multiple modes of intelligence and enable high quality engagements. With this understanding we ought to ensure that all communities have access to the movement practice. If we don't recognise that movement education is needed for all, are we any closer to rectifying the failing of our civilisation that Rudolf Laban spoke of in 1958 when reflecting on the neglect of movement research and movement education as a contributory factor in the failing aspects of our civilisation?

In her understandings of an aspiration for and contribution to dance, Kirsi Monni (2006) succinctly identifies the problem and opportunity that we face if we are to make significant changes. She reminds us that achieving such significant change is about more than introducing 'soft body techniques' and validating new approaches to moving. Her emphasis is towards the more vital concern of addressing how we move and are moved along with others. She argues:

> It is about a change in the understanding of reality ... This ... has brought about new deep ecological ethics where the philosophical horizon is formed by the shared participation in being-in-the-world. (Monni 2006: 170)

To have such rich awareness of the experience of your self and of a 'worlding' of dance remains something of a phantom. In this it is worth remembering that many dance students tend to see their time dancing as something separated from other aspects of their life and do not perceive a reason for this to change. The desire for training in coded languages that prove you can 'dance' has not left the studio. It is part of the profession and cultural industry.

There has of course been a concerted effort from the 17th century onwards to educate us into a belief that there is a divide between body as material matter and mind as an entity with no spatial presence other than that it is located within or occupies the human brain. The body is still hailed by many as a temporary residence for a spirit that has the potential to move into the 'hereafter' once the materiality of the body has been exhausted.

Even in the present expansion of research centred in neuroscience we remain plagued by what is now the subtler dualism that proposes a sentient brain as an organ of awareness and a physical body still portrayed as a mechanical operator that carries the brain/spirit from place to place. What we have to continue to address are the resultant cultural consequences derived from conceiving of our minds as something separate from the whole material world. We have, at least in the West, become used to the idea that we are other than the world; that we reflect upon it rather than exist as a feature of it. Being in it and of it is the essential rationale we require in order to realise our understanding of the realities of our existence. If we are to meet the aspirations of Gill Clarke – who imagined a university Department of Embodiment where dance would be at the core of a curriculum working with a host of other disciplines– these might include: cultural studies, psychology, biology, economics, medicine, history and many others (Burt 2011). We need to help students to embrace more fully the potential dynamism of dance (motion), as an inter-discipline to influence how all of these pursue their goals through its practice and theory.

Relational ethics

To move the discussion forward we want to consider how we might think in terms of being individuals in relation with ourselves and with others in the world. To do this, ethics and aesthetic experience are addressed, offering a possibility to begin to forge an ecology of practice. There can be a tendency to think of ethics in terms of rules, informed by cultural codes to be followed as part of compulsory institutional protocols. Whilst agreement to abide by rules of what might identify acceptable moral conduct is arguably part of a civilising behaviour, it can be used to overshadow individual personal responsibility and accountability. Indeed, the obligatory adoption of codes may well leave insufficient impetus for some people to strive to meet individually attentive and affective aspirations.

What we argue here is that as teachers we are tasked to consider the value inherent in attending to the effect and affect of an individual ethical stance. Such codes are by necessity drawn from lived experiences where each of us is continuously engaged in dialogic relations. It is this fluid state of what is effectively our own *becoming* that gradually reveals what underpins the nature and properties of knowledge. This is something that occurs in relation to others, something situated in the many and varied relationships in which we find ourselves.

For French philosopher Gilles Deleuze (1978) it is this very sense of relation that is the underpinning of identity making. It is the ever diverging and increasing ensemble of relations through an individual life that, when taken together, come to compose how we can each be identified. He argues that if we don't come to know how we can be affected through a process of enriching our own sense of connectivity, then there is little if any chance for a wise life and still less for finding wisdom. What becomes apparent here is the importance placed on articulating what we come to know through mutual connectivity: through being with other people and through exploring or continuous rehearsal of a sense of collectivity. In dance terms this is often found through the processes of choreography or improvisational experiment. It is evident then that relational ethics has a part to play in forging such articulation through engagement in dance practices that attend to moving whether it be solo or communal. Whilst it is a complex way to consider any identifying features of a curriculum, it is worthwhile and significant in terms of an explicit quest for wisdom, as articulated by philosopher Alfred Whitehead, who asserted that, as a basis of knowledge, it is necessary to hope to be wise (1967). However, as Whitehead goes on to argue, this in itself is not sufficient: you need to come to understand, work with and generate new understandings from experiences if you are to have any hope of finding and feeling wisdom.

Viewed from this perspective, ethics concerns our individual behaviour and in turn informs the manner in which we negotiate and establish lived experiences in relation to others. For cultural theorist Sara Ahmed (2000) it is through situated ethics that we forge relations with those things that cannot be measured by the regulative force of rules. In focusing on this more adaptive and responsive form of ethics, there is opportunity to engage with the possibilities made available to us by that which is not-yet-known.

In the understanding and application of responsive ethics there is resonance with experiences during contact improvisation where attention is given to the cultivation of sensitivity to the context through generosity towards (an)other, towards an idea or towards a collective endeavour. A more fluid sense of personal integrity might be realised through such consensual principles where we could identify improvisation more fully as a relational practice that acknowledges interpersonal bonds, where individuals are responsible for their actions and for the consequences that evolve. Perhaps through an open practice that engages an explicit practice of ethics, we might lead to forming non-exploitative learning environments, whether in improvisation, choreography, technical study, movement practice or collaboration.

The influence of Spinoza lies behind these ideas, particularly where he writes that a practice of relational ethics focuses on the question of what a body can do in any given situation or through any decided action. Through Brian Massumi's (2003) readings of Spinozian ethics we can trace ideas that propose that there should be no necessarily positive or negative actions assessed against pre-set classifications or codes. Ethics in these terms involves a practice of working together to secure understanding of the situation that a group may find themselves negotiating at any given time. In dance as in many disciplines, we work within fields of inter-corporeal interactions that are brought to our attention through our own corporeal specificity.

This is always entwined with understandings of self/body, always unstable and culturally variable.

> Ethics in this sense is completely situational ... It happens in *between* people, in the social gaps.... The ethical value of an action is what it brings out *in* the situation, *for* its transformation, how it breaks sociality open. Ethics is about how we inhabit uncertainty, together. It's not about judging right or wrong. (Massumi 2003: 7; original emphasis)

Evident in this trail of thinking is the intention to step beyond ideological moralising and towards what may be perceived as more unorthodox forms of knowledge generation where experiential practice facilitates students in getting to know their way around the detail of their engagements. With the words of Nicholas Ridout (2011) we might frame such experiences as a liquid sense of '*constant becoming*', where learning to work and relate in these ways has a potential to nurture engagement through what is a deep investment in human potential.

Attending to dialogue between aesthetics and ethics

The ideas outlined in this chapter underpinned a recent project undertaken by one of the authors that aimed to explore the use of touch and ethics in learning experiences in dance. The Higher Education Academy (HEA), a UK-based organisation that fosters the quality of delivery in higher education, supported the project under the title *Relational Ethics: dance, touch and learning* (Bannon 2012). The project explored how ethics informs current practice and considered how *relational ethics* might be an effective mode with which to identify the distinct qualitative engagement with ethical concerns that are frequently addressed in teaching and learning in dance.

Working across twelve dance programmes the project was able to identify a considerable range of diligent and responsive practice actively fostering positive ethical practice. In this groundswell of attention there resides an untapped resource that could make significant contribution across programmes, disciplines and institutional boundaries if it were communicated more fully outside the discipline. Within the delivery of dance there is clear evidence of the use of a range of forms of evaluative engagement between colleagues, peers and teachers. This ethos of working is little known beyond the borders of the practice itself and even at times not shared within discreet programme teams. The situation chimes with the observation by Liz Lerman made earlier that little is known beyond the field of dance about the knowledge it generates or contribution that it could make in elucidating good practice elsewhere in the academy and beyond.

As a discipline we would do well to formalise this wealth of experience and disseminate what can be learned by attending to the social structures of people 'on the move'. A number of relevant ideas emerged from the research and are outlined here as propositions ready for further debate. First, dance as a disciplinary area should disseminate and continue to explore how relational ethics informs the practice of teaching and of modes of studio behaviour. As ethics, sustainability and wellbeing increase in profile within the curricula of university programmes the dance sector needs to substantiate its contributions to areas of debate concerning collaboration, collectivity and identity making. Secondly, having experienced the positive advantage of the *dancers' charter* (DanceUK) championed by Peter Brinson (1982), we should refresh and extend the scope of the charter maintaining the commitment to the professional welfare of dancers and further a responsibility towards the social, cultural and wellbeing agendas across our society. Thirdly there is need to heighten engagement with ethics as an explicit part of dance practice, a behaviour that should be fashioned in-dialogue, through the quality of personal practice and in relation with professional purpose. Finally there is benefit in revisiting the ways that we use self-reflection and self-reflexive learning in dance. These modes of evaluative and experiential practice can have distinct roles in helping students to learn how to respond relevantly and critically to evaluate complex situations. What we need is to ensure that we create sustainable positive change incorporating diverse voices as contributory members of the discussion.

It is evident that the sense of the integration of our physical, intellectual, sensory and emotional selves that can occur in learning in dance continues to be advocated by a host of academics and practitioners. Thinking differently about the social context of education and finding a distinct voice for the discipline can happen through choreography with its continual flow of debate between meaning understanding and dissemination.

In terms of aesthetic education there are many avenues of discussion that need further space to rehearse, however Diffey's (1986) argument calling for aesthetics not to be seen as an isolation of elements pertaining only to art or beauty, but rather as a means for exploring experiences of being in the world can serve us well. This again usefully underpins the view that through these processes, seen by many to underpin the discipline of dance, we aim to support individuals to learn how to create themselves (Eisner 2002). It is evidently the case that to attend through moving is to learn through qualitative reasoning that leads to somatic knowledge and to finding ways to appreciate the cohesion of our interconnecting modes of knowing. The purpose of such learning is to understand that one's being in the world effectively unfolds as a series of relational chains, exhibiting qualities that are at once intellectual, sensory and emotional, something that Arnold Berleant (1986) has characterised clearly as ranging from multisensory synaesthesia to somatic action.

The culmination of the relation between ethics and aesthetic sensibility broadens the possibility of generating knowledge through the rich sense of enquiry that it engenders, something that is inevitably situated in an individual's experience of the world. These thoughts echo Clarke's core belief that in dance we have a means to action and a source of knowledge generation.

Earlier in the chapter we spoke of students working within the multifaceted field of dance, learning to synthesise ethical and aesthetic knowing through embodied forms of social engagement. If this connectivity were inscribed in the operation of the broader curriculum drawing in improvisation, choreography and cultural debate, students would have the opportunity to define more fully the rich ensemble of relations that coalesce in the dance discipline. How we make more people aware that this is the substance of learning that goes on in dance education remains a significant task in terms of recruiting students, heightening cultural awareness and convincing senior managers and politicians. There is benefit in the careful articulation of the liberty afforded through an education that enables us to experience the forces within which we all exist. By encouraging versatile thinking as a key identifying feature of learning in dance we can enable the inter-discipline of dance to be recognised as a route to becoming educated persons valued in, and contributing to, civil society.

References

Ahmed, S. (2000) *Strange encounters: Embodied others in post-coloniality,* Routledge

Bannon, F. (2012) *Relational ethics: dance, touch and learning.* York: Higher Education Academy. http://bit.ly/tpMove02

Berleant, A. (1986) 'Experience and Theory in Aesthetics' in *Possibility of Aesthetic Experience* (ed. M.H. Mitias), pp. 91-106, Martinus Nijhoff

Brinson, P. 1992 (1996) *A Dancers' Charter for Health and Welfare*, Dance UK

Burt, R. (2011) 'Resources for Thinking about the Body: An Interview with Gill Clarke', *Dance Theatre Journal,* Vol 24. No 4. pp. 6-10

Cixous, H. (1975) 'The Laugh of the Medusa' in *Feminisms Redux: An Anthology of Literary Theory and Criticism* (eds. R. Warhol-Down & D. Price Herndl) (2009) Rutgers University Press, pp. 416-431

Cvejić, B. (2004) *How Open Are You? Pre-sentiments, pre-conceptions, pro-jections* http://bit.ly/tpMove04

Deleuze, G, & Deleuze, J. (1978) *Gilles Deleuze, Lecture transcripts on Spinoza's Concept of Affect* London: Goldsmiths University. http://bit.ly/tpMove03

Dewey, J. (1934) *Art as Experience,* Minton

Diffey, T. J. (1986) 'The Idea of Aesthetic Experience' in *Possibility of Aesthetic Experience.* (ed. M.H. Mitias) pp. 3-12, Martinus Nijhoff

Forsythe, W. (2008) *Suspense* (ed. M. Weisbeck) Ursula Blickle Foundation

_______ (2012). 'A Meeting with William Forsythe', Dance Biennale, 2012. 8th International Festival of Contemporary Dance http://bit.ly/tpMove62

Geeves, T. (1990) *A Report on Dance Injury Prevention and Management in Australia. Safe Dance Report I.* Canberra: Australia Dance Council (Ausdance)

_______ (1999) *Safe Dance Report III.* Canberra: Australia Dance Council (Ausdance)

_______ (1997) *Safe Dance Report II.* Canberra: Australia Dance Council (Ausdance)

Greene, M. (1988) *The Dialectic of Freedom,* Teachers College Press

Guattari, F. (2006) (reprint) *Chaosmosis: an ethico-aesthetic paradigm* (trans. P. Bains & J. Pefanis), Power Publications

Holt, D. (1997) 'Touching all the bases' in *The 7th International Dance and the Child Conference. The call of forests and lakes* (ed. E. Anttila) pp. 141-45. Dance and the Child International

Illich, I. (1971) *Deschooling Society,* Calder and Boyars

Keats, J. (1817/1970) *The Letters of John Keats* (ed. R. Gittings), Oxford University Press

Kovich, Z. (1994) 'From Intention to Action: Somatic Education and the Dancer' in *The 6th International Dance and the Child Conference. Kindle the Fire* (eds. W. Schiller & D. Spurgeon) Dance and the Child International

Lerman, L. (2011) *Hiking the Horizontal Field Notes from a Choreographer,* Wesleyan Press

Massumi, B. (2003) 'Navigating Movements' http://bit.ly/tpMove01

Monni, K. (2006) 'About the Sense and Meaning in Dance – Ontological Considerations' in *Finnish Dance Research At The Crossroads* (eds. P. K. Pakkanen & A. Sarje) pp. 166-173

Read, A. (2008) *Theatre, Intimacy & Engagement: The Last Human Venue,* Palgrave

Ridout, N. (2011) 'A Prologue' in *A Life of Ethics & Performance* (eds. J. Matthews & D. Torevell) Cambridge Scholars Press

Roy, S. & Lee, R. (2011) 'Gill Clarke Obituary', *The Guardian* 20 Dec. 2011

Schenck, D. (1986) 'The Texture of Embodiment: Foundation for Medical Ethics', *Human Studies* 9: 43-54

Seiber, J. E. (1992) 'Planning Ethically Responsible Research: A Guide for Students and Internal Review Boards', *Applied Social Research Methods Series,* 31, Sage

Whitehead, A.F. (1967) *The Aim of Education* The Free Press

PENNY COLLINSON

Re-sourcing the Body

Embodied presence and self-care in working with others

When we experience the rich complexities of our moving body, our multi-dimensionality becomes available to us. We are awakened, become present to the qualities of movement – feelings and sensations, rhythms, forces and flow. As we sense movement, these qualities, which have perhaps been diminished through our focus on *doing*, become our way of *being*. Whether we simply feel the cycle of our breath coming in and out and moving our chest, or feel the soles of our feet on the ground as we walk, moving can make us aware of our *being-ness* and that we are a living and deeply responsive body. Moving also brings us into the present moment, the ground of fundamental reality and resource. Being present to those we work with is central to dancers and movement educators, and 'listening' is at the heart of it. But what do we really mean by this? Why is presence integral to the work and how can it be cultivated and embodied? Furthermore, how can facilitators take care of themselves when working with others, so that they can be present, resourceful and feel restored through the process? This chapter focuses on somatic movement-based creative practice in one-to-one facilitation.

The central themes and questions involved in presence and self-care in working with others will first be addressed in light of my own practice. These will be contextualised through the experience of meeting the unknown in another, through attunement and resonance. They will be further explored through the somatic perspectives of Sills, Tufnell, Myers, Abrams, *et al*; Juhan's redefinition of ego as 'Witness' to bodily processes, and Wilberg's elucidation of the act of listening as midwife for the emergence of being. Examples are then given of the relational skills inherent in being present as taught on the MA Dance & Somatic Wellbeing: Connections to the Living Body[1] at University of Central Lancashire (UCLan). Distinctions between somatic movement-based creative practice and that of dance

1 MA Dance & Somatic Wellbeing: Connections to the Living Body, is an ISMETA registered programme. Conceived by Amanda Williamson, the course has run at the University of Central Lancashire in Preston, UK since 2007 and in New York City, USA since 2009.

movement, or somatic, therapy are acknowledged. They share many approaches and underpinnings, but their intentions are different, as may be the contexts in which they work and the needs of the client. The final part of the chapter focuses on how the practice of finding simple strategies which illuminate a sense of embodiment – of knowing through the body – may benefit professionals from other disciplines, and how attention to presence and self-care can restore and resource them in their work with clients and service users.

My use of the term 'facilitator' throughout this chapter could be interchangeable with 'educator' or practitioner. Similarly I use the term 'client' to refer to those people with whom I work in a one-to-one context, but this could apply to partner work within group contexts too.

What is the experience of being present with people, what are we doing or not doing in order to experience this, and what are the effects for those we work with? These questions have emerged as central within my work with others, and are concerned with how I attend to my clients, and how this supports them to be more present to their selves. Through my own senses and intuition, my feeling, seeing and listening, I orient towards a state of *being*. 'Seeing' and 'listening' are terms used here as bodily metaphors which include looking and hearing but encapsulate whole-body receptivity. Franklin Sills, author of *Being and Becoming: Psychodynamics, Buddhism and the Origins of Selfhood*, describes 'being' as the awareness which underlies self (the term 'self' refers to an everyday perceptual state, which is generally identified as 'me' or 'I', a conditioned self). "[Being] is the heart of I-am, a spontaneous center of presence that manifests from the moment of conception, is inherently connected to all other beings, and by its nature seeks to know the essence of its own being and the world it finds itself in" (Sills 2009: 5). Being state arises and can be maintained through my capacity to be present. Blackburn and Price (2006) define this process as "presencing", and achieving "a state of awareness that can only be experienced through the body … an awareness of phenomenon as they arise" (Blackburn and Price 2006: 69). For Siegel (2007) presence is our capacity to be open to what is happening as it happens. Sills writes that we "enter a state of presence" and that the facilitator learns to "rest in the truth of the present moment" (Sills 2009: 260-261). He also states that the establishment of presence does not occur by the facilitator's practising presence per se, "but by observing what obscures it" (2009: 261). From an orientation of 'being', I open towards *being with* my clients as fully as I can. In my sessions, I aim to be still and to track my clients' process, their verbal and non-verbal cues, including witnessing/observing their breathing, their sensing, moving and sounding. Being 'open' and listening in this way awakens each of us to our embodied subjective, and intersubjective, experience of the living moment as it manifests and expresses itself. Such receptivity widens our quality of attention and our experience becomes knowable, not conceptually, but experientially and imaginatively.

How do facilitators cultivate presence?

Before I begin working with people I address my own needs, I take care of my self, drawing on my bodily resources in physical/practical preparation. I ensure the studio is warm and clean, and I make space to move myself. I slow down, become still, listening and feeling in to my body. I attend to my energy levels, my capacity to feel myself bodily. I may lie down, rest and join with my breath whilst noticing its rhythm and flow. I may move, tracking my experience and at times sensing movement, at other times being more physically active through stretching, rolling, dancing and running. I am guided by asking, what will help me to feel more present? What do I need to come into relationship with another person? I open towards seeing what is going on right now. This process of self-tracking and reflection is important before meeting others; after all, if I don't know what's going on in my self, how can I support another person's process? My preparation attunes me to the silent, non-verbal realms of being and gets me 'underneath' my thought processes and preoccupations with thinking and knowing.

I tune into my client before they arrive. I imagine in to them – opening to whatever comes back to me. I don't necessarily visualise their face and features but instead I may have sensations, or sense an emotion, or perhaps I will see an image. Whilst still not knowing anything of what's happening for the client this process somehow links and attunes me/us further. The focus towards direct experience continues when we meet to work with each other. My client needs time to arrive. This essentially means coming into the present moment and often there is some dialogue with questions orienting them towards bodily perceptions, and to being in this space, right now: 'Where would you like to be in the space?'; 'As you say [X], how do you feel/where do you sense that in your body?'; 'What would you like to do right now?' During this important transitional stage of navigating from the 'outer' world and towards sensory-feeling-imaginative perception, my spacious presence can help the client settle and become receptive. This process takes time and requires trust. They are learning to self-care, drawing on methods to resource themselves such as breathing, grounding, relaxing and yielding body weight. We are both listening to where movement is emerging and how it wants to unfold. I need to hold steady my attention, intuiting the need perhaps for quiet spaciousness or the potential for physical activity and contact.

Touch (of self or other) plays a fundamental role in somatic learning, heightening support and connection. There is reciprocity in touch; each participant is both touching and touched, and through this flow and interchange both sense connection (Tufnell 2010). Touch is direct and immediate, brings us into relationship, and is a helpful tool in grounding and re-orientation, to locate unexpressed or unfelt areas within the body, and to find new sensory neuromuscular pathways. Other methods may involve supporting the client into slowing down and paying careful attention to breath, sensation, weight, movement impulses, connection to ground, images and feelings. It could also involve active and playful games/tasks or improvisations. This is a spontaneous 'conversation' between both partners in which feelings may appear as metaphor or image. Movement will be varied, subtle and barely visible, or dynamic and gestural; on occasion an individual or collective story or event may unfold (Eddy 2009, Olsen 1993).

This intimacy constantly requires the facilitator to keep resourcing herself – being present to her own bodily needs whilst also staying receptive to the client's unfolding journey. Those I'm working with may experience play, delight and liberation – or their opposites. Hartley reminds us that we do not know exactly what it is we seek in our journeying. She says, "This mysterious balance of 'knowing' and 'not-knowing' drives us to take tentative steps into the unknown. Learning is simultaneously a leap into the new and strange and also a return to what we already know deeply" (Hartley

1995: xxi). What courage and faith we must summon to enter this work! We are adventurers with a calling to encounter the multi-dimensional, multi-faceted nature of being-in-the-world.

Intuitive and improvisatory practices resource our clients because they provide ways to let go of thought and expectation through actions of continuous surrender to what is happening. Stephen Nachmanovitch (1990: 21) describes how we "focus attention on the field we are about to enter, then release the plan and discover the reality of time's flow". And Mary Starks Whitehouse wrote of the process of Authentic Movement as "waiting to be moved" (Whitehouse 1979 in Pallaro 2000: 82). Shaun McNiff writes that the essential ingredient in improvisation is spontaneity, a space in which unplanned expressions can arrive (McNiff 1998: 14). The outcome will be an amalgamation of ideas – things are discovered along the way, as one thing leads to another (1998: 14). As we enter the unknown and turn our attention to our bodily experience, the volume is turned up on processes that are, and have forever been taking place. Many of our bodily processes function below the level of consciousness and self-organisational forces are always at work; the body is constantly self-regulating, renewing and seeking balance (Hanna 2003; Juhan 2002). Bones replace themselves over a three-month cycle, the lining of the stomach renews every four days, skin lacerations heal within days, and all without our conscious willing.

Through these sensory-imaginative processes the door is opened to what Thomas Hanna defines as "somatic learning" (2003: 54), our perceptions of interoceptive, proprioceptive, imaginative and kinaesthetic processes are sharpened and we can become much more attuned to sensory feedback, such as, from the 'special' senses, internal organs, skeletal-musculature, skin, and the gravitational balance through the inner ear (Myers 1998: 103). These process centres are constantly informing us of what is going on in our body, our sense of movement, of balance, as well as our perception of the kinesphere around us, and of our capacity to interact with our environment (Myers 1998; Hanna 2003). Our body's capacity to slow down and moderate sensory-motor responses brings awareness to what's happening – the patterns and responses that are taking place. Slowing down and being aware is then followed up with reflection on the experience, and so goes-forth the loop of attending to self (and other) in which we slow down, listen, open to our experience, and reflect. In this process the facilitator and client find themselves in a dance of being – both listening and responding whilst maintaining awareness to their own needs. Opening to this field of being somehow, mysteriously, brings simplicity – together in the moment, no expectation, no need to make something happen, instead waiting to see what shows its self.

Reflection is an important process in our work as it is about becoming more conscious of what is arising through the body. The meaning-making process includes bridging sensory-imagination and movement into consciousness – not analysis but creative expression – and this can occur in different ways depending on the client's preference. They may want to reflect through creative, poetic or other spontaneous writing, drawing or painting, art-making, or dancing. Rather than being interpretive, these methods are the 'languages' which can convey the multiplicity of being human, such as in this piece of reflective writing which emerged out of a short moving 'warm-up' in preparing to work with my clients:

On ground
on knees
next to them elbows
balancing on points of coral with branches which extend away
head weighed heavy in open palms
the hub of a small boat
caught
rocking in the shallow waters. Breath
you are hidden away
as a tiny pearl
shut tight in its shell.
I hardly know you are here.
Outside I hear the gulls arguing
and the swarm of bees recently moved in to the neighbour's gutter.
(Collinson 2013)

Speaking is important too. Janet Adler suggests that verbalising together after moving, for example, creates a continuation of ritual between mover and witness: "a similar sense of heightened awareness of all that longs to come into form, now into words" (Adler 2002: 77). Clients and educators speak in such a way as to bring their attention to recalling the movement as it is experienced, rather than as remembered and in doing so reflection can be seen as an extension of the movement, and a further unfolding of our self into consciousness. This "harvesting" (Mallon, Tufnell & Rubidge 2005) is often unexpectedly insightful and meaningful to both client and facilitator enabling further layers of creativity and wellbeing.

Through our reflections we can also monitor and assess what we bodily sense. We monitor our energy levels, and consciously balance need for activity and rest, attuning to whatever is useful, helpful and may support our self-care and healing process (Halprin 2003). That aspect of consciousness which 'self-assesses' or monitors oneself, Deane Juhan calls "the Witness" (2002: 350). The Witness, he suggests, knows itself through the body and is connected to all parts. He goes on to suggest, the Witness is "the chair of the internal committee", the committee members being bodily perceptions – interoception, proprioception, kinaesthetic awareness, etc. (2002: 350). The Witness/chairman's job is to listen to the members. This requires a Witness who does not seek to control or direct the situation. She can't, she doesn't have a vote, but must be responsive to that which the members 'tell' her, and act on their behalf. Put another way the inner Witness is also described as (a redefinition of) ego consciousness whereby the ego, having known itself to be sole controller is now, through this process, 'reduced' to being the chair. For the ego, once wilful and controlling, this is demotion; to the Witness it is liberation! In evolving Witness consciousness we become more aware and autonomous. Responses that are based on prior experience and have led to habitual actions or behaviour may no longer be perceived as healthy, and positive adjustments can be made. In this way, as Juhan defines them, our bodies "remain always a work-in-progress" (1987: 350). Our capacity to be self-aware is a fundamental resource and awakens us to the reality that we are always changing, and have the capacity to create change in our own lives (Abrams 2011; Keleman 2011; Tufnell & Crickmay 2004; Hanna 2003).

For many years I have studied the discipline of Authentic Movement, which is described as a Western awareness practice (Adler 2002), and a therapeutic and meditative movement practice (Stromsted 1999). My Masters by Research degree investigated the practice within creative and performance contexts and I identified a main theme of revelation: of how in moving our body reveals that which has been unseen and unknown (Collinson 2005). The parameters of the discipline, for example, invite us to perceive direct experience, to move with eyes closed, to feel sensation, movement, images, to invite that which has been unconscious to consciousness, the formless to form, the impulse to movement. In discovering micro movements alive in my body, my participation in Authentic Movement encouraged me, through periods of stillness and formlessness, to be patient, and to trust the process. I realised that not only had I not known how to listen to my body but also that my body had a lot to tell me … and that being alive to the moment is something to be achieved through my body. The development into being a witness in the discipline primarily grew out of my experience as a mover. Attuning to my self was a resource in attuning to other; tracking my own experience helped me to track another's and verbally describing my experience brought me to my authentic voice when offering Witnessing.

Within the relational field, facilitators/Witnesses become an additional resource for change and transformation within the client's somatic experience (Blackburn and Price 2006). Peter Wilberg writes of the listener as "midwife" in a process called "maieutic listening" (Wilberg 2004: 61). Although it is beyond the scope of this chapter to go into detail, briefly, I find exciting parallels in his description of the therapist as a 'midwife' who 'listens' and leaves silence, a space after the client has spoken, for the gestation and 'birth' of something new. Wilberg suggests that it is through tuning to ourselves that we are then able to tune to our client, as they tune to themselves. Wilberg describes this process as one which enables true professional closeness. For him this is an ethical stance that must be offered, a holding that enables the client to access new experience. Wilberg's theories of maieutic listening can be seen within the sensory-imaginative processes in our field. Miranda Tufnell points out that how effectively we facilitate a session is determined by how we are in our self and the relational field we create with our presence. She goes on to state that our quality of presence may be more potent for the client than anything we actively 'do' (Tufnell 2010). What Tufnell is suggesting here is profound, that our presence may be our most effective source of support to our client. *What are the qualities needed to facilitate presence in this way?*

The facilitator offers an attentive awareness, a quiet spacious 'holding' of her client. Sills reminds us that "In order for basic trust to be established, the therapist [facilitator] must generate a holding environment that is experienced as both safe *and* non-collusive" (Sills 2009: 262). The term 'holding' is used as a metaphor in which the facilitator is directing her attention to the needs of the client including the timing, pace and environment in which the session is taking place. The facilitator [or therapist] orients to her felt experience, her being, she is sensitive, empathic whilst maintaining her awareness of the intimate nature of their connection and their separateness. She is non-directive, non-controlling; she takes her time and offers her presence for the emergence of something new, which is unformed and as yet unknown in her client. In doing so her steady holding, with no expectation or need to change or fix, creates the non-judgemental environment where more of the client can become visible to her or his self. For the facilitator, cultivating embodied presence and the capacity to maintain it in relationship requires patience, love and curiosity. Within this safe holding space lies the potential for the client to enter their being state with another, what Sills calls the "interbeing", and "a being-to-being holding field" (Sills 2009: 9). The sense of recognition that occurs can feel deeply life affirming to the client. Mary Abrams (2013) describes how these qualities of being seen and accepted for who they are can support the client's own capacity to see and to relate to themselves and to others without judgement. For Amanda Williamson (2009: 33), companionship, non-judgement, heart-felt connection, and compassion are all fundamental qualities which shape practice.

Hayes (2007), Stromsted (2001) and Hartley (2005) write of the potency of the relational field. The sense of holding that a client intuits comes about or is dependent upon the facilitator being familiar with encountering her own 'unknown', so that the facilitator needs to 'know herself'. From a Jungian perspective, meeting the unknown may be seen as an encounter with the unconscious that is integral to building 'wholeness' – that which is unknown can become known – the facilitator has journeyed in to the dark regions below, bringing back the fruits of her discoveries to her daily life (Stromsted 2001). The client senses that in travelling to her own depths she will be seen and recognised by her facilitator.

What are the effects of working with someone in this way?

When we strengthen awareness in our body we feel connected – our often fragmented sense of self becomes more whole. Sometimes clients arrive for a session feeling very disconnected. Many say something along the lines of "I feel stressed and all over the place". A useful question might be "where is my attention?" and useful strategies might be orientating to breath, slowing down and focusing on connecting parts of our body which are in contact with the ground. This sense of re-connection can occur relatively quickly, and the use of touch, including compression, holding or more vigorous rubs by the facilitator, can all be helpful possibilities. 'Presencing' in this way is a fundamental resource and enables clients to attend immediately to their bodily needs, calming and reassuring the parts that need this. It is a very simple and obvious method of self-care, offered in much the same way that a mother attends to her baby's needs for containment and communication. Being with another person and giving them the space and time to listen to themselves is very powerful and effective. I recently heard of a doctor in England who asks each of her patients on entering her surgery to sit quietly/contemplatively for one minute before they begin to speak with one another. And of a head teacher who has implemented a period of silent time for all pupils, which he describes as reflection time. Also, whilst I was in dialogue with a social worker, she pointed out that at times just quietly listening can be of most benefit to her service users, many of whom are in vulnerable relationships in which they feel they have no voice.

When we attend to our bodies in a mindful way, we open to our creativity. More options become available to our decision-making process. In a conversation in 2014 Tufnell describes this process as "connecting to the wider landscape of our whole experience ... in which the material and non-material coalesce … become visible". We can't know what it is to be the client, but we need to be able to resonate with what they share with us, to empathise and offer our support. The journey is not always comfortable for the client. Sometimes the body feels an unsafe place, unfamiliar and frightening. As facilitators, our practice helps clients to feel into a tolerance level and notice where support is needed (Gantz 2012).

Speaking at the *Mystery of Embodiment II Summit*, hosted by Meridian University in 2012, somatic practitioner Judy Gantz spoke of supporting clients to feel permission to set their boundaries, such as how much they can move, trust, or wait (2012). As participants we begin to recognise the differences between experiences that are fearful and challenging, and those that are traumatic, and where bodily support feels needed (2012). If an experience is acutely painful and difficult it may be that the participant needs one-to-one work with a psychotherapist (see Musicant 2007). As facilitators we must be discerning and develop clarity about the boundaries beyond which we won't go because we are not trained to do so, for example in trauma work or into the sphere of Dance Movement Psychotherapy. Somatic movement facilitator Ray Johnson (2012) offers useful thoughts around how a somatic approach can be an additional resource within psychotherapy, suggesting that there is a place for building in/on skills, repertoire and somatic literacy as a supplement to exploring the traumatic experience itself, and that bodywork can begin to build a sense of safety in the body. Gantz, (2012), Halprin, (2003) and Keleman (2011), suggest that new experiences coming into the body can build new (neurological) pathways, new kinaesthetic experiences that are not trauma-based.

Studying somatic movement education involves regular and ongoing personal immersion in practice. Familiarity with felt experience is a developmental process and the ground form from which students establish the potential effects and benefits of this approach. Learning often takes place through a process of solo, dyadic and group relational practices, and facilitation skills are therefore learnt through the student's individual experiential participation and through practical delivery to peers.[2] Skills that can be applied to working with people in a variety of ways are further generated through reflective processes and theoretical inquiry.[3] The application of somatic practice across disciplines is growing internationally; there is great need for it. Practitioners from a variety of backgrounds including health, education, social work, social care, medicine, therapy and the performing arts are developing ways to work creatively with the challenges they and their clients/service-users/students face in life. The body is coming much more into focus, and the long-term, effective advocacy and evidenced delivery of practice across disciplines will support its wider visibility and application, perhaps eventually influencing policy change at local and higher levels. Staff on the MA at UCLan have been teaching students on the Psychotherapy course as well as working alongside colleagues in social work and the psycho-social research team. Our work with them offers experiential sessions in embodied presence and the ongoing nature of looking after themselves and attending to their immediate physical and emotional needs. Professions with high burn-out rates, such as teaching and healthcare, may benefit from somatic learning, as it enquires into how we are feeling and also offers strategies for coping. The effects of this may have further direct impact on their clients too, who often remain a 'case' or a 'patient' rather than a 'human being' (Hanna 2003:51). It can be easy for people working with others to forget to recognise and take responsibility for our own needs in the professional context,

---

2 Students at UCLan, on MA Dance & Somatic Wellbeing: Connections to the Living Body, establish the skills throughout the course to deliver peer-led group sessions and one-on-one client sessions.

3 Qualitative research projects undertaken by UCLan students have included a study into the role of breath as a support to school teachers, and into how somatic work can support living with narcolepsy.

through preparing ourselves before seeing clients or attending to what we need to do afterwards. Preparation may be of further help to practitioners in order to help ground and re-stabilise, particularly for those who work in consistently volatile and emotional environments. My colleague, Mary Abrams (2013), points out that the significance of self-care for the facilitator is to model a more holistic approach for the client. In conversation she went on to describe:

> If I as facilitator am not re-sourcing myself with self-care, my client will surely know it on a silent level. Furthermore, my discoveries for self-care become the skills I can pass on to my client, and one more way to facilitate, model, and support self-responsibility on their part. (Abrams 2013)

In offering some concluding thoughts: over time, bodily awareness helps us to be in touch with ourselves both in the studio and in daily life. Our capacity to improvise, to flow, flitter, not to tread a single path but to be flexible and change course is at the root of the work – the unleashing or channelling of our creative spirit. Our relationship with the body conscious and unconscious is a process that can only happen in the body's own time. In this way, our relationship to body changes through our deepening perceptions of who and what we think we are, fostering new insights and bringing with it a sense of personal autonomy or agency (Williamson 2009; Keleman 2011).

However a client has arrived at somatic work; be it through illness, pain or a hunger for creative expression, the journey requires an active participation in the present. Heartfelt presence offered by the facilitator supports clients towards this. Befriending the mysterious nature of the present moment, daring to be seen and heard, enables both client and facilitator alike to drop the masks and roles we have assumed and which may no longer 'fit', or serve us. Such creativity is an antidote to lifestyles that may keep us isolated and sedentary, and which leave us neglecting the rich potential of our humanity.

References

Abrams, M. (2011) 'Feeling Moving: Wandering Through the Flesh of Personal and Human Development', *United States Association of Body Psychotherapy Journal (USABPJ)*, Vol. 10, No 2, pp. 12-21

Adler, J. (2002) *Offering from the Conscious Body: The Discipline of Authentic Movement*, Inner Traditions

Blackburn, J. & Price, C. (2006) 'Implications of Presence in Manual Therapy', *Journal of Bodywork and Movement Therapies* 11, 68-77

Collinson, P. (2005) 'See and Be Seen: A Quality of Presence. An Investigation of Authentic Movement in Creative Process and Performance', Unpublished thesis: Manchester Metropolitan University

_______ (2013) Reflective Somatic journal, Unpublished, Preston: UCLan, UK

Eddy, M. (2009) 'A Brief history of somatic practices and dance historical development of the field of somatic education and its relationship to dance', *Journal of Dance and Somatic Practices* 1: 1, pp. 5-27, doi: 10.1386/jdsp.1.1.5/1

Fraleigh, S. H. (1987) *Dance and the Lived Body*, University of Pittsburgh Press

Gantz, J. (2012) Speaking at the *Mystery of Embodiment II Summit*, Meridian University.

Halprin, D. (2003) *The Expressive Body in Life, Art and Therapy: Working with Movement, Meaning and Metaphor*, Jessica Kingsley Publishers

Hanna, T. (2003) 'What is Somatics? Part 1', *Somatics Spring/Summer*, pp.50-55

Hartley, L. (1995) *Wisdom of the Body Moving: An Introduction to Body-Mind Centering*, North Atlantic Books

_______ (2005) 'Seeking a Sense of Self (The Integration of Authentic Movement and the Body-Mind Centering Approach to Developmental Movement Therapy in Body Psychotherapy Practice)' http://bit.ly/tpMove88

Hayes, J. (2007) *Performing Your Dreams*, Archive Publishing

Johnson, R. (2012) Speaking at the Mystery of Embodiment II Summit, Meridian University. http://bit.ly/tpMove05

Juhan, D. (2002) *Job's Body: A Handbook for Bodywork*, Station Hill Press

Keleman, S. (2011) 'Slow Attending: The Art of Forming Intimacy', *United States Association of Body Psychotherapy Journal (USABPJ)*, Vol. 10, No 2, pp. 5-11

Lawrence, R. L, (2012) 'Intuitive Knowing and Embodied Consciousness', *New Directions for Adult and Continuing Education*, no. 134, Summer, Wiley Periodicals, Inc. doi: 10.1002/ace.20011

Levine, P (2011) *In an Unspoken Voice*, North Atlantic Books

McNiff, S. (1998) *Trust the Process: An Artist's Guide to Letting Go*, Shambhala

Mallon, B., Tufnell, M., & Rubidge, T. (2005), *When I Open My Eyes*, Body Stories

Musicant, S. (2007) 'Authentic Movement in Clinical Work' in *Authentic Movement: Moving the Body, Moving the Self, Being Moved: A Collection of Essays* (ed. P. Pallaro) Jessica Kingsley Publishers

Myers, T. (1998) 'Kinesthetic Dystonia: What bodywork can offer a new physical education', *Journal of Bodywork and Movement Therapies*, 2:2, pp. 101-114

Nachmanovitch, S. (1990) *Free Play: Improvisation in Life and Art*, Jeremy P. Tarcher

Olsen, A. J. (1993, Winter/Spring) 'Being Seen, Being Moved: Authentic Movement and Performance', *Contact Quarterly*, 18, 1, pp. 46-53

Siegel, D. J. (2007) *The Mindful Brain: Reflection and Attunement in the Cultivation of Well-Being*, W.W Norton

Sills, F. (2009) *Being and Becoming, Psychodynamics, Buddhism, and the Origins of Selfhood*, North Atlantic Books

Stromsted, T. (2001) 'Re-inhabiting the female body: Authentic Movement as a gateway to transformation' in *The Arts in Psychotherapy*, 28, (2001) 39, 5, pp. 39

_______ (1999) 'Re-Inhabiting the Female Body: Authentic Movement as a gateway to transformation', Unpublished doctoral dissertation, California Institute of Integral Studies

Tufnell, M. (2010) 'Modular Handbook on Touch', MA Dance & Somatic Wellbeing, UCLan, Preston, UK, Unpublished

Tufnell, M. and Crickmay, C. (2004) *A Widening Field: Journeys into the Body and Imagination*, Dance Books

Whitehouse, M.S. (1979) 'C.G. Jung and Dance Therapy: Two major principles' in *Authentic Movement: Essays by Mary Starks Whitehouse, Janet Adler and Joan Chodorow* (ed. P. Pallaro) (2000) 2nd ed. Jessica Kingsley Publishers

Wilberg, P. (2004) *The Therapist as Listener: Martin Heidegger and the Missing Dimension of Counselling and Psychotherapy Training*, New Gnosis Publications

Williamson, A. (2009) 'Formative support and connection: somatic movement dance education in community and client practice', *Journal of Dance and Somatic Practices* 1:1, pp. 29-45, doi: 10.1386/jdsp.1.1.29/1

NICOLE HARBONNIER-TOPIN and HELEN SIMARD

Towards a Constructive Interaction between Somatic Education and Introspective Verbalisation

Introduction

Somatic practices can contribute to the development of a deeper sense of self, through an attention to, and awareness of, our lived experiences, actions, and sensations (Hanna 1987). In dance education, we have seen that somatic practices can have positive effects on a dancer's level of self-awareness, and can contribute to improving the quality of any learning process (Fortin 1996). But while somatic approaches emphasise the importance of the body in the concept of self, pioneer educator Thomas Hannah (1995) argued that language also played a key role in one's ability to achieve a fuller state of consciousness, underlining the intrinsic links between what he called "sarcal experience" and "lingual experience".

In order for an individual to develop fully this "sarcal experience", bodily experiences, which might be understood at a pre-linguistic level, must be put into words. As Piaget (1948) and Vygostky (1967) have argued, language and verbal evocation are cognitive tools that can be used to learn new artistic or physical skills – be it the altering of perceptions, a memorising task or another type of problem solving. Indeed, in somatic education settings, participants are often encouraged to speak from their movement explorations in order to develop a consciousness of their bodily practices and an awareness of their movement patterns (Adler 2003; Kirsch *et al.* 2009; Grove *et al.* 2005; Opacic *et al.* 2009; Bacon 2012). For example, Martha Eddy explains that she dedicates the last part of her somatic education sessions to a time of "non-verbal and verbal sharing about the experience that day with time for questions and comments" (2006: 88). Similarly, Erskine describes moments of exchange during somatic explorations when students "were asked questions and their own questions were welcomed, they were encouraged to respond with their own thoughts and to the views of others" (2009: 6). Bacon asserts that these verbalisations are "both difficult and imperative" (2012: 118), proposing that somatic educators must develop strategies that facilitate the "discovery and development of language that emerges uniquely *from* the experience of being a moving, perceiving body rather than *about* that experience" (116; original emphasis). Similarly, Smears notes that somatic educators must be aware that these exchanges may at times be "disturbing" to participants, since "giving language to unknown experience requires intention, patience: attention to the subtleties of the lived body and deference to being open to chaos" (2005: 107).

And yet, while students are encouraged to reflect on their embodied experiences during or after somatic education lessons, little empirical research has been conducted on the way in which their verbalisations are formulated, or on the techniques employed by educators to solicit such verbalisations. Since these moments of exchange or verbalisation are often self-guided, and there is no standardised system for how they should be formulated, some students might find it difficult to assess whether or not they have achieved a veritable "transformation from the bodily experience into language" (Bacon 2012: 118). Moreover, as somatic educators, we do not perhaps always evaluate the influence our own choice of words might have on our students' verbalisations of bodily experiences. However, Austin (1970) has noted the "perlocutionary effects of discourse" meaning that the verbalisations of a given speaker will necessarily influence the behaviour and responses of those who bear witness to them. This considered, it seems necessary to consider not only how our students verbalise their experiences, but also how we as educators speak with and guide participants in our somatic education classes, and seek the most appropriate means to assist them.

In the field of psychology, there exists an interview technique called the "explicitation interview". Developed by French researcher (CNRS) Pierre Vermersch (2000, 2012, 1999), this technique proposes an approach to soliciting *a posteriori* introspective verbalisations of performed actions, be they physical, perceptive or mental. Vermersch argues that this process can help individuals gain access to their subjective ,lived experience. Since somatic education and explicitation interview techniques share a common phenomenological base, they both place value on the subjective nature of reality and encourage individuals to plunge into their own concrete, lived experiences to gain a deeper awareness of practice.

As dance researchers and somatic educators trained in explicitation interview techniques, we decided to lead a workshop at the Dance and Somatic Practices Conference at the University of Coventry in July 2013, which combined a somatic exploration with an exercise in introspective verbalisation. In this chapter, we present some of the major themes that were explored in this workshop. We begin by outlining the key principles of a French movement analysis approach known as Functional Analysis of the Dancing Body *(Analyse Fonctionnelle du Corps dans le Mouvement Dansé,* or *AFCMD)*, which informed the explorations we undertook through the workshop. Next, we present the explicitation interview techniques and discuss the reasoning behind our choice of this approach. Having explored the theoretical dimensions of both approaches, we then discuss how we brought these two methods together in practice by reviewing the somatic explorations conducted in our workshop and drawing examples from explicitation interviews conducted with three participants following the workshop. Finally, we conclude the chapter by highlighting the need for further investigation into the modes of verbalisation in the fields of somatic education and dance studies, arguing that the interview techniques proposed by Vermersch's approach to retrospective introspection may prove to be highly effective in movement and practice based research.

An introduction to the principles of Functional Analysis of the Dancing Body

The somatic education lessons offered during our workshop were inspired by a French system of movement analysis called Functional Analysis of the Dancing Body (*Analyse Fonctionnelle du Corps dans le Mouvement Dansé* in French, or *AFCMD*). AFCMD is an approach to movement observation and practice that has developed in France since the late 1980s, when the French government introduced a national diploma programme to train dance teachers, in which dance kinesiology was to play an essential role (Cazemajou 2005). The dance kinaesiology programme itself – which was initiated by Odile Rouquet and carried out by her colleague Hubert Godard – was tailored to give dance educators an integrated training in both somatics and movement sciences, all while bearing in mind how these related to artistic expression in movement (Schulmann 1999). The curriculum of this diploma programme included coursework in anatomy, physiology, neurophysiology, basic biomechanics, movement observation, functional analysis and somatic practices. Although the programme initially drew from Ideokinesis and Structural Integration, it quickly moved to include an understanding of the founding principles of a number of different somatic approaches, such as Feldenkrais, Alexander, and Body-Mind Centering – in order to provide dance educators with an integrative overview of somatic practice, and how various methods could be applied in the field of dance.

Today, AFCMD continues to draw from kinaesiology and somatics and is centred on developing each dancer's perception of his or her own neuromuscular coordination. Unlike pedagogical approaches historically adopted in dance, wherein students must conform to technical or aesthetic norms imposed by different teachers or forms, AFCMD practitioners strive to adjust their teaching approach or lessons to the unique needs of every student (Godard 1990b). As such, each practitioner develops different protocols that help identify their own or their students' unique coordination processes, allowing them to offer neuromuscular facilitation in various movement contexts. Thus, the kind of movement analysis proposed by AFCMD focuses not only on the more easily visible structures of movement, but also on more subtle elements like internal changes related to intentionality of the mover or the postural support system preceding a given movement or gesture (Topin 2001).

An introduction to the introspection interview

After our movement explorations, the participants were introduced to a specific approach to verbalising their workshop experience known as the 'explicitation interview' – a form of "retrospective introspection" (Vermersch 2005; 2009; 1999).

Developed by the psychologist and researcher Pierre Vermersch (*Centre National de Recherche Scientifique-CNRS; Groupe de Recherche sur l'Explicitation-GREX*), this qualitative interview technique was designed to obtain detailed, descriptive verbalisations "based on acts of introspection relating to a past lived experience (in the recent or more distant past)" (Vermersch 2009). Put differently, the explicitation interview is designed to allow individuals to access dimensions of their lived experiences and actions of which they are perhaps not immediately conscious. This technique is often used to interview individuals in professional practices, or those who are engaged in the performance of a specific task; the purpose of conducting this kind of introspection interview is both to allow individuals to gain insight into what actually happened in a given situation or activity, as well as to shed light on implicit knowledge that they have (Vermersch 2000).

Ultimately, the goal of such a verbalisation of lived experience is to assist individuals in auto-informing themselves about the implicit, pre-reflexive knowledge they have with regard to their actions. Since this interview technique is designed to solicit precise verbalisations of lived past experiences, it permits the implicit knowledge contained within a movement to emerge explicitly on the linguistic level and may allow individuals to gain a deeper awareness of their movement practices.

Fig. 1: The authors introduce 'explicitation interview'. Photo: Fresh@CU and C-DaRE

According to Vermersch (2000), some of the defining elements of an introspection interview are that it:

- gains access to the participant's point of view, from a first-person perspective;
- assumes the participant has a pre-reflexive, implicit, practical knowledge of his or her lived experiences
- considers action (both mental and material) as the preferred source of information
- focuses on process or the procedural dimension of said actions
- aims to create the conditions necessary to allow the participant to enter a state of 'evocation' by accessing and describing specific, embodied memories

Rather than simply giving a generalised overview of the entire activity, individuals are encouraged and guided to recount a precise and revealing moment in their actions. The idea is that by providing a genuine description of concrete experience, individuals can deepen their knowledge of their own practice, since actions are not generalised events, but rather specific, complex occurrences that implicate the individual simultaneously in several different levels of lived experience (Vermersch 2009). Of course, through the description of concrete actions (both mental and material), other types of information relating to the activity may emerge over the course of the interview. Vermersch (2000) refers to these other kinds of information as "satellites" of the action, which might include: the context or circumstances in which the action took place; the individual's intentions or motivations with regard to conducting the action; the individual's belief systems or value judgements that influenced the action; and the technical or procedural knowledge the individual drew on to justify or negate the course of action (see Figure 2).

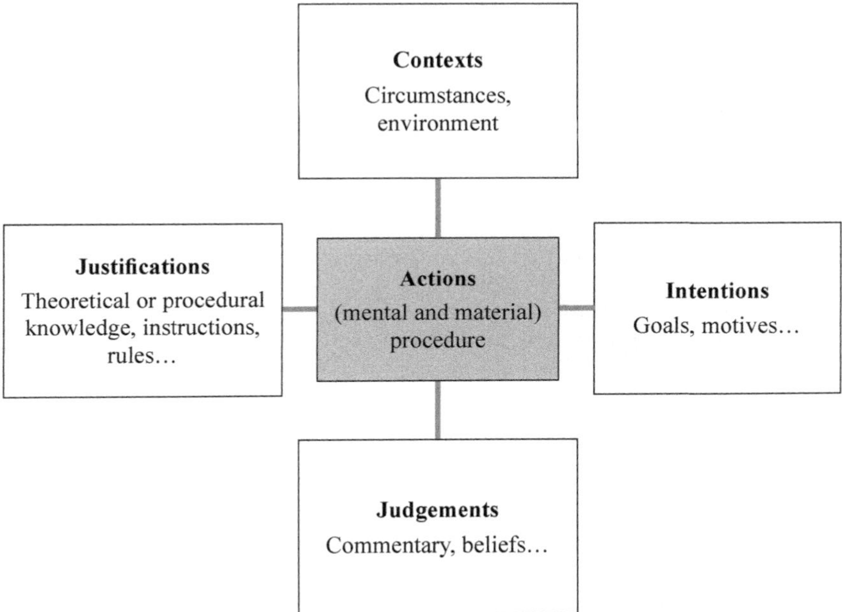

Fig. 2: The System of Lived Experience: Action and Related 'Satellite' Information[1]

According to Vermersch (2000), the introspective interview consists of the six following steps:

1. Initialising: establishing a good interview relationship with the participant and ensuring consent
2. Focusing: targeting a specific moment or experience for discussion
3. Elucidating: soliciting a clear description of the moment or experience in question (this is the heart of the interview)
4. Fragmentation of the description: "going to the level of detail required to make the described action intelligible, in relation to the aims of the study" (Vermersch 2005)
5. Regulating (or guiding the interviewee): resituating the participant in the context; maintaining focus on the specified moment; renegotiating interview relationship as needed
6. Closing: ensuring that the interview wraps up, and confirming that the participant is satisfied with what he or she has said with regard to the experience.

1 (Vermersch 2000: 45)

The interviewer generally begins by asking the participant to walk through some of the contextual information surrounding the activity, such as the circumstances (work, leisure, habitual activity or one-time occurrence), time (day, time, season), and space (home, work, indoor, outdoor, precise location or orientation in a specific room) in which it took place, and might even ask the participant what he or she was wearing that day. Vermersch (2000) argues that examining these kinds of details effectively resituates participants in the moment in question, aiding them to enter a state of evocation in which they may more easily recount details of the event of which they are not consciously aware.

Once the participant is resituated in the moment, the rest of the interview focuses on a precise and minute description of the action in question. Thus, it is important for the interviewer to recognise if and when the participant slips into providing other kinds of information (context, intentions, judgements or procedural knowledge) in order to assist him or her to remain focused on the description of his or her mental and material actions. Since qualitative studies often focus on understanding why individuals engage in various social activities (Husserl 1970), this insistence on focusing on what people do, as opposed to why they do it, may seem counter-intuitive. However, Vermersch proposes that human beings create meaning from action, as opposed to actions being dictated by meanings. Thus, he argues that this retrospective verbalisation of actions can provide a 'fertile ground' from which the meaning of the activity can emerge.

A somatic education lesson on the influence between relation to gravity and walking coordination

Our workshop began with movement explorations inspired by what Godard refers to as an individual's "functional predisposition" (*terrain fonctionnel*), which he defines as an "innate tendency, orienting (ascending or descending dynamics) our way of dealing with gravity, physically and symbolically" (Godard 1990a; McHose & Godard 2006; Newton 1995; Godard *et al.* 1994). Godard proposes that posture is a base coordination through which each individual builds his or her preferred relationship to gravity, and by which all other movement patterns can be understood or analysed (Godard 1990b).

The participants were invited to begin to identify their own functional predisposition using three different tests: first, by gesturing towards the ceiling with their index finger; second, by bending and extending their legs while gliding their backs along a wall; and third, by jumping, feet together, while a partner either emphasised the down accent of the jump by pushing down on their shoulders, or emphasised the up accent of the jump by gently lifting their ribcage from behind on the up accent. Godard's (1990a) hypothesis is that an individual who initiates the gesture towards the ceiling from the pelvis, the extension of the legs while gliding the back along the wall by pushing the feet into the floor, or feels more comfortable jumping when a partner pushes on his or her shoulders is probably orienting his or her relationship to gravity in an ascending dynamic. On the other hand, he proposes that the person who initiates the gesture towards the ceiling with the upper body, the extension of the legs while gliding the back along the wall by reaching with the head, or feels more comfortable jumping when a partner lifts his or her ribcage is more likely orienting his or her relationship to gravity in a descending dynamic.

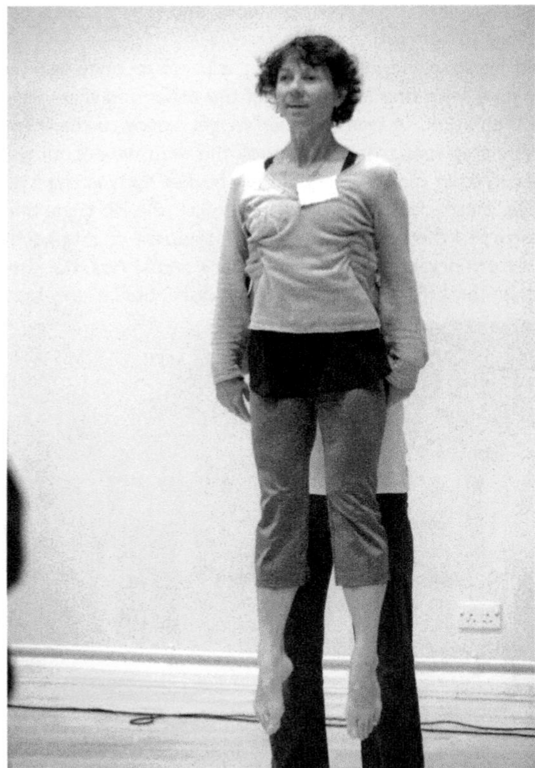

Fig. 3: A descending dynamic during the jump. Photo: Fresh@CU and C-DaRE

Having begun to identify their own functional predispositions, we then invited the participants to explore their walking patterns through two different exercises. First, we asked them to walk around the room in order to take note of their usual or "natural" walking patterns. We proposed they could take note of different elements of the movement such as the speed of their gait, how weight was distributed through their feet, and the manner in which the swing of the arms was coordinated with their steps. Once they had identified key elements of their own walk, the participants were asked to close their eyes and listen to one volunteer walking around the room, all the while considering how this individual's walk differed from their own. Was the gait faster or slower than theirs had been? Did the step have a heavier heel strike or articulate lightly through the toes? Did the volunteer seem to favour one foot over the other in their stride?

Once they had taken note of these differences, the participants were asked to open their eyes and attempt to recreate the walk that they had just heard. In order to accomplish this, they might have to slow down or speed up their gait, shift their weight into the heel or ball of the foot, adjust which part of their body initiated the movement, or even change their whole posture. The exercise was repeated several times with different volunteers, with the participants alternating between their own walking patterns and the patterns of others. In taking note of and attempting to mimic the walking patterns of others, the participants began to reorganise what defined their own postural alignment and functional predispositions, and thus gained a deeper awareness of their own walking patterns.

In the second exercise, we invited the participants to once again stand with their eyes closed, this time with one foot ahead of the other and their weight on the back foot. They were then asked to transfer their weight slowly to the front foot, lifting the back foot to take a step forward. As they took this step, we encouraged them to note what changes occurred in various parts of their bodies, such as: the front foot, the back foot, the front leg, the back leg, the pelvis, the spine, the rib cage, the head and their breathing. What part of the body initiated the movement or advanced first? How was their breathing pattern organised in relation to their steps? Was their stride propelled by one foot more than the other, or was the weight distributed evenly between both feet?

Fig. 4: Participants walk with eyes closed. Photo: Fresh@CU and C-DaRE

As the participants crossed the room, slowly building awareness of the mechanics of their walking pattern, we encouraged them to explore how they could alter or reorganise this habitual pattern in a different way. Could they change the point of initiation of the movement or the chronology of which parts of the body advanced first? For example, could a participant who had initiated their walk from a lengthening of the spine or forward inclination of the ribcage instead begin the movement with a forward propulsion of the hips, or a grounding of the feet? Did such changes cause them to lose balance, or actually give them more stability? By exploring both subtle and drastic changes that could be made to their walk, the participants were able to gain awareness of this highly complex, yet pedestrian and often unconscious, movement pattern. As such, they gained further insight into their functional predisposition, or how they organised their posture in relation to gravity.

Verbalising the somatic experience through retrospective introspection

Immediately following our somatic explorations, we invited participants to take a moment to reflect individually on the workshop, to see if any particular moment came back as being particularly significant or marking to them. By significant, we explained that it could be a moment that they had found particularly enjoyable, one during which they felt they had learned something about their own movement processes, or simply a moment that struck them spontaneously as being relevant. Some participants chose to conduct this reflection mentally, while others wrote down the key points that they had retained from the exercises. Following this reflection time, we asked if any of the participants wanted to participate in short explicitation interviews in order to revisit and further explore a moment they felt was important. A few participants volunteered, and scheduled appointments to meet with us over the rest of the conference. The examples in this section are points of interest that emerged from some of these interviews.

We began each interview by asking the participants to walk us through the moment they had chosen, and employed several different strategies to regulate the manner in which their verbalisation occurred. For instance, we asked a number of contextual questions with regard to the experience: where had they been standing in the room at this moment? What direction were they facing? Who were they standing next to? Did anyone in their field of consciousness say or do anything noteworthy at that moment. While these details may seem unimportant or trivial, Vermersch (2000) argues that reviewing them can assist participants in resituating themselves in the experience, thus allowing them better to elucidate their experiences.

Another strategy that can be employed is that once the specific, significant moment has been identified, the participant is asked to go back a few seconds, and describe what had happened just before this moment. As Vermersch explains, bringing participants to describe what had happened just before the revelatory moment allows them to further fragment the experience, permitting them to take into account minute details of which they might not have been consciously aware. For example, one participant wanted to be interviewed in order to discuss a moment that had occurred during the first walking exercise, where, along with the group, he had tried to mimic the walking pattern of another participant he had listened to walking around the room while his eyes were closed. He explained that he had felt relieved when he opened his eyes and confirmed his feeling that his own walking pattern was nothing like the other participant's. In this moment, he had suddenly felt he was able to explore his own walk more freely, and was interested in understanding what had caused this sensation of release. When he was asked to describe what had happened directly before this, the participant described standing with his eyes closed, listening to the other participant walking. He said that when he attempted to recreate this walking pattern, he felt pressed down or crushed, and that his throat was constricted. In contrast, he was able to identify that when he saw the other person walking he experienced a feeling of relief, which he specified was on a somatic level linked to a sensation of blood flowing through his body, a dropping in his abdomen, more freedom in his breath and throat, and a mobility in his eyes. It is interesting to note that while this experience could have been seen primarily as an emotional reaction or value judgement on the participant's part, we see that verbalising the experience allowed him to deepen his kinaesthetic awareness, and identify a number of precise, minute internal physical changes that took place in his experience.

In another interview, a participant made an interesting discovery about the way that she stored, processed and recalled information relating to her somatic experiences. This participant wanted to talk about a step she took during the second walking exercise, when she transferred her weight from her back foot onto her front foot. In this moment, she had suddenly felt unstable, and was interested in understanding both what had thrown her off balance and also how she had managed to steady herself. In order to describe the moment in which she took the step forward and felt unbalanced, the participant explained that she was drawing from a visual sense of watching herself walking from behind. As she viewed herself in this way, she felt that something was missing from the image, as if part of her body vital to the action could not be seen from this perspective. At this point, a different interview strategy was employed, and she was asked to describe the movement from the perspective of her physical sensations of her actions instead of from her visual sense of the event. As she described where she felt the movement was taking place in her body, the participant was able to identify that her heel was the body part that was missing from her visual image, and from where the instability originated: she could sense that her weight was shifted too far forward, and that her heel was not fully coming into contact with the ground. Here, it is interesting to note that verbalisation allowed the participant not only to gain a deeper awareness about the instability in her walking pattern, but to recognise that she could draw on different kinds of sensorial data (in this case, physical and visual sensations) to recall and analyse her somatic experiences.

Fig. 5: The recall of sensations during a transfer of weight in a step forward.
Photo: Fresh@CU and C-DaRE

While these two examples show how explicitation interview techniques can be used immediately following or soon after a somatic exploration to solicit a precise description of the experience, this approach can also be used to revisit experiences that took place much further in the past. For example, another participant wanted to be interviewed following the workshop in order to revisit a moment she remembered from a performance that had taken place quite some time previously. She remembered this performance as being particularly enjoyable but was not sure what exactly gave her this impression. Through her interview, she was able to identify that her pleasure in the performance was related to an expanded awareness of the space around her. She was able to describe the moment when she changed direction, turning to face the audience. In this moment, she felt conscious of her whole environment (other dancers, audience, stage markings) and did not feel restricted by the demands of the choreography. Whereas this sense of expansiveness might normally make her feel anxious, she was at this moment able to manage the details of the performance without losing a sense of ease and relationship to the audience and fellow dancers. Following the interview, this participant told us that verbalising her experience in this way had allowed her to take note of a number of details concerning the event that she had either forgotten, or of which she had not consciously taken note at the time of the performance. As such, she felt that Vermersch's approach to retrospective introspection and verbalisation of lived experiences could be particularly valuable tools in her practice-based research.

Conclusion: Towards a 'phenomenological pedagogy'

Describing or defining somatic experiences is never an easy task. In this chapter, we have proposed that the use of introspective verbalisation techniques drawn from Vermersch's explicitation interview approach may allow somatic educators to solicit minute and precise descriptions of actions performed by students in the context of somatic education lessons. Making reference to examples drawn from our workshop at the Dance and Somatic Practices Conference, we have shown how using this interview technique allowed participants to gain a deeper awareness of their kinaesthetic experiences. As such, unlike mental imagery or visualisation techniques often used in dance and movement education, where participants are encouraged to use imagined metaphorical or technical images to improve performance (Hanrahan and Vergeer 2001), we have argued that verbalisations based on retrospective introspection of lived experience can permit somatic practitioners to gain subtle yet highly relevant information that they could draw on in future somatic explorations, learning situations or performances.

As we have mentioned, Vermersch's position that awareness of an experience is best developed through a precise and minute description of the actions involved in the process may seem counter-intuitive to individuals unfamiliar with his approach; additionally, it should be mentioned that several of the workshop participants wondered if the technique might not potentially elicit strong emotional responses through the revisiting of past lived experiences, and felt it at times resembled interview techniques that might be employed in psychological analysis or therapeutic settings. As such, we recommend that somatic practitioners interested in using Vermersch's approach to retrospective introspection receive formal training in the technique before integrating formal explicitation interviews into their lesson plans. However, without going as far as conducting formal interviews with each and every one of our students, we as somatic educators may find that adopting a mode of reflection centred on a retrospective introspection on and verbalisation of precise actions performed at a particular moment can aid student and teacher alike to achieve a greater capacity for autonomous learning and reflexive self-awareness. By recognising that each action is a unique and complex process, we are also reminded that each student is a unique individual with particular needs. Thus, by providing our students (and ourselves) with the tools needed to verbalise their somatic experiences, we allow them to bring the implicit knowledge contained in their movement explorations to a linguistic level, encouraging them to bring the lessons learned through their movement practices out of the dance studio and into their everyday lives. After twenty-five years of development, and with more than fifty certified instructors in France, Switzerland, Italy and Canada continuing to train students in explicitation interview techniques, we are persuaded that Vermersch's approach to retrospective introspection can provide somatic education and practitioners with those tools.

Acknowledgements

We would like to thank the participants of the Dance and Somatic Practices Conference 2013 who very generously shared their somatic experiences with us, and authorised their description in this chapter.

References

Adler, J. (2003) 'From Autism to the Discipline of Authentic Movement', *American Jnl. of Dance Therapy*, 25(1), 5-16

Austin, J. L. (1970) *Quand dire, c'est faire*, Éditions du Seuil

Bacon, J. (2012) 'Her body finds a voice: Authentic Movement in an imaginal world', *Body Movement and Dance in Psychotherapy*, 7(2), 115-127

Cazemajou, A. (2005) *Analyse du mouvement. Une nouvelle vision du corps en mouvement*, Centre national de la danse, unpublished

Eddy, M. (2006) 'The Practical Application of Body-Mind Centering® (BMC) in Dance Pedagogy', *Jnl. of Dance Education*, 6(3), 86-91

Erskine, S. (2009) 'The integration of somatics as an essential component of aesthetic dance education', in *Dance dialogues: Conversations across cultures, artforms and practices* (ed. C. Stock)

Fortin, S. (1996) 'L'éducation somatique: nouvel ingrédient de la formation pratique en danse', *Nouvelles de Danse*, 28, 14-29.

Glaser, B. G. & Strauss, A. L. (2010) *La découverte de la théorie ancrée : stratégies pour la recherche qualitative, Individu et société*, Armand Colin

Godard, H. (1990a) 'À propos des théories sur le mouvement', *Marsyas*, 16, 109-111

_______ (1990b) 'L'empire des sens... La kinésiologie, un outil d'analyse du mouvement', *Nouvelles de Danse*, 4, 101-105

Godard, H., Newton, A. & Barnes, R. (1994) 'Reading The Body in Dance', *Rolf lines*, 37-41

Grove, R., Stevens, C. & McKechnie, S. (2005) *Thinking in Four Dimensions: Creativity and cognition in contemporary dance*, Melbourne University Press

Hanna, T. (1987) 'What is Somatics? Part Three', *Somatics Magazine*, 6(2), 57-61

_______ (1995) 'What is Somatics?' in *Bone, Breath and Gesture* (ed. D.H. Johnson) North Atlantic Books, 341-352

Hanrahan, C. & Vergeer, I. (2001) 'Multiple uses of Mental Imagery by Professional Modern Dancers', *Imagination, Cognition and Personality*, 20(3), 231-255

Husserl, E. (1970) *L'idée de la Phénoménologie* (trans. A. Lowit), Presses Universitaires de France

Kirsch, D., et al. (2009) 'Choreographic Methods for Creating Novel, High Quality Dance', in *5th Int. Workshop on Design & Semantics of Form & Movement*, 188-95

McHose, C. and Godard, H. (2006) 'Phenomenological space, interview with Hubert Godard', *Contact Quarterly*, 31(2), 23-38

Newton, A. (1995) 'Basic Concepts in the Theory of Hubert Godard', *Rolf Lines*, 32-43

Opacic, T., Stevens, C. & Tillmann, B. (2009) 'Unspoken knowledge: implicit learning of structured human dance movement', *Jnl. of Experimental Psychology: Learning, Memory and Cognition*, 35(6), 1570-1577

Piaget, J. (1948) *La Naissance de l'Intelligence Chez l'Enfant*, Delachaux & Niestlé

Schulmann, N. (1999) 'Définition: L'analyse fonctionnelle du corps dans le mouvement dansé' in *Dictionnaire de la Danse* (ed. P. Le Moal) Larousse

Topin, N. (2001) 'L'Analyse du mouvement, une danse du regard: l'enseignement d'Hubert Godard', *Nouvelles de Danse*, 46-47, 100-113.

Vermersch, P. (1999) 'The View from Within. Introspection as Practice', *Jnl. of Consciousness Studies*, 6(2-3), 17-42

_______ (2000) *L'entretien d'explicitation*, 3rd ed. ESF

_______ (2005) 'Aide à l'explicitation et retour réflexif', *Expliciter*, 59, 26-31

_______ (2009) 'Describing the Practice of Introspection', *Jnl. of Consciousness Studies*, 16, 20-57

_______ (2012) *Explicitation et Phénoménologie, Formation et Pratiques Professionnelles*, Presses Universitaires de France

Vygotsky, L. S. (1967) *Thought and Language*, MIT Press

PART FIVE

Lived Lineages

JENNY ROCHE

Disorganising Principles

Corporeal Fragmentation and the Possibilities for Repair

Introduction

Dancers investigate ever-expanding relationships to embodiment through the variety of idiosyncratic choreographic signatures that are continually emerging in professional practice. They live fragmented lineages that are interrupted and redirected as they traverse between various projects led by different choreographers or the same choreographer pursuing different creative goals. As contemporary dance continues to reconceive ways of moving, the dominant lineages of dance training are less useful as reference points through which dancers can recalibrate bodily activity and thus rebalance. In this chapter, I examine the impulse towards fragmentation in contemporary dance and explore how moments of agency for dancers might arise and be seized within the complexities of this environment. These issues are discussed in relation to my encounter with a bodywork therapy of Japanese origin, Amatsu, which I studied throughout 2012 and through the teaching principles of Gill Clarke as illuminated through the *Minding Motion* project, which explored Clarke's pedagogy for Tanzplan, Germany 2010 (Diehl and Lampert 2011). My experiences in performance and bodywork practice are offered as examples throughout the chapter.

Fragmenting Corporeality

A key characteristic of contemporary dance is the desire to rupture the stability of previous choreographic vocabularies in order, as choreographer William Forsythe (2011: 90) describes it, "to detach ourselves from positions of certainty". In the endeavour to expand established paradigms and increase creative agency, contemporary choreographers rupture the stability of the familiar so as to avoid pre-conditioned and repetitive movement responses. One way to achieve this has been through interdisciplinary research with cognitive psychologists and neuroscientists.

Over the last decade there has been an increased interest in augmenting choreographic creativity through such collaborations.[1] Dee Reynolds (2007) describes "*kinesthetic imagination*" as the means whereby dominant patterns of directing and using energy, which influence the kinaesthetic habits of individuals, are overthrown in cultural shifts. She names dance as the art form that can effectively anticipate and demonstrate these energetic transformations and this potentiality situates dance at the vanguard of culturally significant artistic practices (2007: 1). In contemporary dance we witness a continuous evolution of movement vocabularies and choreographic methodologies that describe and establish innovative corporeal relationships between body and world.

The embodied subject seeks stability and over a lifetime, repeated movements congeal into a habitual body. However, for the dancer new movement experiences interrupt this stability. Guided by the choreographer's conceptual framework, the dancer *disorganises* at the beginning of a creative process, only to re-organise differently to incorporate new choreographic schema. Thus dancers vacillate between the stability of the habitual and its rupture when forming new movement pathways. When working as a dancer I relished opportunities to embody concepts that disorganised and re-ordered my corporeality. For example, when working with North American choreographer John Jasperse in 2005, he asked me to improvise with the image of "*the femur bones like jet sprays of water on top of which the pelvis floats like a ball*" (Roche 2009: 101). Taking turns improvising with this image we worked on translating it into rhythm and sensation to create a new logic of pelvic motion with all the subsequent impulses that this concept evoked: pressure rising vertically from both femurs and resonating upwards through the torso until it became amplified in the movement responses of the head. We improvised with this idea until Jasperse solidified the material into a choreographed phrase.

Longtime dancer with Forsythe, Dana Casperson (2011), writes of her experience of corporeal fragmentation in the creative process and the quest to find bodily wholeness even when engaged in actively decomposing the body. Casperson (2011:93) alludes to other layers of physical restriction in her spine – "unusual twists and shifts in it that can have the effect of dis-integrating my body, causing it to act as separate parts" – that have added to the complexity of her negotiation of fragmentation. In the following passage, she describes a movement task developed by Forsythe for the piece *Decreation,* which gives an example of purposefully seeking to disorganise normative corporeal alignments within a choreographic process:

> Bill [Forsythe] created the task of walking while setting in motion a sort of diachronic physical ricochet in the body, which was accomplished by sending the eyes in one direction, jaw in the other, rib cage in one direction, hips in the other, etc. (Casperson 2011: 97)

Dancing bodies are ordered in specific ways through adopting thought concepts with corporeality. Susan Leigh Foster (1992: 482) refers to this when she describes a body disciplined through participation in a dance technique as a 'body—of—ideas' as does Ann Cooper Albright (1997: 54) when she highlights "the meanings sewn into the neuromusculature of the [dancing] body". Casperson (2011: 93) says, "even when we are not aware of it, we are always already engaged in some thought version of our bodies". So the uncertainty that Forsythe outlines above not only describes

1 Choreographer Wayne McGregor has been one of the main advocates of this enquiry through his R-Research project with Random Dance (http://bit.ly/tpMove89). Also see Delahunta (2009: 58).

destabilising fixed corporeal positions but perhaps also includes the search for new conceptual lenses through which embodiment can be experienced.[2]

But why fragment the body in this way? At her keynote speech for the Dance and Somatic Practices Conference 2013 at the University of Coventry, choreographer and scholar Carol Brown spoke of how attractive corporeal fragmentation can be for emerging choreographers, proposing that oftentimes "destruction is more exciting than repair". The impulse towards disorganisation is appealing because it enables the subject to destabilise her/his molar identity and decompose the alignments that correspond to a stable version of self. Approaching this from another perspective, Casperson (2011: 99) writes of the possibility to perceive and represent wholeness through embodying choreography that produces fragmentation. The mechanics are not visible when integration is seamless and without effort. However, displaying the rerouting of connections through the body that are required for communication between the different parts foregrounds the potential to experience wholeness (*ibid*).

Dancers inevitably embody uncertainty. Secure company jobs are increasingly rare and the majority of dancers must develop a freelance career path through the independent sector.[3] The economic reality of the dancer's career demands supreme versatility in order to survive. This requires the capability of transforming across the differing stylistic approaches of various choreographers and could be described as 'destratification' from Deleuze and Guattari's (1987: 159–160) theory of how subjects can transgress the normative relationship to the three major social strata, "the organism, significance, and subjectification". Deleuze and Guattari (1987) identify the complex networks of social connections that impose a dominant reality on subjects and enclose them within molar identities. In contrast, the Deleuzean *Body without Organs* imagines a destratified body interrelating across networks of desire in processes of becoming as these impulses allow the formation of various relationships within the body and between body and world (*ibid*). This body is not organised according to the authority of cultural norms but is instead free to contravene these boundaries. Similarly, destratification could describe the dancer's potential to transgress and disorder bodily wholeness, so that new corporeal configurations can be realised. As a survival strategy this adaptive tool enables dancers to negotiate the complexity of remaining employable in an increasingly diverse milieu.

Embodying choreographic movement is not a free destratification for the dancer but engendered through a creative process that is generally led by a choreographer. At its most liberated, this process involves a meta-positioning of concepts that stimulate movement responses and at its most controlled, it involves a series of prescribed movements that must be accurately embodied. Butterworth (2004:55) describes the spectrum of choreographic processes as ranging from "choreographer as expert – dancer as instrument" to "choreographer as collaborator – dancer as co-owner". I suggest that the dancer's destratification is a result of embodying externally originating rules that lead to the formation of a particular movement vocabulary for each choreographic piece, wherever on the continuum of methodologies (expert to collaborator) the choreographer falls. In this chapter, I am specifically discussing choreographic processes that lie within this broad framework with the understanding that the choreographic role normally involves directing the dancer in and out of choreographic investigations.

---

2 Sandra Reeve (2011) explored nine of these conceptual lenses, from the *object body* to the *ecological body*.

3 For an account of this from the perspective of a dancer in New York City, see Dittman (2008).

In as much as Deleuze and Guattari (1987) offer the potential to destratify, Rosi Braidotti (2000: 158–160) in her critique of Deleuzean concepts from a feminist perspective, stresses that the transformative capability of *becoming* is not limitless but is constrained by the "ecology of the self". This is not to say that she posits an essential natural body, but that she recognises the body as matter, rather than as a site capable of endless change. She outlines the Deleuzean body as "a field of transformative effects whose availability for changes of intensity depends, first, on its ability to sustain and, second, to encounter the impact of other forces or affects" (Braidotti 2000: 159). Thus Braidotti evokes the material limits of the body, which brings into focus the potential strain on dancing bodies in their requirement to be continually available to change.

Riding Movement Impulses

Since I began studying Amatsu[4] body therapy, I have questioned how the dancer's transformative capabilities, which are driven by conceptual reconfiguration of corporeality, impact on the material body. As Braidotti (2000) explains above, the ability to transform depends on the capacity to endure other forces, while remaining open to alteration. I now explore through the frame of Amatsu how these transformations might impact on deeper experiences of bodily organisation.

Amatsu is "a modern adaptation of a [Japanese] soft tissue therapy" with a two-thousand-year lineage (O'Connor 2006). In 1995, master of the school of Hi Chi Bu Ku Goshin Jutsu, Dr Masaaki Hatsumi gave Dennis Bartram and two fellow students[5] from the British Isles the rights to teach his techniques, which they developed into Amatsu (ibid)[6]. Through this system, the focus is on bringing the body back to homeostasis, to a state in which it can perform self-healing. As this system derives from a martial art, movement is at the core of this practice that centres on the mobilisation of soft tissue. Practitioners work with the innate intelligence of the nervous system through muscle testing to identify broken links in the neuromuscular chain of connections. The purpose of muscle testing is to check neurological functioning. It is not to test whether the muscle is weak or strong, but rather to see if there is any disturbance in the messaging system which instigates and relays muscular action.

Core to the Amatsu training is the notion of biotensegrity, which is the understanding that the skeleton is suspended in a matrix of soft tissue, muscles, ligaments and tendons through a tensile integrity relationship. The concept of tensegrity – tension and integrity combined – refers to organic structures in architecture and originates with American architect Buckminster Fuller who designed the geodesic dome (Heller 2002). In Amatsu, the fascia is understood to move according to impact or injury into particular holding patterns that start to pull on other structures. Over time, these settle into an adaptive pattern that maintains the imbalance. Bartram (2009: 1) says, "the elastic property of tissue can deform as a result of ... stress and [can] allow it to reshape after the force has ceased". However, he continues, "when the stress force is greater than the elastic deformity of the tissue, the response is called plastic and the deformation of tissue is continuous and permanent" (Bartram 2009: 1).

4 Throughout 2012, I studied and am now certified in Anma massage, which is the first stage of the Amatsu body therapy training.

5 William Doolan and Christopher Roworth were the two other students (O'Connor 2006).

6 For more information on Amatsu, see Dennis Bartram's website at http://bit.ly/tpMove97

Bartram (2005b) advises balancing movement practices equally on both sides of the body, so that the winding up of fascia in one direction can be unwound and rebalanced. However, it is rare that choreographic movements will be practised equally on both sides as asymmetry delivers choreographic novelty. This is one simple example of the way in which dancing can create organisational imbalances. Returning to Casperson's description of the choreographic task instigated by Forsythe for *Decreation*, I imagine how this might present a worrying diagnosis within an Amatsu session,

> *Client has suffered an unknown trauma to the body that has caused the eyes to move in one direction, jaw to displace in the other (check if this is indicative of a sacral misalignment), rib cage in one direction and hips in the other (test the Quadratus Lumborum and Psoas muscles).*

In Amatsu, the treatment protocol is to rebalance the pelvis first in most cases. This is achieved with as little intervention as possible and through working distally from the point of immobility so that the process of realignment can sequence through the body.

In explorative dance rehearsal and performance practice, bodily discontinuities are created without opportunities to bring these to resolution. For example, in my PhD research, I commissioned solo works from three choreographers[7] and performed these works together in a full-length programme in 2008. The purpose of this was to map each creative process and to explore traversing between different choreographic environments in succession in order to examine my transformative capabilities in the extreme. Moving from one process to the next in rehearsal required a clear change in attention and body attitude making me aware of how each process solicited a different dancing body. Drawing on this experience, I noted:

> After the performances, I stopped 'dead'. I stilled my dancing body out of my perceived need to reclaim it again. I hardly moved or explored my physicality beyond treatments for my back, which felt quite strained afterwards … [the Amatsu practitioner] treating me said that the right side of my body was 'locked', from my neck down through the spine to my pelvis. The left psoas muscle was constricting my left kidney and when he released it, I felt exhausted for a number of weeks. This gave me a sense of the tension I had been holding physically and perhaps the conflict of surrendering my embodied self to these various processes simultaneously. (Roche 2009: 132)

The choreographic impulse to rupture the stability of the known has material implications for the bodies of the dancers that research into these realms. This may be more significantly so because dancers relinquish control over the direction these explorations take while working within the choreographer's creative framework. As mentioned previously, dancers do not usually instigate the conceptual framings of their corporeality within a dance piece but rather respond and react to given tasks within a choreographic process. So, what strategies are available to dancers to enact embodied agency within these externally instigated processes and how might these strategies allow dancers to re-establish equilibrium within an unpredictable environment in which they can never fully prepare for what the choreographer might ask of them? Through responding to and directing the micro-events in the compositional process of choreography, the dancer has the possibility to exercise agency. Casperson (2011: 94) describes this when she explains how dancers manage the challenges inherent in this role:

---

7 These choreographers were John Jasperse (US), Jodi Melnick (US) and Liz Roche (Ire) and the programme was commissioned by and performed in Dublin Dance Festival 2008.

> [Dancers] practice understanding that freedom is not the absence of external pressure, but an internal ability to remain fluid and engaged under demanding circumstances ... [they] become accustomed to riding multiple, sometimes apparently conflicting, energetic waves to find out where they might go. (Casperson 2011: 94)

So, if dancers can ride the waves of the choreographic process, they will remain fluid rather than straining against the tasks at hand. Following the micro-events, which may have ruptured the previous state of stability and moved them into uncertainty, they exercise what Alain Badiou (2005b) terms a *fidelity to the event*. Badiou writes about the emergence of truth from the interruptive nature of the singular event. According to Badiou (2005b: 47), because the event is the result of a chance occurrence its course is not regulated, that is, "the axiom that supports it has arbitrated outside of any rule of established knowledge". He states that a truth is a new occurrence and as knowledge in itself produces repetition of the known, it is the unpredictable rupture by the event that opens up new instances of truth. These words could be describing the emergent properties of a creative choreographic process and the endeavour to detach from the stability of the known. Indeed, Badiou (2005a: xii) defines the event as a break in continuum, stating that it is not only open to the militant but also, "the artist-creator, the scientist who opens up a new theoretical field, or the lover whose world is enchanted".

It should be noted that Badiou (2000) offers a different political standpoint to Deleuze on how subject-hood is attained. He critiques Deleuze's approach as hierarchical, as it requires a kind of self-determination that Badiou believes is not accessible to all in order to move beyond limitations. Badiou (2000) proposes that, in response to the event, anyone can be brought into new ways of perceiving, regardless of whether they seek these possibilities out. Adkins (2012: 514) writes that for Deleuze "any and every change in intensity" is new and a situation that is capable of producing difference, whereas "for Badiou the new must be *ex nihilo*, miraculous in order to be new". In the dancer's encounter with new ways of conceptualising corporeality, continuity is interrupted as new movement possibilities are discovered and in that rupture, new insights are possible. Maintaining fidelity to these new insights requires the dancer to inhabit the uncertainty of this position, to operate between fixed positions and to stay in motion. Strategies that could support this would be tools that enable the dancer to situate her/himself within a continuity of dancing practice and that repair the relationship to the body's flow. For example, Casperson (2011:93) outlines how she practises "thinking my body into a whole, even in situations where my body was not actually whole" as a means to overcome corporeal fragmentation.

To give an example of how challenging this might be I will explain an encounter I had during my Amatsu training. For one of my case studies, I worked on a fellow dancer's foot. According to her physiotherapist, the talus bone in her foot was out of alignment. After the first Amatsu treatment it seemed to realign but when she danced a particular section of a piece in performance, which involved her purposely bumping into other dancers, it came out of alignment again. Although the jarring and jolting did not hurt her, she felt that this was the moment when the injury occurred each time in performance. The improvised collisions seemed to momentarily confuse her nervous system and her weak point (the talus at that time) was not able to hold the realignment. There is a technique in Amatsu that allows the practitioner to simulate a jolt to the nervous system, such as would occur in a trip or fall, in order to integrate the possibility of a surprise event throwing the body out of homeostasis. In our next session, I used this technique and subsequently my colleague was able to dance that section without any problem arising in her foot. In this way, it was possible to prepare her nervous system for the unexpected and integrate this performance moment.

Campbell Edinborough (2013: 117-118) writes about cultivating the performer's resilience through the frame of Feldenkrais Method. He describes resilience, after Moshe Feldenkrais, as the ability to manage the unexpected, such as a fall or push, without activating self-protecting impulses and draws parallels between a sudden loss of equilibrium and the pressures engendered through the performance environment. Edinborough (2013: 116) explains that a sudden disorientation, "or any action performed without awareness, is accompanied by undifferentiated excitement of neurons in the motor cortex" and this will trigger the impulse of muscular contraction. This creates resistance to the flow of movement through the body and perhaps, to look at this from the perspective of Amatsu, limits the plasticity of the soft tissue in reshaping after the sudden and unexpected contraction.

In Edinborough's (2013) outline, awareness is a key factor in managing unpredictability. It could be that in the dancer's case, it is a matter of preparing for the unknown by integrating the potential for the fragmentation that disrupts normative alignments. Dancers navigate highly complex states of stability and change when operating in uncharted choreographic territories. In the case of my colleague's foot, the sudden disorganisation caused by a particular choreographic task exposed an underlying physical vulnerability. It is continually challenging for dancers to manage these issues when working under the pressures of professional practice.

Rewind and Repair

I propose that Gill Clarke's pedagogical approach cultivates a type of dancing awareness and the resulting agency that might allow dancers to manage the unexpected but before I explore this I would like to address briefly Bartram's description of global bodily intelligence. He describes this as the intelligence that coordinates movement beyond the simple level of acquisition and automatic enactment of a skill. He refers to this as *proprioception* in order "to equate with Western concepts of body, mind coordination" (2009: 5). Describing his experience with Hatsumi, Bartram (2009: 2) explains that when observing a master in movement, "they appear to float through their actions". Bartram describes this bodily intelligence as the ability to "relax inside the act", so that individual steps are not apparent but rather are experienced as continuous movement. He writes, "inside this flow the limbs of the body can be explorative, decisive and evasive in a synaesthesia of motion" (Bartram 2009: 4). This is the state that Bartram encourages the practitioner to embody while treating a client. Indeed, when teaching Amatsu, much of the focus is on the movement quality of the practitioner, in the understanding that this quality is communicated to the client through touch. Bartram (2005a: 9) explains, "I utilise and explain the virtues of this kind of movement to the therapists I train. Firstly, it encompasses a high level of ergonomic safety for the practitioner and secondly becomes the generator of the tactile power and feeling for the psychomotor skill of the therapy".

After I experienced Bartram's techniques throughout the training process, I was surprised to learn how much they corresponded with Clarke's practices. When exploring these ideas through the frame of Clarke's approach, I found correlations between Bartram's description of this embodied state and Clarke's idea of an "agreement" in the system that allows movement to sequence through from one body part without obstruction (Clarke, Cramer & Müller 2011: 215). This is achieved through not holding unnecessary tension in subsequent parts and, "reliant upon the elasticity of the fascia to support a sliding sequencing of movement, or to facilitate a simple simultaneous agreement by the integrated system so it might be directed as a whole" (*ibid*: 215). Similarly, Bartram (2005b) describes how creating a "fixed fulcrum" (or locked joint) blocks the passage of movement through the soft tissue and the other joints. The 'agreement' Clarke seems to be referring to denotes more than just the movement of the fascia, but could be expanded to include a global coherence, or synchronous effort that works in tandem with Braidotti's 'ecology of the self' and Bartram's bodily intelligence, so that everything is firing together. In both paradigms, the subject is encouraged to embody a state that incorporates a global bodily awareness, preparedness for the unexpected and the ability to allow movement to sequence through the body without creating obstruction. This creates possibilities for the subject to think globally through movement to manage potential fragmentation.

Clarke, Cramer & Müller (2011: 215) identify that within Clarke's approach "there might even be a technical ideal: being clear, easeful and 'light' in doing integrated movements", evoking Bartram's description of 'relaxing inside the act'. The description of Clarke's approach refers to relaxing extraneous muscles that are not immediately involved in the action. This state is familiar to those working within the field of somatics, whereby awareness in movement creates coherence through the whole system. It makes possible a kind of readiness to integrate new movement possibilities and to encounter the unknown in the way that Edinborough (2013) outlines above. He writes, "intelligence in the context of live performance demands walking a fine line between action and reflection" (Edinborough 2013: 118). Clarke's strategies involve the use of imagination and metaphor to form connections in the body and this supports the notion that dancing and conceptual framing are central for the ability to move the body in agreement towards a goal, producing a kind of embodied agency (Clarke, Cramer and Müller 2011: 215).

One of the most prominent themes in Clarke's work is the dancer as central to the creation of a dance piece, bringing expertise as a mover to choreographic research and the communication of the work as a live agent in performance. Highlighting this role of dancer as researcher and movement innovator, Clarke's (2011: 212) pedagogical practice enables this kind of creative and autonomous learning, so that the dancer can develop as an "investigative artist". Circling back to Deleuze and Guattari, we could imagine how this approach gives a *line of flight* for the dancer, a possibility to extend beyond the dominant lineages in dance through establishing techniques that situate her/him at the centre of a creative dancing practice. The operation of a line of flight is "the movement by which 'one' leaves the territory", whether that may be a social grouping or a system that subjugates the individual (Deleuze & Guattari 1987: 508). When applied to this context, it is an opportunity for dancing subjects to renegotiate their position *within* the power relations of dancing practices.

When learning the protocols and ethos of Amatsu from Bartram, I became aware of how his teaching could circulate and function as an embodied toolkit for support and recuperation. The emphasis on the practitioner's embodied state in training directly communicated the texture of Bartram's physicality and resonated as a movement practice might, calling to mind significant dance teachers and choreographers I have encountered throughout my career (Clarke being one of these in open classes in

London in the 1990s). During rehearsals for a recent performance of a choreography entitled *Shared Material on Dying*[8], I found myself influenced by Bartram's approach and applying some of his principles during my preparations. The piece is five years old and we have performed it in a number of different venues over that period of time.

> *We dance the material in absolute unison together in separate parts of the stage, but I am in the centre and the only dancer who is fully lit. The other two dancers are like my shadows throughout the piece. One of the key instructions for this work is to keep the fluidity of the transitions while maintaining a clear unison without musical accompaniment. The movement is detailed and requires a lot of upper body flexibility, which is counterbalanced by a solid relationship to the floor through the legs and feet. In rehearsals while re-embodying this material, I became aware of how the movement used the right side of the body more dominantly and turned mainly towards the right, finishing in what I could describe as an endpoint. This seemed similar to the feeling when working with a client in Amatsu, of blocked tissue at a juncture where there was no further movement possible. The choreography seemed to wind up in one direction without offering the possibility to unwind. I contemplated what it meant to walk around for five years with this movement trace travelling in only one direction. Applying Bartram's suggestion of working bilaterally, I painstakingly transferred the material to the other side, which felt counterintuitive because of the familiarity of the original movement patterns. The first sensation on dancing the material on the other side was a rush of energy into the right side of my head, which I felt like tangible relief. After spending some time on this task, I returned to the original version of the material. I felt I had more choice than just following the habitual movement pathways of the first side. The additional bodily knowledge seemed to release feelings of tightness on the right side of my body, giving me a 'global' sense of the whole body even when predominantly moving the right side. I could maintain my movement awareness more easily when dancing the material. More generally, this exercise seemed to remove any accumulated strain in dancing the choreography. Whatever endpoint had been formed over five years, I now had a fluid pathway through it.*

The process of interrogating movement that comes directly from the choreographer is seen in *Minding Motion* as similar to "'trying on someone else's clothes', seeing how that feels and then exploring how one could make them one's own" (Clarke, Cramer & Müller 2011: 223). This approach acknowledges the different movement patterns that choreography produces and can impose on the dancer, while creating a frame through which the dancer can maintain a role of movement researcher. My example above demonstrates how dancers might investigate choreographic movement in ways that increase agency and ownership, while being faithful to the choreographic score, so that there is a sense of choice and possibility even while adhering to the rules of the game. The experience of Amatsu as an approach introduced me to the global bodily intelligence that Clarke also references. While not wishing to conflate the two – one is clearly a therapeutic body technique and the other a dance pedagogical practice – I have found how the framing of embodiment in each approach allows for the cultivation of a kind of embodied agency. This could be a challenge for dancers to achieve when operating in systems that may require them to work counter-intuitively

8 Performances took place in Dance Exchange, Birmingham in February 2013, Liz Roche choreographed the piece in 2008 and I danced it with Katherine O'Malley and Lucia Kickham for this iteration.

and disorder a sense of wholeness. Perhaps dancing agency could be defined as the possibility to remain fluid, engage a global bodily intelligence and anticipate the unexpected within the uncertain environment of performance and the longer-term unpredictability of how each new choreographer might ask the dancer to organise or disorganise their corporeality. Clarke's knowledge of corporeality is embedded in a pedagogy that could support the agency of the dancer in negotiating working environments that are necessarily complex, novel and unpredictable. By equipping them with strategies drawn from her legacy, dancers might develop dancing practices that offer possibilities for fragmentation but equally enable repair.

References:

Adkins, B (2012) "Deleuze and Badiou on the Nature of Events" *Philosophy Compass* 7 (8)

Albright, A. C. (1997) *Choreographing Difference: The Body and Identity in Contemporary Dance*, Wesleyan University Press.

Badiou, A. (2005a) *Being and Event*, (trans. O. Feltham) Continuum

______ (2005b) *Infinite Thought* (trans. O. Feltham & J. Clemens) Continuum

Bartram, D. (2005a) 'The Journey Towards Tensegrity', http://bit.ly/tpMove63

______ (2005b) 'Working in the Space' http://bit.ly/tpMove65

______ (2009) 'From Palpation to Inhibition' http://bit.ly/tpMove66

Braidotti, R. (2000) 'Teratologies' in *Deleuze and Feminist Theory* (ed. I. Buchanan & C. Colebrook) Edinburgh University Press

Butterworth, J. (2004) 'Teaching Choreography in Higher Education: A Process Continuum Model', *Research in Dance Education* 5 (1): 45-67

Casperson, D. (2011) 'Decreation' in *William Forsythe and the Practice of Choreography* (ed. S. Spier) Routledge

Clarke, G., F.A. Cramer & G. Müller (2011) 'Minding Motion' in *Dance Techniques: 2010 Tanzplan Germany*, (ed. I. Diehl & F. Lampert) Henschel Verlag

Delahunta, S., P. Barnard & W. McGregor (2009) 'Augmenting Choreography: Insights and Inspiration from Science' in *Contemporary Choreography: A Critical Reader*, (ed. J. Butterworth & L. Wildschut) Routledge

Deleuze, G. & Guattari, F. (1987) *A Thousand Plateaus: Capitalism and Schizophrenia* (trans, B. Massumi) 10th ed., University of Minnesota Press

Diehl, I. & F. Lampert (eds.) (2011) *Dance Techniques 2010: Tanzplan Germany*, Henschel Verlag

Dittman, V. (2008) 'A New York Dancer' in *The Body Eclectic: Evolving Practices in Dance Training* (eds. M. Bales & R. Nettl-Fiol) University of Illinois Press

Edinborough, C. (2013) 'Developing Resilience and Presence Using the Feldenkrais Method' in *Body and Performance* (ed. S. Reeve) Triarchy Press

Forsythe, W. (2011) 'Choreographic Objects' in *William Forsythe and the Practice of Choreography* (ed. S. Spier) Routledge

Foster, S. L. (1992) 'Dancing Bodies' in *Incorporations* (ed. J. Crary & S. Kwinter) Zone 6.

Heller, M. (2002) 'Tensegrity Models' *Dynamic Chiropractic* 20 (26): 30

O'Connor, K. (2006) 'Amatsu Therapy Explained' http://bit.ly/tpMove64

Reeve, S. (2011) *Nine Ways of Seeing a Body*, Triarchy Press

Reynolds, D. (2007) *Rhythmic Subjects: Uses of Energy in the Dances of Mary Wigman, Martha Graham and Merce Cunningham*, Dance Books

Roche, J. (2009) 'Moving Identities: Multiplicity, Embodiment and the Contemporary Dancer', PhD thesis, Roehampton University, UK

JENNIFER MACKERRAS and JANE TOMS

Myth-Busting

Using the Alexander Technique to free yourself from detrimental misconceptions in the performing arts

Introduction

Creative arts practitioners who use their bodies do so as a means of expression, as a form of communication and as a vehicle for meaning, metaphor and other forms of discourse. These practitioners depend upon their ability to use their bodies, their training and their knowledge of themselves to portray their ideas reliably and accurately. Yet so often practitioners can be limited, not so much by their body, or by their technical knowledge, but by their deeply held but mistaken beliefs. These self-imposed 'myths' can impede practitioners and prevent them from achieving their desired goals.

This chapter describes a workshop that explored how the Alexander Technique has helped creative practitioners move past their personal 'myths'. It covers content delivered during the workshop, along with ideas that emerged as a result of preparing, delivering, interacting and reflecting on the workshop.

Both authors have experience in working with performers. Jane Toms taught dancers on a Masters programme through Coventry University and continues to work with performers in her private Alexander Technique teaching practice. Jennifer Mackerras works with all manner of performers, and teaches Alexander Technique on various programmes at the Royal Welsh College of Music and Drama. We have both worked with performers whose talent and expertise have been limited by their beliefs about the nature of their activity and what they need to do to successfully achieve their aims.

The genesis of our characterisation of the Alexander Technique as 'myth-busting' was in response to a presentation by Natalie Garrett Brown at the Alexander Technique and Performing Arts Conference in Melbourne, Australia (Garrett Brown and Toms 2012). Garrett Brown spoke of 'dancerly myths', a term which appealed to us as a means of describing both the mistaken nature of some of the ideas held by performers about their craft, and the degree of attachment with which they are held. It occurred to us that 'myth-busting' might be an engaging and informative way of describing Alexander Technique, and we began to explore this in our teaching practice. We originally conceived of the workshop as a means of exploring this idea with other performers and educators. However, through the preparation and delivery of the workshop, we came to realise that the concept of 'myth-busting' could operate on many levels – even influencing the way we as Alexander Technique teachers conceive of our own heritage and teach our work. This chapter is a continuation and deepening of our investigation of myth-busting.

Background

F.M. Alexander began 'myth-busting' when he had a performance-related problem that couldn't be resolved by the usual means. His exploration revealed that a common cause of poor performance and physical difficulty were the 'erroneous preconceived ideas' (Alexander 1918/1997: 109) – the faulty beliefs or 'myths' – that people held. Since its development, the Alexander Technique has been used by performing artists across the world as a powerful tool for self-development and change.

For the purpose of the workshop the term 'myth' was considered as a concept that can encompass many forms: metaphor, parable, analogy, belief or fairy tale, as well as ancient tales with a spiritual or religious significance. Some myths may have started as 'true' stories, situated in an actual time and place, but as they were told and re-told sections may have been altered or had their focus changed in ways that made them less factually 'true'. Their continuing value then becomes a function of the perceived usefulness of their underlying message or belief structure after these changes.

Stories can gain the status of myth because they are useful. They tell a 'truth'. Even when the story is no longer factually accurate, something remains that is 'true', or that provides an 'identity'. That is to say, a myth can provide a shorthand means of expressing identity. It is easier to refer to 'the little engine that could' (a classic American fairy tale) than to say 'I'm small and insignificant, and maybe a bit of a failure, but I try really hard.' As such, myths become a poetic descriptor of self-image that enables a person to live at a remove from the possibly unpalatable bald truth. A story thus doesn't need to be factually true necessarily, but it does need to be useful. When the story stops being useful it not only ceases to help us, but, at times, it could even hinder our progress.

Often our behaviour can be informed by a commonly held but erroneous belief which gains its power through its widespread prevalence that gives a kind of social 'proof'. For example in our teaching practice we encounter a number of students who hold the belief 'I didn't succeed immediately, so therefore I'm not naturally talented.' A belief such as this may have a multitude of 'myths' underpinning it.

Another example of a social 'proof' would be the belief in the high value of getting a correct answer (and getting it quickly). According to Kiyosaki (1993: 82-3) this commonly held belief is foundational to the structure of conventional school systems. Placing a high value on getting the 'right' answer may not be a problem. But if this belief is then joined with another prevalent idea in Western society – that talent is a gift of birth, fixed and unchanging and not able to be taught – then we have created a belief structure that may limit a student's willingness to experiment and risk failure, placing a cap on their potential development.

The workshop

We began the workshop by sharing our stories about how we came into the Alexander Technique and about how exploring our own stories, using the Technique, had revealed some personal myths. We both had pain-related performance problems, connected, it appeared, to medical issues, but both had come to realise that it was our belief systems that really were our limiting factor. Having shared something about ourselves we then led an activity for the fifteen workshop participants.

The 'Fruit Salad' game, an activity used by teachers "to build up group trust through shared laughter and movement" (UNICEF 1999), was adapted in order to learn about the group, to introduce some key ideas about the ethos of the workshop and to explore personal myths. With that in mind we asked a series of 10 questions sequentially of the group, who were sitting in a circle, with the instruction 'Move into the middle and high five if you ...

- love marmite (vegemite!)
- hate marmite
- have reached your potential
- travelled to Coventry by train
- have some idea of what the Alexander Technique is
- believe people swallow spiders in their sleep
- are a dancer or work with dancers
- love the sun
- have had Alexander Technique lessons
- love experimenting with new ideas'

There was much laughter, movement and learning. Some things that were learnt about the group were that there were many Alexander Technique pupils; there was one person who had no Alexander Technique experience and that everyone was involved in dance. Some key ideas were introduced and in addition it was discovered that only one person in the workshop believed you swallowed spiders in your sleep, and that person was one of the presenters. A participant from America helped the presenter feel less foolish by sharing that only a few weeks ago her daughter came back from school proclaiming 'Mummy did you know that you swallow spiders in your sleep?'

'Myths' debunked

The workshop continued by exploring the concept of myths further. As a light-hearted introduction to that exploration, we read sections from the book *Don't Swallow Your Gum and Other Medical Myths Debunked* (Carroll & Vreeman 2009) which includes examining the myth that 'the average person swallows 8 spiders a year'.

We shared that, according to the authors, this myth originated with a 1954 book about insect folklore and was ridiculed in a 1993 magazine article. The article was then used "in classic myth spinning form" as a source supporting the myth (*ibid*: 23). Group discussion followed: Why would such a myth develop? Who would believe it? It was suggested that it might be a way to get children to tidy their room or a way to encourage other behaviours. At the beginning of the book Carroll and Vreeman say:

> Many things you believe about your health, things you were told as a child, are simply unproven... It's in our best interest to understand where these unproven beliefs came from, and then judge whether they are useful (2009: 2).

They also warn:

> Discovering that something you believed in is not true can be disturbing and unsettling (2009: 4).

When personal 'myths' 'go bad'

The workshop then moved on to F.M. Alexander, his work and its role in personal 'myths' and 'myth-busting'. We explained that Alexander talked about the "erroneous preconceived ideas" (the 'myths') that we bring to everything we do, saying "every defective action is the result of the erroneous preconception of the doer" (Alexander 1997(1918): 120). So we asked 'where do these erroneous preconceived ideas, these 'myths', come from?' We shared a myth commonly held by performers: 'my lungs are situated in my belly.' This type of myth, in our experience, frequently comes about through a failure in communication. The teacher may see something in a student's performance that leads them to wish to discourage shallow breathing. They tell their student to 'breathe into their belly'.

The teacher knows that this is not anatomically possible, but is using the phrase metaphorically to encourage the student to allow movement in their abdominal area (a response to the diaphragm contracting and descending). The student may not have sufficient anatomical knowledge to recognise this as metaphor, or may not be listening closely, or may simply decide that the teacher is speaking literally. Whatever the reason, the student mistakes the metaphor and takes the phrase as anatomical truth: 'my lungs are in my belly'. The student will then act upon that knowledge and (very likely) perpetuate it.

We led participants into another activity where they shared some myths they had encountered by writing them on post-it notes and sticking them on the wall. We then divided the participants into groups and tasked them with collecting myths that fell into a particular category: physical, conceptual, performance-based or miscellaneous. The groups then shared some of the myths they had collected. Box 1 shows some of the myths that were written on the post-its. The collecting of them and the sharing generated much discussion.

Box 1: Some of the myths shared by the workshop participants	
Bad posture is hereditary If it's difficult it's good Carry an umbrella to keep the rain away If you break a mirror ... 7 years' bad luck Throwing salt over your shoulder if spilt Black cat crossing means bad luck If you walk under a ladder you will get 7 years' bad luck Bad luck to walk under a ladder Accidents come in threes (break a match-stick) Don't put new shoes on the table Good girls go to heaven What you give is what you get When the hips are referred to as the top of the pelvis	Women can't be pilots because their ovaries would explode Practice makes perfect You need a strong core If I stand in the back of the room no-one will notice me Dance is a universal language 'They' don't like dancing Not everyone can sing You can't swim for 4 hours after eating No pain no gain The spine is straight It is important to sit up at the table Shoulders back, head up Stage fright is normal and instinctive

This led to the next part of the workshop and a series of questions:

1. How can we decide which myths or stories are still useful?
2. What criteria can we use to decide?
3. Would using an already existing framework, like the Alexander Technique, be worth exploring?

The group said yes to question 3 and the exploration began.

Alexander's Story

We now discussed the story of F.M. Alexander and the evolution of the work that came to be known as the Alexander Technique. The choice of narrative structure comes from Alexander himself: his chapter 'Evolution of a Technique' from *Use of the Self* is in narrative form. This structure allows Alexander to do two things. It gives him a basis to describe some of the detailed experimental nature of his investigations – the importance of this will become more apparent in a moment. The progression of Alexander's narrative also gives readers a framework to help them begin to learn the principles of his work and to identify with his struggles.

We chose the following key elements of Alexander's story to cover in the workshop:

- Alexander as a questioner
- Alexander as someone who realised his problems were caused by his own erroneous beliefs and actions
- Alexander as an experimenter

Alexander was a questioner from an early age. He was even forced to leave school and enter into private tutoring because his questioning disrupted lessons (Vineyard 2007: 7). However what proved disruptive in a classroom was key to instigating his investigations into the cause of the vocal troubles that threatened his acting career. When Alexander could find no relief from either medical approaches or theatrical/vocal coaching, he asked a question of his doctor that forms the starting point for the investigations that are the foundation of the Alexander Technique:

> was [it] something I was doing that evening in using my voice that was the cause of the trouble? (Alexander 1932/1997: 412)

This question is fundamental because by asking it Alexander firmly took responsibility for his problems. He was no longer looking for a pathological or medical explanation, nor was he looking for improvements in vocal or acting technique. Rather, he was putting forward the hypothesis that it was *something he was doing* that was the cause of his trouble. As mentioned earlier, Alexander also spoke of "every defective action being the result of the erroneous preconception of the doer" (Alexander 1918/1997: 120). Thus he saw the something that he was 'doing' as causally linked to his erroneous preconceived ideas.

From this starting point, Alexander became an experimenter and scientist, in that he made a succession of hypotheses about what was causing his trouble and how to proceed, and then designed practical tests to see if he was correct (Weed 2004: 16). For example, his experience had shown him that his vocal troubles only affected his voice on stage, not during ordinary speech. He hypothesised that he must be doing something different when reciting, and watched himself in a mirror while reciting and while speaking normally to identify the differences (Alexander 1932/1997: 412). Later this initial hypothesis of "doing something different when reciting" was reframed when, as he continued to observe himself, he detected that the three tendencies he had noticed when reciting "were also present, though in a lesser degree, in my ordinary speaking" (*ibid*: 413). When reading Alexander's account of his investigations, it is hard not to be impressed by the persistence and inventiveness of his experimentation, and his willingness to change his ideas.

Setting out the big ideas

Even though it is written primarily in a narrative style, in 'Evolution of a Technique' Alexander sets out many of the main ideas of the Alexander Technique in such a way as to begin to deal with potential erroneous ideas and preconceptions. At this point in the workshop, we gave an example of the introductory material common to our training background in the Interactive Teaching Method (ITM), in order to demonstrate how setting out the big ideas as a preliminary step can have a tremendous impact upon myths and erroneous beliefs. A fuller description of that introductory material can be found in *Reach Your Dreams: An ITM introduction to the Alexander Technique* (Weed 2012: 25-42). In what follows we share two of those big ideas that were explored in the workshop.

The first is the starting definition that, in the ITM, teachers typically give new students:

The Alexander Technique
is the study
of
thinking
in relation to
movement.

This definition speaks to many of the foundational principles of Alexander's discoveries, for example, the close connection between thinking and movement. It also implies a physiologic truth, i.e. that every movement is generated by some sort of thought. For voluntary movements, this means that what you think is pretty much what you get.

Because thinking – and changing one's relationship to thinking – is so much at the heart of Alexander's work, in the Interactive Teaching Method the second big idea we start classes with is called the 'One Thought' which is:

The poise of the head
in relation with the body
in movement
is the key
to freedom
and ease of motion.

This 'Thought' speaks to another of the fundamental principles of Alexander's work: that the relationship of the head and the body is so important that one might almost call it primary. Based on another physiologic truth, that we are reflexly organised in a cephalo-caudal manner, F.M. Alexander's work demonstrates how, by changing the way in which one thinks about how to move, the resulting changes in the relationship of one's head with one's body can have dramatic impacts on the freedom, fluidity and organisation of one's movement.

Having established some key elements of Alexander's story – questioning, self-responsibility, and experimentation – and setting out some big ideas, the workshop moved on to the key benefits of Alexander Technique in dealing with personal myths and self-limiting erroneous preconceptions i.e:

- The Alexander Technique as a means of rescuing ourselves from the clutches of mistaken beliefs
- The Alexander Technique as a paradigm for honouring and using what is useful from our heritage.

Rescue from mistaken beliefs

In the workshop we argued that the benefit of the Alexander Technique as a method of rescue from mistaken beliefs arises directly from the significance of Alexander's questioning nature. Throughout his writing, Alexander places a tremendously high value on the use of questioning, and the benefits of open mindedness. Alexander's definition of open mindedness, however, is not a *laissez faire* acceptance of any point of view, however poorly expressed or fallacious. Rather, Alexander says:

> What I intend by the open mind ... is the just use and exercise of conscious reason (1918/1997: 57).

For example, as previously highlighted, in Alexander's own story he faced a problem: his vocal troubles. He applied his 'open mind' to the situation and in applying his open mind he began with a question, "was [it] something I was doing ...?" (1932/1997: 412). In other words, Alexander uses questioning as a tool for exploring and clarifying his thinking.

A practical demonstration of this occurred in the workshop, when one of the participants came forward for an experiential 'hands-on' turn. Upon coming up for the turn, the participant stated that she had been having problems with soreness in her neck, but had no diagnosed pathology that would account for it. When hands-on work began with the participant, it became very clear that the participant's neck was not moving as freely as it might. This suggested that the participant very likely had a belief (or cluster of beliefs) that were limiting the function of her neck. When asked what her neck was for, the participant replied, 'for holding my head on'.

This answer made complete sense of what she was doing physically. She was using muscles in her neck to 'hold her head on' in a manner that was not merely unnecessary, but unnecessarily strong and painful. Through the use of one simple question, and the 'myth-busting' discussion of neck functioning and anatomy that followed, the participant was able to regain the free functioning in her neck. This demonstration was a fine example of Alexander's idea that "a changed point of view is the royal road to reformation" (Alexander 1918/1997: 44).

As a result of this 'hands-on' turn one member of the group volunteered that when she heard the question 'what is your neck for?' – although she 'knew theoretically' it wasn't for 'holding her head on' – her instinct was to respond with the same answer as the one given by the person who was having the hands-on experience. This illustrated how the group environment can stimulate individual learning, even when you are not the person having the individual hands-on experience.

AT as a paradigm for honouring and using what is useful from our heritage

So far we have seen that F.M. Alexander's work is invaluable in uncovering myths that we may hold about our psycho-physical selves. In the hands-on demonstration in the workshop, the participant came to realise that she had a belief about her neck that led to sub-optimal functioning. In the course of the demonstration, she chose to move away from that belief. However, we may make another decision. Having examined what we are doing and why we believe it to be correct, we may find no reason why we should jettison our beliefs or our practices at that moment. If this is so, then the question becomes: how are we best to use our myths or beliefs? This is where F.M.'s strengths as an experimenter and his belief in the importance of reasoning come into play.

The lesson available to us in F.M. Alexander's account of his investigations is clear. We, like him, should keep playing, testing and experimenting. We, like him, should form a hypothesis, test it out and evaluate it. We, like him, should not be concerned if we fail many times, but should use our failures to inform our next attempts (Matson 2013). F.M. found his failures emotionally trying, but he still kept experimenting (Alexander 1932/1997: 417). If Alexander kept going, then so should we. And we should not be concerned if, in the process, we do not feel comfortable. A quote from Fred Astaire that was used in the workshop and much liked by the participants is relevant here:

> This search for what you want is like tracking something that doesn't want to be tracked. It takes time to get a dance right, to create something memorable (Astaire).

Roughly speaking, we know what it is that we want to achieve. We analyse where we are at the moment. We reason out a means that we think will get us to our goal, and then we test it. We practise it, both by carrying out our plan and by holding our plan in our minds without attempting to do it. Our experiments are not merely trial and error, but are informed by our goals and the qualities of our successes and failures (Alexander 1932/1997: 423).

So what did you like? What did you learn?

Towards the end of the session, as is typical in an ITM workshop, we asked the group to note down what they had liked or learnt. We then offered the opportunity for people to share some of these thoughts. One person shared 'the importance of beliefs in spite of knowledge' as they reflected on the hands-on experience where it was evident that 'knowing theoretically' and 'believing practically' were different things. This was a reminder that 'knowing' your myths is one thing, but being able to 'bust' them is something different entirely.

Another participant shared that they liked the 'lack of mystery' evidenced by the workshop and this approach to the Alexander Technique. This was particularly interesting to us as we reviewed our pre-workshop preparation. As part of the workshop preparation we had considered including a segment on Alexander Technique 'myths', but decided that our focus in the workshop was to be personal myths. Indeed we had highlighted during our preparation:

> The most pervasive Alexander Technique myth that I can think of is that the Alexander Technique is mysterious. So often people want to bewitch

> themselves with their use of language. They want to have the sense that the teacher is doing something mysterious and special. But the true value of the Alexander Technique lies in its clarity.

What intrigued us was that by exploring myths with a personal focus, more universal, less personal myths had also been questioned, like the 'mysterious' Alexander Technique.

Post-workshop thoughts

The positive reception to the workshop was encouraging, but also spurred us on to think more broadly about myth-busting in regards to the Alexander Technique itself. We identified one myth about the Technique – that it is considered mysterious – but does it have its own myths within itself, and could these myths prove to be unhelpful in the long term?

It is certainly the case that there are different teaching traditions within the Alexander Technique, and that these traditions hold different beliefs about not just how to teach, but what principles, concepts and procedures should be taught. In this chapter we have presented the Alexander Technique from the standpoint of our own teaching tradition, the Interactive Teaching Method, because it formed the basis of our training. But could there be myths within the Interactive Teaching Method for the teaching of the work of F.M. Alexander? Could even such ideas as the 'One Thought' one day prove to be a non-useful 'myth'?

The question for us is in essence how one categorises the different elements that make up the work, and whether any of these different elements may take on the characteristics of myth that we described at the beginning of the chapter. As Alexander Technique teachers, we follow Alexander's lead in using stories as a teaching tool; we also use other tools (such as hands-on work) in order to put before the student the concepts and principles of the Alexander Technique as we currently comprehend them. According to Stephen Covey, "principles are deep, fundamental truths that have universal application" (Covey 1989: 35). This is a powerful definition, but also a tall order. Is the guideline under which you are basing your behaviour really a principle, or just something you believe? Ultimately, you won't know until you start using it and discovering its limits. This is the reason why in this chapter we have suggested that experimentation is one of the fundamental principles of Alexander's work. We all need to be alive to the possibility that even those ideas that we hold most dear may have limitations. They may be useful on one level but not another; they may simply cease to be correct past a certain level of expertise. One needs to use what one knows, but hold on to it lightly. It is not for nothing that F.M. Alexander valued the open mind (Alexander 1918/1997: 56-7).

But is experimentation really a principle, or is it just a part of the myth of F.M. Alexander that may prove to be unhelpful in the long term? This is a real and useful question, but it does leave us open to the problem of infinite regress: where do we stop questioning what is true and what is helpful. The paradox of infinite regress is well explained with (appropriately) another myth, in this retelling made famous by Stephen Hawking. Bertrand Russell (or William James, or some other scientist, depending on the myth-teller) was giving a lecture about astronomy and encountered a woman at the end of the talk who said that what Russell had said was rubbish. According to the woman, the world was really a giant plate carried on the back of a giant tortoise. Russell was amused and asked, thinking to catch the woman out, "And what is the tortoise standing on?" The woman replied, "You're very clever, young man, very clever, but it's tortoises all the way down!" (Hawking 1988: 1).

Part of experimentation and the quest for understanding is being prepared to ask the difficult question, to jettison unhelpful ideas. But equally, we cannot question or understand anything without choosing a 'place to stand'. At the beginning of his quest to discover the cause of his vocal problems, Alexander began with assumptions about how his vocal mechanisms worked. He needed to start from somewhere. But equally, he was always aware that these assumptions existed, and said that he would be willing to amend his theories, and even alter his premises, should new facts demonstrate that he had made false assumptions (Alexander 1997/1918: 38).

What we present as true principles of the Alexander Technique may not be absolute truths. They may not even be partially or contextually true. But they are currently useful and beneficial, not just to us (the authors) but to our students past and present. Perhaps we should place a high value not so much on truth as on utility. And are there limits to the usefulness of the principles we have identified in the Alexander Technique? Possibly. We haven't found them yet. But we'll keep looking, and invite readers of this chapter to do the same.

Concluding remarks

So if Alexander was a myth-buster, as we have argued, and if we wish to move past our myths and reach our potential, then the Alexander Technique is a powerful tool. Alexander is reported to have said "you can do what I do, if you will do what I did, but none of you want anything mental" (Barlow 1995: 284). The workshop and this chapter have acted as an introduction to what Alexander did. We hope workshop participants and readers of this chapter will find useful ways to experiment as they bust their own 'myths' and lift their self-imposed limits on their potential.

References

Alexander, F.M. (1997) *The Books of F Matthias Alexander*, IRDEAT. (Comprising *Man's Supreme Inheritance* (1918), *Constructive Conscious Control of the Individual* (1923), *The Use of the Self* (1932), and *The Universal Constant in Living* (1941))

Astaire, F. quotation online at http://bit.ly/tpMove06, It was paraphrased by Ronald Reagan in a speech from 21 May 1988, available online at http://bit.ly/tpMove07

Barlow, M. (1995), 'The Alexander Memorial Lecture' in Barlow, M. & Davies, T.A. (2002), *An Examined Life*, Mornum Time Press

Carroll, A & Vreeman, R. (2009) *Don't Swallow Your Gum and Other Medical Myths Debunked*, Penguin

Covey, S.R. (1989), *The Seven Habits of Highly Effective People*, Business Library

Garrett Brown N & Toms J (2012) 'Collaborative teaching in the dance studio; facilitating self agency and reflexivity through group learning in the Alexander Technique', Platform presentation at The Alexander Technique and the Performing Arts Conference, 19-21 September, 2012 Melbourne, Australia.

Hawking, S.W. (1988), *A Brief History of Time*, Bantam

Kiyosaki, R. & Bennett, H.Z. (1993) *If You Want to be Rich and Happy, Don't Go to School*, rev.ed., Aslan

Matson, J. (2013) 'CIC Genesis: Chapter 7 – A Triumph' Online at http://bit.ly/tpMove08

UNICEF (1999) 'Co-operation games: Fruit salad', online at http://bit.ly/tpMove09

Vineyard, M. (2007) *How You Stand, How You Move, How You Live*, Da Capo

Weed, D.L. (2004) *What You Think is What You Get*, 3rd ed. ITM Publications

_______ (2012) *Reach Your Dreams*, ITM Publications

DUNCAN HOLT

A Moving and Touching Career in Dance and Chiropractic

Introduction

The experiences under discussion in this chapter span two sophisticated forms of touch, each considering movement-centred activity in the inter-relationships that rely upon the knowledge gained through interpersonal touch and movement. These two forms are *dance* and *chiropractic*. Through physical touching/contact with each other and with themselves in the environment, dancers can explore and discover their dancing purposes with their collaborators. Through palpation, which is the inquiring and therapeutic use of touch, chiropractors can explore and discover with their patients the nature of their situations and attend to ways forward with regard to treatment, recovery or wellbeing. In both it is the soma of the embodied dancer or chiropractor that is the prime mover. As both a dancer and a chiropractor, I experience my world through a merger of knowledge and experience that continues through both contexts to make a sometimes-indistinguishable combination of knowledge, skill and practice.

In this chapter, through an auto-ethnographic process, I interweave a personal narrative that draws together the differences or indeed anomalies of practice between these two seemingly disparate disciplines. In it I observe some of the common aspirations and inspirations that embody these two practices, each of which contains aspects of somatic education that now are part of the breadth of many dance practices. In this way,

> Auto-ethnography renames a familiar story of divided selves longing for a sense of place and stability in the fragments and discontinuities of modernity (Neumann 1996: 173-74).

In this process is an auto-ethnographic exploration of the development of my career in dance and my parallel career as a chiropractor in which I observe the connected histories that produced it. The process of this combination or mingling is a worldly outcome of the particular circumstances of a 'divided self' that in the midst of these divisions have drawn together these modern 'fragments and discontinuities' towards a notion of the 'sense of place and stability' that Neumann evokes.

I begin with a personal contextualisation of both disciplines and integrate this with a discussion of how I first engaged with each discipline. Thereafter I describe the manner in which these two separate disciplines came to merge in one person, as they have gradually become entwined, interactive and interdependent aspects of my career and my identity. The discussion is perhaps of use for those torn or confused about their seemingly irreconcilably divergent directions in life. This is a feature of this life that may resonate with others who find themselves in pursuit of goals that exist in or shift through more than one discipline or form of life. This is such that in composing this life I have come to understand and benefit from the ways that each trajectory can be found to support the other.

What emerges is the symbiotic manner in which these two multifaceted practices have influenced, been influenced and are framed by, the creation of dance art works for performance and dance teaching and therapeutic work with chiropractic patients whether for addressing current discomforts or for the reassuring maintenance of bodily integrity.

I have also had significant academic engagement with higher educational institutions that deliver training and education in both disciplines. One of these journeys has involved a career as a university lecturer in dance in several institutions. I have, in addition to my roles as teacher, mentor and academic, acquired significant experience in the ways and means of quality assurance within and across academic institutions.

For the other I am engaged as an external examiner to a major UK chiropractic training college able to offer this knowledge of institutional processes in combination with my own chiropractic knowledge and experience, hopefully to the benefit of the chiropractic community. I have through these dual practices found that the synergies between dance and chiropractic are numerous. In the combination of the two I am for one a Fellow of the McTimoney Chiropractic Association and for the other a Senior Fellow of the Higher Education Academy (UK).

However it is important to stress at an early stage that it is not my purpose in this chapter to promote the particular virtues or merits of any one or more of the many techniques of chiropractic that are practised around the world – and there are many – any more than it is to promulgate one or another form of dance, again there are many. That said, I have had personal experience of several chiropractic techniques, just as I have had personal experience of a wide range of dance genres and forms. It is these experiences in both dance and chiropractic that are the foundation of my personal choices as a patient, as a practitioner and as a dance professional. It is in the context of these chosen forms that this discussion takes place.

To orient those who are unfamiliar, it is worth noting that chiropractic is viewed governmentally in the UK as a primary Health Care System. As such it is governed by an Act of Parliament that is executed and administered by the General Chiropractic Council (GCC). The GCC is the parallel of other similar statutory bodies such as the General Medical Council or the General Osteopathic Council. It has legal responsibilities:

- To *protect* the public by establishing and operating a scheme of statutory regulation for chiropractors
- To *set the standards* of chiropractic education, conduct and practice

- To *ensure the development* of the profession of chiropractic, using a model of continuous improvement in practice (GCC 2011)

In performing its duties the GCC has borrowed the definition of the World Federation of Chiropractic to describe the profession in its own terms:

> Chiropractic is concerned with the diagnosis, treatment and prevention of mechanical disorders of the musculoskeletal system and the effects of these disorders on the function of the nervous system and general health. There is an emphasis on manual treatments including spinal manipulation or adjustment. (World Federation of Chiropractic)

This definition is the crux of much debate within the chiropractic profession as various belief systems cross over this anodyne description into what is for some an extreme and zealous attachment to particular aspects of the work at near religious levels of enthusiasm and fervour. This level of personal zeal will be familiar to many who work in dance. The manner in which chiropractors work, is, like dance, one of bodily engagement and it is perhaps the case that this aspect of interaction through the body and the trust required to maintain this level of intimacy is the premise upon which this zeal exists. It is through the many interactions of physical contact/touch that these practices might be seen to have common foundations.

When regarding the influence of touch we can probably agree that it is the manner and quality of the touch that is of primary importance and that these qualities are made manifest by the movement in the touch – in the type of friction in its initiation, duration and disengagement (Bannon & Holt 2011).

The movement involved in touch determines the manner in which touch is encoded and decoded. It ranges from violent and unwanted abuse to the consented movement of connected bodies in space such as in a Contact Improvisation duet or in the case of the chiropractor, a patient/practitioner therapeutic interaction. The knowledge formed through touch informs simultaneously both the person touching and the person who is touched and in this transaction of sensation there is a revelation of humanly-/bodily-generated perceptions and features. It is then through our socialisation and our culturalisation, including the manner and content of our education, that we come to interpret and understand these interactions.

It is the case that the experiences of both dance and chiropractic have in my career; each in their distinctive forms, influenced the practices of the other. For instance the depth of information of anatomy, pathologies and the application of treatment modalities that are the body of knowledge of the chiropractor can be transferred straightforwardly to many dance contexts. This could include that I as a teacher recognise students' issues of alignment or fitness and potentially direct such students to practices through which they might address these.

Similarly, much of the detailed experience of living and working as a dancer and a dance teacher is transferable to the treatment context. The deep experience of working in my body supports my understanding in empathising with my non-dancing patients. Throughout the forty-five years of my dance career I also have been in the midst of the range of somatic practices – Alexander Technique, Body Mind Centering, the Feldenkrais Method – that in addition to their independent and unique applications as treatments and counselling in their own right, have also become very prevalent if not central to the dance industry in the UK as ways of addressing individual dancers' issues or in enhancing performance and experience. On meeting Gill Clarke OBE I found a colleague whose understanding of this field and its application to the dance context was inspirational in guiding me to finding ways in which my understanding of these approaches was to become inseparable from my understanding of dance and eventually of chiropractic (Clarke 2014).

Starting to Dance

My dancing days were preceded by a fairly undistinguished series of attempts to become an athlete. Attempts at basketball, Judo, surfing, Canadian football and ice hockey had all rather floundered upon my general lack of a cutthroat competitive edge. In spite of these setbacks in seeking a significant engagement with my physicality, I found a powerful outlet for this desire when dancing. It started with about a thousand Friday and Saturday nights between the ages of 12 and 20, dancing for two or three hours at a time to Motown, Beatles and Beach Boys. For much of my teens this ecstatic experience, combined with the pursuit of social encounters with girls, was enough. On the way through this I became secure with rhythm and with floor craft: the art of finding and using space on a crowded dance floor. In addition to these I also began to see myself as a performer, someone who is 'at home' on the dance floor and comfortable with being watched.

With this sense of performance in mind I sought to engage with dance in a more formal and progressive manner. Then a little ballet! I say little because the others in the class were approximately a dozen 12 year old girls and I was already 19. The social impact was too much and though the teacher was supportive I was not at that time able to identify myself in the context of that aspect of dance – the little girl ballet culture.

I then joined a small and loose group of part time 'hippy' dancers led by a graduate of Bennington College, where Graham and Cunningham teachers had begun to be included in higher education. I started at a very basic level of dance technique but under this particularly avant-garde influence we worked at what I now know to have been a high level of sophistication with regard to improvisation exercises and improvised performances. Eventually, I migrated to Toronto where the *Toronto Dance Theatre* (TDT), led by Patricia Beatty, Peter Randazzo and David Earl, all former dancers with the Martha Graham Dance Company, became my introduction to the rigors of formal dance training.

Things start to mingle

On one occasion during the early days of my training in the Graham tradition of modern dance at the Toronto Dance Theater (TDT) I eagerly threw myself into a travelling 'combination' with a myriad turns, jumps, changes of direction and level across the studio. I put my foot down to turn and it stayed where it was while the rest of me continued to turn. Whether this was because of sticky feet, sticky floor or both; combined with a significant lack of experience, is undeterminable. The result was a serious knee injury.

It was the kind of displacement injury wherein the medial epicondyle of the knee appears to protrude beyond the normal contours of the leg. After several days of hobbling I visited, for the first time, a chiropractor. He palpated and studied the area, took x-rays and diagnosed the damage. Then: an adjustment; with a loud crack he relocated the elements of the joint– tibia and femur – and sent me on my way. Several more treatments and four months of rest later, I returned to dancing, though I was far more cautious about my movement and somewhat reticent about the reliability of my knee.

This was a man chiropractor named David Drum. I mention him specifically because his work and his manner were inspirational and because of the parallels that occur through our careers. He, like me, grew up on the east coast of Canada. This is a region from which many people in search of a more expansive life style travel to cities such as Toronto. He had through his career not only become the favoured chiropractor of the Toronto dance community, but he also had an extensive practice in New York where he worked closely with the Joffrey Ballet. Beyond his chiropractic work and his knowledge of dance and dancers, he also sustained a career as a highly regarded artist working in oil paints and creating works in the realist traditions (Drum 2014). His straightforward approach to his chiropractic work impressed and resonated with me and I knew then that, when the opportunity arrived, I too would engage in two careers.

Four years and a considerable amount of dance training later, I achieved my first professional dance job in 'Cycles Dance Company'. In 'Cycles' I found colleagues who were participating in the beginning of the British New Dance scene. We with others of our generation, found our way to the creation of works that were choreographed by or resonated with practitioners such as Emlyn Claid, Fergus Early and Royston Maldoom. We performed at the earliest events in the formation of the genre at *Action Space* for the Festival of the Association of Dance and Mime Artists and later at *X6* (Jordan 1992).

During this period of intense dancing and rehearsing I felt limited by what appeared to me to be a reoccurrence of my trepidations with my knee in pliés, balances and various shifts of weight. This seemed also to impact upon my ankle leading to further inhibition in my dancing, especially jumping. To address this I visited the dance company's recommended chiropractor. This experience was extremely different from my first encounter with the profession.

This time it was a whole-body technique with somatic aspects of attending to sensation by both the practitioner and the patient. It worked beyond symptoms and the location of the complaint to a holistic approach that corrected the jointed alignment from the atlas bone that supports the skull on the neck and proceeded through a structural analysis of all the joints of the spine and limbs adjusting along the way towards a corrected alignment of the essential three-dimensional pelvis and then through to the distal appendages of fingers and toes. As a result of this intervention I was more secure with my now pain-free knees, my ankles no longer burned with every jump, my neck was freer and my shoulders dropped their usual culturally/self-imposed characteristic macho tension. What was most impressive to me at the time, in addition my now confident use of my knee, was the quality of touch.

Fascination with Chiropractic

Though this work was distinctly different from my experiences with David Drum in Toronto I found myself enthralled by the processes of chiropractic and soon became a regular at the clinic. Chiropractic is based firstly upon palpation: a deep and apprehending touch that reputedly can distinguish inflamed flesh from normal through the full depth of a buttock. It is a use of touch that differentiates the reception of sensation in a manner that can be likened to listening or seeing; each of these senses requires us to learn to interpret and distinguish information as part of the process of perceiving a touch sensation, sight or sound. It is through this use of touch that the information required to address chiropractic issues is gathered. It provides an accurate perception of the 'located'ness' of parts and their situations in relation to the surrounding structures that informs and guides further investigation, to provide the practitioner with sufficient understanding of the case to make the appropriate judgements and adjustments.

The new and unique knowledge found by touch is formed by the accumulation of the knowable information that is gathered by *observation* through touch. It is this observation of the body – *with*in which the particular arrangements of parts and features in the unique 'liveness' of the individual can be understood – that is the substance of the knowledge and therefore of the facility by which the chiropractor is able to engage with the patient. In conjunction with the verbal recording of the patient's medical/chiropractic history, the practitioner apprehends information from manual contact with the client and this guides the decisions and informs the actions that constitute the treatment.

The second aspect of touch involved in the treatment is the adjustments themselves. These are done by the hand with a light touch and without the levering techniques associated with many other manipulation practices. This touch, and its associated movement, is deft and dexterous in the full meaning of these words; it is skilful in its physical movements, especially those of the hands. This touch is also adroit, being adept in action or thought. These are all terms that are also used to describe dancers of exceptional ability.

With permission I was allowed to observe my fellow dancers being treated. The dexterous nature of the chiropractic work was as fascinating to me to watch, as it was to receive. My conjecture here was that it might also be as fascinating to do. The memories of my Toronto encounter and the leftover thought that it was in some way connected to my future came back like a shout from the past. I came to the realisation that I wanted to have this skill. I took the opportunity to study the discipline and to acquire the qualifications.

To facilitate my study at the McTimoney Chiropractic College (Harding 1997) I abandoned my performance career and sought to fund my training by working as a community dance artist. This work was to give me a deeper connection with dance as I entered a new phase of engagement with amateur dancers, part time professional dancers, student dancers, child dancers and a host of other interested sectors of my community. Rather than end my dance career, chiropractic gave it a fresh start and a new direction in dance. From this point, instead of trading one career for another, I had two careers. There have of course been conflicts and synergies, I have at times been confused as to whether I was a chiropractor who incidentally danced or a dancer who has incidentally trained in chiropractic.

However, I now know that the somatic learning that I had encountered with Gill Clarke (Burt 2011) and others in my dance career has provided, through my study of my soma, a deeply felt empathy for the patients I work with in my chiropractic practice. From my personal experience as a dancer working with injury I share empathetically with my patients those sensations of pain, discomfort and frustration that come with the range of complaints and disorders that chiropractors address.

It is clear that many practices of the body can maintain and restore wellbeing, whether through yoga practice, a keep fit programme, a sophisticated sports regimen, dancing or any of the many other physical endeavours. However there are circumstances in which one is unable to make sufficient difference to address particular issues. I am confident in my understanding of chiropractic work that it has the potential to repair and restore an individual's optimum well being or improve one's ability to live with many conditions whether or not a full repair or cure can be achieved. It is likely that, whatever the condition, one will benefit from having one's alignment restored or significantly improved. For some the treatment is a giant step in self-realisation. To be told or to discover, by drawing attention to the variability, particularity and indivisibility of the physical state, that the body is not just something that one has but rather that we are our bodies and that we live in and of them, often hits home as the reality of the situation. Often this realisation arrives with an affliction that might have been avoided had the realisation occurred earlier, perhaps through attending to the embodied self as a matter of course.

I also have knowledge of things that might help clients that are outside of my chiropractic training derived instead from my dance training and life in dance including improvisation, the practice of choreographic organisation and a vast array of bodily experiences of dance forms and techniques. This list includes aspects of bodily alignment, the action of the joints, centring, grounding, stretching, turning, twisting, moving with a range of dynamics, ways of resting constructively and the creation of regimens of training, exercise and remedial planning that can maintain wellbeing or aid recuperation. It is a life in a moving body. This dancing business is very sophisticated!

Working through Touch

Other aspects of my research into the nature of touch in dance are clearly associated with my work as both a chiropractor and a dance practitioner (Bannon & Holt 2011). There is a looping of information and experience here with chiropractors working through touch and dancers who work somatically (whether consciously or not) to know and do what they do in practice, in performance or in creative play. To grasp one's experience and to apply the knowledge gleaned through that experience in a purposeful process is an intrinsic aspect of both chiropractic and dance.

Using chiropractic terminology the following protocols of chiropractic practitioner/patient interaction describe sensorially apprehended knowledge that could easily be applied to many dance contexts.

Palpation is the act of feeling, primarily by the hand: the application of the fingers with light pressure to the surface of the body for the purpose of determining the condition and location of parts of the body beneath the skin (surface anatomy) in acts of chiropractic diagnosis.

This is particularly important for those chiropractors that do not use x-ray equipment as a matter of course. After explaining the nature of chiropractic and taking a comprehensive and chiropractic-based case history, I as the chiropractor approach a new and sometimes apprehensive client. I start what is now a familiar monologue, where I say something like:

> If I may, I am just going to make contact with my hands on your shoulders in order to start to come to know you and your situation. I want to find out what I can about **muscle tone**, **temperature**, **humidity**, **tension**

and the **relationship of parts**: their **alignment**, **integrity** and **location** with regard to site of the bones in their joints (Andrews & Courtney 1999).

All of this information arrives in seconds and is crucial in terms of what comes next with regard to adjustment and treatment. Although the intrusion of this first contact is minimal and often received as a comfort, the impact of this act of touch is of course far greater than the understated notion of 'just going to make contact' suggests, but rather a complex wealth of interaction.

- **Muscle tone** can tell me where to look next – if the tension goes to the neck or to the scapula this will give me information in the form of clues that I may confirm elsewhere. If the tone is flaccid or hyper, other issues may be apparent that could determine how to proceed or whether it might be best not to proceed. Contra-indications can make themselves apparent in many ways and at any time.
- **Temperature** can suggest inflammation or fever or shock. Again, these are important to identify at an early stage of the examination and can determine whether or not to proceed.
- **Humidity** – is the client having a diabetic sweat or is there dryness in one area and not another? Is there a dermatological issue here that didn't emerge during the taking of the medical history?
- Is there **tension** in the neck or in the shoulders that dissipates on touch or increases in an apprehensive cringe from being touched at all?
- The **relationship** of parts is a significant determinant of what is at the root of the initial cause for seeing a chiropractor. One may find that the distance between the clavicles or the scapulae is disproportionate – too wide, too close or too horizontally or vertically asymmetrical.
- The **alignment** of the clavicles might vary from left to right as they approach the sternum or in their vertical orientation or their shape might indicate through size and form a previous breakage that has repaired with overgrowth that has left these structures out of balance.
- The **integrity of the structures,** whether a broken bone, a disintegrating joint or a torn muscle or tendon or ligament, is worth knowing about as you start to work with a client. They might tell their chiropractor that this has happened. They might not know or be able to differentiate their sensations sufficiently well as to be able to say with any confidence what is going on.
- The **location** of the structures is significant. It may reveal whether a joint is intact and from this suggest to the chiropractor to explore the range of movement or test the nerves as the next procedure to determine whether an adjustment could be efficacious in improving symptoms or preventing deterioration.

All of this is information that arrives from the first encounter in touch. Other senses are also at work. From looking at the client, some of the information above will have been predicted or confirmed. From scent, one might find an odour that starts another line of investigation that might lead to discovering that the client has diabetes. The sound of the patient, either qualitatively or in terms of what they say – both during the taking of their history and what they say during the examination or the treatment – can continue to inform the chiropractor at work.

Returning to the list above and focusing upon the **relationship of parts** it is clear that this concept is complex. In a human body it cannot be otherwise. For example with regard to the knee injury described above, it is not sufficient to think merely of the reuniting of the tibia and the femur. Their dislocation from one another has implications for all the other components of the joint and for the other structures of the region, for the body and its physiology as a whole.

In terms of bones of the region, the kneecap and the fibula also need to be considered and potentially adjusted in relation to the newly relocated larger bones. This may happen of the body's own accord but in most cases further intervention will be needed. Further implications for the structure as a whole are also to be considered – if the imbalance in the knee is distorting the alignment of the pelvis then there is much more work to do. With regard to the soft tissues – the tendons, ligaments, cartilage and muscles – these may well have been traumatised during the original incident and in the aftermath of the event or in the aftermath of the relocation of the joint. They too may be in need of recuperative treatment, as might the further joints and tissues that are dependent upon the secure location of these parts for their stability. This all suggests the value and significance of a whole-body treatment.

Back to Dance

The ways in which we as dancers and as dance teachers or choreographers touch each other both in mutuality and in ways more reflective of power relations such as directed instructions make significant differences to the work of our students and colleagues and in the gathering and giving of information. This is information that is simultaneously cognitive and sensorial in its perpetration and its reception.

Demonstration between teacher/choreographer and student/performer is still the dominant way in which dancers exchange movement information. In that process, a significant aspect and proportion of the exchange is often done through touch. The tutor who manually rearranges the student's feet or shapes their spine, the choreographer who works out a lift with one then the other of a duet, is engaging in touch. These, as stated at the beginning of the chapter, are done with close attention to the quality of that touch, such that it will convey both the importance of the content of the touch and also the content itself. Here content would include manual guidance concerning body shape, dynamic movement intention, points of partner engagement and a multitude of dance information.

In both professions there is something primal occurring between the two parties. It is the shared touch that informs, through the rich and significant understandings of the circumstance of the shared experience that give mutual cognisance to the profound understandings of the shared event.

I have had times in my Contact Improvisation experience where, during a large group-based exercise, an unseen partner has emerged from a crowd of ten or more in the *jam* and through touch alone (eyes closed perhaps) I have been able to identify who it is. It is a phenomenon that is, I believe, quite common among experienced 'contacters'.

What comes to be known in that situation might be recognition of:

- muscle tone
- temperature
- humidity
- tension
- the relationship of parts:
    - their alignment
    - their integrity
    - their location (e.g. the site of the bones in their joints).

All of these in their totality are unique to the person and thereby contribute to that person's identity and therefore to the ability of others to identify them.

Many of these indicators will give clues as to their identity but in dancing over time there are also other aspects that will inform us on many other levels:

- height
- weight
- dynamism
- gender
- context
- a variety of announced and unannounced intentions including:
    - relations with these intentions – with contextual regard to the exercise
    - the person's experience in performing these acts

During the moments of this arrival we experience the phenomena of individuality.

- Weight
  This person has weight in the form of a unique heft, or delicacy, and a range that is characteristic of them.
- Height
  They have a height that may at first be deceptive but as one relates the recognisable parts, an understanding begins to emerge. There are recognisable parts: a foot, a head, a back.

There is a distance between such recognisable parts and a nearly measured knowledge of the length of a forearm or a shin or the length of the spine. With this we apply our experience of the world and make an estimate that might be stated in feet and inches, centimeters or just where to place our own weight to manage their centre of gravity in conjunction with our own in the shared centre that emerges in this work.

A person's dynamism is quickly apparent and no doubt recognisable from the last time you saw them or contacted with them. Continuing with eyes closed one might determine:

- the strength or not of the contact (weight)
- the suddenness or continuity of the action (time)
- the boundedness or freedom of the action (flow)
- whether they are moving directly or indirectly (space).

This is what Laban (Laban & Ullman 1966) might see as a revealing of a characteristic dynamic range or analysis that is made available and can be gleaned by this touch.

What I have come to understand is that the chiropractic information stands as a healthy inclusion and underpinning to my dance teaching. My dance work underpins my chiropractic.

The information, about spinal alignment for instance, as with the many other facets of these two disciplines, now merges in my 'knowing' what it is that I am doing. Whether that knowledge is sourced through dance or chiropractic is of interest but it is not essential. Telling a dance student that the verticality of their joint alignment through the spine will have a positive axial impact upon their rotational action when performing turns is not different from telling an aging chiropractic client that this alignment will help them in reversing the car. Telling a dance student that sharing a common gravitational centre with a partner will help in lifting and being lifted is not too different from saying the same thing to a client whose daily work includes lifting heavy objects. I say these things to both groups of people on a daily basis. A runner who works to lengthen his neck during a marathon will find more space between his ribs that in turn offers him greater lung capacity as he meets the 'wall' in the 21st mile. As Ken Robinson suggests in his TED talk;

> I think math is very important, but so is dance. Children dance all the time if they're allowed to, we all do. We all have bodies, don't we? Did I miss a meeting?" (2006)

These details, observances and attitudes are now an embedded aspect of my self and my self-perception, such that I know myself in these ways as an indistinguishable whole. Dance that starts as an embodied practice connects with other embodiments and other disciplines whilst at its core through the interaction of person/s with space, movement and sound dance exists as an inter-discipline. The interconnections are similar to those suggested by Gill Clarke (Burt 2011) in her imagined (University) Department of Embodiment with dance at its centre. From this centre of dance-focused embodiment, studies of the body could reach out to the various ways in which movement as the central function of the body would be observed, treated and exercised for all manner of intrinsic and extrinsic purposes such as therapeutic engagements ranging from massage to surgery or community interactions that might include sociological research and interactions to a breadth of cultural, multicultural and intercultural endeavours that support a society that is conscious of the integrity of humans who are their indivisible bodies: their indivisible entities.

In returning to Neumann, whose words helped to open this chapter, I realise my integration as a person in the world who is of both things and many more. What has at times been obscure is the impact of the disparate cultures in which these two forms exist. In the ongoing of my life and work it has become more an issue of getting the calendars to work than one of identity or purpose.

Dancing as a career does not necessitate being a chiropractor, nor does chiropractic as a career necessitate being a dancer. However the richness of these in the context of a common embodiment is a fascination. The science paradigm and the art paradigm are not mutually exclusive nor are they in opposition to one another. The creativity and precision of the one feeds the other. Both are creative and precise. Both are embodied.

The divided self is a myth; I am one entity in all that I do and the longed for 'sense of place and stability' is inherently present in being. I suggest that the quest is to have and to maintain a critical awareness of 'self' in the context of questioning the implied certainties that are the work of a lifetime. As I stand in the classroom, studio or clinic, I realise my many selves and acknowledge that being many selves is to be human. We are, as with our anatomies, as with our thoughts, complex; and this complexity enriches us all.

References

Andrews, E. & Courtney, A. (1999) *The essentials of McTimoney Chiropractic*, Thorsens

Bannon, F.C. & Holt, D. (2011) 'Touch, experience and knowledge' *Journal of Dance & Somatic Practices* Volume 3: Numbers 1+2, pp. 215-227, doi: 10.1386/jdsp.3.1-2.215_1

Burt, R. (2011) 'Resources for thinking about the body: an interview with Gill Clarke', *Dance Theatre Journal*, Vol. 24. No 4. pp. 6-10.

Clarke, G., 'Mind is as in motion', Independent Dance, http://bit.ly/tpMove10

Drum, D., 'David Drum fine art' online at http://bit.ly/tpMove11

General Chiropractic Council, 'What is the GCC?' online at http://bit.ly/tpMove12

Harding, S., (1997) *McTimoney Chiropractic: The first 25 years*, McTimoney Chiropractic College

Jordan, S., (1992) *Striding out*, Dance Books

Laban, R. & Ullman L. (eds.) (1966) *Choreutics* MacDonald & Evans

Neumann, M. (1996) 'Collecting ourselves at the end of the century' in *Composing ethnography: Alternative forms of qualitative writing* (eds. C. Ellis & A.P. Bochner) AltaMira pp. 172-198

Robinson, K. , (2006) TED Talk online at http://bit.ly/tpMove13

World Federation of Chiropractic (2001) online at http://bit.ly/tpMove14

MARTHA EDDY

Early Trends

Where Soma and Dance Began to Meet – Keeping the Meeting Alive

My intent for this chapter was to discuss the wonderful growth of somatic movement in the context of the larger field of somatic education and how dance programmes and professionals have been a centre point in this growth. Indeed this is what I discussed in my article in the inaugural issue of the *Journal of Dance and Somatic Practices* (Eddy 2009). That article begins with a survey of the historical influences on the field and demonstrates how dance has supported the growth of somatic education in the arts world (performance), in the private sector (studio programs) and in academia. The July 2013 conference in Coventry was critical as an international exchange of scholarship and practice across somatic disciplines.

My remarks shifted because I lost my father on 21st June 2013. Indeed, I was unable to give a keynote address and workshop at 'the other' Dance and Somatics conference in 2013 held on our planet – at the University of Brockport in New York State. Norm Eddy at age 93 died the day that conference launched. He had been leading a normal life two days before. While I am saddened by the circumstances that kept me away from Brockport, his passing raised questions that I now direct towards our field. Reflecting on my personal experience of legacy given from parent to child gave me pause; I found analogous questions regarding the living or absorbing of somatic dance today as our somatic leaders pass on. I felt compelled to ask relatives within the circles of somatic dance – "What is our legacy?"; "What is our responsibility to keep the specific values that emerge from shared experience alive?" and "How much do we move on to new language and perspectives as key thinkers/movers/influencers of our lives die?" Does the history of somatic thinking and somatic dance have a particular place in our current dance experience? If so, what is it? If not, what is the legacy to be remembered, and, in what form, by whom? How does somatic thinking from the past live in us today? Is it at all useful to invoke 'past somatics' now? Is reflecting upon and honouring the past useful to 'being in the present with personal authority', as we do while engaging in somatic dance experiences?

Even more, expansion of somatic dance supports a growing question: Is 'somatics' in the 21st century necessary? Should we do anything to buoy its growth and even its survival? Regular convening of the somatic dance community as a whole went missing in the United States for about 20 years. The National Dance Association (NDA) used to sponsor The Science and Somatics of Dance conferences in the early 1990s. The papers are published in issues of the *Kinesiology & Medicine for Dance* journal (1992). While the National Dance Education Organization (NDEO) is including somatic thinking in many of its projects and has dozens of presentations with the word somatic included in its titles and descriptions, it has not created a separate forum for somatic dialogue. Could this be because somatic education in dance has become so widespread, so common, that it no longer needs to be recorded as such, identified, cited? As early as 1994, Sylvie Fortin of the University of Quebec in Montreal predicted that the concept of somatics might become obsolete as it is absorbed into 'mainstream dance' (Fortin 1994).

While somatic dancing is locatable throughout contemporary dance it often arises in unspoken/unidentified formats. Is this mysteriousness good enough? Does a lack of language about somatic origins signal the dying down of somatics in dance? I think not, as we also see the trend is towards more talking about somatic dance. Indeed I feel it is a call to claim and declare somatic legacies.

More recently, there have been small symposia of somatic dance burgeoning in many places. In New York City alone the Alexander and Feldenkrais leadership are now sponsoring annual workshops on dance and their particular brand of somatic education (annual Freedom of Movement conferences among others). There must be other such 'convenings', and it would be good to know about them. It is not easy to locate all information about how our field grows. Might the lack of roadmaps to somatic information being used in dance be related to the minimal amount of verbal or written credit shared about dance roots and developments in general?

My scholarship strives to show how the work of many people has formed a living lineage of somatic knowledge, passed down from one generation to the next, always with changes, new discoveries and interconnected threads that weave together tradition and emerging ideas (Eddy 2009).

My thinking is this: dance, and guided somatic dance experience, exists as part of an oral-kinaesthetic tradition. Unless we speak our dance influences we may not know what tradition a set of movements comes from. Just three or four decades (two generations) ago we used to know we were dancing Jooss' or Martha Graham's movement because we registered for a Jooss-Ledeer or Graham class, respectively. With the advent of contemporary dance there has been a wondrous merging of methods in most classes, including sometimes distinct and often a mix of somatic influences. Often we are taught or guided to move in particular ways and not informed of the source. In my informal investigations I find that many dance teachers do not know an original source of the particular movement they teach but they can usually identify a person who taught them a movement or led them to discover it on their own. As late as the 1970s and 1980s we usually knew what style of dance we were studying. As I take classes at festivals today, in universities and at dance studios alike, I experience somatic movement and dance motifs from diverse traditions: somatic and dance. Rarely does the teacher inform us of the source. I contend that it is easy to change this, affording a 'connecting of the dots' and a way to keep gratitude for our inheritances, or lineages and legacies, alive. Perhaps this tracking of influences does not matter, or perhaps it does. At least, it deserves investigation. A reason to choose to investigate legacy and to name it is simply to honour the individuals who have brought us here, who guided our journeys as dancers, somatic educators and artists. Another reason is to gain access to the original movement concept and the underlying context and meaning of it.

What is important about a somatic legacy, if anything? Is somatic dance distinct from contemporary dance? Why is it important to gather, move and engage in dialogue about somatics?

When I was unable to attend the June 2013 Brockport conference due to my father's sudden death I worked with Conference Director Cynthia Williams to prepare an exercise that she could read aloud and guide conference participants to explore: "As part of your history as a mover there have been teachers, both formal and informal, along the way. I invite you to take time to pay verbal homage to those people who have entered into your embodiment process: your teachers, your friends, your colleagues, who are living through you – their movement or movement ideas are alive in your movement. (I invite you to move this.) As you move begin to notice movements in your living body that conjure up specific people who have been influences in your dance and movement history. As a movement reminds you of a specific person say his or her name out loud."

This activity echoed an exploration I led at the beginning of the presentation of the paper 'Access to Somatics: Socio-Political Concerns' (Eddy 2000) at the combined conference amongst the Society of Dance Scholars, Congress on Research in Dance, the National Dance Education Organization, the Laban Institute and other dance organisations in 2000. I attempted to enliven the talk through a taste of embodied practice as it relates to the scholarship of somatics. Here again in this chapter I take the liberty of weaving together my own personal experience, to honour my legacy from my parents as activists, movers and shakers and to summon you to shift from reader to explorer by 'touching in' to your soma. I especially bid you to remember your teachers and how they live in you, through your memory, your movement, your cells.

I propose that whenever we teach, as educators, choreographers or lecturers, we honour the individuals who influenced our dance, our somatic and our somatic dance development by giving voice to the people who have guided our journeys as dancers, somatic educators and artists. I encourage you to spend some time now in reflection about your own journey, and if leading groups to then gather into small groups to hear one another, and then to share findings back together as a whole. The key tenet is to give voice to some of the formative movement experiences you have had and to verbally honour those individuals and mentors whose influence you feel as you move, embodying the sages of your own lineage.

This leads to the interconnectedness of our field. In my own cross-case research of 36 different somatic movement certification programmes and their founders' influences (Eddy 2005), we see many interwoven lineages. In Figure 1 you can see how the work of many people has been shaped by the work of the somatic founders – identified as 'the first generation' (*ibid*). This living lineage of body knowledge, like dance forms, has passed down from one generation to the next, always with changes, new discoveries and interconnected threads. These living stories of human experience weave together our somatic tradition and foster the emergence of new ideas.

We do not have time to review fully this original investigation of somatic education but we can summarise with a note that somatic movement emerged from some rather distinct phenomena: illnesses, physical limitations, diaspora and displacement (Eddy 2009). These experiences of difference 'from the norm' led to exposure to, or discovery of, unfamiliar physical and/or spiritual practices. In the case of the somatic pioneers these conditions combined with a love of movement and/or curiosity about the body, and often a background in both the arts and the sciences. The positive outcomes of this enquiry gave credence to seeking internal awareness through attentive dialogue with oneself.

From the 2009 article, I want to highlight three concepts: branches within somatics; generations of somatic movement leadership; and the need to acknowledge somatic innovators as sources through the somatic and dance landscape.

1. THREE KEY BRANCHES: In Dynamic Embodiment lectures since 2004 and in my *Journal of Dance and Somatic Practices* article (2009: 7) I posited that there are three key branches of somatic enquiry/different forms of somatic investigation: somatic psychology, somatic bodywork and somatic movement. I like to emphasise that somatic movement has been formalised into the field of Somatic Movement Education & Therapy by the International Somatic Movement Education and Therapy Association (ISMETA). Somatic movement involves listening to the body and responding with varied movement interplay, inhibiting limiting habits (Alexander), differentiating the movement potential of distinct body areas (Feldenkrais), embracing old and new 'body attitudes' (Bartenieff) and sometimes simply awakening the ineffable kinaesthetic experience and allowing it to resonate both inwards and outwards.

Of course there are exceptions. How do these exceptions of source impact the experience of somatic dance? For example, if your first experience of somatic dance was from the somatic psychology lineage (perhaps through the field that overlaps into somatic movement – dance/movement therapy, also referred to as movement psychotherapy, or even more specifically through the practice of Authentic Movement) how does it differ from somatic dance that came from studies with Feldenkrais Awareness Through Movement, or how does it differ from the individualised experience of Functional Integration – a type of Feldenkrais somatic education that might be seen as a form of somatic bodywork?

2. FOUR GENERATIONS: Within the realm of somatic movement over the past 100 years I identified at least four active generations of people who began their own 'brand' of somatic movement and shaped it into a certification programme for training others in somatic movement inquiry. They are:

A. The Pioneer generation: F.M. Alexander, Irmgard Bartenieff, Moshe Feldenkrais, Gerda Alexander (Eutonie), Ida Rolf (Rolf Movement), Charlotte Selver, Mabel Todd and Milton Trager.

B. The Dance generation: Anna Halprin, Elaine Summer, Sondra Fraleigh, Emilie Conrad, Bonnie Bainbridge Cohen, Joan Skinner and Nancy Topf, with Judith Aston hovering nearby as dancer become fitness leader.

C. The Amalgam generation: In 2005 I identified 20 other ongoing training programmes (Eddy 2005) and referred to them as 'amalgam systems', since they call upon a blend of various influences. This generation is still growing, especially as seen in the number of organisations that are now part of ISMETA.

D. The Now and Future Next generation: The ongoing evolution of new amalgams and personal discoveries based on a century of somatic scholarship, sometimes uncovering or accessing systems long in place such as Steiner or Gurdjieff, all with new purposes and applications.

In what seems a spontaneous manner, new areas of enquiry are also being generated from somatic movement exploration. To name a few: social somatics, dance somatics, eco-somatics, spirituality and somatic dance. Mostly I see somatic dance stemming from the somatic movement disciplines, however that can vary. Has it for you? Again, has your lineage of somatic dance been from psychology, medicine, arts, philosophy or education?

3. NAMING SOURCES: To reiterate – in order to keep this somatic history alive and growing, and to support the development of somatic dance, I find it is important to name our sources. It strengthens our scholarship whilst respecting that we are predominantly a non-verbal field. Informing students of our lineages is imperative in dance because whether teaching or performing we are oral-kinaesthetic communicators. We leave a strong visual impact in our communication, yet the auditory component is often weaker, especially when music or text only plays a supportive function. We are capable of amplifying our impact by including more oral action, and aural perception of rhythmic/voiced/spoken experience. This is actually easy in dance class and can be quick as in the activity practised above. In performance it would need to be well-managed to say the least. However, choosing to include our somatic training in our dance performance biographies would be one step out of silence and invisibility. Unless we speak our movement influences we may not know much about the movements we practise day in and day out. With reflection we are better able to awaken curiosity about the movement, and its purposes. With a little information about sources we can follow curiosity further, finding more classes, books, articles and films about this concept or movement and its lineage.

A Social Schema for Our Somatic Dance Legacy?

An overlapping phase in my research includes the arena of social somatics and is firmly planted in dance somatics. It has been to assess the potency and placement of 'somatic dance' in a global schema. This desire emerged out of a series of discussions with Michael Roguski, post-colonial theorist. We reflected on the cultural roots of and influences on Somatic Movement Education and Therapy. One of the emergent themes from analysis of my interviews of Emilie Conrad and Bonnie Bainbridge Cohen (Eddy 2002) was that the somatic process is not only a journey of awareness and self-acceptance, but also that the somatic process can lead to cultural empathy and societal balance.

Our discussions benefited greatly from Roguski's self-confessed ignorance of the somatic theory and practices. However, his position as a New Zealand expatriate provided a specific platform of inquiry.

> I was born and raised in Aotearoa/New Zealand, a nation that is in continual flux as we come to terms with the impact of colonialism, the sovereignty of Te Iwi Māori and our rights to parallel development with Pākehā [Europeans]. Perhaps because Aotearoa/New Zealand has been colonised relatively recently, the technologies of colonisation, such as practices of assimilation within education, our stolen lands, over-representation ofTe Iwi Māori in the prison system, unemployment figures, and our under-representation in the modern conceptions of professional (educational) success, as examples, are well documented, and are continually voiced in the media and through daily discussions. It is this process that has brought me to colonialist theory and my epistemological position of guarding against confiscation of a culture's heritage, whether that is land, artistic systems, dance forms, philosophies and/or holistic approaches to health and education.
>
> (Roguski, personal communication, October 2002)

In contrast, my viewpoints have been inspired through my early exposure to rhythms and dance and the need for the development of a strong sense of cultural attunement for survival in Spanish Harlem, New York.

Having grown up in Spanish Harlem, alive with rhythm and beat, an intimate neighborhood of thousands was filled with individuals often pulled into deep hunger and interpersonal conflicts due to lack of resources. Drugs, switchblade fights, mattress fires, wild dogs and gambling bookies on the corner, and kids scrambling for candy amongst roaches and rats were all elements of daily life. These conditions live in my personal history of home. Given this, I forever see the somatic process as a profound luxury, including the privileges of clean and warm floors as well as the time to relax deeply on them in relative quiet and safety guided by another vantage point on life – one that could direct away from basic survival using hyper-vigilance, to awareness within. All this was supported by another privilege – that of advanced schooling supporting excellent understanding of the scientific aspects of movement and the science of the body.

Michael Roguski, with his Māori heritage, helped me forge the following dialogue on the subject of honorary lineages and cultural roots of somatics after he lived in New York City for some years. He works as a post-colonialist theorist trained in psychology and cultural anthropology and states "But surely the well-being of the individual cannot be separated or compartmentalised from our genealogies, our Wairua [spirit], our emotional, mental, and physical bodies, our families – both nuclear and extended – our connection to Papatuanuku [Mother Earth], and our responsibilities to society. So why American society's consternation with the concept of the somatic?" As such, Roguski forwarded his impression that somatic movement, as an approach to the self as a whole appears to be a reclamation of a 'lost self', and that such approaches "are far from new, and are really a reclamation of our natural or innate sense of well-being." (Personal communication, October 2002) At the heart of these discussions emerges a socio-political view of somatic movement/practice as experienced in the USA.

Working with Roguski, I analysed four of the interviews that I conducted with as many of the progenitors of somatic movement disciplines that are alive today – the Second Generation – all dancers, all women, all influenced by either Asian or Pan-African experiences. One finding is that through these systems there appears to be a natural resistance to the prevalent alienation of the Western self, caught in the stress and duress of such socio-political forces as industrialisation, technological shifts, a decreased sense of social capital/social cohesion[1] and associated alienation from spiritual foundation/rootedness/other. Again, these somatic approaches are notable because they are profoundly active – they are therefore called systems of 'somatic movement'. In these systems the experience of the ever-changing soma is supported by a mandate to move, move out for what is true to the natural core of the lived process. In this mandate for movement, action is taken; the centre (of breath, of weight, of the body) moves in response to what is known from somatic wisdom to be best for the whole.

These somatic dancers model the power of the corporeal, embodied, kinaesthetic, lived experience and are willing to work for its voice – no matter how raw. Of note is that they do not all cite their global influences in their descriptive literature or lectures. The search for 'the universal' or 'the humanistic' as a through-line of body-mind investigation has encouraged a mono-cultural approach to somatic pedagogy and the promotion of the field. However, I have found that through the work of those founders of somatic disciplines who are women, it has become possible to more easily retrace some of these global influences on 21st-century somatic studies because they are also willing to tell their stories. I posit that, through the lives and experience of the second generation of female somatic leaders, more of an emotional voice also entered the holistic paradigm of somatic education, and somatic movement, through somatic dance. Furthermore, emotions were expressed and fuelled expressions of discontent and in some cases supported activism. I am often discouraged that the seminal history of a person's movement experience that has been based in another culture does not make it into the somatic classroom. For example, the inclusion of Emilie Conrad's studies in Haiti and Bonnie Bainbridge Cohen's influences from living in Japan would enrich the learning experience (Eddy 2002).

Roguski has a different analysis. He feels by not stating that their work has arisen out of a particular indigenous culture, these somatic leaders are not actually claiming the movement phenomenon or experience, and in this way they are therefore not co-opting it. They have simply found their own truths within the experiences of each of these rich cultural immersions and if asked will gladly share it.

I still ask the question – how in somatic education, a moving feeling sensing educational setting, do participants get the information to learn more about the underlying sources? How can people know where to go for more without stopping the flow of the kinaesthetic exploration? Out of this urgency, I have devised the above "movement to language" legacy practice that seems to work, bringing historical clarity out quickly (Eddy 2000).

These questions 'of authority' and from where it should and does arise have led to further questions: To what degree is the sharing of somatic findings or wisdom important? What are the healthiest processes for the verbal exchange of 'personal somatic wisdom'? How does the need to be witnessed within community find its place within the deep somatic experience? Is it important to view somatic experience in larger cultural contexts?

---

1 Social capital and social cohesion are used here in reference to the notion that social interaction and community, and the capability to achieve these, are resources that have value in society; they can even promote the fiscal advancement of a culture and certainly enhance the wellbeing of a group. (Portes 1998)

Once again, dance emerges as a way to externalise somatic discoveries and to bring them to visible dialogue, with the option to further engage in verbal exchange as well. But, questions remain: Does the world of somatic dance education help or hinder acculturation? Is the complementary health field an asset? Does somatic movement and dance fit in here? With the advances of the wellness industry and even the dance academy are we in jeopardy of once again commercialising the somatic experience and that which is simply natural and human?

Being set apart, giving 'somatics' its distinct place, is also an honouring, but it can lead once again to confusion of authority. Roguski reminds us that repositioning of authority is a subset of colonialism. He sees this also in how authority is set apart in medical institutions. Somatic education is set apart because it places the authority in the person, who can then seek scientific and medical information and facilitation for the ultimately personal decisions that need to be made. If we allow voice for all that emerges from within we find a place with a profound acceptance of cultural pluralism. The resulting dialogue can be a cross-cultural interchange that includes the passage out of the comfortable or the uncomfortable, and into a new set of values and rules.

Hence this 'movement' movement, built on the consciousness of somatic practice, has the inherent elements of a political movement that actually moves. The dancing is what catapults the awareness into action. The dance drives the community building and strengthens the network, and values the 'giving back' to the world. It is needed to move us away from fears of not moving. It reinforces that we are three-dimensional beings and, as such, that we need to navigate complexity. What secures this solidity within the ephemeralness of somatic dance is to allow for emergent (non-hegemonic) language – words, names and honouring – to accompany softly the dancing self.

It is important to see the need for gathering and sharing, and for moving into community. Great thanks are due to all groups who work together to organise conferences as well as any informal convenings. These advance our community, our scholarship, our communication, our understanding, and hence our wisdom. I hope each reader will share her or his legacy and that we, as a community, can continue to share movement into the future.

References

Eddy, M. (2000) 'Access to Somatic Theory and its Application: Socio-Political Concerns', *Dancing in the Millennium* Joint Conference Proceedings of CORD/SDHS/LIMS/WDA: Washington DC, July 19-23

_______ (2002) 'Somatic Practices and Dance: Global Influences', *Dance Research Journal*. 34.2.46–62

_______ (2005) Dynamic Embodiment course materials. New York, NY: Moving On Center.

_______ (2009) 'A Brief History of Somatic Practices and Dance: Historical Development of the Field of Somatic Education and Its Relationship to Dance', *Journal of Dance and Somatic Practices* 1(1). doi: 10.1386/jdsp.1.1.5/1

Fortin, S (1994) 'Final Plenary', ESTIVALE, University of Quebec, Montreal

Portes, A. (1998) 'Social Capital: Its Origins and Applications in Modern Sociology', *Annual Review of Sociology* 24: 1-24. Retrieved from http://bit.ly/tpMove15

ABOUT THE EDITORS

Editors

Natalie Garrett Brown is principal lecturer and contributes to the BA (Hons) Dance course while coordinating postgraduate provision at Coventry University. She is an Associate Editor of the *Journal of Dance and Somatic Practices* and Vice Chair of Dance HE, an organisation representing Dance across Higher Education in the UK. Natalie undertook her Somatic Movement Educator's Training in Body-Mind Centering with Embody Move Association, UK She is a founding member of *enter & inhabit*; a collaborative performance project and has published on somatic-informed performance practices.

Sarah Whatley is Professor of Dance and Director of the Centre for Dance Research (C-DaRE) at Coventry University. Her research interests include dance and new technologies, dance analysis, somatic dance practice and pedagogy, and inclusive dance practices; she has published widely on these themes. The AHRC, the Leverhulme Trust and European Union fund her current research. She led the AHRC-funded Siobhan Davies digital archive project, *RePlay* and continues to work with Davies on other artist-initiated research projects. She is also Editor of the *Journal of Dance and Somatic Practices* and sits on the editorial boards of several other journals.

Kirsty Alexander is co-director of Independent Dance, an artist-led organisation providing a responsive framework to support, sustain and stimulate dance artists in their ongoing development as professionals. She has been an influential advocate for the furtherance of somatic-informed pedagogies within the conservatoire sector and regularly acts as an advisor, both in the UK and internationally, on the development of university dance programmes. Her research interests centre around the contribution dance and somatic practices can make to the broader field of educational philosophy. Kirsty is an Associate Editor of the *Journal of Dance and Somatic Practices*.

Assistant Editor

Emma Meehan is a research assistant at the Centre for Dance Research (C-DaRE) at Coventry University. She received her BA and PhD from the Drama Department, Trinity College Dublin. She is a co-convenor of the Performance as Research working group at the International Federation for Theatre Research and Editorial Assistant on the *Journal of Dance and Somatic Practices*. Her research interests are in somatic practices in performance, contemporary dance in Ireland and performance as research.

Series title: Ways of Being a Body

Nine Ways of Seeing a Body ~ Sandra Reeve

In the first book in this series, Sandra Reeve tracks Western approaches to the body from Descartes onwards. The nine ways of seeing a body that she describes are:

> ***The body as object ~ The body as subject ~ The phenomenological body ~ The somatic body ~ The contextual body ~ The interdependent body ~ The environmental body ~ The cultural body ~ The ecological body***

This admirably short little book has been very widely welcomed as a guide and stimulus for teachers, students and practitioners.

> *"I love your book and ...I am now using it ... as a text in one of my courses."*
> Don Hanlon Johnson, Professor of Somatics, California Inst. of Integral Studies
>
> *"...for anyone who has ever trawled through philosophies of the body it is a welcome relief to have them laid out so clearly. ...essential reading for anyone interested in dance, in movement, in philosophies of the body; for dancers, researchers, students, somatic movement practitioners and for dance movement therapists. Wonderful."*
> Polly Hudson: Senior Lecturer, Dance Performing Arts, Coventry University
>
> *"a delightful, readable set of ...lenses through which to consider and reconsider embodied practice..."* Phillip Zarrilli: Artistic Director, The Llanarth Group

Series title: Ways of Being a Body

Body and Performance ~ Sandra Reeve (editor)

The second book in this series brings together 12 contemporary approaches to the body that are being used by performers or in the context of performance training.

The intention is for students, dancers, performers, singers, musicians, directors and choreographers to locate their own preferred approach(es) to the body-in-performance amongst the lenses described here. The collection is also designed to facilitate further research in that direction as well as to signpost alternatives that might enrich their current vocabulary.

The 12 approaches represent the praxis and research of their authors. They are: ***The Ontogenetic Body*** (BMC) ~ ***The Intersubjective Body*** (body in flux, Corporeal Feminism and somatic-informed movement practice) ~ ***The Autobiographical Body*** (Object Relations) ~ ***The Resonant Body*** (Sounding Dance Improvisation) ~ ***The Learnt Body*** (Merleau-Ponty, Edward Casey, Jaana Parviainen and Rudolf Laban) ~ ***The Resilient Body*** (the Feldenkrais Method.) ~ ***The Imaginal Body*** (the Alexander technique) ~ ***The Kinetic Body*** (*kudiyattam*) ~ ***The Cognitive Body*** (Damasio's 'body-minded brain' and 'somatic marker hypothesis') ~ ***The Vocal Body*** (an integrative approach to physiovocal unity) ~ ***The Dwelling Body*** (inter-relationship of place and identity) ~ ***The Musical Body*** (a choreography shaped through the musical body).

Series title: Ways of Being a Body

Body and Awareness ***(forthcoming)***

www.triarchypress.net/BeingaBody

A Sardine Street Box of Tricks

Crab Man and Signpost (Phil Smith & Simon Persighetti)

This is a handbook for anyone who wants to make their own 'mis-guided' tour, walk or walk-performance. Written by two members of the Exeter-based Wrights & Sites group, the book is based on the mis-guided 'Tour of Sardine Street' that they created for Queen Street in Exeter during 2011.

Designed to help anyone who makes, or would like to make, walkperformances or variations on the guided tour, the book describes a range of different approaches and tactics, and illustrates them with examples from the Queen Street tour. For example:

- Wear something that sets you apart and gives others permission to approach you: "Excuse me, what are you supposed to be?"
- Take a can of abject booze from the street or a momentary juxtaposition of a dove and a plastic bag and mould them, through an action, into an idea
- Attend to the smallest things
- Examine the cracks in your street and the mould on its walls, note its graffiti, collect its detritus, observe how its pavements are used and abused
- Set yourself tasks that passers-by will be intrigued by: they will enjoy interrupting and even joining in with you
- Draw upon ambiguous, ironical or hollowed-out rituals to complement the multiplicity of your walk with intensity of feeling or depth of engagement.

walking's new movement

Phil Smith

In ***walking's new movement*** Phil Smith (of *Mythogeography*, Counter-Tourism, Wrights & Sites and *On Walking ...and Stalking Sebald*):

- unravels the history of psychogeography and looks forwards/around to what might come next
- maps the 'evolution' of walking and looks at 'stages' in that evolution
- offers a helicopter view for walking artists to place themselves in historical and artistic context
- offers important new ideas about abusive semi-public spaces (in the wake of recent scandals) and suggests how radical walking can act against 'the spectacle' and power
- presents a compelling theory about romanticism and the postmodern in relation to walking
- suggests a World Brain for walking
- lists strategies, tactics and a full manifesto for Radical Walking.

Both books are for anyone who makes, or wants to make, walking art or walk-performances - and for anyone interested in psychogeography, radical walking, drift and dérive, site-specific performance, and the use/abuse of public space in the shadow of Jack the Ripper, Jimmy Savile and others.

www.triarchypress.net/smithereens

ALSO FROM TRIARCHY PRESS

Embodied Lives

Reflections on the Influence of Suprapto Suryodarmo and Amerta Movement

edited by: Katya Bloom, Margit Galanter and Sandra Reeve

30 movement performers, therapists, artists, teachers and colleagues from around the world describe the impact of Prapto's Amerta Movement on their lives and work.

Since the mid-80s, Prapto's moving/dancing has inspired many thousands of people in the West, and many more in his native Java, who have witnessed, worked with or been otherwise influenced by his Amerta Movement practice.

But what is this non-stylised Amerta Movement practice? And what is it about Prapto's work that so touches the lives of therapists, artists, musicians, dancers, teachers, performers, monastics and laypeople from all walks of life?

To answer these questions, this new book brings together the experiences of 30 movement practitioners from Indonesia, Europe, North and South America and Australasia. As their chapters show, their personal and professional lives have all been affected by their long-term studies and interactions with Prapto.

The common denominator for all the authors is the exploration of their own movement as a way of deepening their connection to themselves, to each other and, at the same time, to their respective worlds.

These chapters all also share the potency that comes from writing from lived experience, rather than writing about something with distance.

www.triarchypress.net/EmbodiedLives

Triarchy Press is an independent publisher of new, alternative thinking (altThink) about government, finance, organisations, society, movement, somatics, performance and the creative life.

www.triarchypress.net

Lightning Source UK Ltd.
Milton Keynes UK
UKOW07f0451090816

280274UK00011B/36/P

9 781909 470637